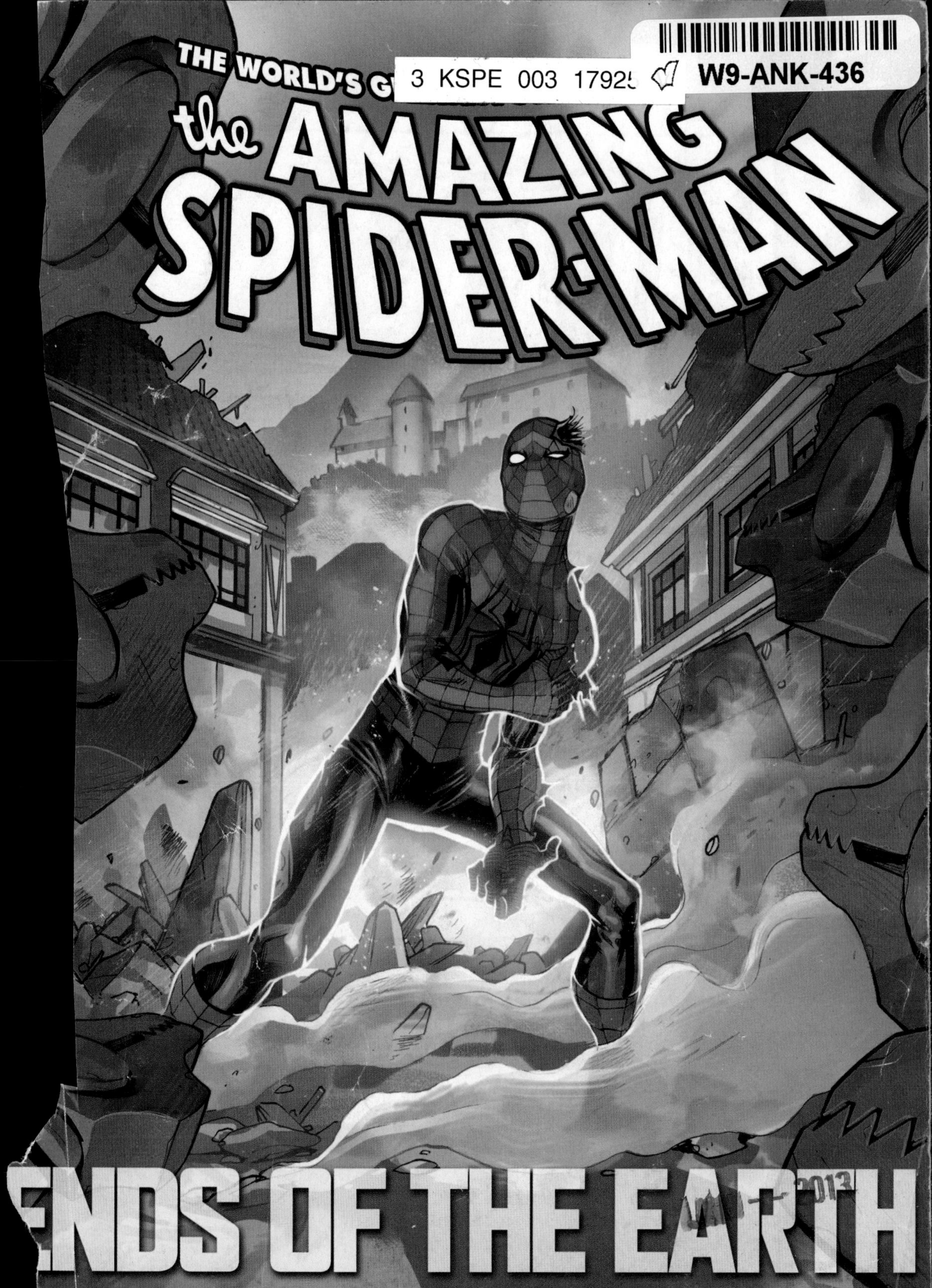

THE AMAZING SPIDER-MAN

THE WORLD'S G...

ENDS OF THE EARTH

SPIDER-MAN: ENDS OF THE EARTH. Contains material originally published in magazine form as ENDS OF THE EARTH #1, AMAZING SPIDER-MAN #682-687 and AVENGING SPIDER-MAN #8. First printing 2013. ISBN# 978-0-51-6006-9. Published by MARVEL WORLDWIDE, INC., a subsidiary of MARVEL ENTERTAINMENT, LLC. OFFICE OF PUBLICATION: 135 West 50th Street, New York, NY 10020. Copyright © 2012 and 2013 Marvel Characters, Inc. All rights reserved. All characters featured in this issue and the distinctive names and likenesses thereof, and all related indicia are trademarks of Marvel Characters, Inc. No similarity between any of the names, characters, persons, and/or institutions in this magazine with those of any living or dead person or institution is intended, and any such similarity which may exist is purely coincidental. **Printed in the U.S.A.** ALAN FINE, EVP - Office of the President, Marvel Worldwide, Inc. and EVP & CMO Marvel Characters B.V.; DAN BUCKLEY, Publisher & President - Print, Animation & Digital Divisions; JOE QUESADA, Chief Creative Officer; TOM BREVOORT, SVP of Publishing; DAVID BOGART, SVP of Operations & Procurement, Publishing; RUWAN JAYATILLEKE, SVP & Associate Publisher, Publishing; C.B. CEBULSKI, SVP of Creator & Content Development; DAVID GABRIEL, SVP of Publishing Sales & Circulation; MICHAEL PASCIULLO, SVP of Brand Planning & Communications; JIM O'KEEFE, VP of Operations & Logistics; DAN CARR, Executive Director of Publishing Technology; SUSAN CRESPI, Editorial Operations Manager; ALEX MORALES, Publishing Operations Manager; STAN LEE, Chairman Emeritus. For information regarding advertising in Marvel Comics or on Marvel.com, please contact Niza Disla, Director of Marvel Partnerships, at ndisla@marvel.com. For Marvel subscription inquiries, please call 800-217-9158. **Manufactured between 11/14/2012 and 12/24/2012 by R.R. DONNELLEY, INC., SALEM, VA, USA.**

10 9 8 7 6 5 4 3 2 1

the AMAZING SPIDER-MAN
ENDS OF THE EARTH

AMAZING SPIDER-MAN #682-683 & #686-687
Writer: **DAN SLOTT**
Artist: **STEFANO CASELLI**
Color Artist: **FRANK MARTIN JR.**

AMAZING SPIDER-MAN #684-685
Writer: **DAN SLOTT**
Penciler: **HUMBERTO RAMOS**
Inker: **VICTOR OLAZABA**
Colorist: **EDGAR DELGADO**

AMAZING SPIDER-MAN: ENDS OF THE EARTH #1
Writers: **ROB WILLIAMS** (PART 1) **& BRIAN CLEVINGER** (PART 2)
Penciler: **THONY SILAS**
Inker: **VICTOR OLAZABA**
Colorist: **WIL QUINTANA**
Special thanks to Dan Slott

AVENGING SPIDER-MAN #8
Writers: **TY TEMPLETON** WITH **DAN SLOTT**
Penciler: **MATTHEW CLARK**
Inker: **SEAN PARSONS**
Colorist: **WIL QUINTANA**

Letterer: **VC'S JOE CARAMAGNA** • Assistant Editor: **ELLIE PYLE**
Senior Editor: **STEPHEN WACKER** • Executive Editor: **TOM BREVOORT**

Collection Editor: **JENNIFER GRÜNWALD** • Assistant Editors: **ALEX STARBUCK** & **NELSON RIBEIRO**
Editor, Special Projects: **MARK D. BEAZLEY** • Senior Editor, Special Projects: **JEFF YOUNGQUIST**
Senior Vice President of Sales: **DAVID GABRIEL** • SVP of Brand Planning & Communications: **MICHAEL PASCIULLO**

Editor in Chief: **AXEL ALONSO** • Chief Creative Officer: **JOE QUESADA** • Publisher: **DAN BUCKLEY** • Executive Producer: **ALAN FINE**

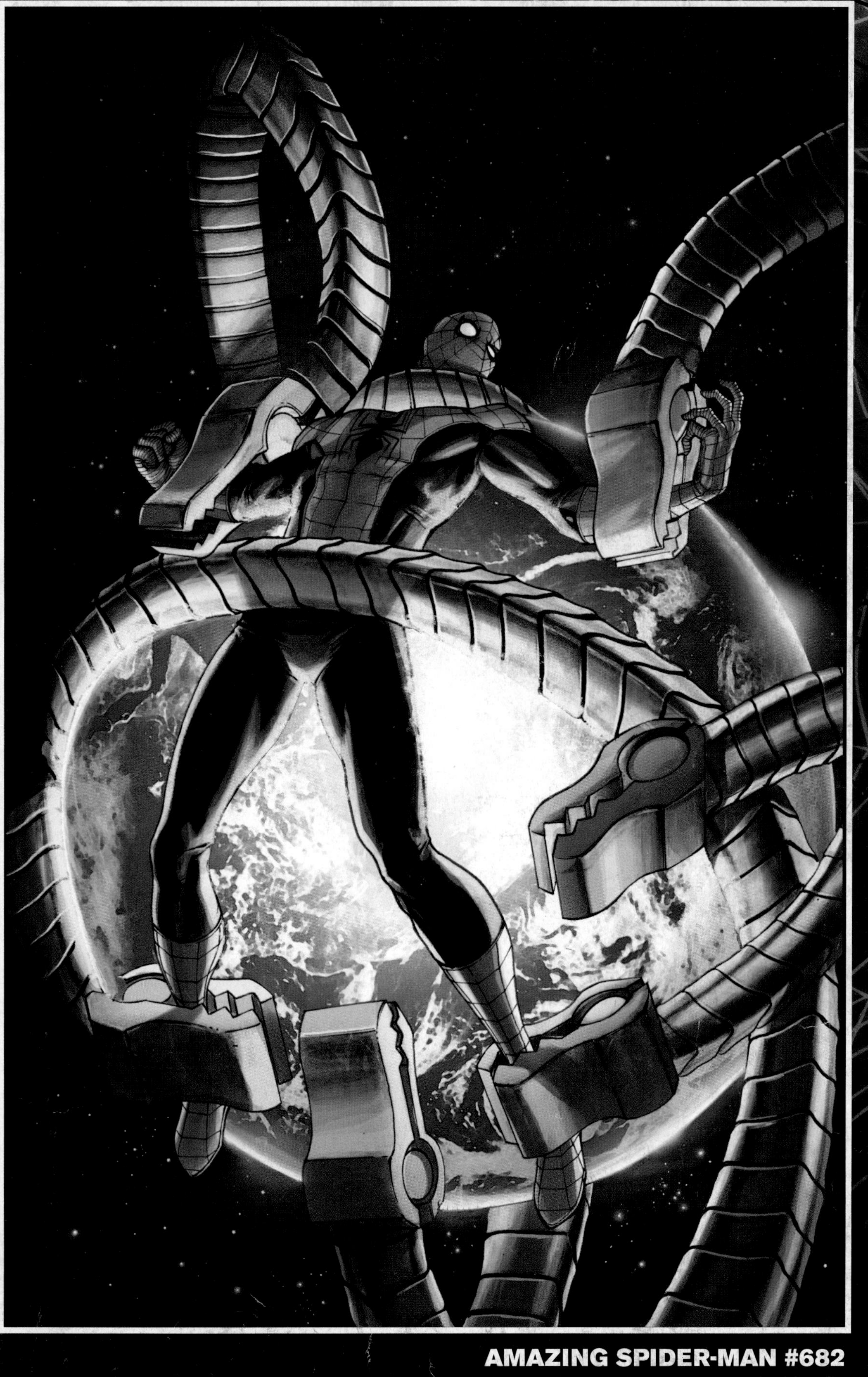

AMAZING SPIDER-MAN #682
COVER BY STEFANO CASELLI & FRANK MARTIN JR.

While attending a demonstration in radiology, high school science student Peter Parker was bitten by a spider that had accidentally been exposed to radioactive rays.

Through a miracle of science, Peter soon found that he had gained the spider's powers...and had, in effect, become a human spider! Currently, he works as a top researcher at Horizon Labs, but he remains...

the AMAZING SPIDER-MAN

Doctor Otto Octavius was a nuclear physicist who constructed a set of mechanical arms, controlled by a brain/computer interface, that helped him with his atomic research. But something went wrong with his experiment and a radioactive explosion fused the arms to his body and mind. He became Doctor Octopus, one of Spider-Man's most sinister foes! Now, his body is dying and the time has come for his final master plan...

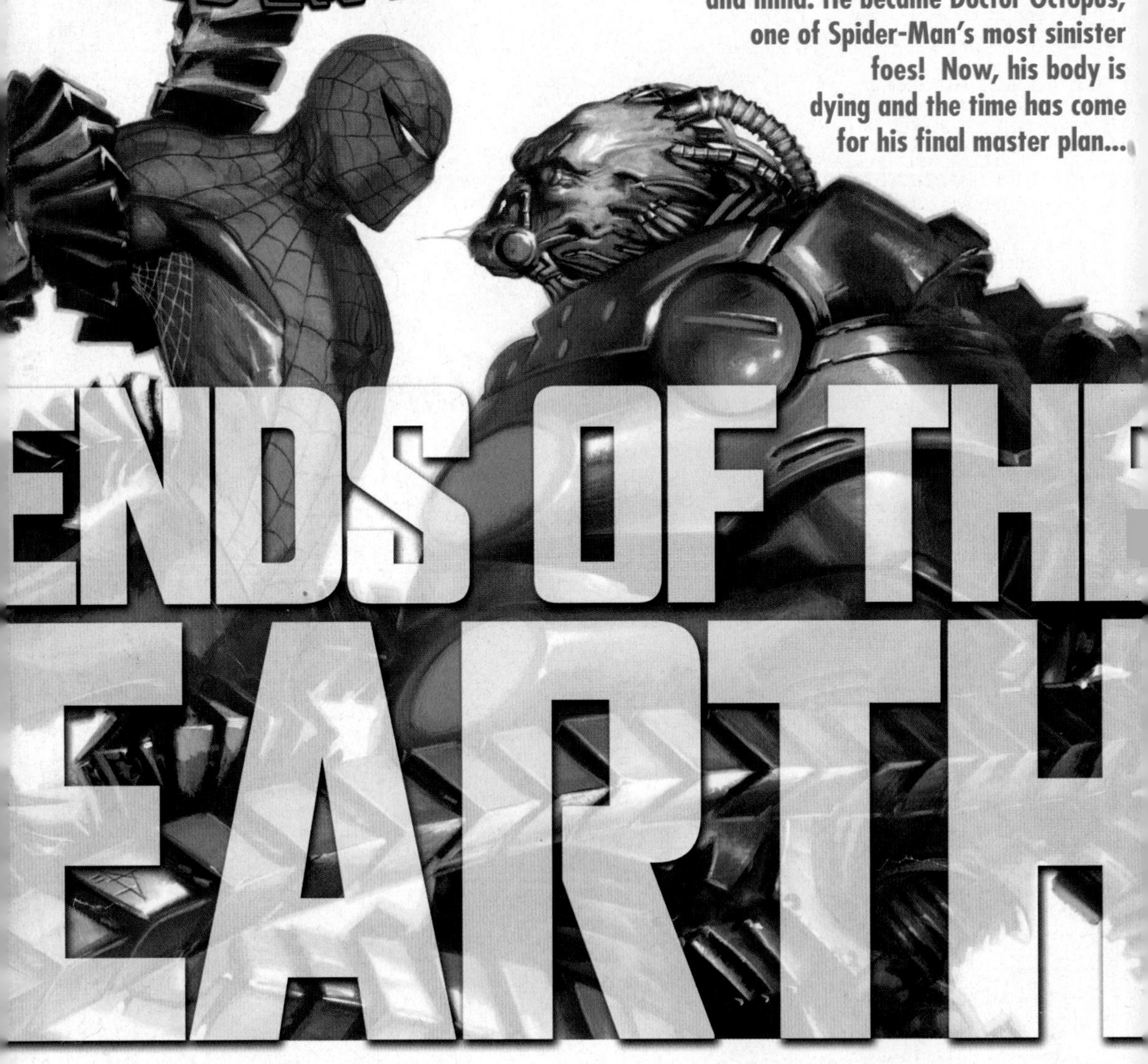

ENDS OF THE EARTH

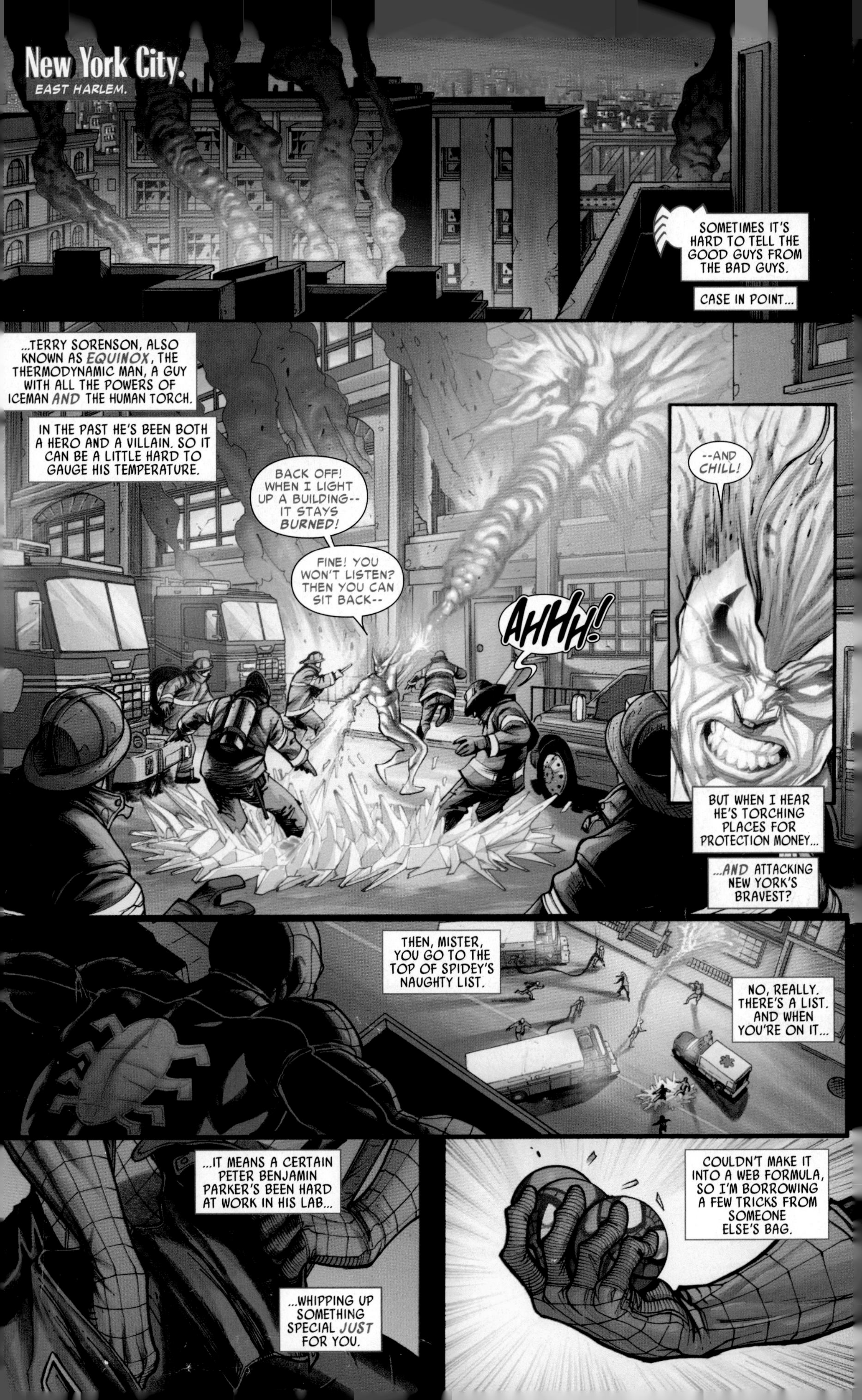
New York City.
EAST HARLEM.
SOMETIMES IT'S HARD TO TELL THE GOOD GUYS FROM THE BAD GUYS.
CASE IN POINT...
...TERRY SORENSON, ALSO KNOWN AS EQUINOX, THE THERMODYNAMIC MAN, A GUY WITH ALL THE POWERS OF ICEMAN AND THE HUMAN TORCH.
IN THE PAST HE'S BEEN BOTH A HERO AND A VILLAIN, SO IT CAN BE A LITTLE HARD TO GAUGE HIS TEMPERATURE.
BACK OFF! WHEN I LIGHT UP A BUILDING-- IT STAYS BURNED!
FINE! YOU WON'T LISTEN? THEN YOU CAN SIT BACK--
--AND CHILL!
AHHH!
BUT WHEN I HEAR HE'S TORCHING PLACES FOR PROTECTION MONEY...
...AND ATTACKING NEW YORK'S BRAVEST?
THEN, MISTER, YOU GO TO THE TOP OF SPIDEY'S NAUGHTY LIST.
NO, REALLY. THERE'S A LIST. AND WHEN YOU'RE ON IT...
...IT MEANS A CERTAIN PETER BENJAMIN PARKER'S BEEN HARD AT WORK IN HIS LAB...
...WHIPPING UP SOMETHING SPECIAL JUST FOR YOU.
COULDN'T MAKE IT INTO A WEB FORMULA, SO I'M BORROWING A FEW TRICKS FROM SOMEONE ELSE'S BAG.

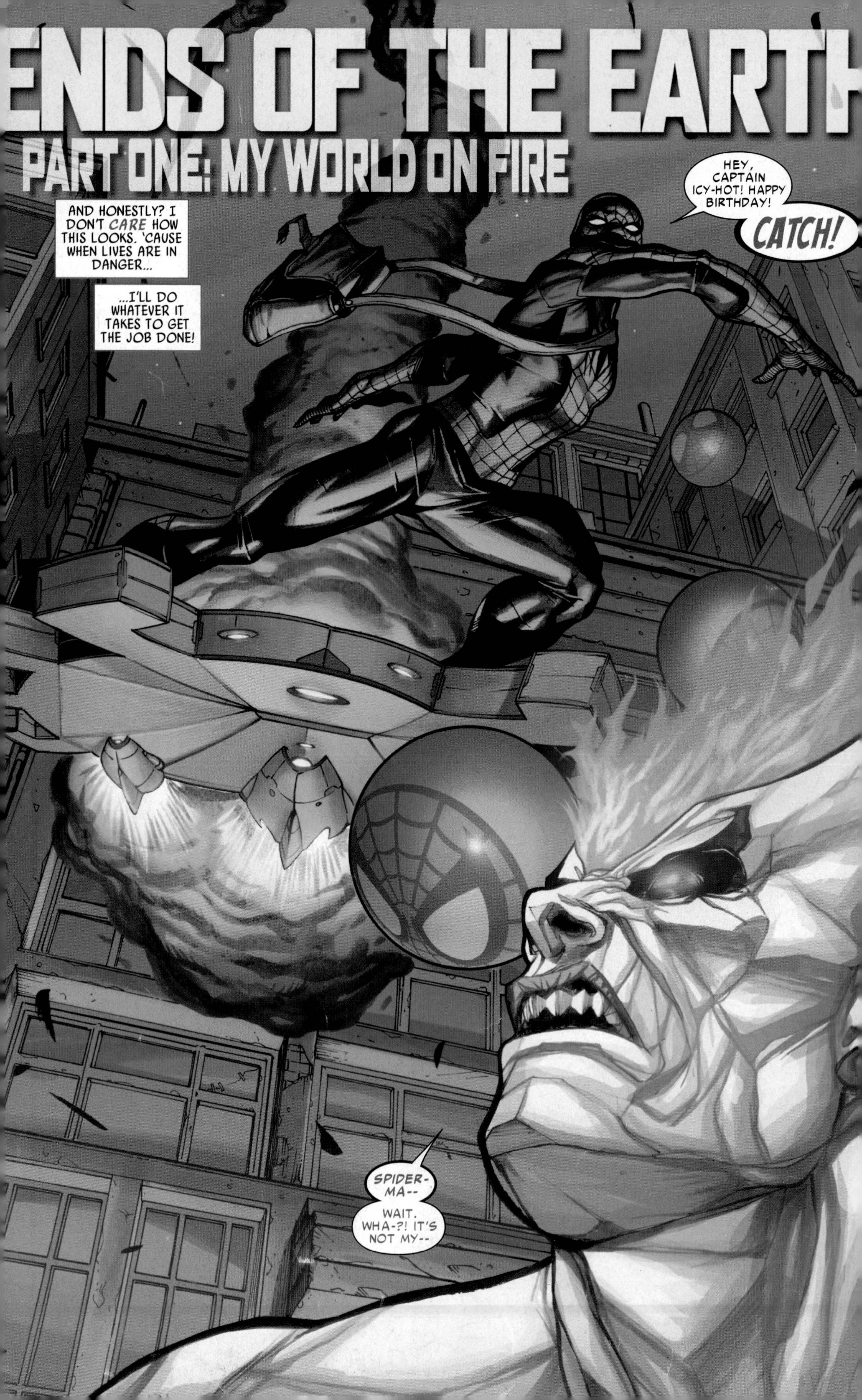
ENDS OF THE EARTH
PART ONE: MY WORLD ON FIRE
AND HONESTLY? I DON'T CARE HOW THIS LOOKS. 'CAUSE WHEN LIVES ARE IN DANGER...
...I'LL DO WHATEVER IT TAKES TO GET THE JOB DONE!
HEY, CAPTAIN ICY-HOT! HAPPY BIRTHDAY!
CATCH!
SPIDER-MA--
WAIT. WHA-?! IT'S NOT MY--

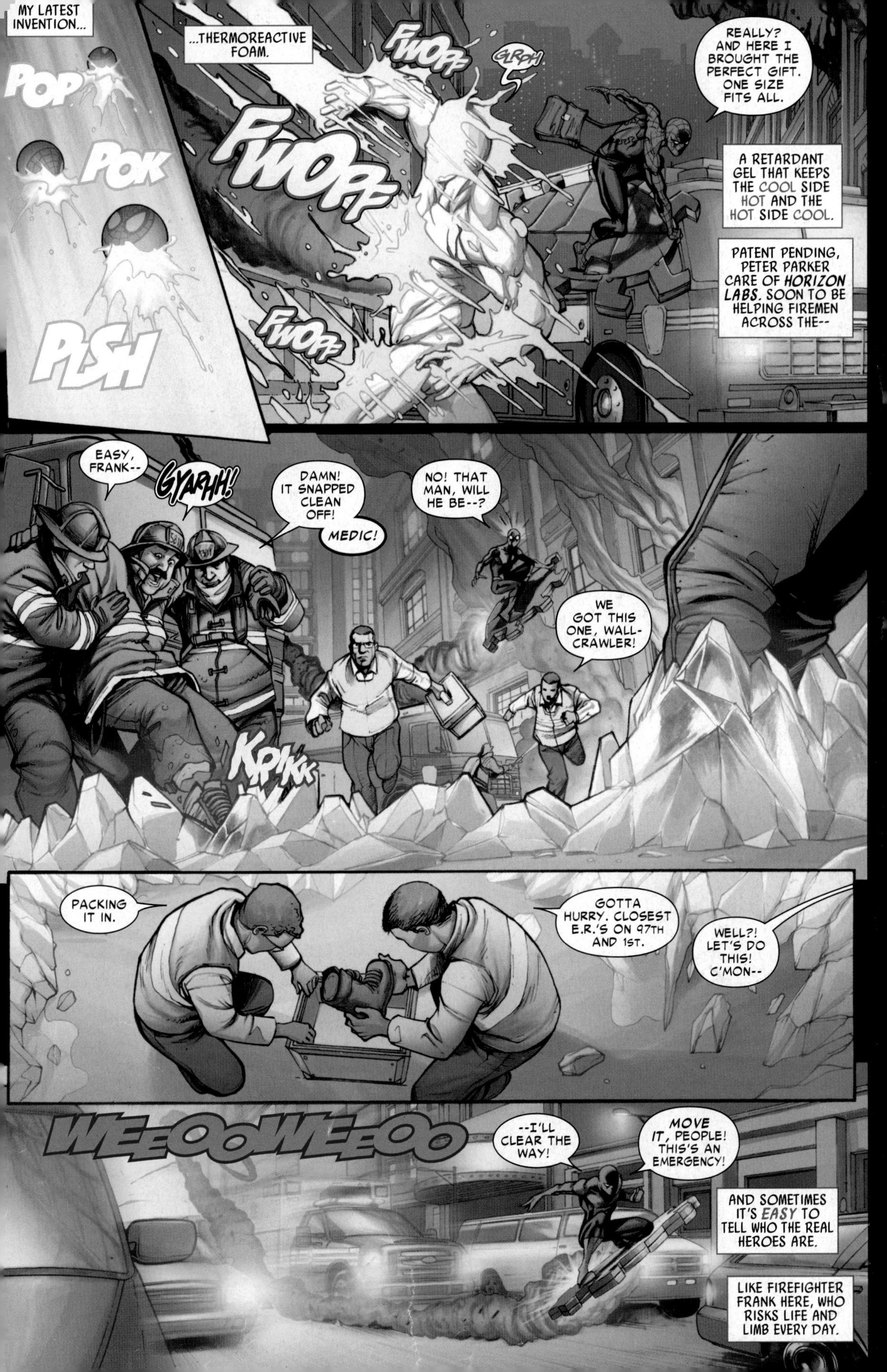
MY LATEST INVENTION...
POP
POK
PLSH
...THERMOREACTIVE FOAM.
FWOFF
GLRDH
FWOFF
FWOFF
REALLY? AND HERE I BROUGHT THE PERFECT GIFT. ONE SIZE FITS ALL.
A RETARDANT GEL THAT KEEPS THE COOL SIDE HOT AND THE HOT SIDE COOL.
PATENT PENDING, PETER PARKER CARE OF HORIZON LABS. SOON TO BE HELPING FIREMEN ACROSS THE--
EASY, FRANK--
GYARHH!
DAMN! IT SNAPPED CLEAN OFF!
MEDIC!
NO! THAT MAN, WILL HE BE--?
WE GOT THIS ONE, WALL-CRAWLER!
KRIKK
PACKING IT IN.
GOTTA HURRY. CLOSEST E.R.'S ON 97TH AND 1ST.
WELL?! LET'S DO THIS! C'MON--
WEEOOWEEOO
--I'LL CLEAR THE WAY!
MOVE IT, PEOPLE! THIS'S AN EMERGENCY!
AND SOMETIMES IT'S EASY TO TELL WHO THE REAL HEROES ARE.
LIKE FIREFIGHTER FRANK HERE, WHO RISKS LIFE AND LIMB EVERY DAY.

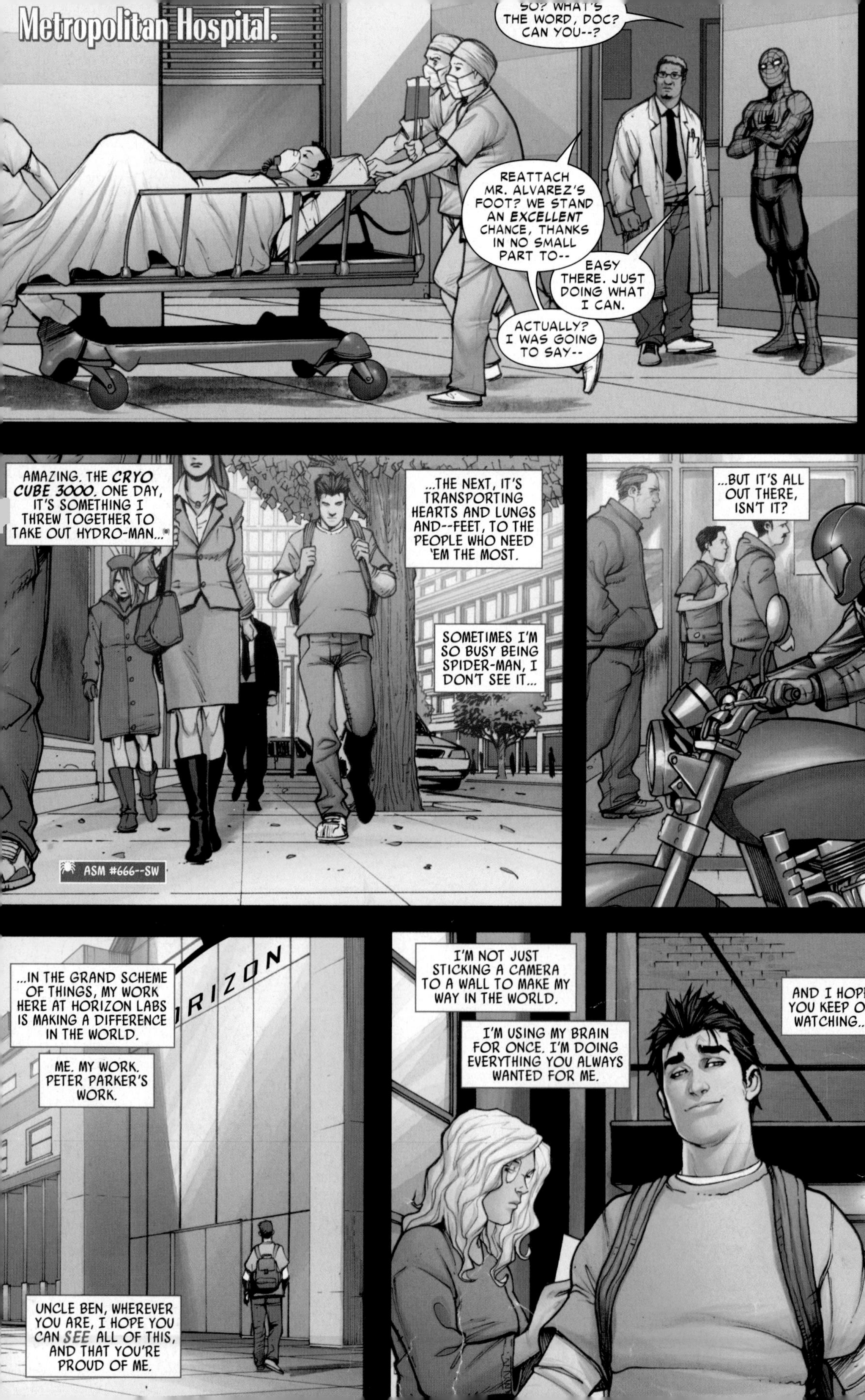
Metropolitan Hospital.
SO? WHAT'S THE WORD, DOC? CAN YOU--?
REATTACH MR. ALVAREZ'S FOOT? WE STAND AN EXCELLENT CHANCE, THANKS IN NO SMALL PART TO--
EASY THERE. JUST DOING WHAT I CAN.
ACTUALLY? I WAS GOING TO SAY--
AMAZING. THE CRYO CUBE 3000. ONE DAY, IT'S SOMETHING I THREW TOGETHER TO TAKE OUT HYDRO-MAN...
ASM #666--SW
...THE NEXT, IT'S TRANSPORTING HEARTS AND LUNGS AND--FEET, TO THE PEOPLE WHO NEED 'EM THE MOST.
SOMETIMES I'M SO BUSY BEING SPIDER-MAN, I DON'T SEE IT...
...BUT IT'S ALL OUT THERE, ISN'T IT?
...IN THE GRAND SCHEME OF THINGS, MY WORK HERE AT HORIZON LABS IS MAKING A DIFFERENCE IN THE WORLD.
ORIZON
ME. MY WORK. PETER PARKER'S WORK.
UNCLE BEN, WHEREVER YOU ARE, I HOPE YOU CAN SEE ALL OF THIS, AND THAT YOU'RE PROUD OF ME.
I'M NOT JUST STICKING A CAMERA TO A WALL TO MAKE MY WAY IN THE WORLD.
I'M USING MY BRAIN FOR ONCE. I'M DOING EVERYTHING YOU ALWAYS WANTED FOR ME.
AND I HOPE YOU KEEP ON WATCHING...

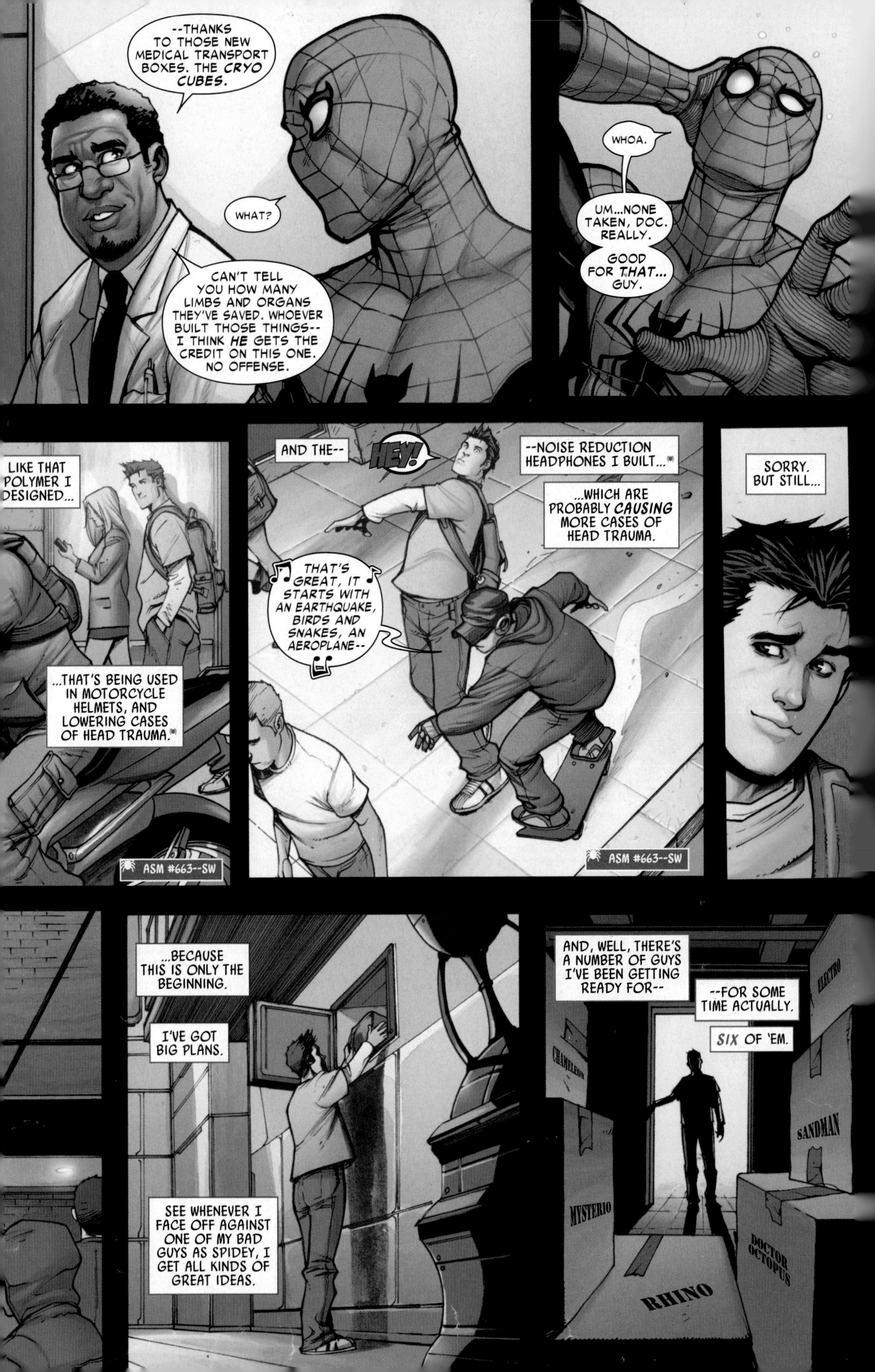
--THANKS TO THOSE NEW MEDICAL TRANSPORT BOXES. THE CRYO CUBES.
WHAT?
CAN'T TELL YOU HOW MANY LIMBS AND ORGANS THEY'VE SAVED. WHOEVER BUILT THOSE THINGS-- I THINK HE GETS THE CREDIT ON THIS ONE. NO OFFENSE.
WHOA.
UM...NONE TAKEN, DOC. REALLY.
GOOD FOR THAT... GUY.
LIKE THAT POLYMER I DESIGNED...
...THAT'S BEING USED IN MOTORCYCLE HELMETS, AND LOWERING CASES OF HEAD TRAUMA.
ASM #663--SW
AND THE--
HEY!
--NOISE REDUCTION HEADPHONES I BUILT...
...WHICH ARE PROBABLY CAUSING MORE CASES OF HEAD TRAUMA.
THAT'S GREAT, IT STARTS WITH AN EARTHQUAKE, BIRDS AND SNAKES, AN AEROPLANE--
ASM #663--SW
SORRY. BUT STILL...
...BECAUSE THIS IS ONLY THE BEGINNING.
I'VE GOT BIG PLANS.
SEE WHENEVER I FACE OFF AGAINST ONE OF MY BAD GUYS AS SPIDEY, I GET ALL KINDS OF GREAT IDEAS.
AND, WELL, THERE'S A NUMBER OF GUYS I'VE BEEN GETTING READY FOR--
--FOR SOME TIME ACTUALLY.
SIX OF 'EM.
ELECTRO
CHAMELEON
SANDMAN
MYSTERIO
DOCTOR OCTOPUS
RHINO

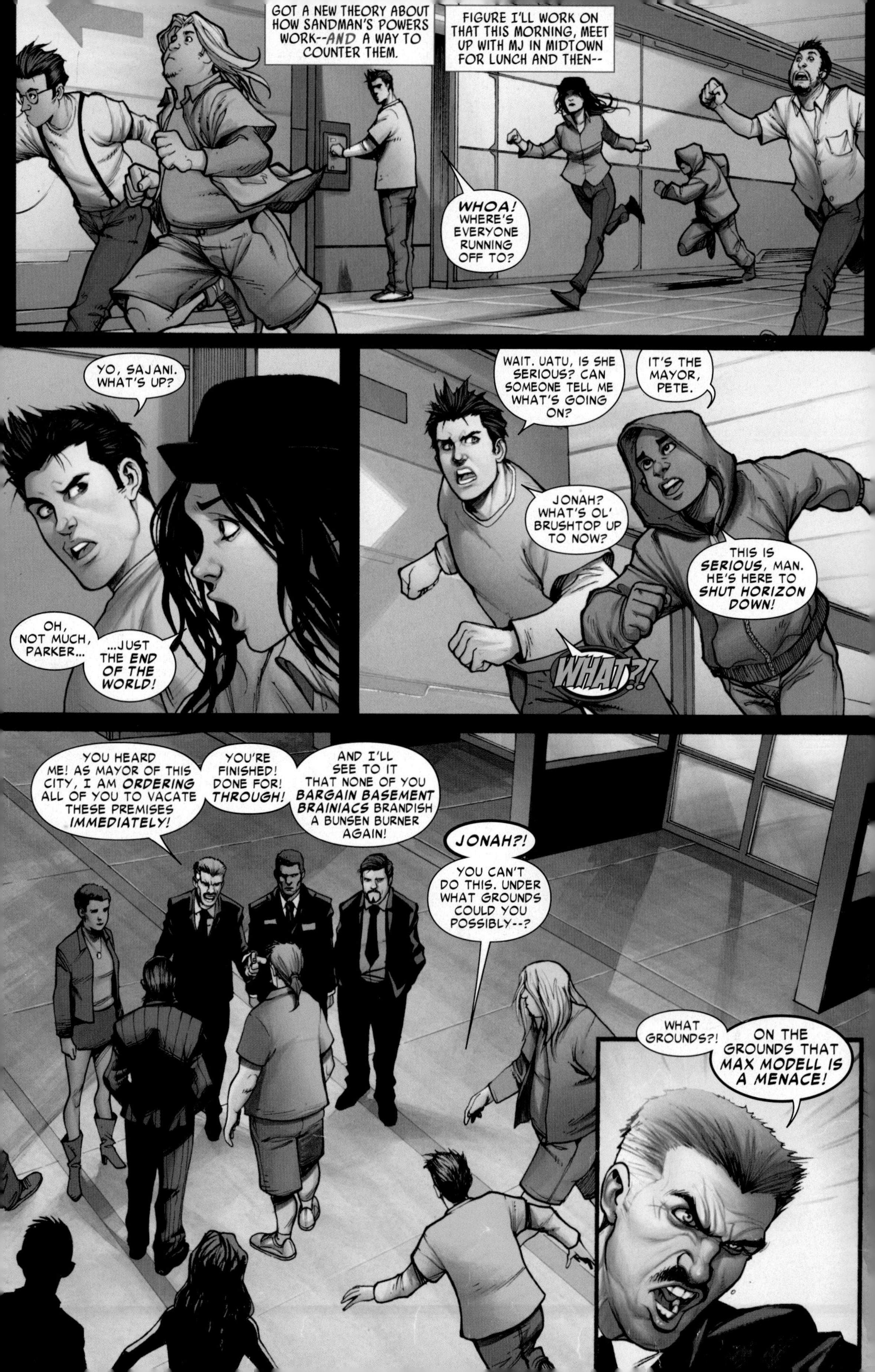
GOT A NEW THEORY ABOUT HOW SANDMAN'S POWERS WORK--AND A WAY TO COUNTER THEM.
FIGURE I'LL WORK ON THAT THIS MORNING, MEET UP WITH MJ IN MIDTOWN FOR LUNCH AND THEN--
WHOA! WHERE'S EVERYONE RUNNING OFF TO?
YO, SAJANI. WHAT'S UP?
OH, NOT MUCH, PARKER...
...JUST THE END OF THE WORLD!
WAIT. UATU, IS SHE SERIOUS? CAN SOMEONE TELL ME WHAT'S GOING ON?
IT'S THE MAYOR, PETE.
JONAH? WHAT'S OL' BRUSHTOP UP TO NOW?
THIS IS SERIOUS, MAN. HE'S HERE TO SHUT HORIZON DOWN!
WHAT?!
YOU HEARD ME! AS MAYOR OF THIS CITY, I AM ORDERING ALL OF YOU TO VACATE THESE PREMISES IMMEDIATELY!
YOU'RE FINISHED! DONE FOR! THROUGH!
AND I'LL SEE TO IT THAT NONE OF YOU BARGAIN BASEMENT BRAINIACS BRANDISH A BUNSEN BURNER AGAIN!
JONAH?!
YOU CAN'T DO THIS. UNDER WHAT GROUNDS COULD YOU POSSIBLY--?
WHAT GROUNDS?!
ON THE GROUNDS THAT MAX MODELL IS A MENACE!

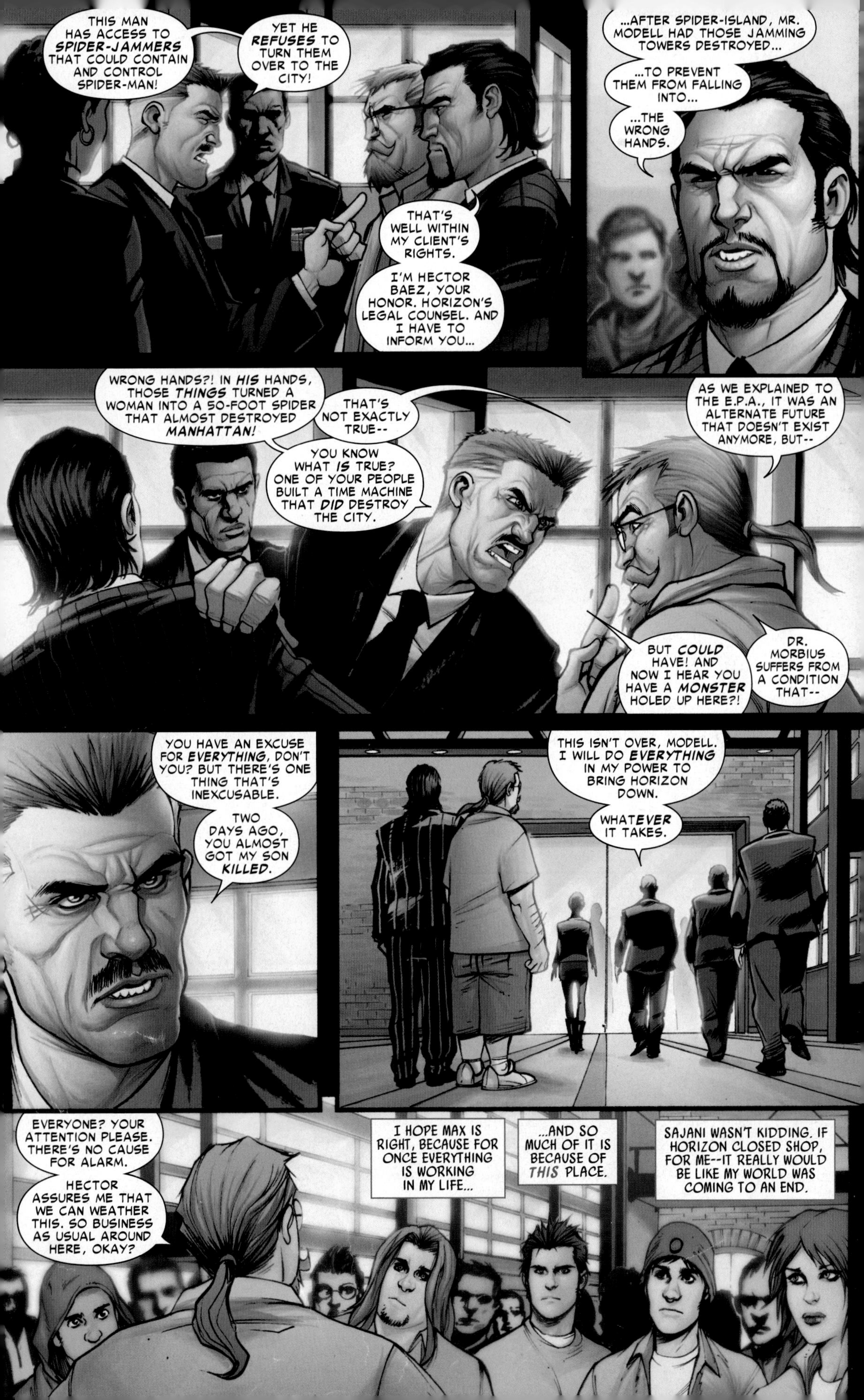
THIS MAN HAS ACCESS TO SPIDER-JAMMERS THAT COULD CONTAIN AND CONTROL SPIDER-MAN!
YET HE REFUSES TO TURN THEM OVER TO THE CITY!
THAT'S WELL WITHIN MY CLIENT'S RIGHTS.
I'M HECTOR BAEZ, YOUR HONOR. HORIZON'S LEGAL COUNSEL. AND I HAVE TO INFORM YOU...
...AFTER SPIDER-ISLAND, MR. MODELL HAD THOSE JAMMING TOWERS DESTROYED...
...TO PREVENT THEM FROM FALLING INTO...
...THE WRONG HANDS.
WRONG HANDS?! IN HIS HANDS, THOSE THINGS TURNED A WOMAN INTO A 50-FOOT SPIDER THAT ALMOST DESTROYED MANHATTAN!
THAT'S NOT EXACTLY TRUE--
YOU KNOW WHAT IS TRUE? ONE OF YOUR PEOPLE BUILT A TIME MACHINE THAT DID DESTROY THE CITY.
AS WE EXPLAINED TO THE E.P.A., IT WAS AN ALTERNATE FUTURE THAT DOESN'T EXIST ANYMORE, BUT--
BUT COULD HAVE! AND NOW I HEAR YOU HAVE A MONSTER HOLED UP HERE?!
DR. MORBIUS SUFFERS FROM A CONDITION THAT--
YOU HAVE AN EXCUSE FOR EVERYTHING, DON'T YOU? BUT THERE'S ONE THING THAT'S INEXCUSABLE.
TWO DAYS AGO, YOU ALMOST GOT MY SON KILLED.
THIS ISN'T OVER, MODELL. I WILL DO EVERYTHING IN MY POWER TO BRING HORIZON DOWN.
WHATEVER IT TAKES.
EVERYONE? YOUR ATTENTION PLEASE. THERE'S NO CAUSE FOR ALARM.
HECTOR ASSURES ME THAT WE CAN WEATHER THIS. SO BUSINESS AS USUAL AROUND HERE, OKAY?
I HOPE MAX IS RIGHT, BECAUSE FOR ONCE EVERYTHING IS WORKING IN MY LIFE...
...AND SO MUCH OF IT IS BECAUSE OF THIS PLACE.
SAJANI WASN'T KIDDING. IF HORIZON CLOSED SHOP, FOR ME--IT REALLY WOULD BE LIKE MY WORLD WAS COMING TO AN END.

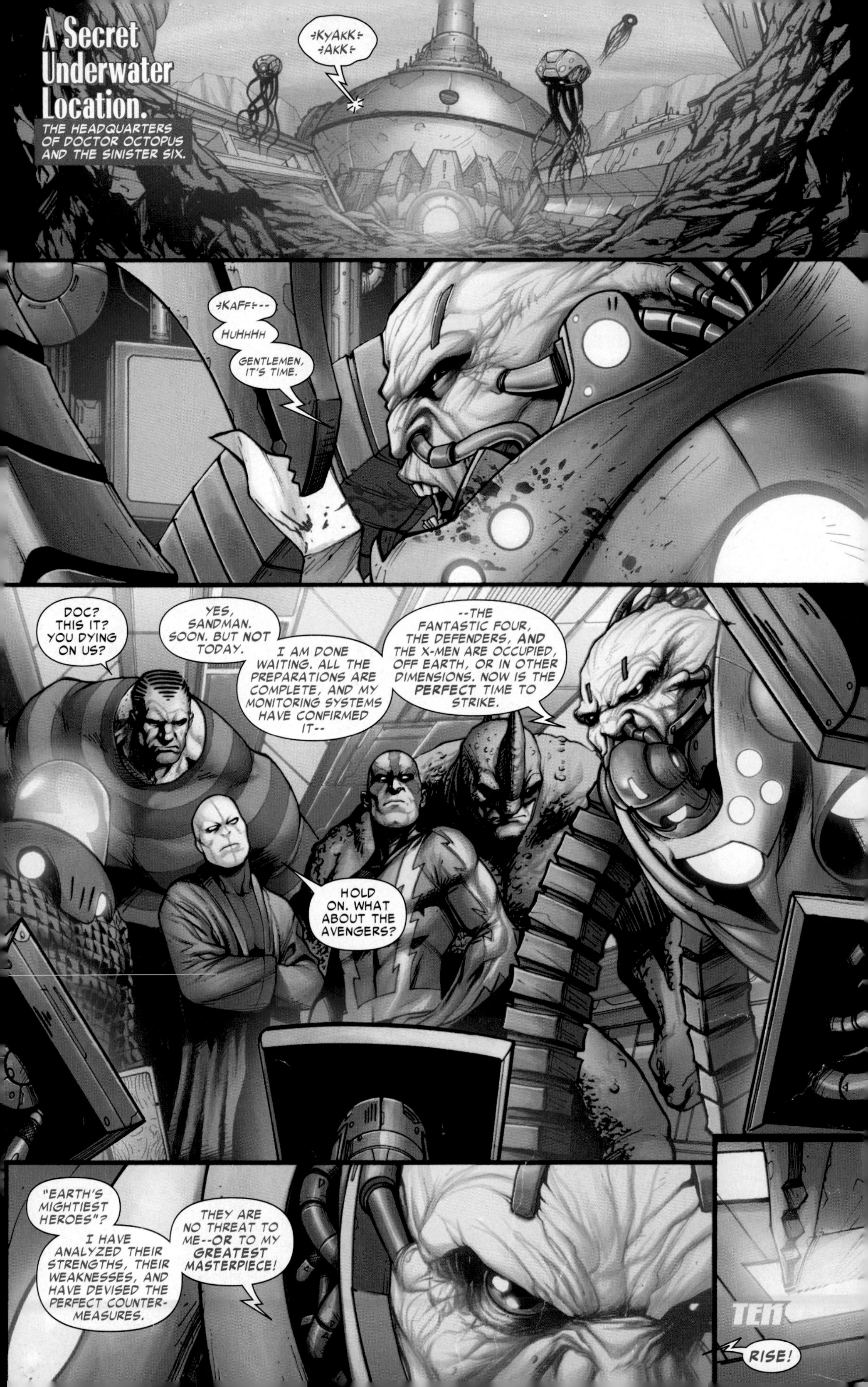
A Secret Underwater Location.
THE HEADQUARTERS OF DOCTOR OCTOPUS AND THE SINISTER SIX.
KYAKK AKK
KAFF--
HUHHHH
GENTLEMEN, IT'S TIME.
DOC? THIS IT? YOU DYING ON US?
YES, SANDMAN. SOON. BUT NOT TODAY.
I AM DONE WAITING. ALL THE PREPARATIONS ARE COMPLETE, AND MY MONITORING SYSTEMS HAVE CONFIRMED IT--
--THE FANTASTIC FOUR, THE DEFENDERS, AND THE X-MEN ARE OCCUPIED, OFF EARTH, OR IN OTHER DIMENSIONS. NOW IS THE PERFECT TIME TO STRIKE.
HOLD ON. WHAT ABOUT THE AVENGERS?
"EARTH'S MIGHTIEST HEROES"?
I HAVE ANALYZED THEIR STRENGTHS, THEIR WEAKNESSES, AND HAVE DEVISED THE PERFECT COUNTER-MEASURES.
THEY ARE NO THREAT TO ME--OR TO MY GREATEST MASTERPIECE!
TEN
RISE!

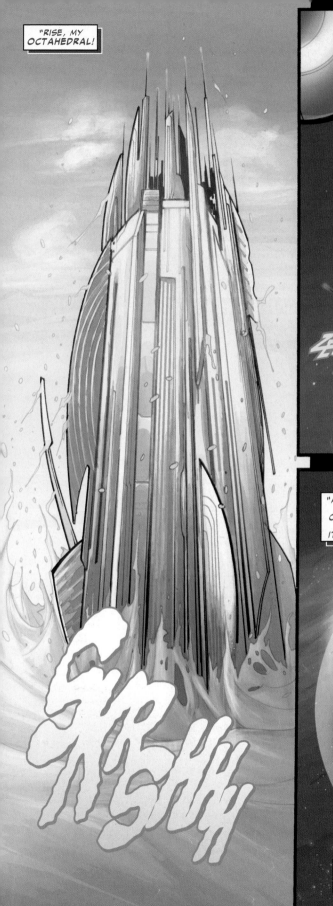

"RISE, MY OCTAHEDRAL!"

"THROUGH YOU, I SHALL CONDUCT MY 'CHOIR INVISIBLE.'

MY HOST OF ANGELS, LYING PATIENTLY IN WAIT, DYING TO SING.

"AND WITH THEM I, OTTO OCTAVIUS, WILL SET HEAVEN ITSELF ALIGHT...

"...AND PURGE THIS WORLD WITH FIRE!"

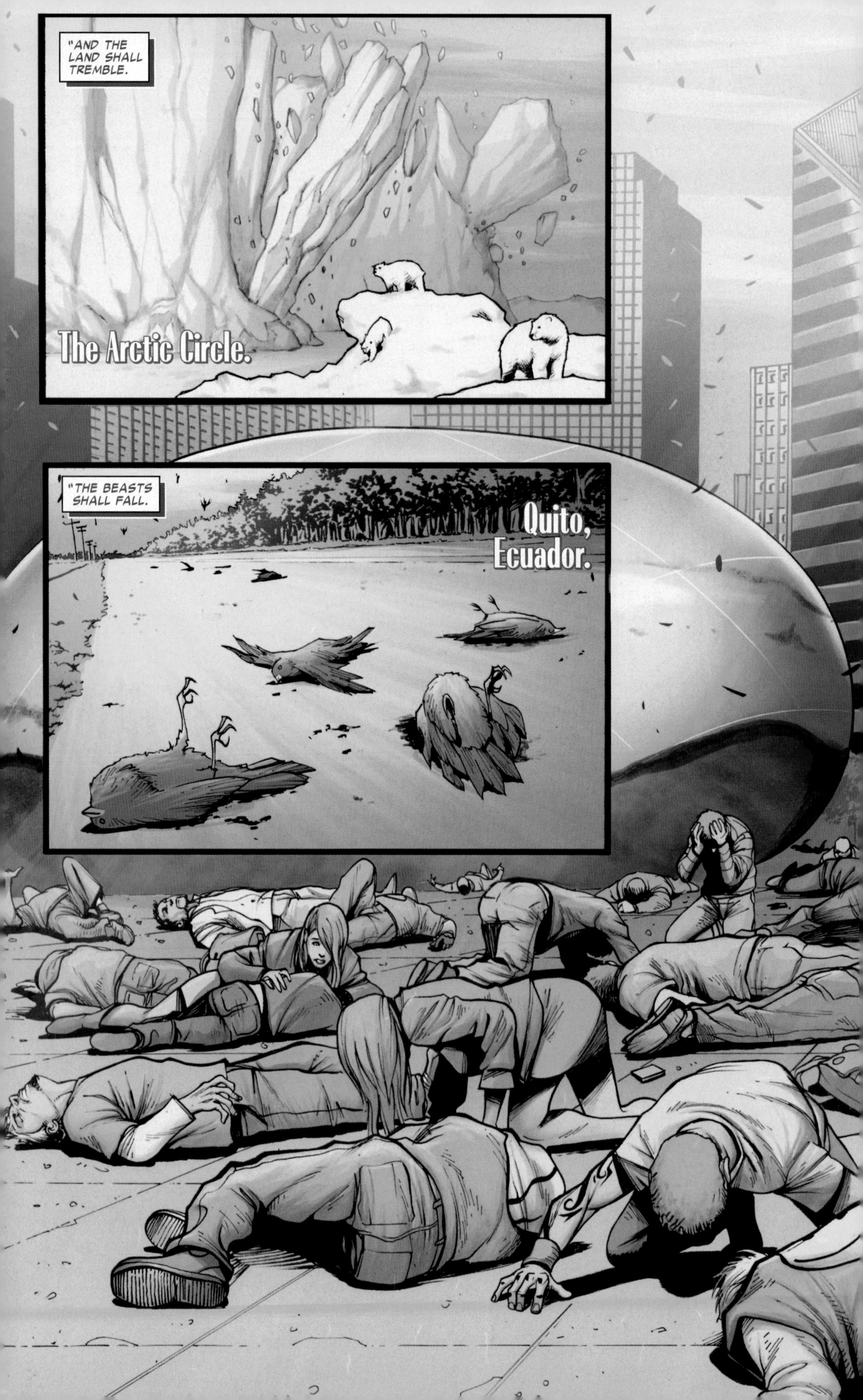
"AND THE LAND SHALL TREMBLE.
The Arctic Circle.
"THE BEASTS SHALL FALL.
Quito, Ecuador.

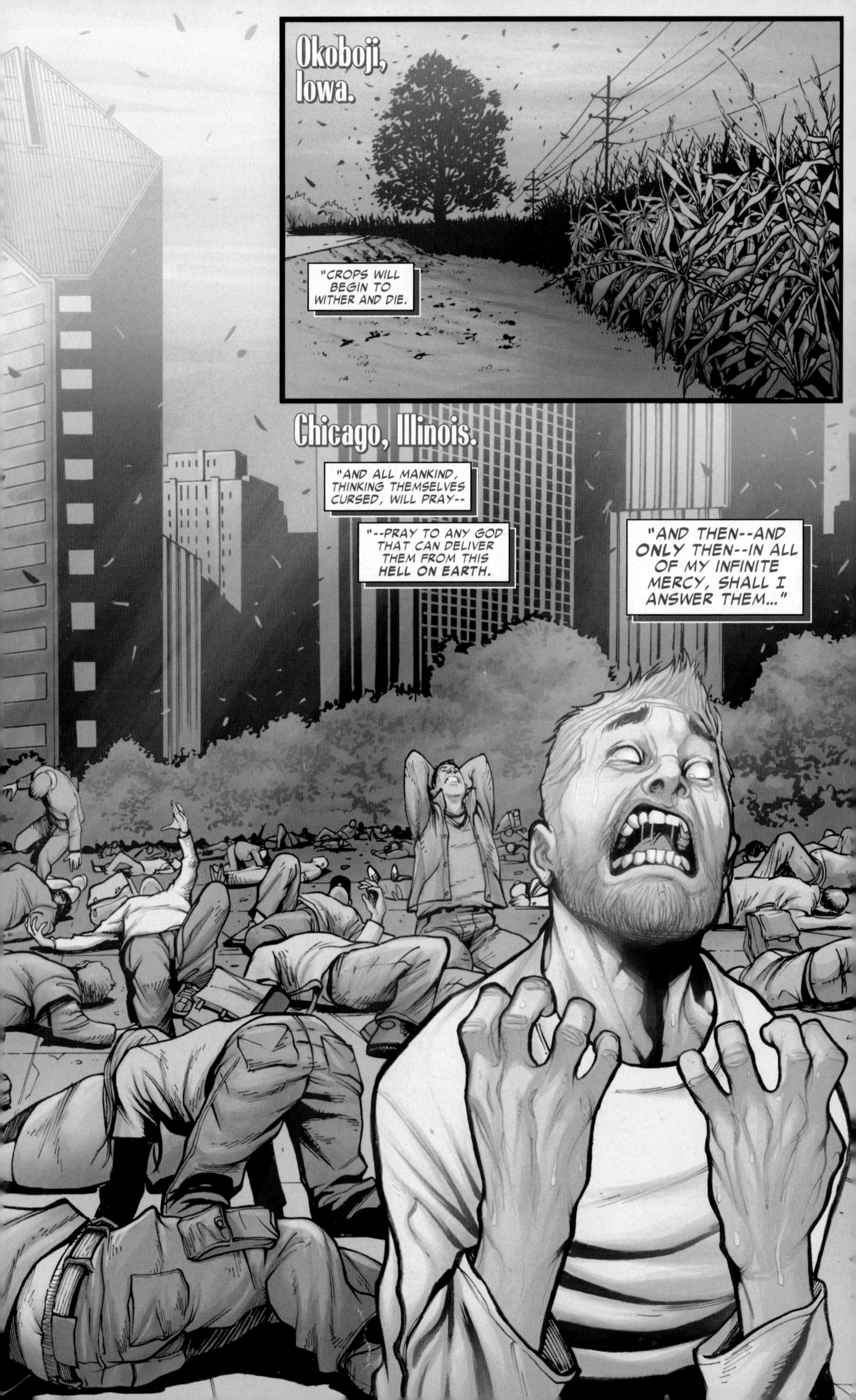
Okoboji, Iowa.
"CROPS WILL BEGIN TO WITHER AND DIE.
Chicago, Illinois.
"AND ALL MANKIND, THINKING THEMSELVES CURSED, WILL PRAY--
"--PRAY TO ANY GOD THAT CAN DELIVER THEM FROM THIS HELL ON EARTH.
"AND THEN--AND ONLY THEN--IN ALL OF MY INFINITE MERCY, SHALL I ANSWER THEM..."

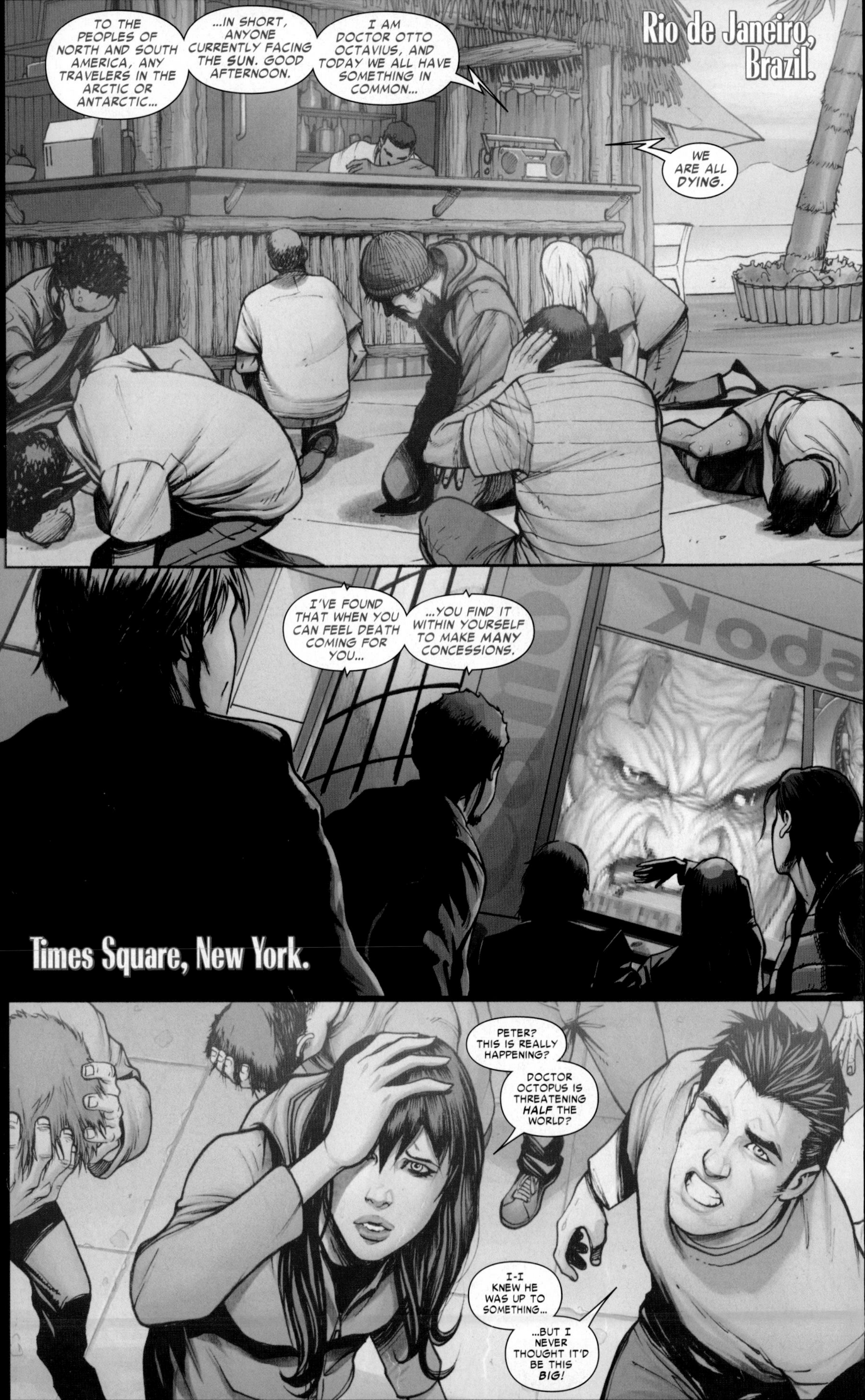
Rio de Janeiro, Brazil.
TO THE PEOPLES OF NORTH AND SOUTH AMERICA, ANY TRAVELERS IN THE ARCTIC OR ANTARCTIC...
...IN SHORT, ANYONE CURRENTLY FACING THE SUN. GOOD AFTERNOON.
I AM DOCTOR OTTO OCTAVIUS, AND TODAY WE ALL HAVE SOMETHING IN COMMON...
WE ARE ALL DYING.
I'VE FOUND THAT WHEN YOU CAN FEEL DEATH COMING FOR YOU...
...YOU FIND IT WITHIN YOURSELF TO MAKE MANY CONCESSIONS.
Times Square, New York.
PETER? THIS IS REALLY HAPPENING?
DOCTOR OCTOPUS IS THREATENING HALF THE WORLD?
I-I KNEW HE WAS UP TO SOMETHING...
...BUT I NEVER THOUGHT IT'D BE THIS BIG!

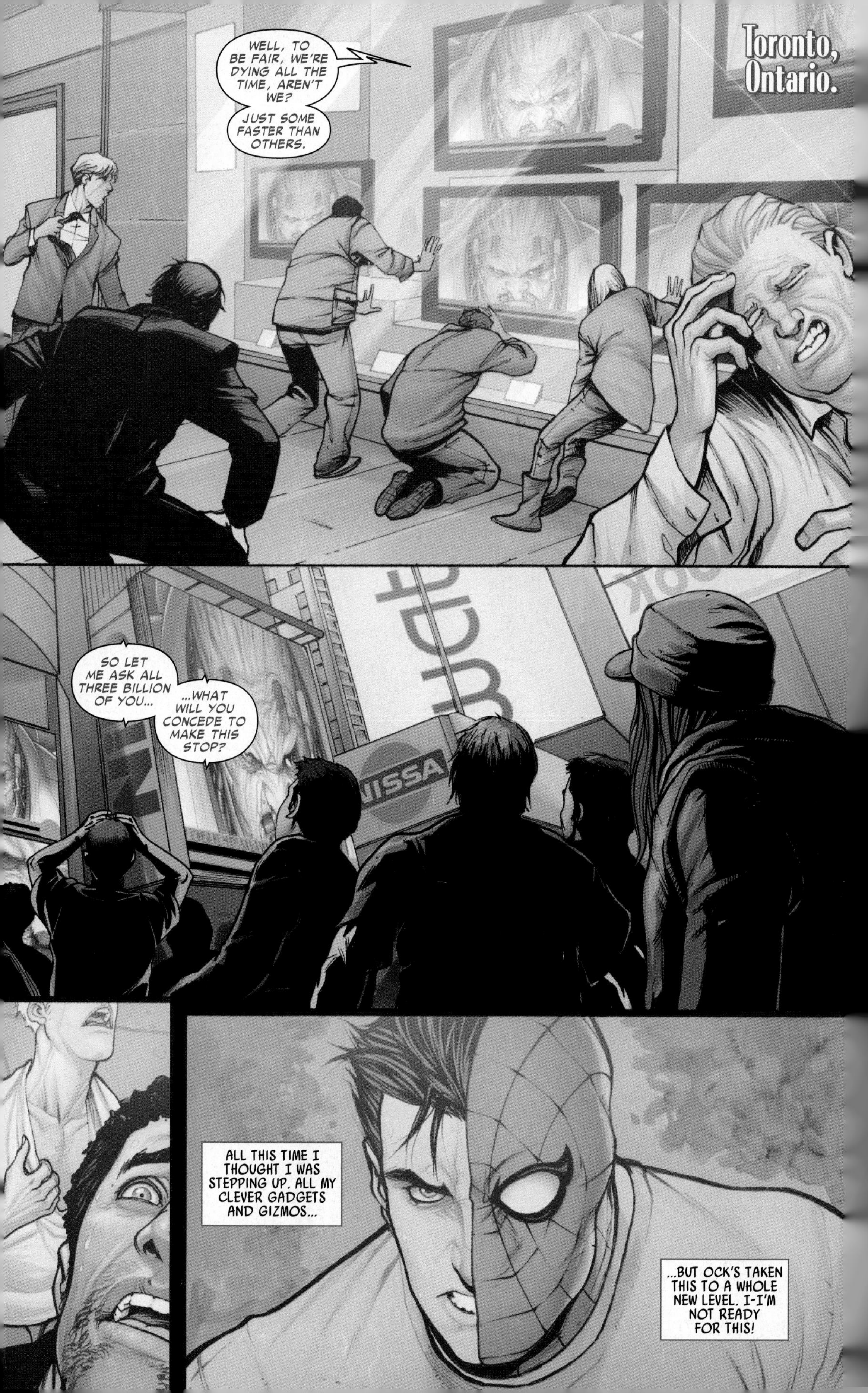
Toronto, Ontario.
WELL, TO BE FAIR, WE'RE DYING ALL THE TIME, AREN'T WE?
JUST SOME FASTER THAN OTHERS.
SO LET ME ASK ALL THREE BILLION OF YOU...
...WHAT WILL YOU CONCEDE TO MAKE THIS STOP?
ALL THIS TIME I THOUGHT I WAS STEPPING UP. ALL MY CLEVER GADGETS AND GIZMOS...
...BUT OCK'S TAKEN THIS TO A WHOLE NEW LEVEL. I-I'M NOT READY FOR THIS!

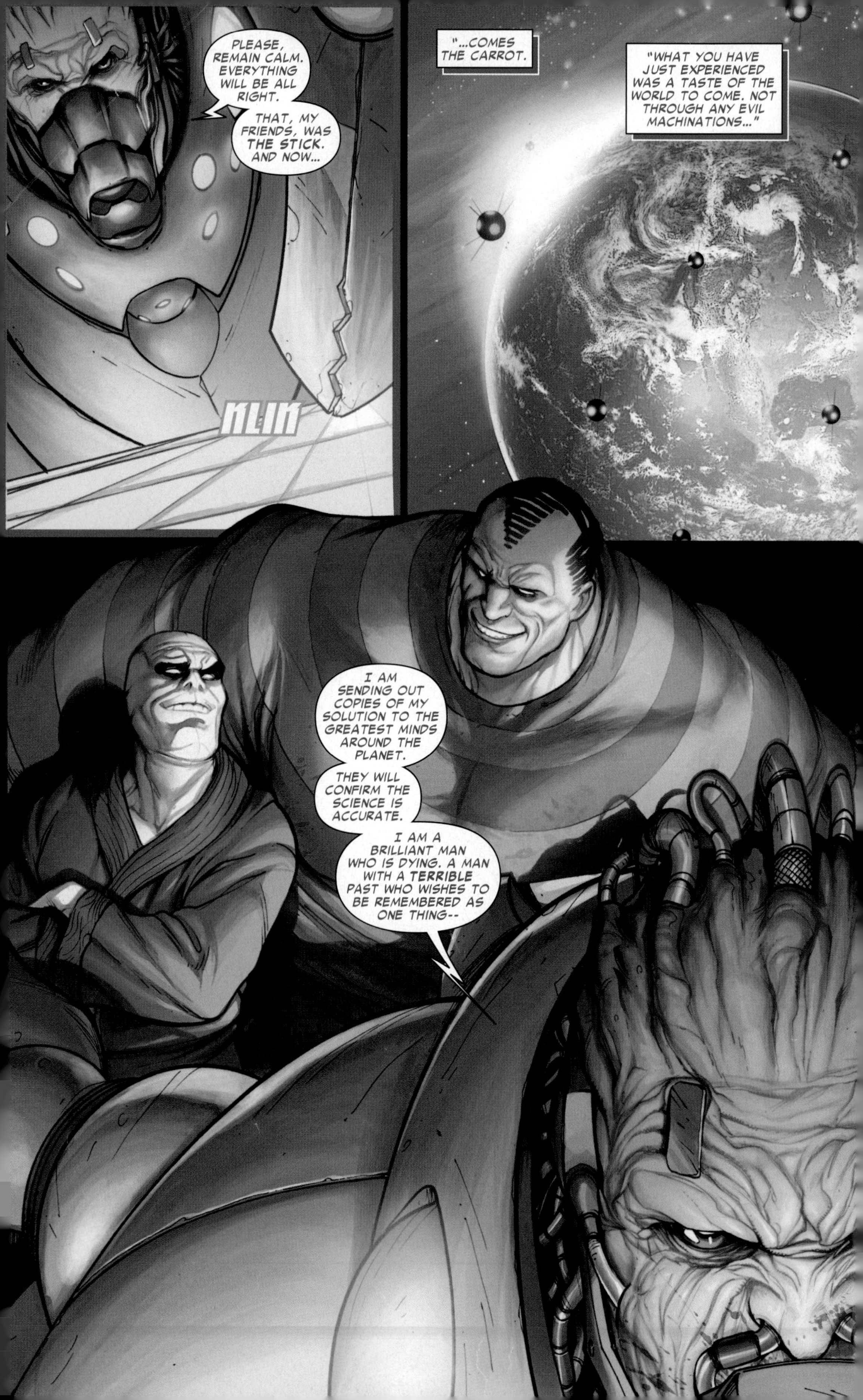
PLEASE, REMAIN CALM. EVERYTHING WILL BE ALL RIGHT.
THAT, MY FRIENDS, WAS THE STICK. AND NOW...
KLIK
"...COMES THE CARROT.
"WHAT YOU HAVE JUST EXPERIENCED WAS A TASTE OF THE WORLD TO COME. NOT THROUGH ANY EVIL MACHINATIONS..."
I AM SENDING OUT COPIES OF MY SOLUTION TO THE GREATEST MINDS AROUND THE PLANET.
THEY WILL CONFIRM THE SCIENCE IS ACCURATE.
I AM A BRILLIANT MAN WHO IS DYING. A MAN WITH A TERRIBLE PAST WHO WISHES TO BE REMEMBERED AS ONE THING--

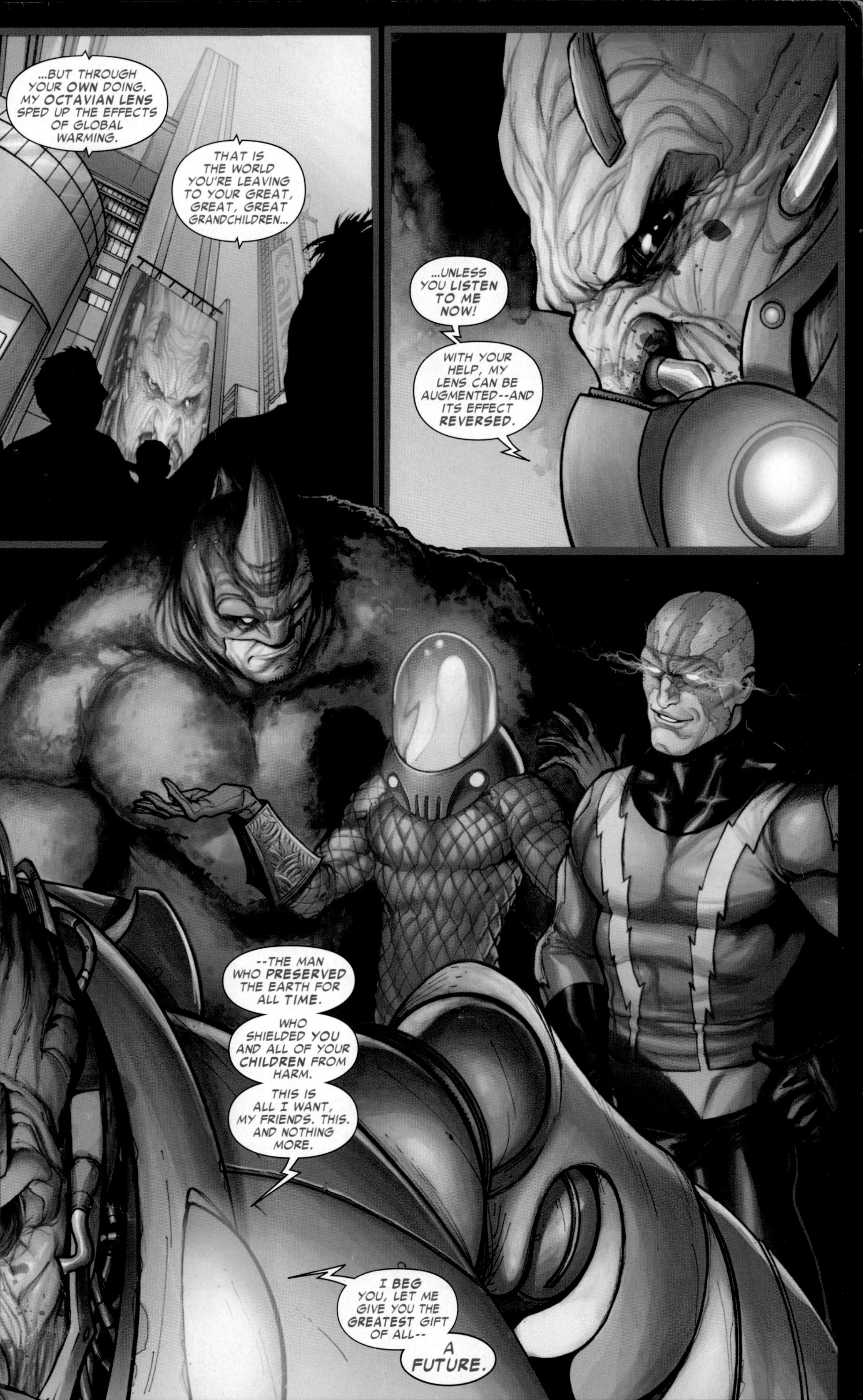
...BUT THROUGH YOUR OWN DOING. MY OCTAVIAN LENS SPED UP THE EFFECTS OF GLOBAL WARMING.
THAT IS THE WORLD YOU'RE LEAVING TO YOUR GREAT, GREAT, GREAT GRANDCHILDREN...
...UNLESS YOU LISTEN TO ME NOW!
WITH YOUR HELP, MY LENS CAN BE AUGMENTED--AND ITS EFFECT REVERSED.
--THE MAN WHO PRESERVED THE EARTH FOR ALL TIME.
WHO SHIELDED YOU AND ALL OF YOUR CHILDREN FROM HARM.
THIS IS ALL I WANT, MY FRIENDS. THIS. AND NOTHING MORE.
I BEG YOU, LET ME GIVE YOU THE GREATEST GIFT OF ALL-- A FUTURE.

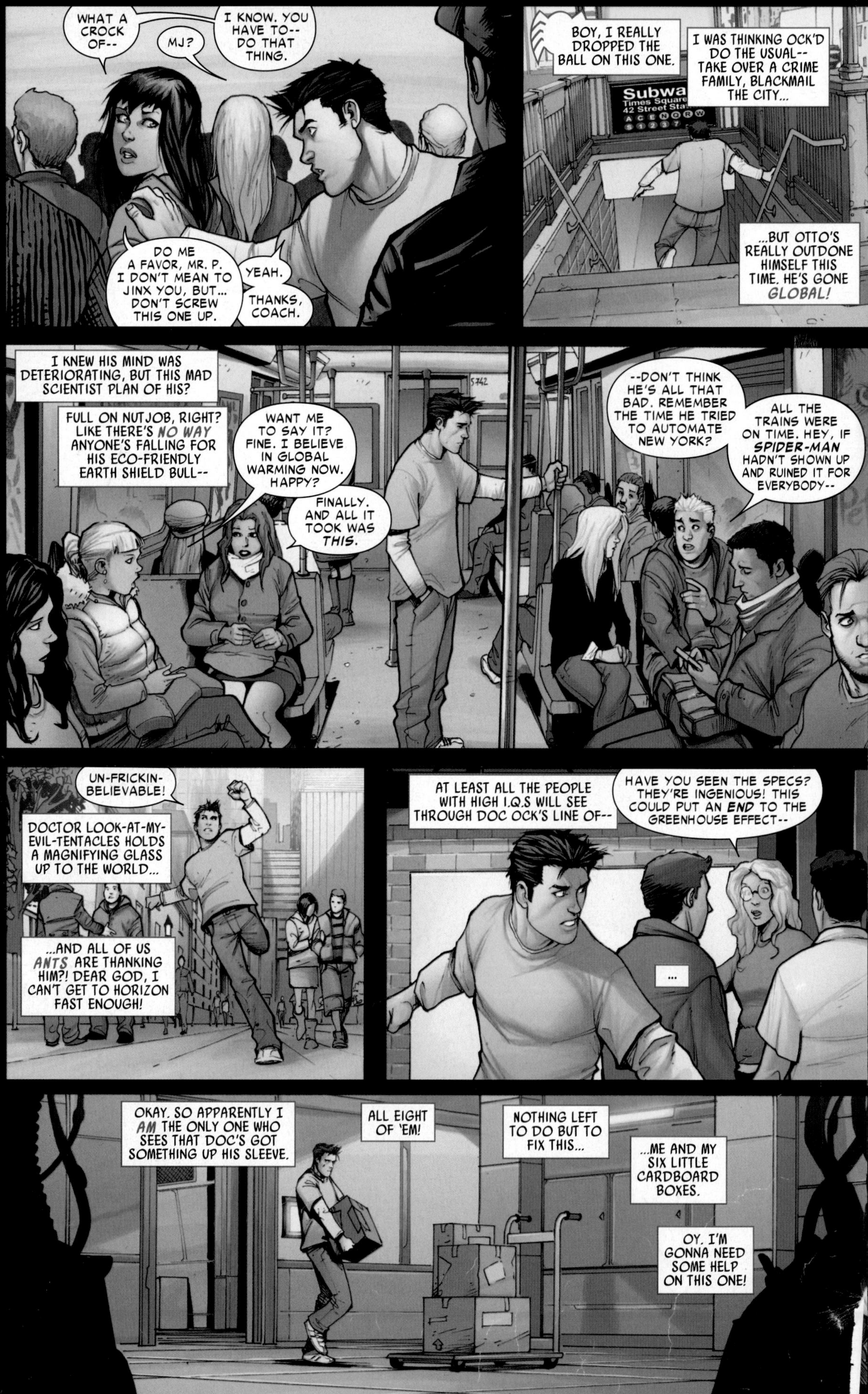

WHAT A CROCK OF--
I KNOW. YOU HAVE TO--
MJ?
DO THAT THING.
DO ME A FAVOR, MR. P. I DON'T MEAN TO JINX YOU, BUT... DON'T SCREW THIS ONE UP.
YEAH.
THANKS, COACH.
BOY, I REALLY DROPPED THE BALL ON THIS ONE.
I WAS THINKING OCK'D DO THE USUAL-- TAKE OVER A CRIME FAMILY, BLACKMAIL THE CITY...
Times Square
...BUT OTTO'S REALLY OUTDONE HIMSELF THIS TIME. HE'S GONE GLOBAL!
I KNEW HIS MIND WAS DETERIORATING, BUT THIS MAD SCIENTIST PLAN OF HIS?
FULL ON NUTJOB, RIGHT? LIKE THERE'S NO WAY ANYONE'S FALLING FOR HIS ECO-FRIENDLY EARTH SHIELD BULL--
WANT ME TO SAY IT? FINE. I BELIEVE IN GLOBAL WARMING NOW. HAPPY?
FINALLY. AND ALL IT TOOK WAS THIS.
5742
--DON'T THINK HE'S ALL THAT BAD. REMEMBER THE TIME HE TRIED TO AUTOMATE NEW YORK?
ALL THE TRAINS WERE ON TIME. HEY, IF SPIDER-MAN HADN'T SHOWN UP AND RUINED IT FOR EVERYBODY--
UN-FRICKIN-BELIEVABLE!
DOCTOR LOOK-AT-MY-EVIL-TENTACLES HOLDS A MAGNIFYING GLASS UP TO THE WORLD...
...AND ALL OF US ANTS ARE THANKING HIM?! DEAR GOD, I CAN'T GET TO HORIZON FAST ENOUGH!
AT LEAST ALL THE PEOPLE WITH HIGH I.Q.S WILL SEE THROUGH DOC OCK'S LINE OF--
HAVE YOU SEEN THE SPECS? THEY'RE INGENIOUS! THIS COULD PUT AN END TO THE GREENHOUSE EFFECT--
...
OKAY. SO APPARENTLY I AM THE ONLY ONE WHO SEES THAT DOC'S GOT SOMETHING UP HIS SLEEVE.
ALL EIGHT OF 'EM!
NOTHING LEFT TO DO BUT TO FIX THIS...
...ME AND MY SIX LITTLE CARDBOARD BOXES.
OY. I'M GONNA NEED SOME HELP ON THIS ONE!

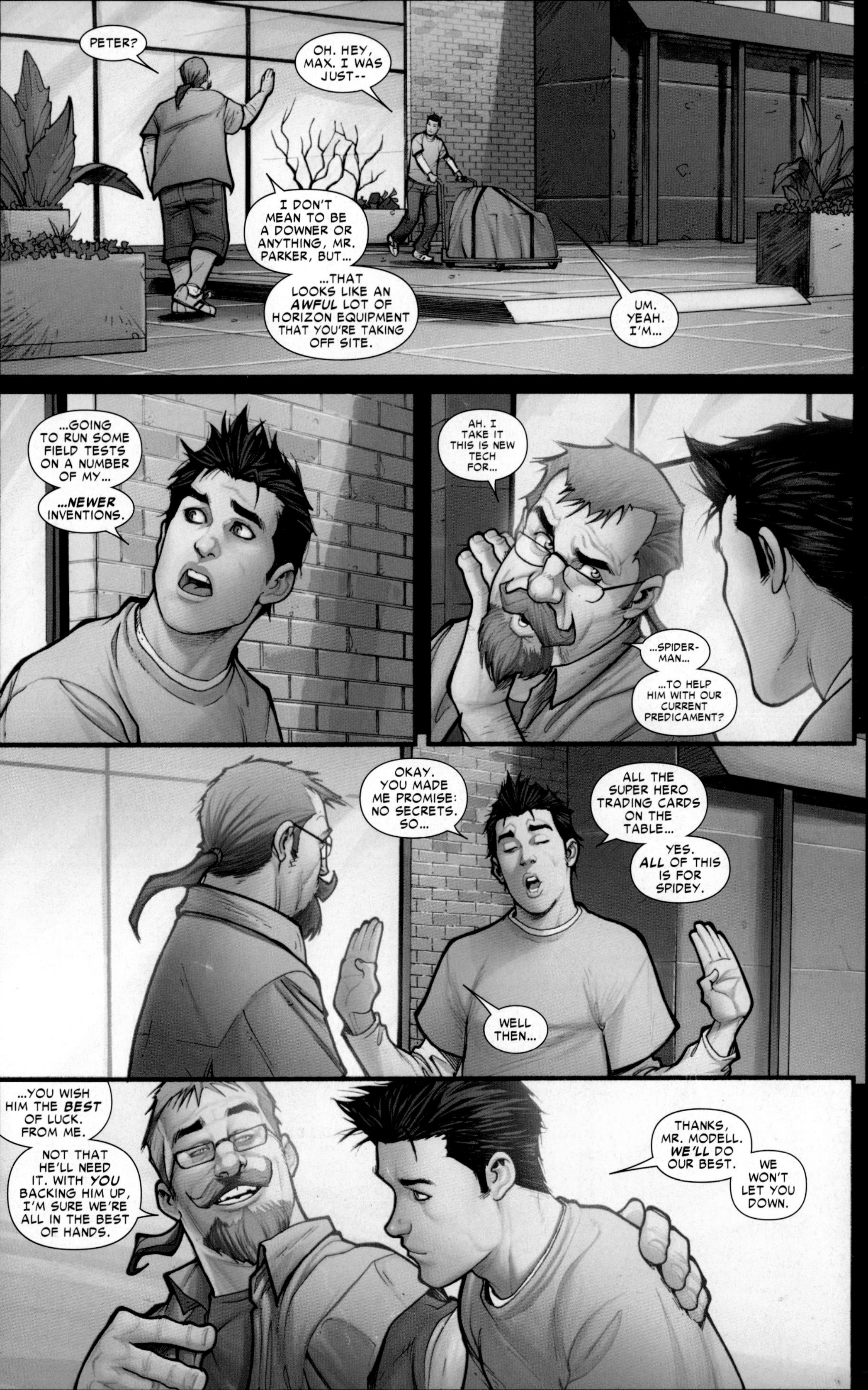
PETER?
OH. HEY, MAX. I WAS JUST--
I DON'T MEAN TO BE A DOWNER OR ANYTHING, MR. PARKER, BUT...
...THAT LOOKS LIKE AN AWFUL LOT OF HORIZON EQUIPMENT THAT YOU'RE TAKING OFF SITE.
UM. YEAH. I'M...
...GOING TO RUN SOME FIELD TESTS ON A NUMBER OF MY...
...NEWER INVENTIONS.
AH. I TAKE IT THIS IS NEW TECH FOR...
...SPIDER-MAN...
...TO HELP HIM WITH OUR CURRENT PREDICAMENT?
OKAY. YOU MADE ME PROMISE: NO SECRETS. SO...
ALL THE SUPER HERO TRADING CARDS ON THE TABLE...
YES. ALL OF THIS IS FOR SPIDEY.
WELL THEN...
...YOU WISH HIM THE BEST OF LUCK. FROM ME.
NOT THAT HE'LL NEED IT. WITH YOU BACKING HIM UP, I'M SURE WE'RE ALL IN THE BEST OF HANDS.
THANKS, MR. MODELL. WE'LL DO OUR BEST.
WE WON'T LET YOU DOWN.

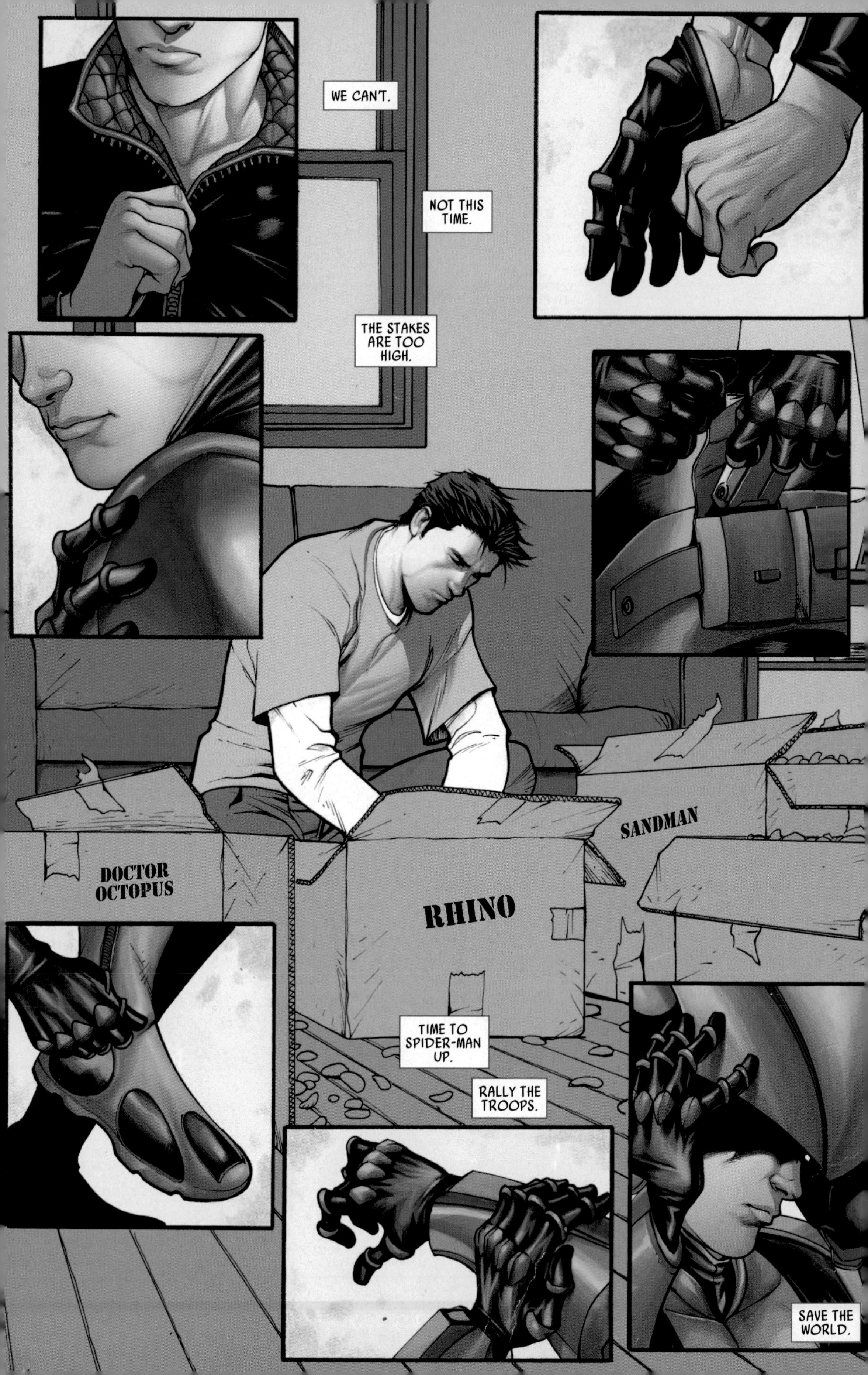

WE CAN'T.
NOT THIS TIME.
THE STAKES ARE TOO HIGH.
SANDMAN
DOCTOR OCTOPUS
RHINO
TIME TO SPIDER-MAN UP.
RALLY THE TROOPS.
SAVE THE WORLD.

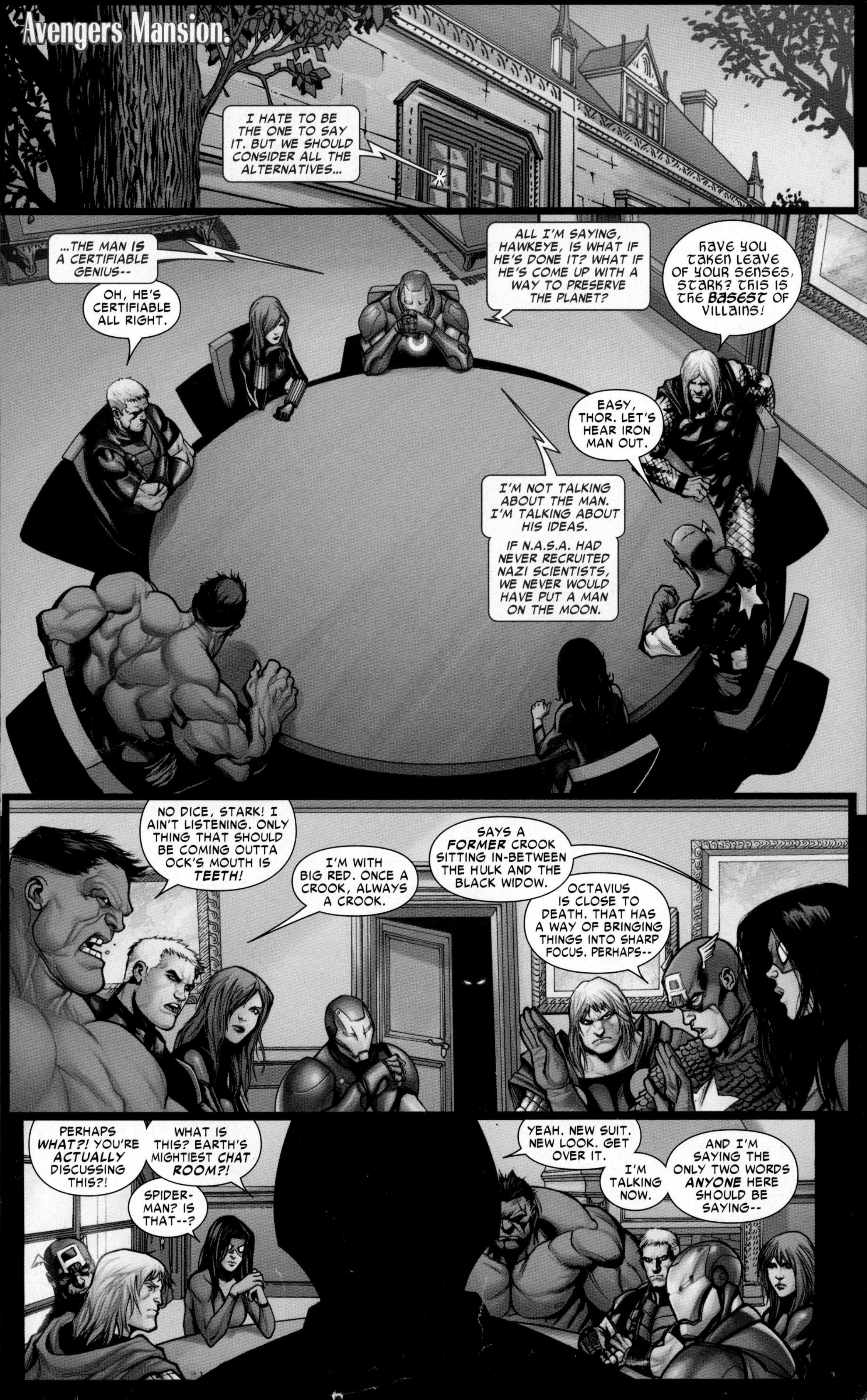
Avengers Mansion.
I HATE TO BE THE ONE TO SAY IT. BUT WE SHOULD CONSIDER ALL THE ALTERNATIVES...
...THE MAN IS A CERTIFIABLE GENIUS--
OH, HE'S CERTIFIABLE ALL RIGHT.
ALL I'M SAYING, HAWKEYE, IS WHAT IF HE'S DONE IT? WHAT IF HE'S COME UP WITH A WAY TO PRESERVE THE PLANET?
HAVE YOU TAKEN LEAVE OF YOUR SENSES, STARK? THIS IS THE BASEST OF VILLAINS!
EASY, THOR. LET'S HEAR IRON MAN OUT.
I'M NOT TALKING ABOUT THE MAN. I'M TALKING ABOUT HIS IDEAS.
IF N.A.S.A. HAD NEVER RECRUITED NAZI SCIENTISTS, WE NEVER WOULD HAVE PUT A MAN ON THE MOON.
NO DICE, STARK! I AIN'T LISTENING. ONLY THING THAT SHOULD BE COMING OUTTA OCK'S MOUTH IS TEETH!
I'M WITH BIG RED. ONCE A CROOK, ALWAYS A CROOK.
SAYS A FORMER CROOK SITTING IN-BETWEEN THE HULK AND THE BLACK WIDOW.
OCTAVIUS IS CLOSE TO DEATH. THAT HAS A WAY OF BRINGING THINGS INTO SHARP FOCUS. PERHAPS--
PERHAPS WHAT?! YOU'RE ACTUALLY DISCUSSING THIS?!
WHAT IS THIS? EARTH'S MIGHTIEST CHAT ROOM?!
SPIDER-MAN? IS THAT--?
YEAH. NEW SUIT. NEW LOOK. GET OVER IT.
I'M TALKING NOW.
AND I'M SAYING THE ONLY TWO WORDS ANYONE HERE SHOULD BE SAYING--

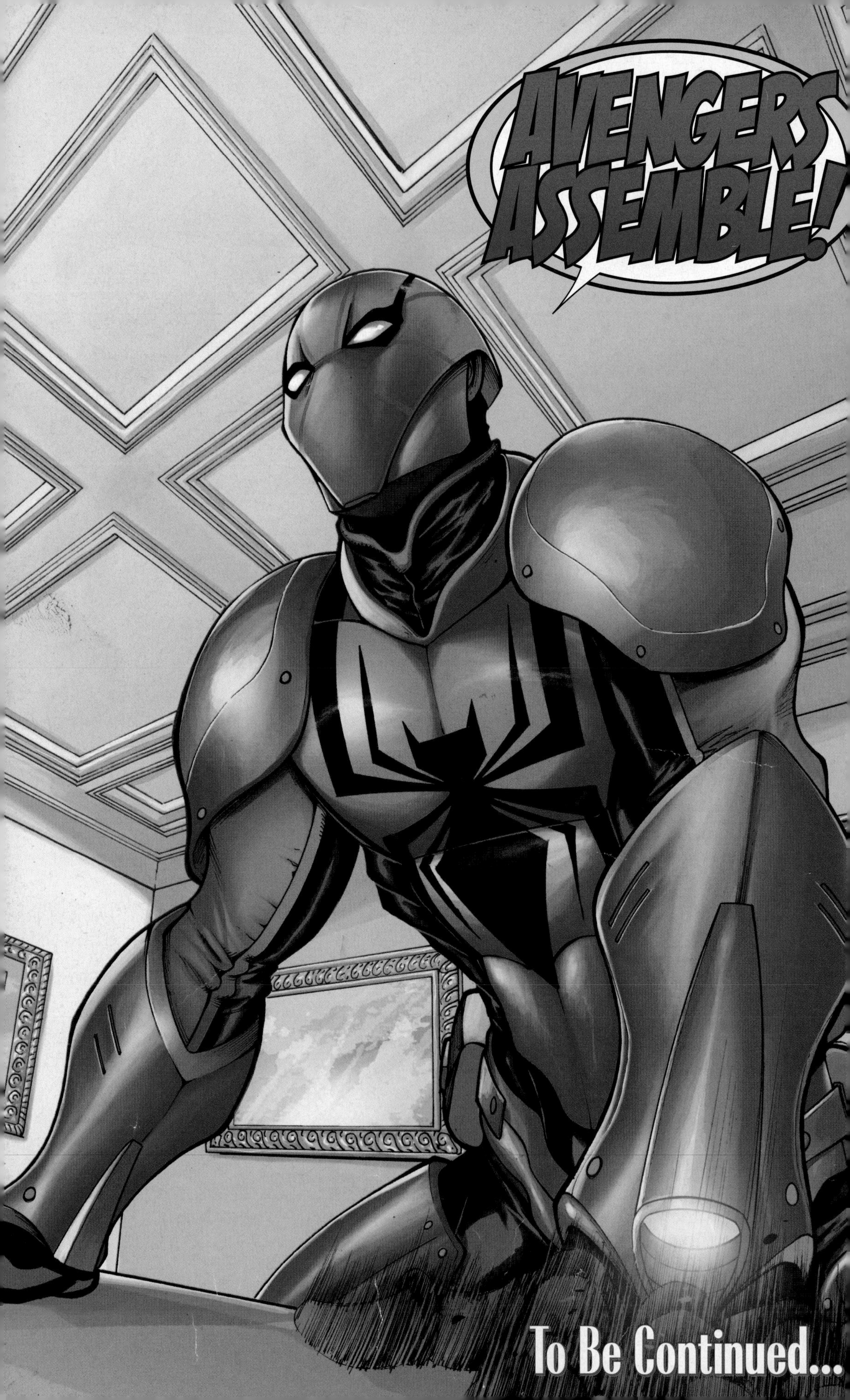
AVENGERS ASSEMBLE!
To Be Continued...

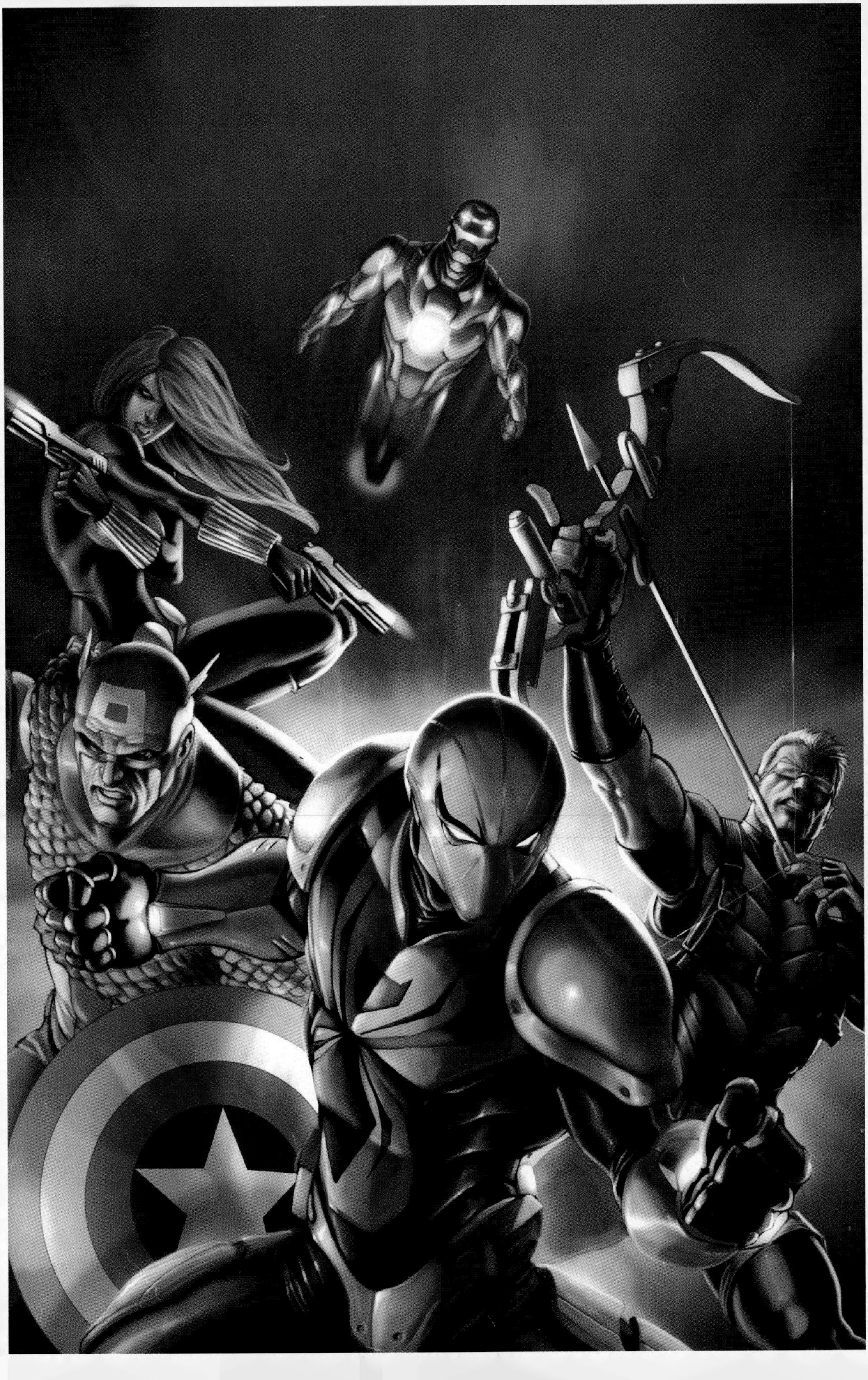

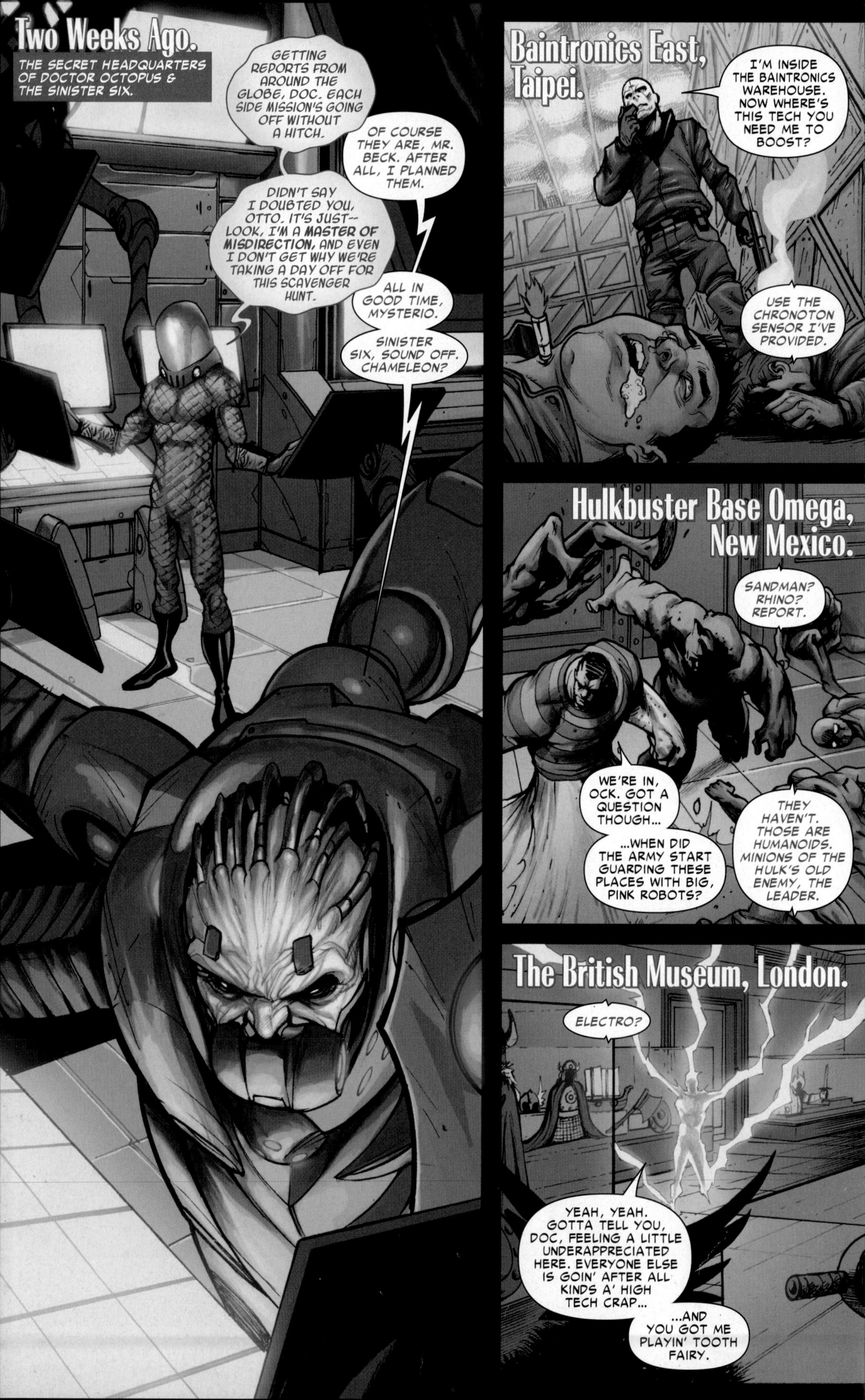
Two Weeks Ago.
THE SECRET HEADQUARTERS OF DOCTOR OCTOPUS & THE SINISTER SIX.
GETTING REPORTS FROM AROUND THE GLOBE, DOC. EACH SIDE MISSION'S GOING OFF WITHOUT A HITCH.
OF COURSE THEY ARE, MR. BECK. AFTER ALL, I PLANNED THEM.
DIDN'T SAY I DOUBTED YOU, OTTO. IT'S JUST-- LOOK, I'M A MASTER OF MISDIRECTION, AND EVEN I DON'T GET WHY WE'RE TAKING A DAY OFF FOR THIS SCAVENGER HUNT.
ALL IN GOOD TIME, MYSTERIO.
SINISTER SIX, SOUND OFF. CHAMELEON?
Baintronics East, Taipei.
I'M INSIDE THE BAINTRONICS WAREHOUSE. NOW WHERE'S THIS TECH YOU NEED ME TO BOOST?
USE THE CHRONOTON SENSOR I'VE PROVIDED.
Hulkbuster Base Omega, New Mexico.
SANDMAN? RHINO? REPORT.
WE'RE IN, OCK. GOT A QUESTION THOUGH...
...WHEN DID THE ARMY START GUARDING THESE PLACES WITH BIG, PINK ROBOTS?
THEY HAVEN'T. THOSE ARE HUMANOIDS. MINIONS OF THE HULK'S OLD ENEMY, THE LEADER.
The British Museum, London.
ELECTRO?
YEAH, YEAH. GOTTA TELL YOU, DOC, FEELING A LITTLE UNDERAPPRECIATED HERE. EVERYONE ELSE IS GOIN' AFTER ALL KINDS A' HIGH TECH CRAP...
...AND YOU GOT ME PLAYIN' TOOTH FAIRY.

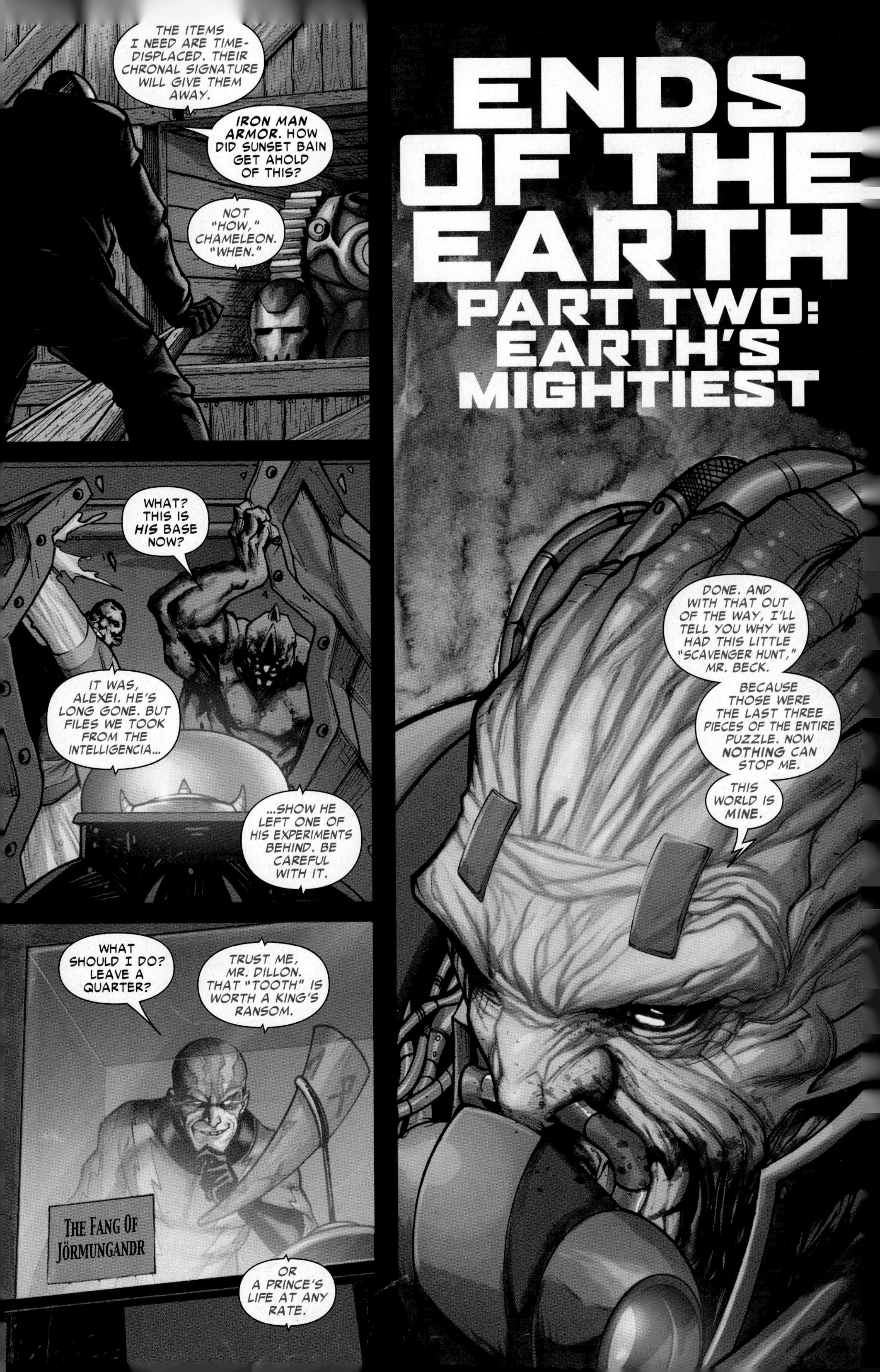
THE ITEMS I NEED ARE TIME-DISPLACED. THEIR CHRONAL SIGNATURE WILL GIVE THEM AWAY.
IRON MAN ARMOR. HOW DID SUNSET BAIN GET AHOLD OF THIS?
NOT "HOW," CHAMELEON. "WHEN."
ENDS OF THE EARTH
PART TWO: EARTH'S MIGHTIEST
WHAT? THIS IS HIS BASE NOW?
IT WAS, ALEXEI. HE'S LONG GONE. BUT FILES WE TOOK FROM THE INTELLIGENCIA...
...SHOW HE LEFT ONE OF HIS EXPERIMENTS BEHIND. BE CAREFUL WITH IT.
WHAT SHOULD I DO? LEAVE A QUARTER?
TRUST ME, MR. DILLON. THAT "TOOTH" IS WORTH A KING'S RANSOM.
THE FANG OF JÖRMUNGANDR
OR A PRINCE'S LIFE AT ANY RATE.
DONE. AND WITH THAT OUT OF THE WAY, I'LL TELL YOU WHY WE HAD THIS LITTLE "SCAVENGER HUNT," MR. BECK.
BECAUSE THOSE WERE THE LAST THREE PIECES OF THE ENTIRE PUZZLE. NOW NOTHING CAN STOP ME.
THIS WORLD IS MINE.

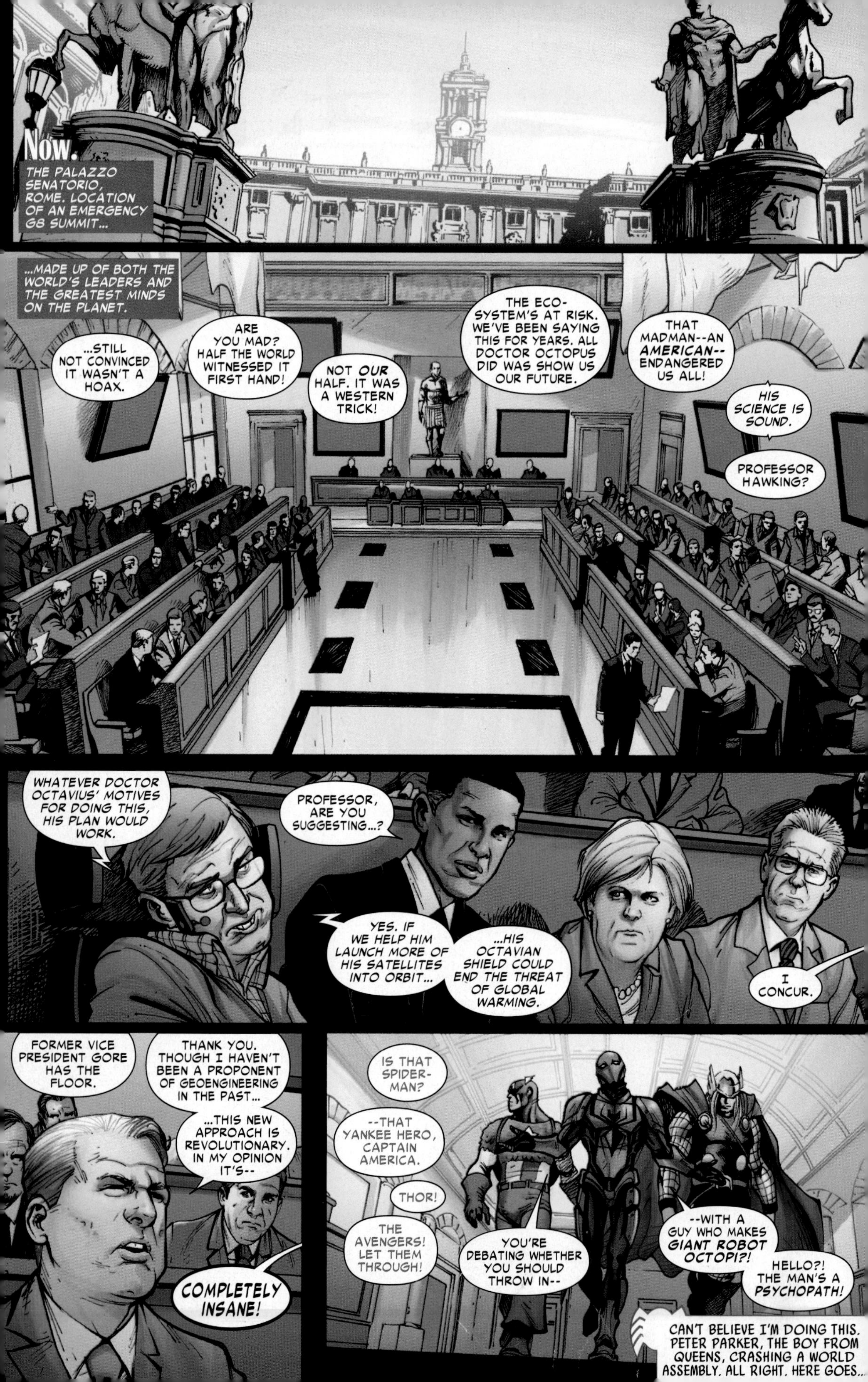
Now.
THE PALAZZO SENATORIO, ROME. LOCATION OF AN EMERGENCY G8 SUMMIT...
...MADE UP OF BOTH THE WORLD'S LEADERS AND THE GREATEST MINDS ON THE PLANET.
...STILL NOT CONVINCED IT WASN'T A HOAX.
ARE YOU MAD? HALF THE WORLD WITNESSED IT FIRST HAND!
NOT OUR HALF. IT WAS A WESTERN TRICK!
THE ECO-SYSTEM'S AT RISK. WE'VE BEEN SAYING THIS FOR YEARS. ALL DOCTOR OCTOPUS DID WAS SHOW US OUR FUTURE.
THAT MADMAN--AN AMERICAN--ENDANGERED US ALL!
HIS SCIENCE IS SOUND.
PROFESSOR HAWKING?
WHATEVER DOCTOR OCTAVIUS' MOTIVES FOR DOING THIS, HIS PLAN WOULD WORK.
PROFESSOR, ARE YOU SUGGESTING...?
YES. IF WE HELP HIM LAUNCH MORE OF HIS SATELLITES INTO ORBIT...
...HIS OCTAVIAN SHIELD COULD END THE THREAT OF GLOBAL WARMING.
I CONCUR.
FORMER VICE PRESIDENT GORE HAS THE FLOOR.
THANK YOU. THOUGH I HAVEN'T BEEN A PROPONENT OF GEOENGINEERING IN THE PAST...
...THIS NEW APPROACH IS REVOLUTIONARY. IN MY OPINION IT'S--
COMPLETELY INSANE!
IS THAT SPIDER-MAN?
--THAT YANKEE HERO, CAPTAIN AMERICA.
THOR!
THE AVENGERS! LET THEM THROUGH!
YOU'RE DEBATING WHETHER YOU SHOULD THROW IN--
--WITH A GUY WHO MAKES GIANT ROBOT OCTOPI?!
HELLO?! THE MAN'S A PSYCHOPATH!
CAN'T BELIEVE I'M DOING THIS. PETER PARKER, THE BOY FROM QUEENS, CRASHING A WORLD ASSEMBLY. ALL RIGHT. HERE GOES...

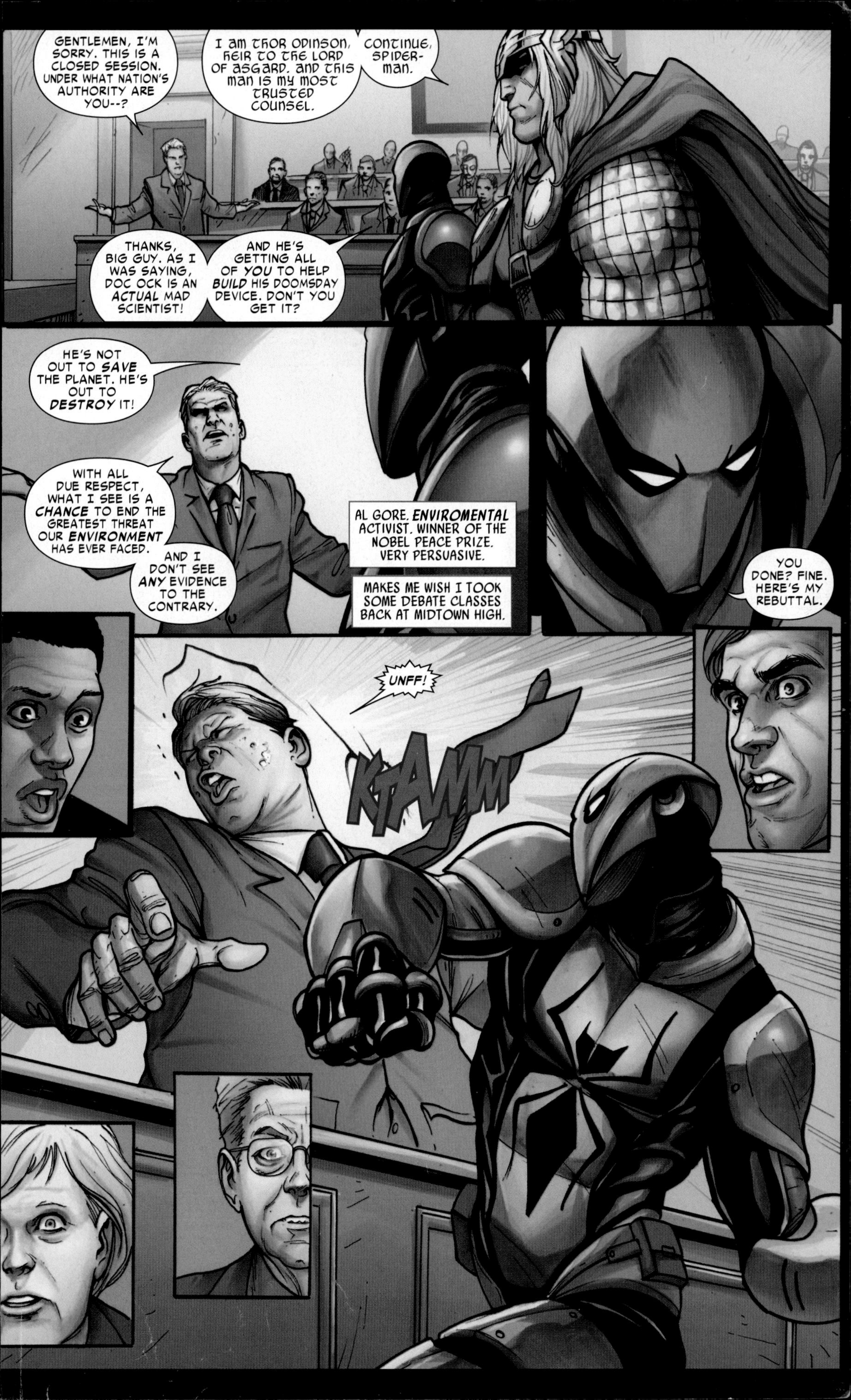
GENTLEMEN, I'M SORRY. THIS IS A CLOSED SESSION. UNDER WHAT NATION'S AUTHORITY ARE YOU--?
I AM THOR ODINSON, HEIR TO THE LORD OF ASGARD. AND THIS MAN IS MY MOST TRUSTED COUNSEL.
CONTINUE, SPIDER-MAN.
THANKS, BIG GUY. AS I WAS SAYING, DOC OCK IS AN ACTUAL MAD SCIENTIST!
AND HE'S GETTING ALL OF YOU TO HELP BUILD HIS DOOMSDAY DEVICE. DON'T YOU GET IT?
HE'S NOT OUT TO SAVE THE PLANET. HE'S OUT TO DESTROY IT!
WITH ALL DUE RESPECT, WHAT I SEE IS A CHANCE TO END THE GREATEST THREAT OUR ENVIRONMENT HAS EVER FACED.
AND I DON'T SEE ANY EVIDENCE TO THE CONTRARY.
AL GORE. ENVIROMENTAL ACTIVIST. WINNER OF THE NOBEL PEACE PRIZE. VERY PERSUASIVE.
MAKES ME WISH I TOOK SOME DEBATE CLASSES BACK AT MIDTOWN HIGH.
YOU DONE? FINE. HERE'S MY REBUTTAL.
UNFF!
KTAMM

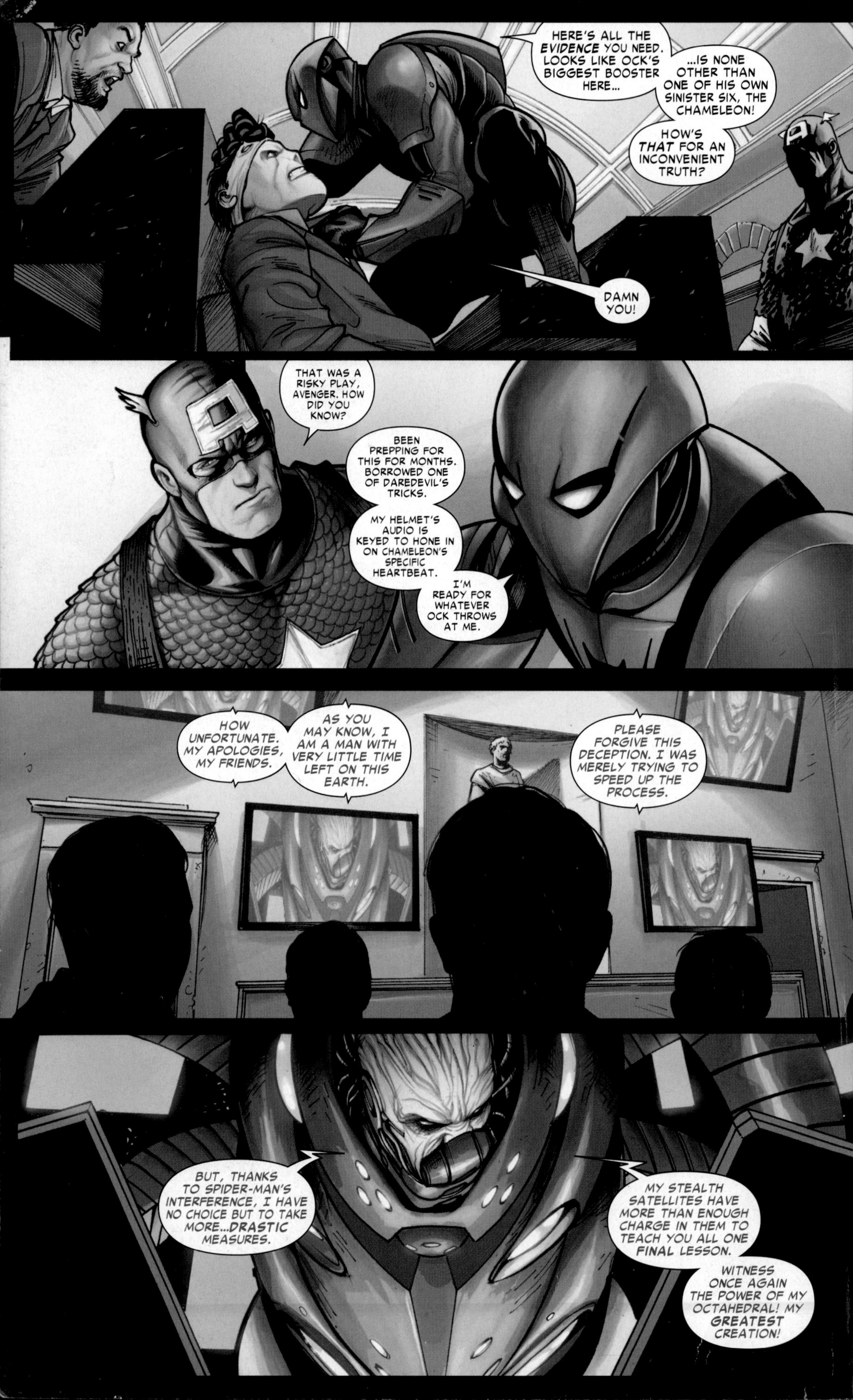
HERE'S ALL THE EVIDENCE YOU NEED. LOOKS LIKE OCK'S BIGGEST BOOSTER HERE...
...IS NONE OTHER THAN ONE OF HIS OWN SINISTER SIX, THE CHAMELEON!
HOW'S THAT FOR AN INCONVENIENT TRUTH?
DAMN YOU!
THAT WAS A RISKY PLAY, AVENGER. HOW DID YOU KNOW?
BEEN PREPPING FOR THIS FOR MONTHS. BORROWED ONE OF DAREDEVIL'S TRICKS.
MY HELMET'S AUDIO IS KEYED TO HONE IN ON CHAMELEON'S SPECIFIC HEARTBEAT.
I'M READY FOR WHATEVER OCK THROWS AT ME.
HOW UNFORTUNATE. MY APOLOGIES, MY FRIENDS.
AS YOU MAY KNOW, I AM A MAN WITH VERY LITTLE TIME LEFT ON THIS EARTH.
PLEASE FORGIVE THIS DECEPTION. I WAS MERELY TRYING TO SPEED UP THE PROCESS.
BUT, THANKS TO SPIDER-MAN'S INTERFERENCE, I HAVE NO CHOICE BUT TO TAKE MORE...DRASTIC MEASURES.
MY STEALTH SATELLITES HAVE MORE THAN ENOUGH CHARGE IN THEM TO TEACH YOU ALL ONE FINAL LESSON.
WITNESS ONCE AGAIN THE POWER OF MY OCTAHEDRAL! MY GREATEST CREATION!

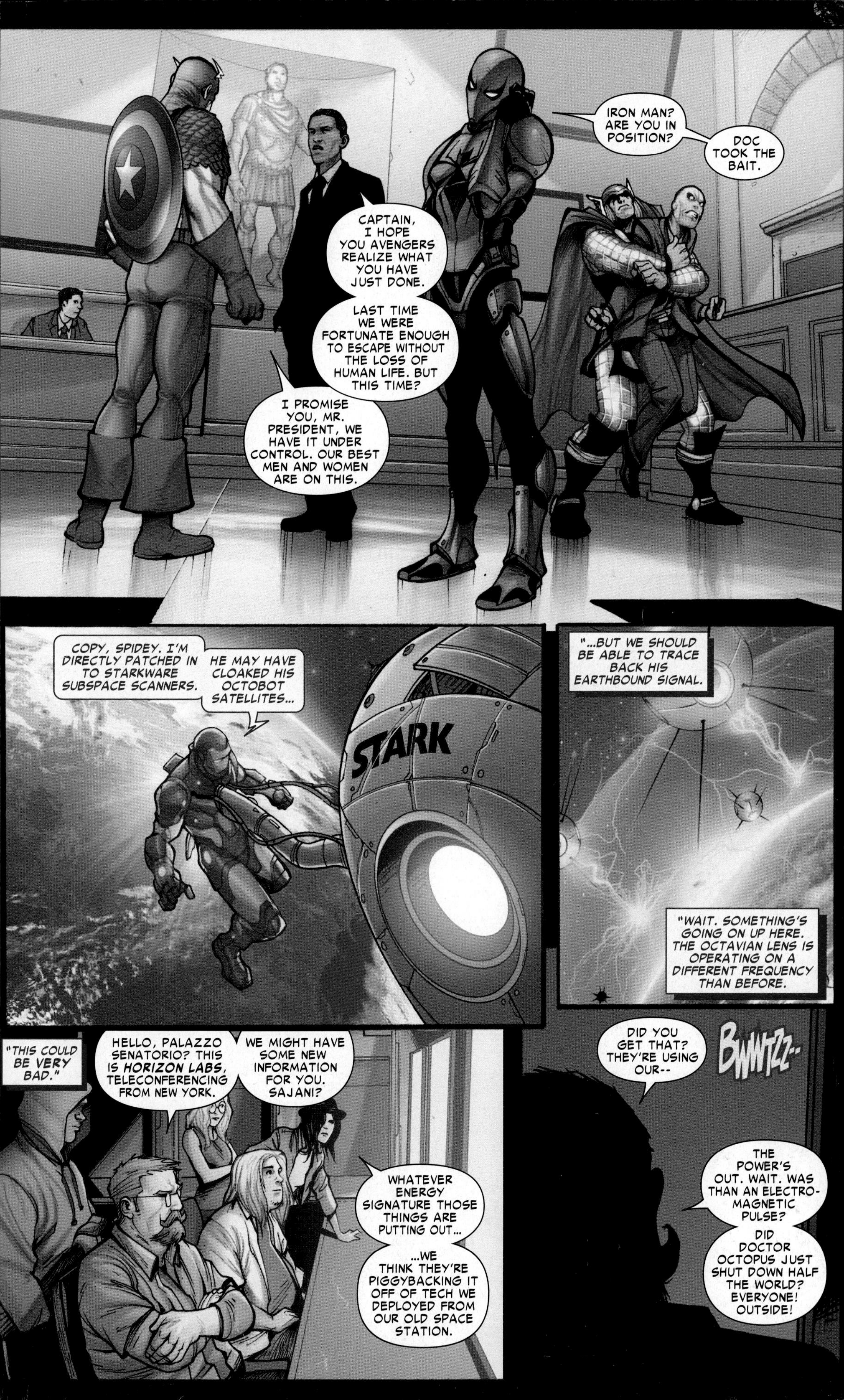
IRON MAN? ARE YOU IN POSITION?
DOC TOOK THE BAIT.
CAPTAIN, I HOPE YOU AVENGERS REALIZE WHAT YOU HAVE JUST DONE.
LAST TIME WE WERE FORTUNATE ENOUGH TO ESCAPE WITHOUT THE LOSS OF HUMAN LIFE. BUT THIS TIME?
I PROMISE YOU, MR. PRESIDENT, WE HAVE IT UNDER CONTROL. OUR BEST MEN AND WOMEN ARE ON THIS.
COPY, SPIDEY. I'M DIRECTLY PATCHED IN TO STARKWARE SUBSPACE SCANNERS.
HE MAY HAVE CLOAKED HIS OCTOBOT SATELLITES...
STARK
"...BUT WE SHOULD BE ABLE TO TRACE BACK HIS EARTHBOUND SIGNAL.
"WAIT. SOMETHING'S GOING ON UP HERE. THE OCTAVIAN LENS IS OPERATING ON A DIFFERENT FREQUENCY THAN BEFORE.
"THIS COULD BE VERY BAD."
HELLO, PALAZZO SENATORIO? THIS IS HORIZON LABS, TELECONFERENCING FROM NEW YORK.
WE MIGHT HAVE SOME NEW INFORMATION FOR YOU. SAJANI?
WHATEVER ENERGY SIGNATURE THOSE THINGS ARE PUTTING OUT...
...WE THINK THEY'RE PIGGYBACKING IT OFF OF TECH WE DEPLOYED FROM OUR OLD SPACE STATION.
DID YOU GET THAT? THEY'RE USING OUR--
BWWTZZ--
THE POWER'S OUT. WAIT. WAS THAN AN ELECTRO-MAGNETIC PULSE?
DID DOCTOR OCTOPUS JUST SHUT DOWN HALF THE WORLD? EVERYONE! OUTSIDE!

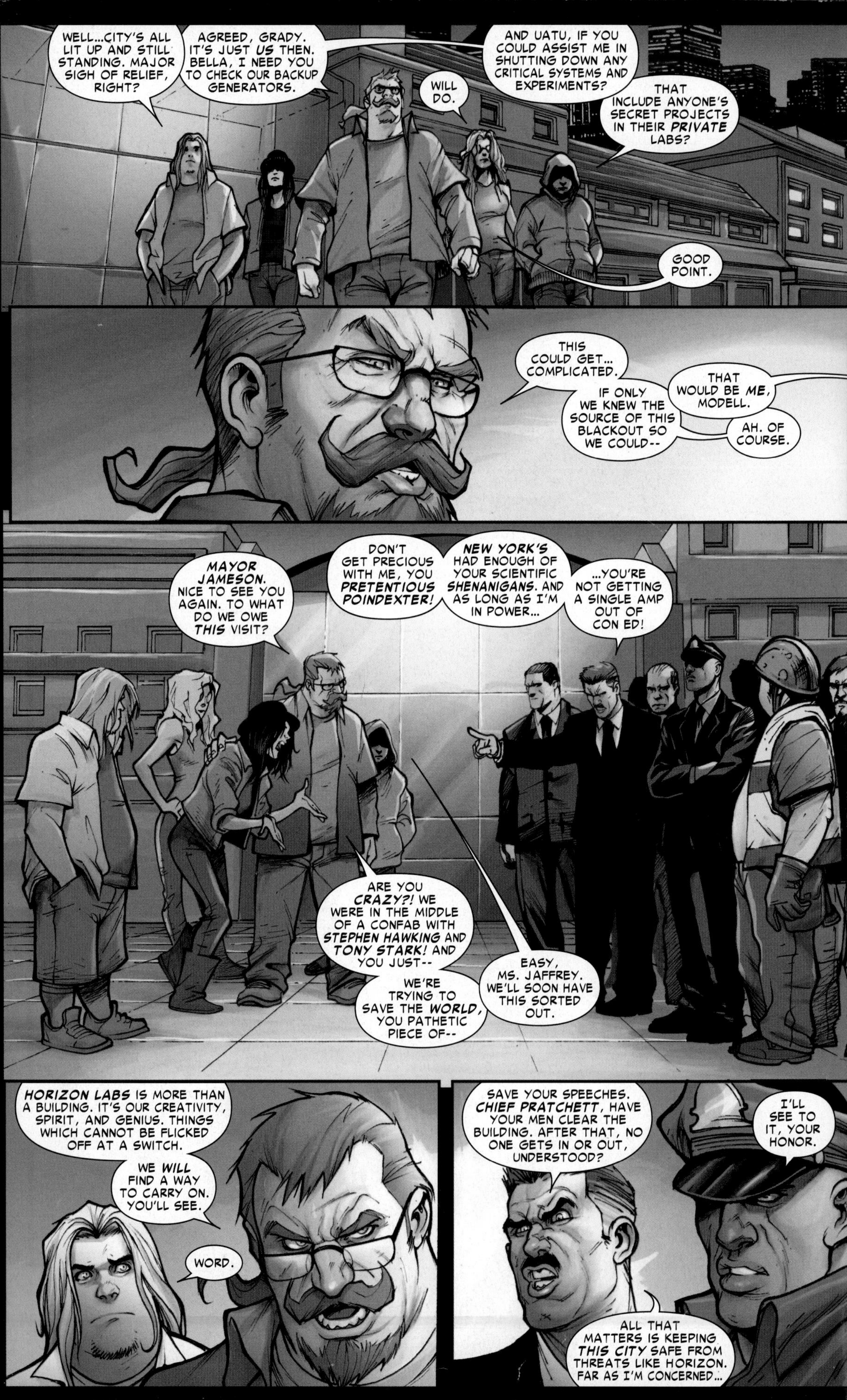
WELL...CITY'S ALL LIT UP AND STILL STANDING. MAJOR SIGH OF RELIEF, RIGHT?
AGREED, GRADY. IT'S JUST US THEN. BELLA, I NEED YOU TO CHECK OUR BACKUP GENERATORS.
WILL DO.
AND UATU, IF YOU COULD ASSIST ME IN SHUTTING DOWN ANY CRITICAL SYSTEMS AND EXPERIMENTS?
THAT INCLUDE ANYONE'S SECRET PROJECTS IN THEIR PRIVATE LABS?
GOOD POINT.
THIS COULD GET... COMPLICATED.
IF ONLY WE KNEW THE SOURCE OF THIS BLACKOUT SO WE COULD--
THAT WOULD BE ME, MODELL.
AH. OF COURSE.
MAYOR JAMESON. NICE TO SEE YOU AGAIN. TO WHAT DO WE OWE THIS VISIT?
DON'T GET PRECIOUS WITH ME, YOU PRETENTIOUS POINDEXTER!
NEW YORK'S HAD ENOUGH OF YOUR SCIENTIFIC SHENANIGANS. AND AS LONG AS I'M IN POWER...
...YOU'RE NOT GETTING A SINGLE AMP OUT OF CON ED!
ARE YOU CRAZY?! WE WERE IN THE MIDDLE OF A CONFAB WITH STEPHEN HAWKING AND TONY STARK! AND YOU JUST--
WE'RE TRYING TO SAVE THE WORLD, YOU PATHETIC PIECE OF--
EASY, MS. JAFFREY. WE'LL SOON HAVE THIS SORTED OUT.
HORIZON LABS IS MORE THAN A BUILDING. IT'S OUR CREATIVITY, SPIRIT, AND GENIUS. THINGS WHICH CANNOT BE FLICKED OFF AT A SWITCH.
WE WILL FIND A WAY TO CARRY ON. YOU'LL SEE.
WORD.
SAVE YOUR SPEECHES. CHIEF PRATCHETT, HAVE YOUR MEN CLEAR THE BUILDING. AFTER THAT, NO ONE GETS IN OR OUT, UNDERSTOOD?
I'LL SEE TO IT, YOUR HONOR.
ALL THAT MATTERS IS KEEPING THIS CITY SAFE FROM THREATS LIKE HORIZON. FAR AS I'M CONCERNED...

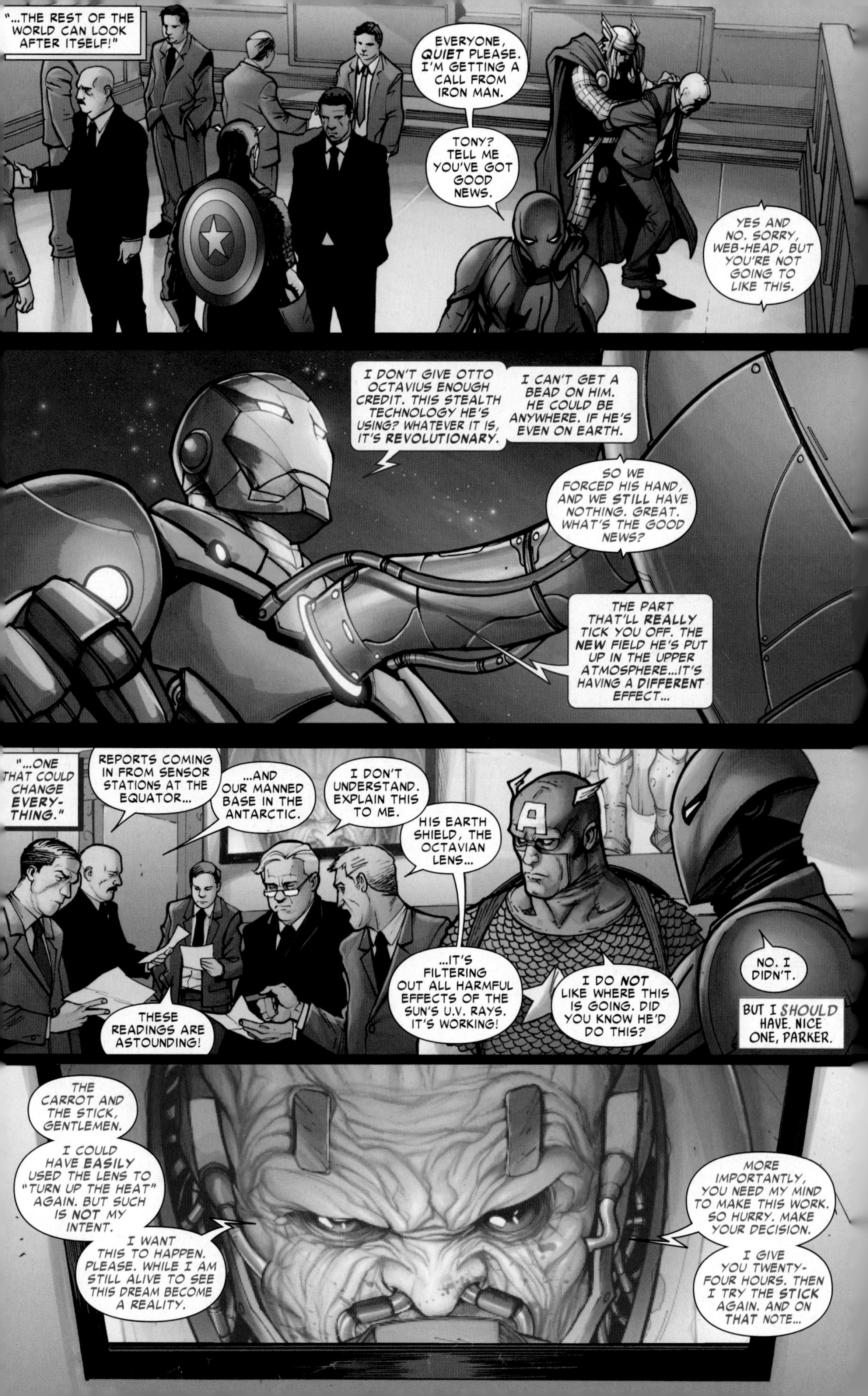
"...THE REST OF THE WORLD CAN LOOK AFTER ITSELF!"
EVERYONE, QUIET PLEASE. I'M GETTING A CALL FROM IRON MAN.
TONY? TELL ME YOU'VE GOT GOOD NEWS.
YES AND NO. SORRY, WEB-HEAD, BUT YOU'RE NOT GOING TO LIKE THIS.
I DON'T GIVE OTTO OCTAVIUS ENOUGH CREDIT. THIS STEALTH TECHNOLOGY HE'S USING? WHATEVER IT IS, IT'S REVOLUTIONARY.
I CAN'T GET A BEAD ON HIM. HE COULD BE ANYWHERE. IF HE'S EVEN ON EARTH.
SO WE FORCED HIS HAND, AND WE STILL HAVE NOTHING. GREAT. WHAT'S THE GOOD NEWS?
THE PART THAT'LL REALLY TICK YOU OFF. THE NEW FIELD HE'S PUT UP IN THE UPPER ATMOSPHERE...IT'S HAVING A DIFFERENT EFFECT...
"...ONE THAT COULD CHANGE EVERYTHING."
REPORTS COMING IN FROM SENSOR STATIONS AT THE EQUATOR...
...AND OUR MANNED BASE IN THE ANTARCTIC.
I DON'T UNDERSTAND. EXPLAIN THIS TO ME.
HIS EARTH SHIELD, THE OCTAVIAN LENS...
...IT'S FILTERING OUT ALL HARMFUL EFFECTS OF THE SUN'S U.V. RAYS. IT'S WORKING!
THESE READINGS ARE ASTOUNDING!
I DO NOT LIKE WHERE THIS IS GOING. DID YOU KNOW HE'D DO THIS?
NO. I DIDN'T.
BUT I SHOULD HAVE. NICE ONE, PARKER.
THE CARROT AND THE STICK, GENTLEMEN.
I COULD HAVE EASILY USED THE LENS TO "TURN UP THE HEAT" AGAIN. BUT SUCH IS NOT MY INTENT.
I WANT THIS TO HAPPEN. PLEASE. WHILE I AM STILL ALIVE TO SEE THIS DREAM BECOME A REALITY.
MORE IMPORTANTLY, YOU NEED MY MIND TO MAKE THIS WORK. SO HURRY. MAKE YOUR DECISION.
I GIVE YOU TWENTY-FOUR HOURS. THEN I TRY THE STICK AGAIN. AND ON THAT NOTE...

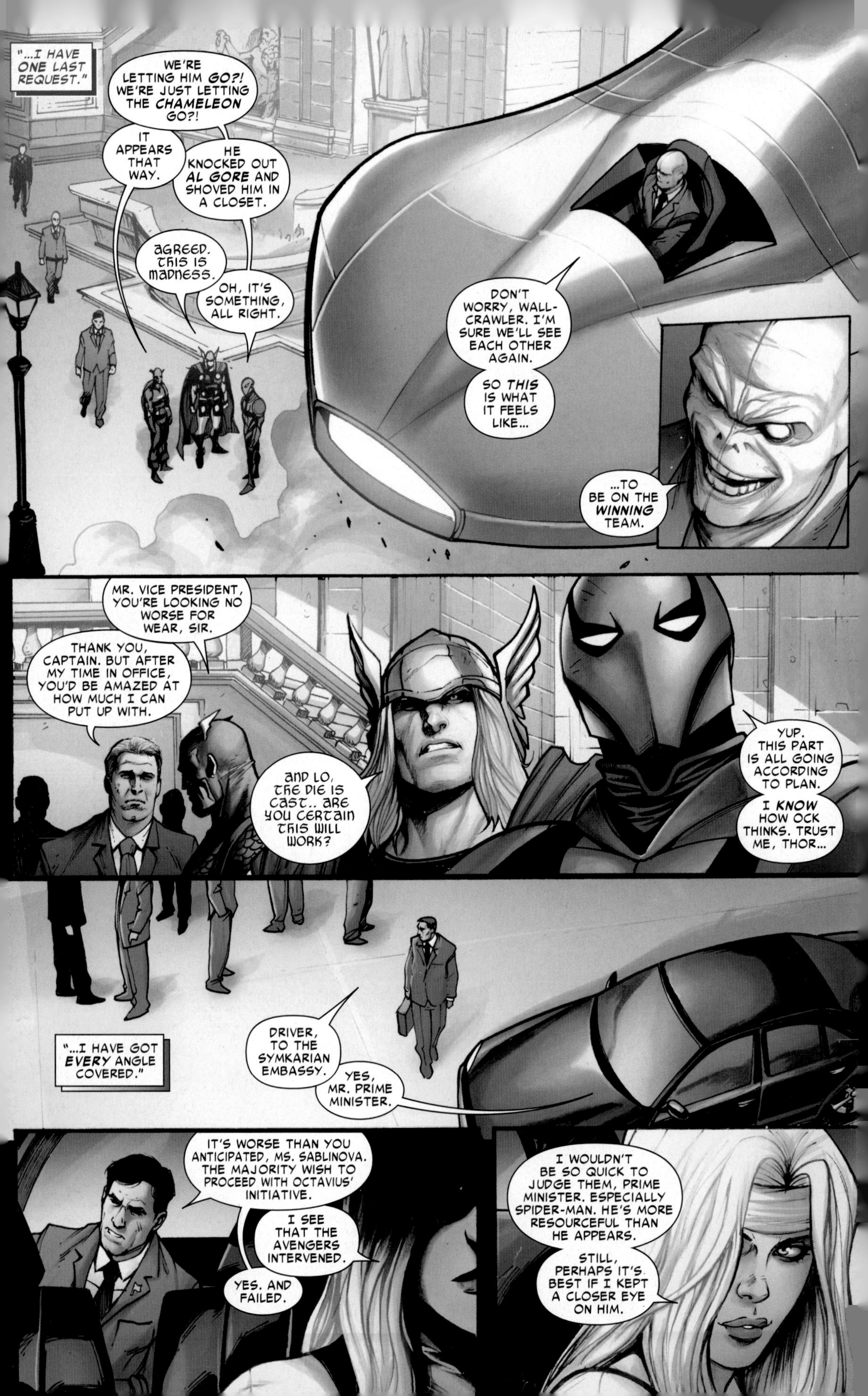
"...I HAVE ONE LAST REQUEST."
WE'RE LETTING HIM GO?! WE'RE JUST LETTING THE CHAMELEON GO?!
IT APPEARS THAT WAY.
HE KNOCKED OUT AL GORE AND SHOVED HIM IN A CLOSET.
AGREED. THIS IS MADNESS.
OH, IT'S SOMETHING, ALL RIGHT.
DON'T WORRY, WALL-CRAWLER. I'M SURE WE'LL SEE EACH OTHER AGAIN.
SO THIS IS WHAT IT FEELS LIKE...
...TO BE ON THE WINNING TEAM.
MR. VICE PRESIDENT, YOU'RE LOOKING NO WORSE FOR WEAR, SIR.
THANK YOU, CAPTAIN. BUT AFTER MY TIME IN OFFICE, YOU'D BE AMAZED AT HOW MUCH I CAN PUT UP WITH.
AND LO, THE DIE IS CAST.. ARE YOU CERTAIN THIS WILL WORK?
YUP. THIS PART IS ALL GOING ACCORDING TO PLAN.
I KNOW HOW OCK THINKS. TRUST ME, THOR...
"...I HAVE GOT EVERY ANGLE COVERED."
DRIVER, TO THE SYMKARIAN EMBASSY.
YES, MR. PRIME MINISTER.
IT'S WORSE THAN YOU ANTICIPATED, MS. SABLINOVA. THE MAJORITY WISH TO PROCEED WITH OCTAVIUS' INITIATIVE.
I SEE THAT THE AVENGERS INTERVENED.
YES. AND FAILED.
I WOULDN'T BE SO QUICK TO JUDGE THEM, PRIME MINISTER. ESPECIALLY SPIDER-MAN. HE'S MORE RESOURCEFUL THAN HE APPEARS.
STILL, PERHAPS IT'S BEST IF I KEPT A CLOSER EYE ON HIM.

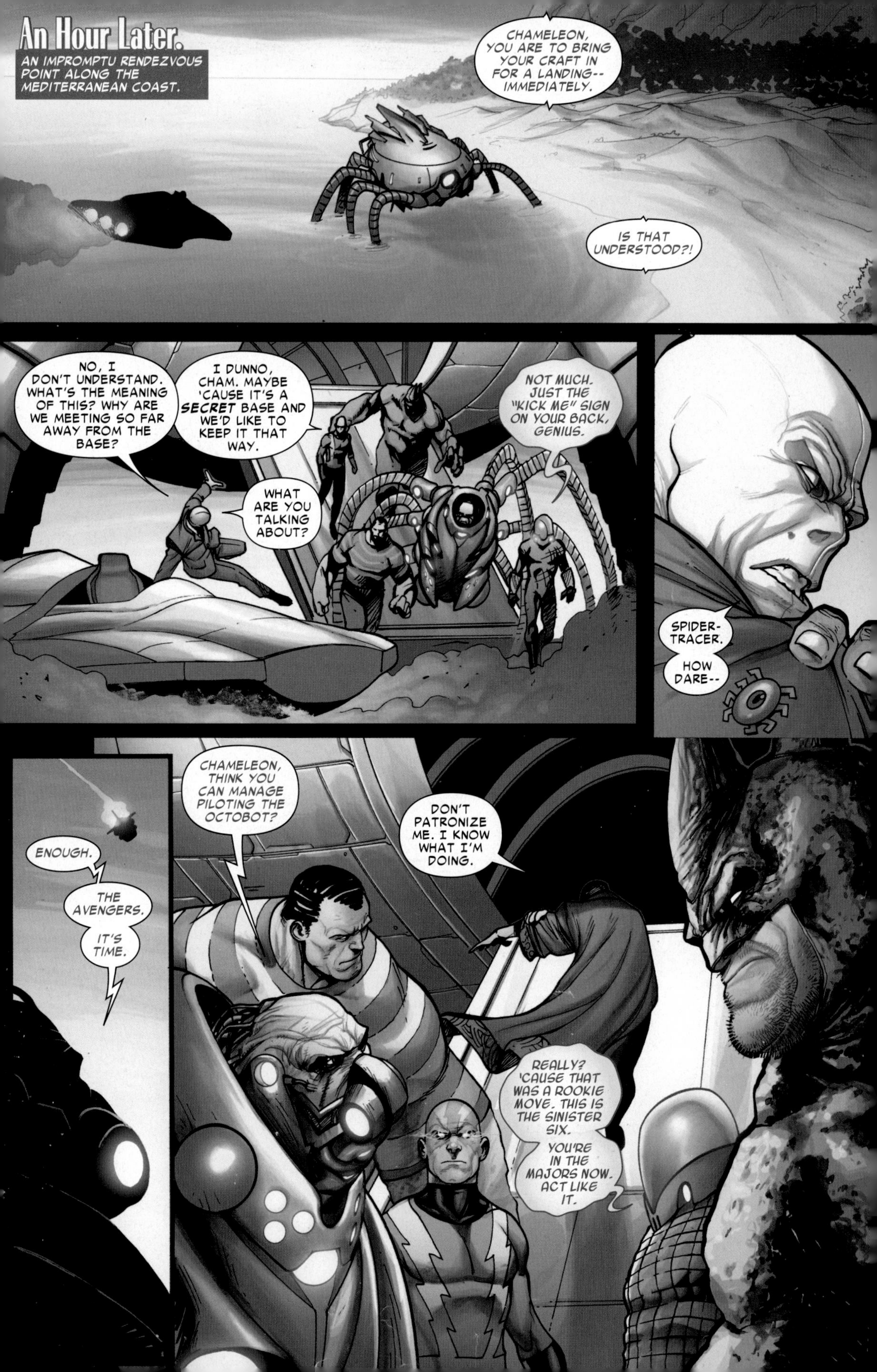
An Hour Later.
AN IMPROMPTU RENDEZVOUS POINT ALONG THE MEDITERRANEAN COAST.
CHAMELEON, YOU ARE TO BRING YOUR CRAFT IN FOR A LANDING-- IMMEDIATELY.
IS THAT UNDERSTOOD?!
NO, I DON'T UNDERSTAND. WHAT'S THE MEANING OF THIS? WHY ARE WE MEETING SO FAR AWAY FROM THE BASE?
I DUNNO, CHAM. MAYBE 'CAUSE IT'S A SECRET BASE AND WE'D LIKE TO KEEP IT THAT WAY.
WHAT ARE YOU TALKING ABOUT?
NOT MUCH. JUST THE "KICK ME" SIGN ON YOUR BACK, GENIUS.
SPIDER-TRACER.
HOW DARE--
ENOUGH.
THE AVENGERS.
IT'S TIME.
CHAMELEON, THINK YOU CAN MANAGE PILOTING THE OCTOBOT?
DON'T PATRONIZE ME. I KNOW WHAT I'M DOING.
REALLY? 'CAUSE THAT WAS A ROOKIE MOVE. THIS IS THE SINISTER SIX.
YOU'RE IN THE MAJORS NOW. ACT LIKE IT.

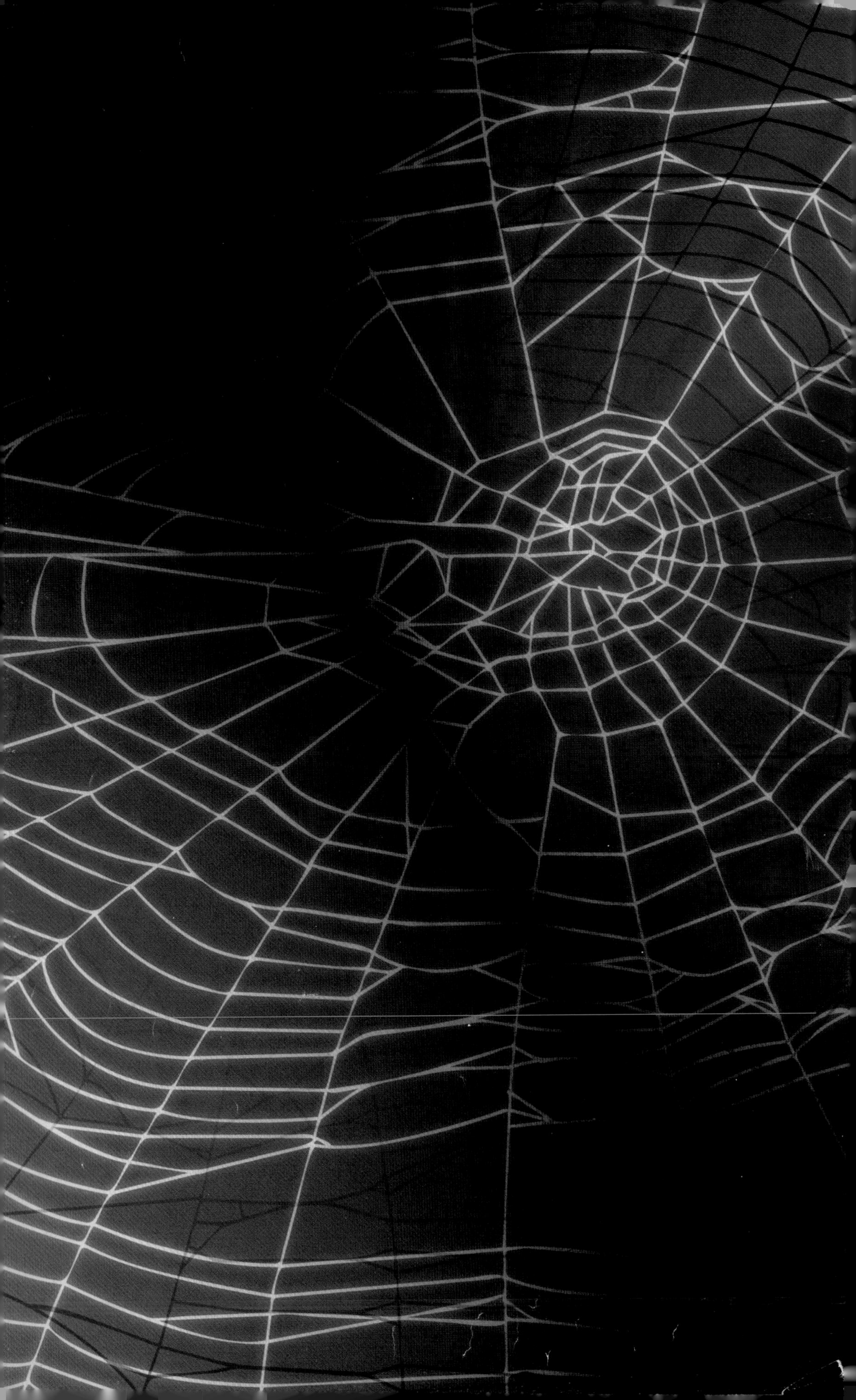

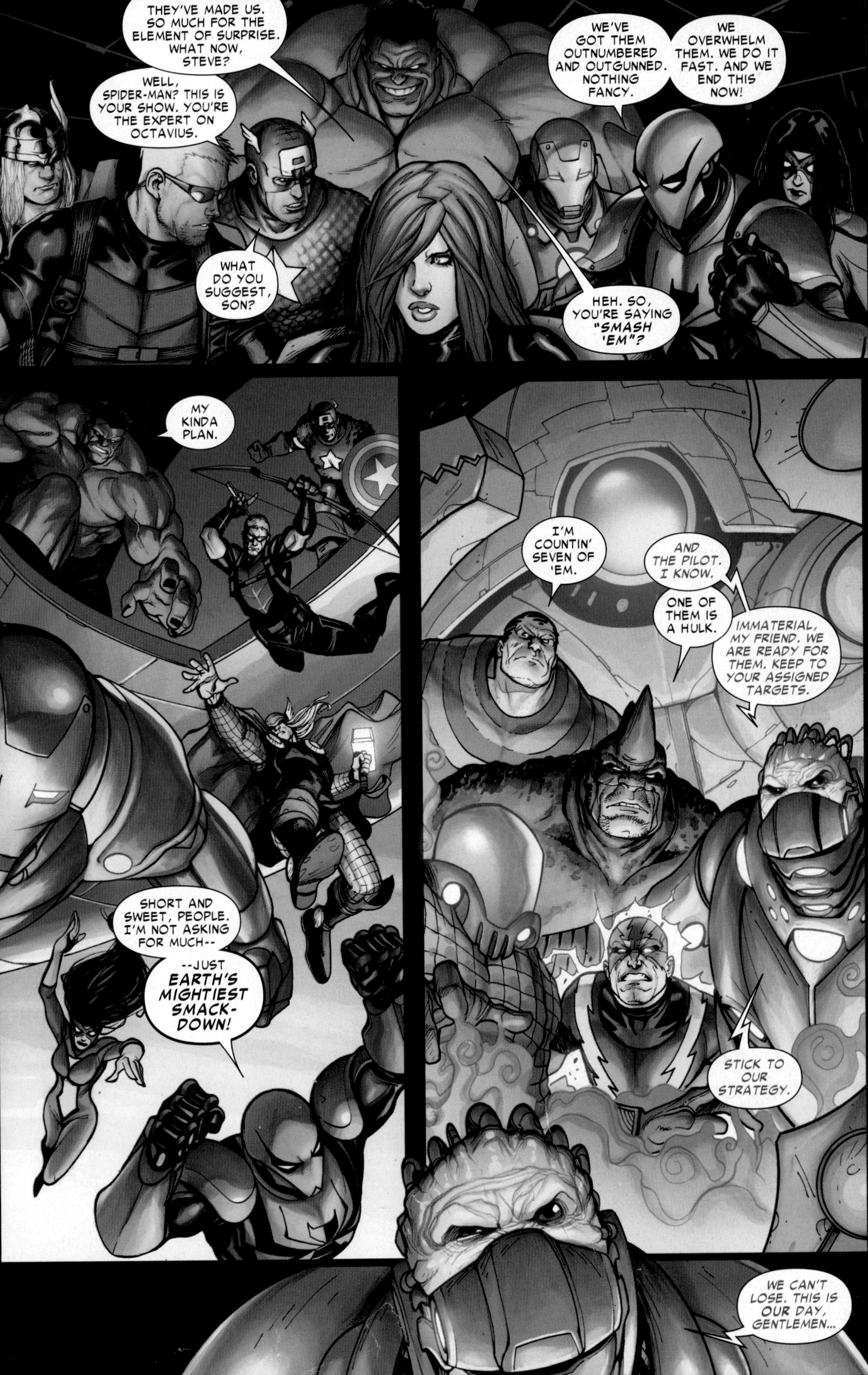
THEY'VE MADE US. SO MUCH FOR THE ELEMENT OF SURPRISE. WHAT NOW, STEVE?
WELL, SPIDER-MAN? THIS IS YOUR SHOW. YOU'RE THE EXPERT ON OCTAVIUS.
WHAT DO YOU SUGGEST, SON?
WE'VE GOT THEM OUTNUMBERED AND OUTGUNNED. NOTHING FANCY.
WE OVERWHELM THEM. WE DO IT FAST. AND WE END THIS NOW!
HEH. SO, YOU'RE SAYING "SMASH 'EM"?
MY KINDA PLAN.
SHORT AND SWEET, PEOPLE. I'M NOT ASKING FOR MUCH--
--JUST EARTH'S MIGHTIEST SMACK-DOWN!
I'M COUNTIN' SEVEN OF 'EM.
AND THE PILOT. I KNOW.
ONE OF THEM IS A HULK.
IMMATERIAL, MY FRIEND. WE ARE READY FOR THEM. KEEP TO YOUR ASSIGNED TARGETS.
STICK TO OUR STRATEGY.
WE CAN'T LOSE. THIS IS OUR DAY, GENTLEMEN...

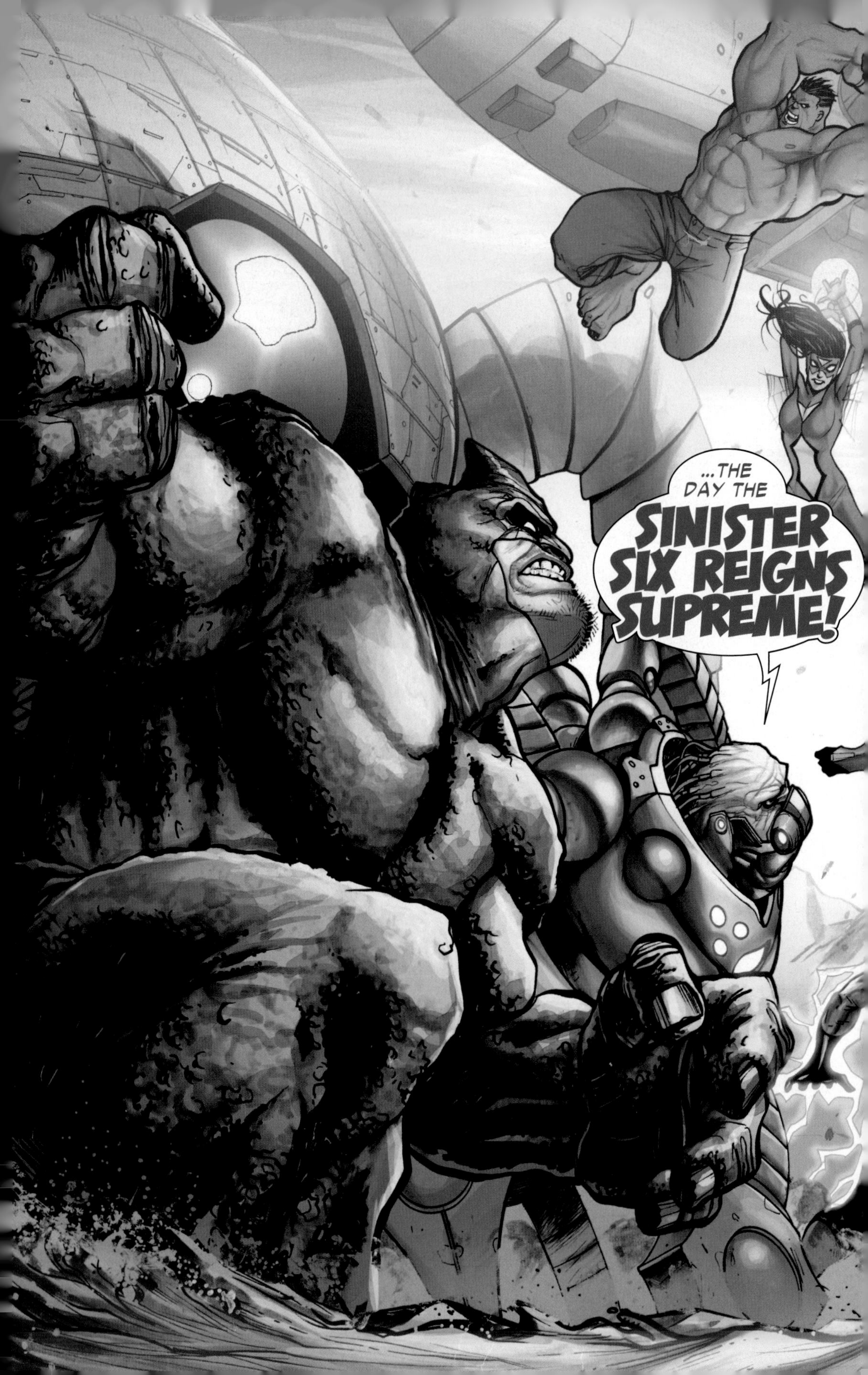
...THE DAY THE SINISTER SIX REIGNS SUPREME!

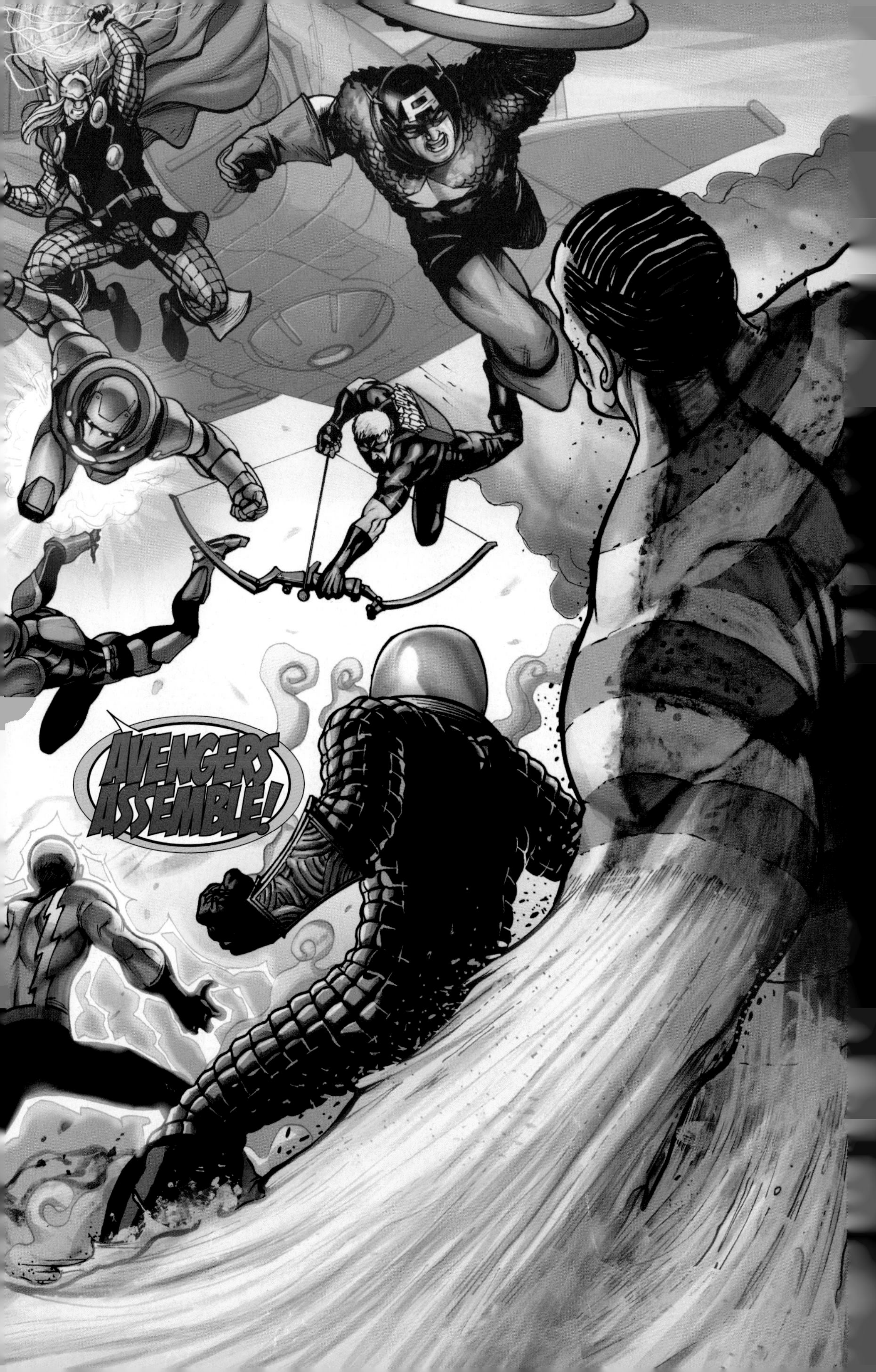
AVENGERS ASSEMBLE!

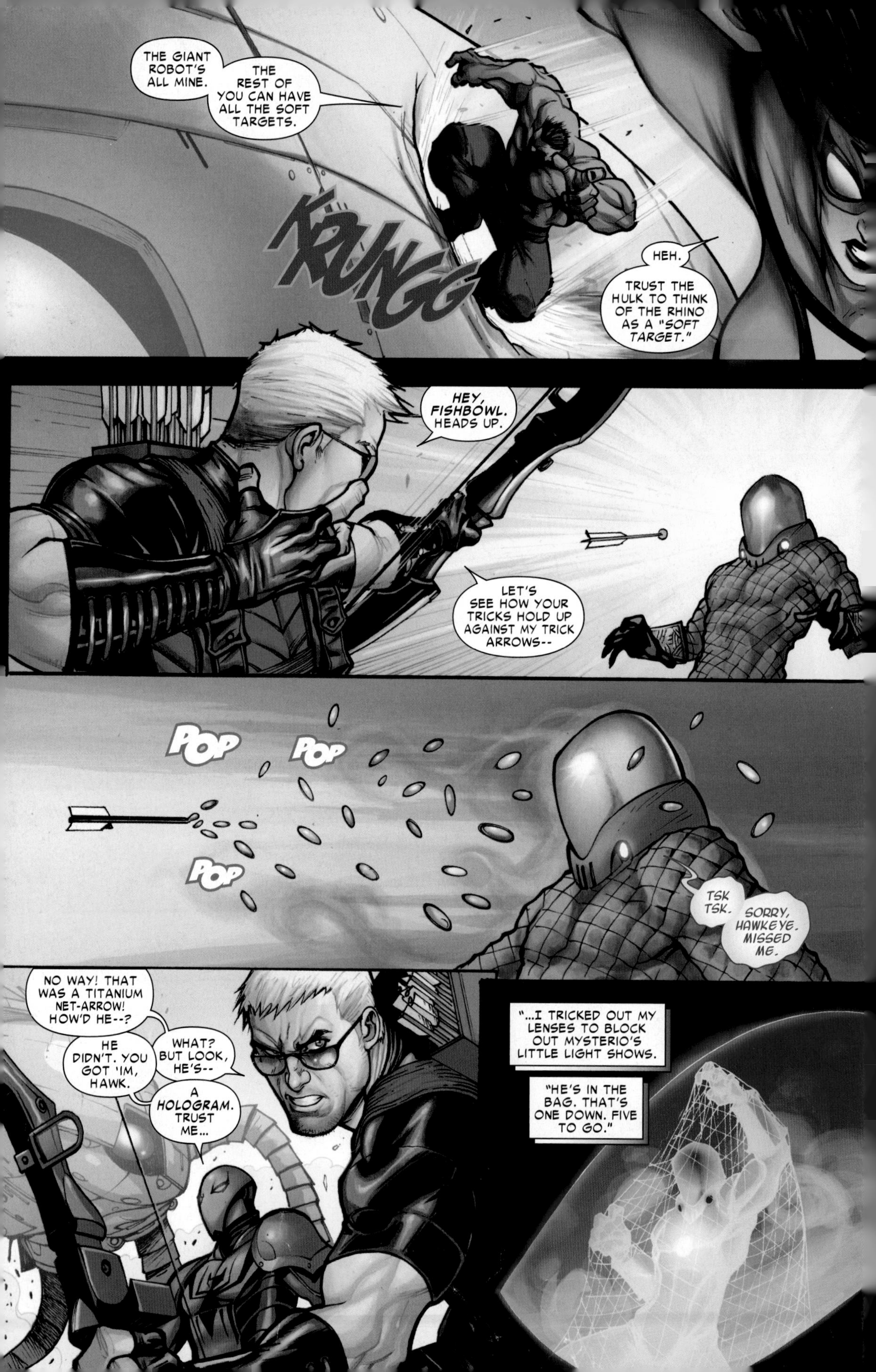
THE GIANT ROBOT'S ALL MINE.
THE REST OF YOU CAN HAVE ALL THE SOFT TARGETS.
KRUNGG
HEH.
TRUST THE HULK TO THINK OF THE RHINO AS A "SOFT TARGET."
HEY, FISHBOWL. HEADS UP.
LET'S SEE HOW YOUR TRICKS HOLD UP AGAINST MY TRICK ARROWS--
POP
POP
POP
TSK TSK.
SORRY, HAWKEYE. MISSED ME.
NO WAY! THAT WAS A TITANIUM NET-ARROW! HOW'D HE--?
HE DIDN'T. YOU GOT 'IM, HAWK.
WHAT? BUT LOOK, HE'S--
A HOLOGRAM. TRUST ME...
"...I TRICKED OUT MY LENSES TO BLOCK OUT MYSTERIO'S LITTLE LIGHT SHOWS.
"HE'S IN THE BAG. THAT'S ONE DOWN. FIVE TO GO."

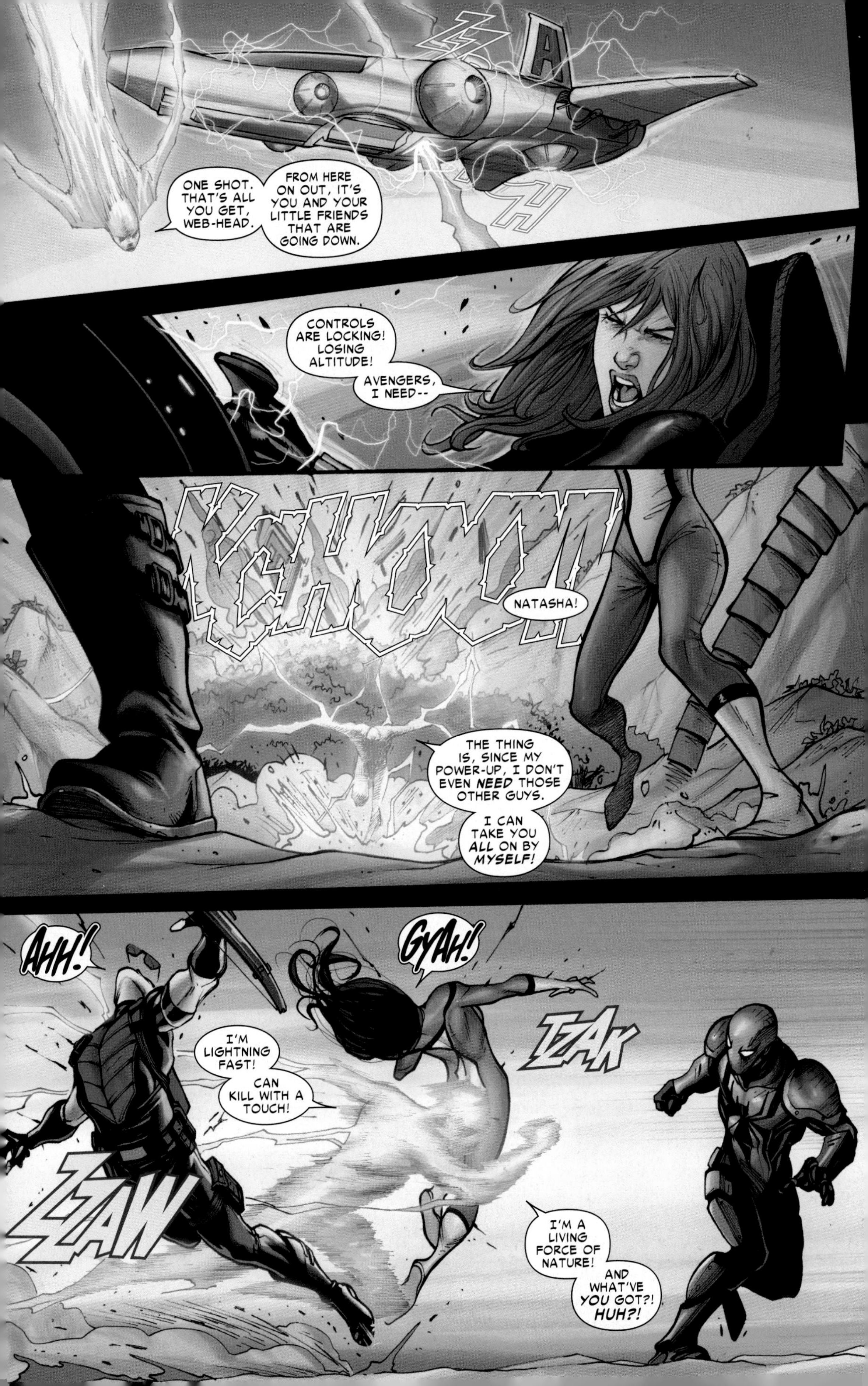
ZZZ
A
ONE SHOT. THAT'S ALL YOU GET, WEB-HEAD.
FROM HERE ON OUT, IT'S YOU AND YOUR LITTLE FRIENDS THAT ARE GOING DOWN.
CONTROLS ARE LOCKING! LOSING ALTITUDE!
AVENGERS, I NEED--
KA-WOOM
NATASHA!
THE THING IS, SINCE MY POWER-UP, I DON'T EVEN NEED THOSE OTHER GUYS.
I CAN TAKE YOU ALL ON BY MYSELF!
AHH!
GYAH!
TZAK
I'M LIGHTNING FAST!
CAN KILL WITH A TOUCH!
ZZAW
I'M A LIVING FORCE OF NATURE!
AND WHAT'VE YOU GOT?! HUH?!

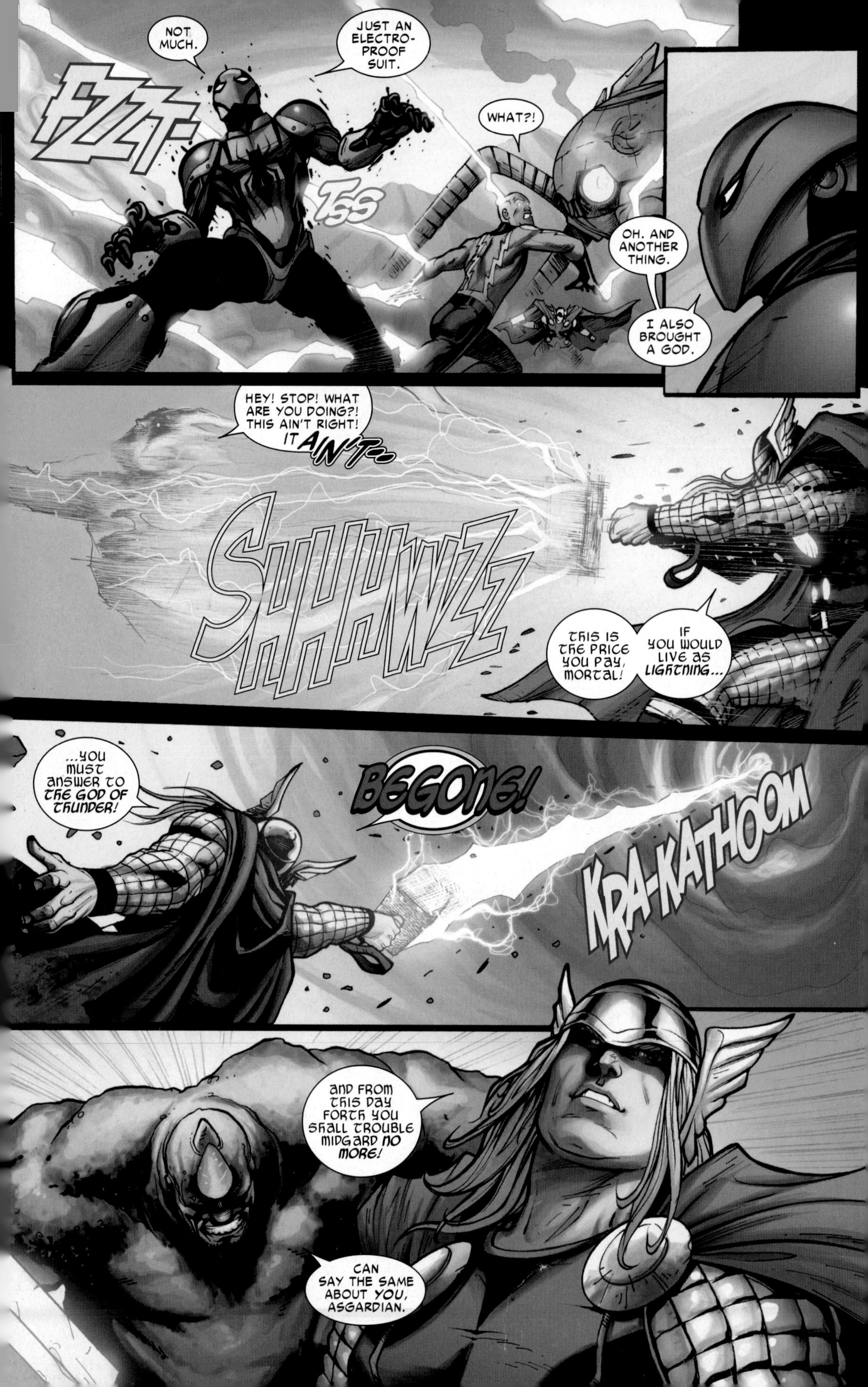

NOT MUCH.
JUST AN ELECTRO-PROOF SUIT.
FZZT
TSS
WHAT?!
OH. AND ANOTHER THING.
I ALSO BROUGHT A GOD.
HEY! STOP! WHAT ARE YOU DOING?! THIS AIN'T RIGHT! IT AIN'T--
SHHHWZZ
IF YOU WOULD LIVE AS LIGHTNING...
THIS IS THE PRICE YOU PAY, MORTAL!
...YOU MUST ANSWER TO THE GOD OF THUNDER!
BEGONE!
KRA-KATHOOM
AND FROM THIS DAY FORTH YOU SHALL TROUBLE MIDGARD NO MORE!
CAN SAY THE SAME ABOUT YOU, ASGARDIAN.

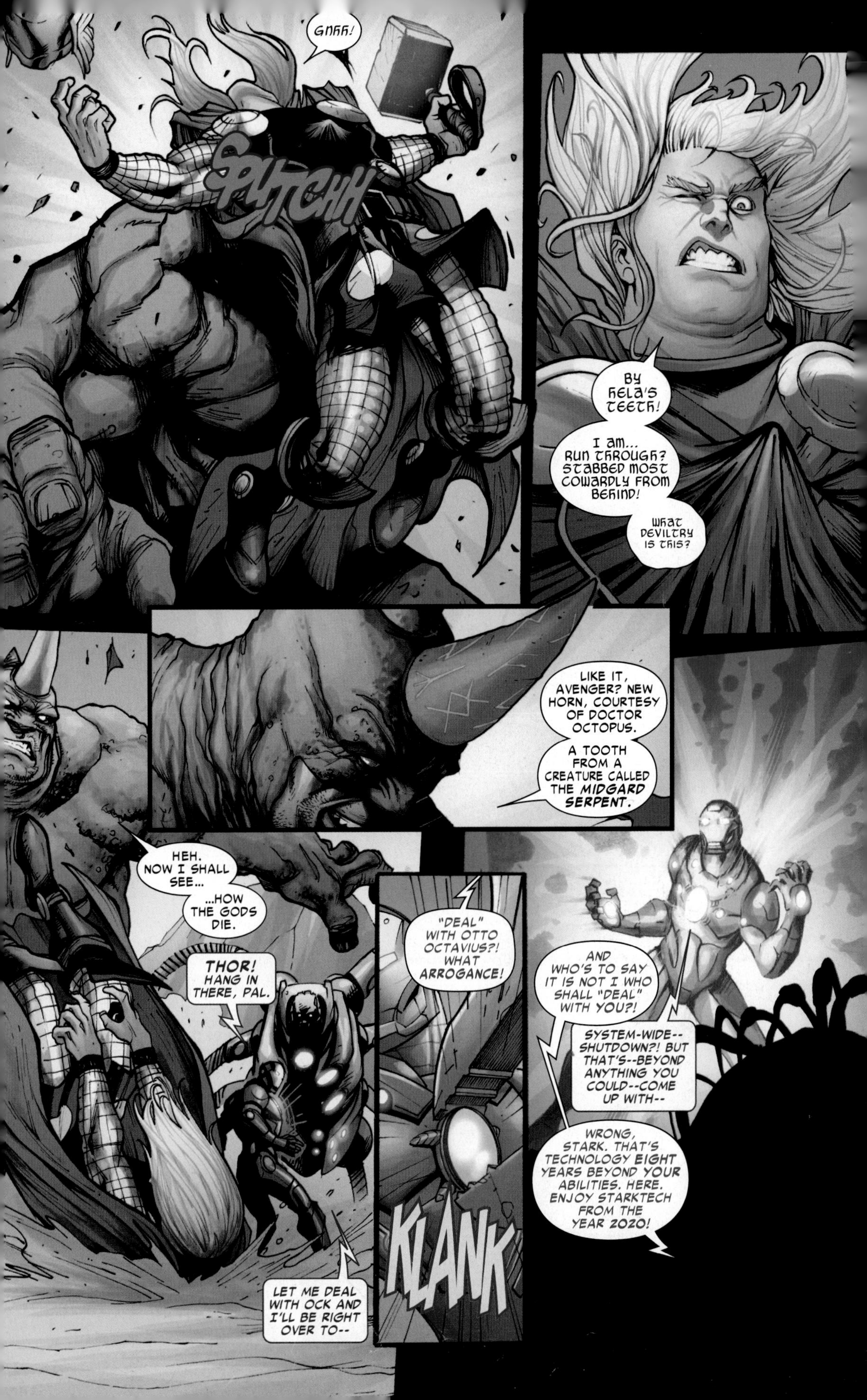
GNHH!
SPLITCHH
BY HELA'S TEETH!
I AM... RUN THROUGH? STABBED MOST COWARDLY FROM BEHIND!
WHAT DEVILTRY IS THIS?
LIKE IT, AVENGER? NEW HORN, COURTESY OF DOCTOR OCTOPUS.
A TOOTH FROM A CREATURE CALLED THE MIDGARD SERPENT.
HEH. NOW I SHALL SEE...
...HOW THE GODS DIE.
THOR! HANG IN THERE, PAL.
LET ME DEAL WITH OCK AND I'LL BE RIGHT OVER TO--
"DEAL" WITH OTTO OCTAVIUS?! WHAT ARROGANCE!
KLANK
AND WHO'S TO SAY IT IS NOT I WHO SHALL "DEAL" WITH YOU?!
SYSTEM-WIDE--SHUTDOWN?! BUT THAT'S--BEYOND ANYTHING YOU COULD--COME UP WITH--
WRONG, STARK. THAT'S TECHNOLOGY EIGHT YEARS BEYOND YOUR ABILITIES. HERE. ENJOY STARKTECH FROM THE YEAR 2020!

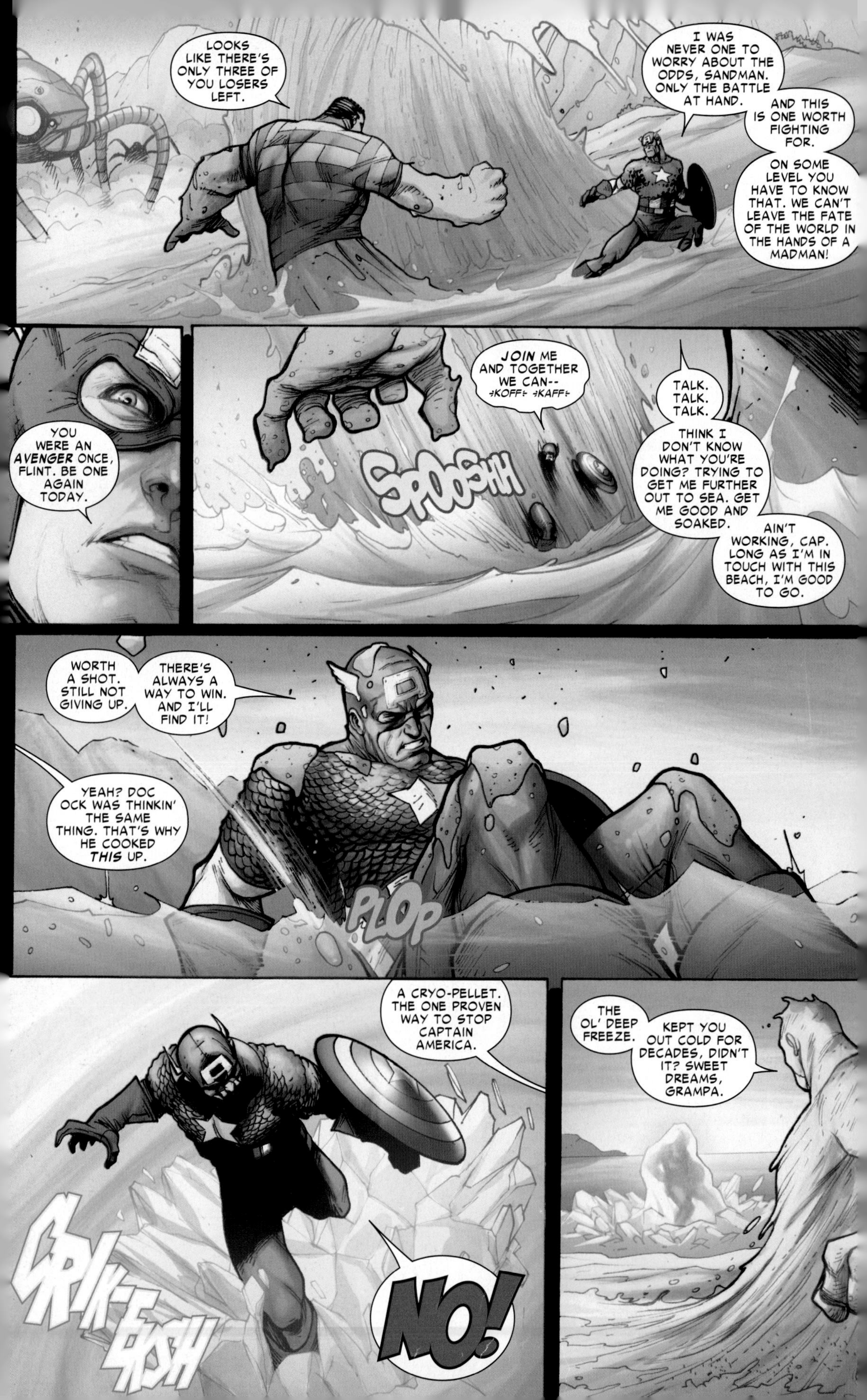
LOOKS LIKE THERE'S ONLY THREE OF YOU LOSERS LEFT.
I WAS NEVER ONE TO WORRY ABOUT THE ODDS, SANDMAN. ONLY THE BATTLE AT HAND.
AND THIS IS ONE WORTH FIGHTING FOR.
ON SOME LEVEL YOU HAVE TO KNOW THAT. WE CAN'T LEAVE THE FATE OF THE WORLD IN THE HANDS OF A MADMAN!
YOU WERE AN AVENGER ONCE, FLINT. BE ONE AGAIN TODAY.
JOIN ME AND TOGETHER WE CAN-- KOFF KAFF
SPOOSHH
TALK. TALK. TALK.
THINK I DON'T KNOW WHAT YOU'RE DOING? TRYING TO GET ME FURTHER OUT TO SEA. GET ME GOOD AND SOAKED.
AIN'T WORKING, CAP. LONG AS I'M IN TOUCH WITH THIS BEACH, I'M GOOD TO GO.
WORTH A SHOT. STILL NOT GIVING UP.
THERE'S ALWAYS A WAY TO WIN. AND I'LL FIND IT!
YEAH? DOC OCK WAS THINKIN' THE SAME THING. THAT'S WHY HE COOKED THIS UP.
PLOP
A CRYO-PELLET. THE ONE PROVEN WAY TO STOP CAPTAIN AMERICA.
CRIK-EKSH
NO!
THE OL' DEEP FREEZE.
KEPT YOU OUT COLD FOR DECADES, DIDN'T IT? SWEET DREAMS, GRAMPA.

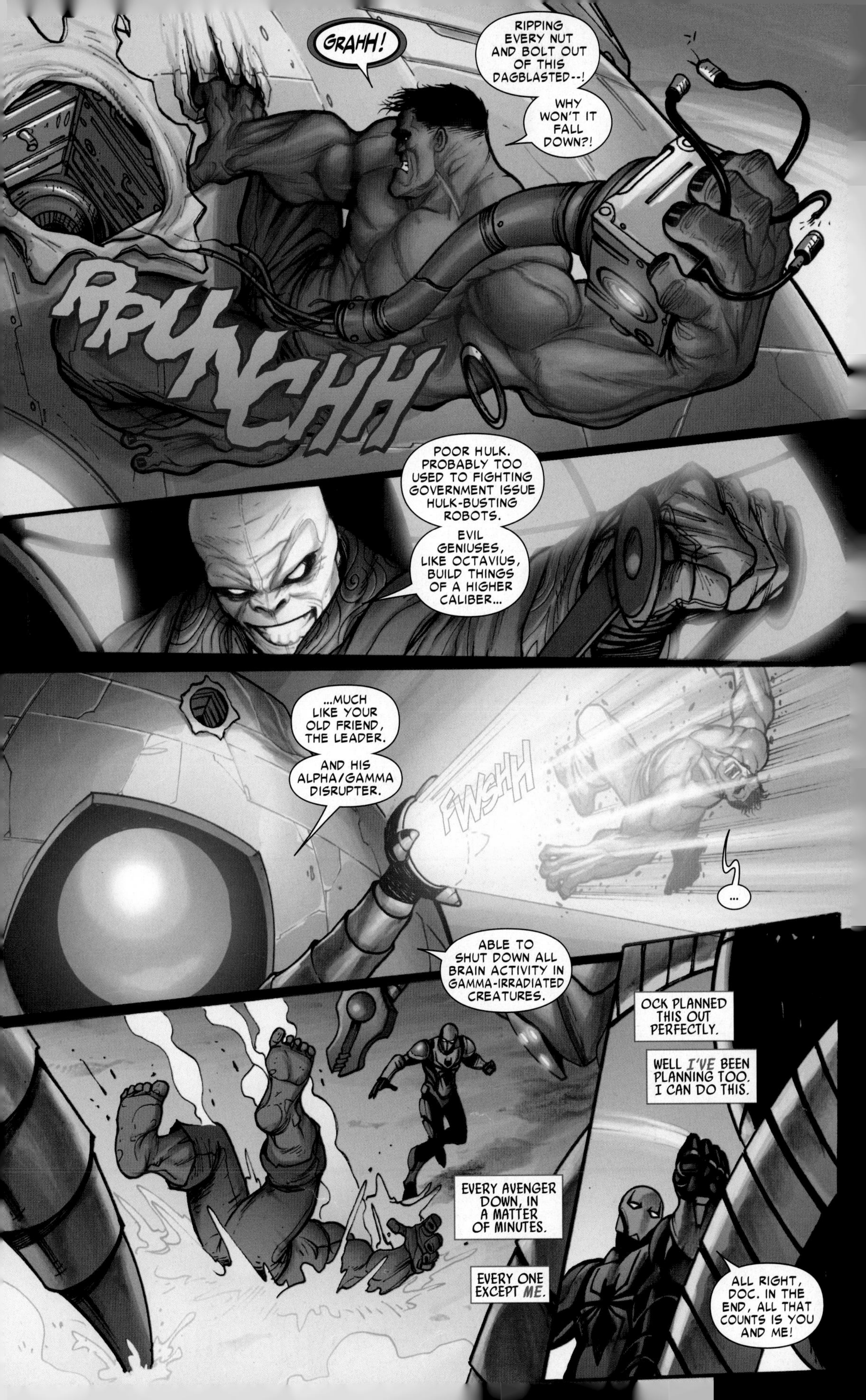
GRAHH!
RIPPING EVERY NUT AND BOLT OUT OF THIS DAGBLASTED--!
WHY WON'T IT FALL DOWN?!
RRUNCHH
POOR HULK. PROBABLY TOO USED TO FIGHTING GOVERNMENT ISSUE HULK-BUSTING ROBOTS.
EVIL GENIUSES, LIKE OCTAVIUS, BUILD THINGS OF A HIGHER CALIBER...
...MUCH LIKE YOUR OLD FRIEND, THE LEADER.
AND HIS ALPHA/GAMMA DISRUPTER.
FWSHH
...
ABLE TO SHUT DOWN ALL BRAIN ACTIVITY IN GAMMA-IRRADIATED CREATURES.
OCK PLANNED THIS OUT PERFECTLY.
WELL I'VE BEEN PLANNING TOO. I CAN DO THIS.
EVERY AVENGER DOWN, IN A MATTER OF MINUTES.
EVERY ONE EXCEPT ME.
ALL RIGHT, DOC. IN THE END, ALL THAT COUNTS IS YOU AND ME!

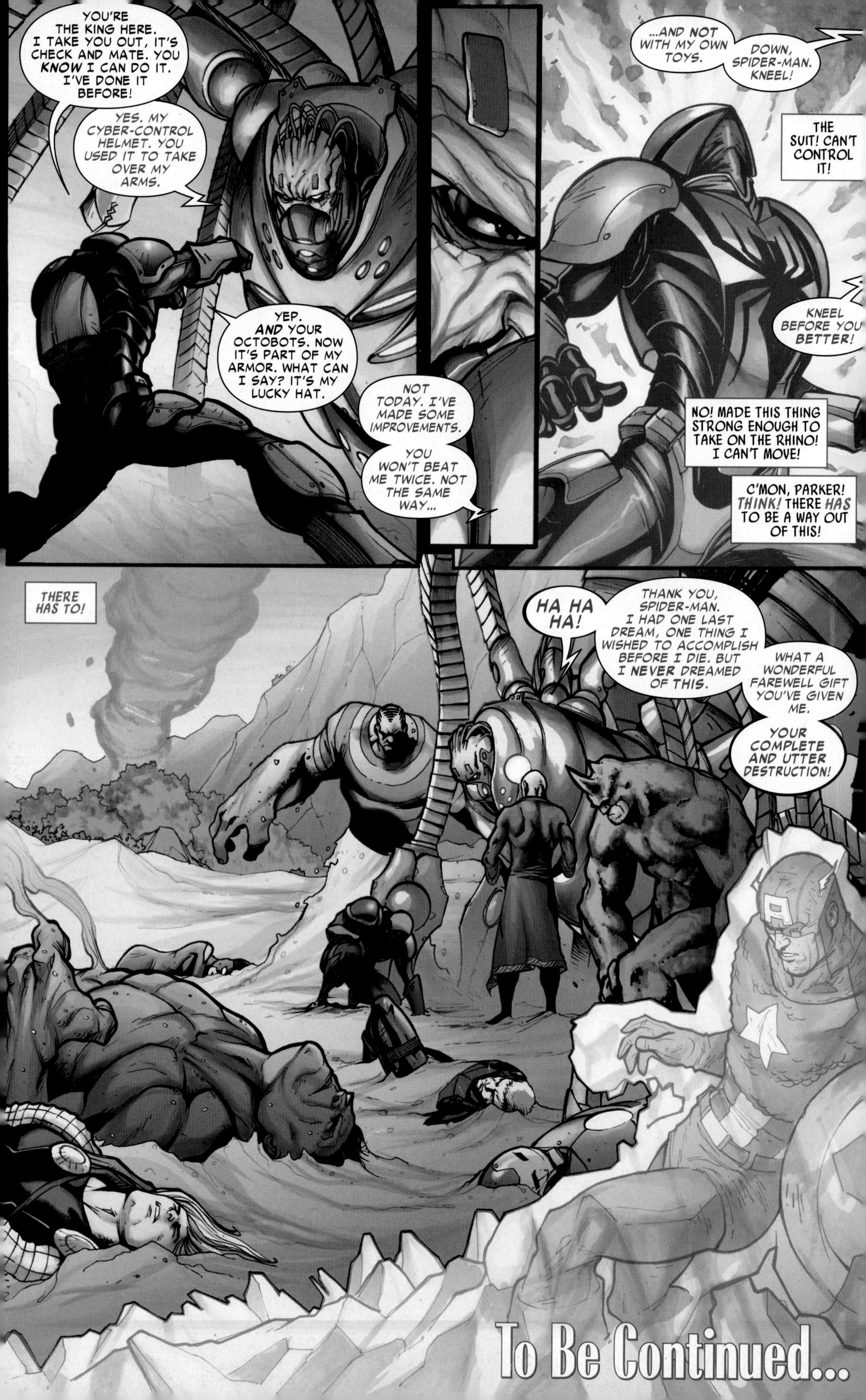

YOU'RE THE KING HERE. I TAKE YOU OUT, IT'S CHECK AND MATE. YOU KNOW I CAN DO IT. I'VE DONE IT BEFORE!
YES. MY CYBER-CONTROL HELMET. YOU USED IT TO TAKE OVER MY ARMS.
YEP. AND YOUR OCTOBOTS. NOW IT'S PART OF MY ARMOR. WHAT CAN I SAY? IT'S MY LUCKY HAT.
NOT TODAY. I'VE MADE SOME IMPROVEMENTS.
YOU WON'T BEAT ME TWICE. NOT THE SAME WAY...
...AND NOT WITH MY OWN TOYS.
DOWN, SPIDER-MAN. KNEEL!
THE SUIT! CAN'T CONTROL IT!
KNEEL BEFORE YOUR BETTER!
NO! MADE THIS THING STRONG ENOUGH TO TAKE ON THE RHINO! I CAN'T MOVE!
C'MON, PARKER! THINK! THERE HAS TO BE A WAY OUT OF THIS!
THERE HAS TO!
HA HA HA!
THANK YOU, SPIDER-MAN. I HAD ONE LAST DREAM, ONE THING I WISHED TO ACCOMPLISH BEFORE I DIE. BUT I NEVER DREAMED OF THIS.
WHAT A WONDERFUL FAREWELL GIFT YOU'VE GIVEN ME.
YOUR COMPLETE AND UTTER DESTRUCTION!
To Be Continued...

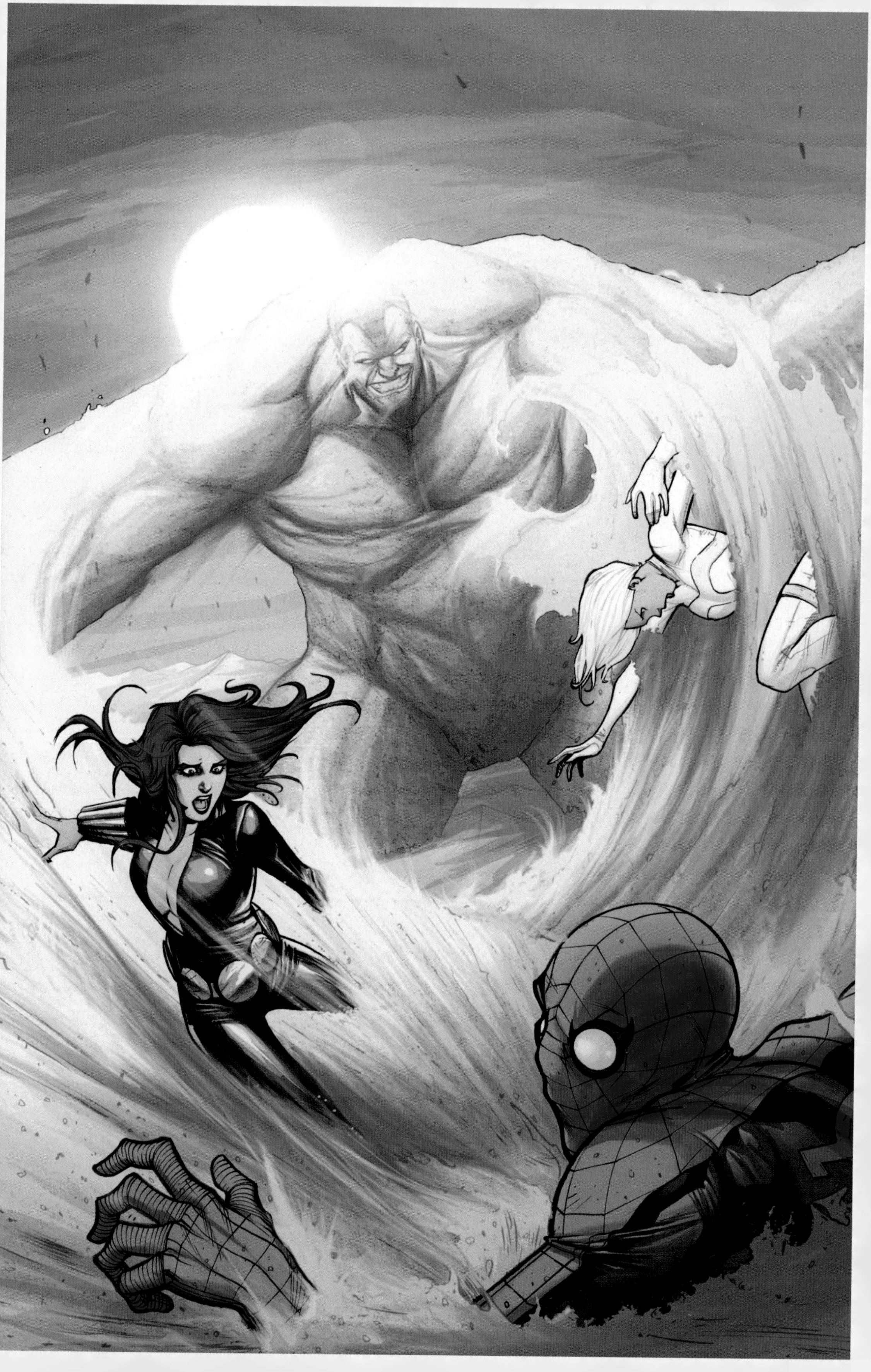

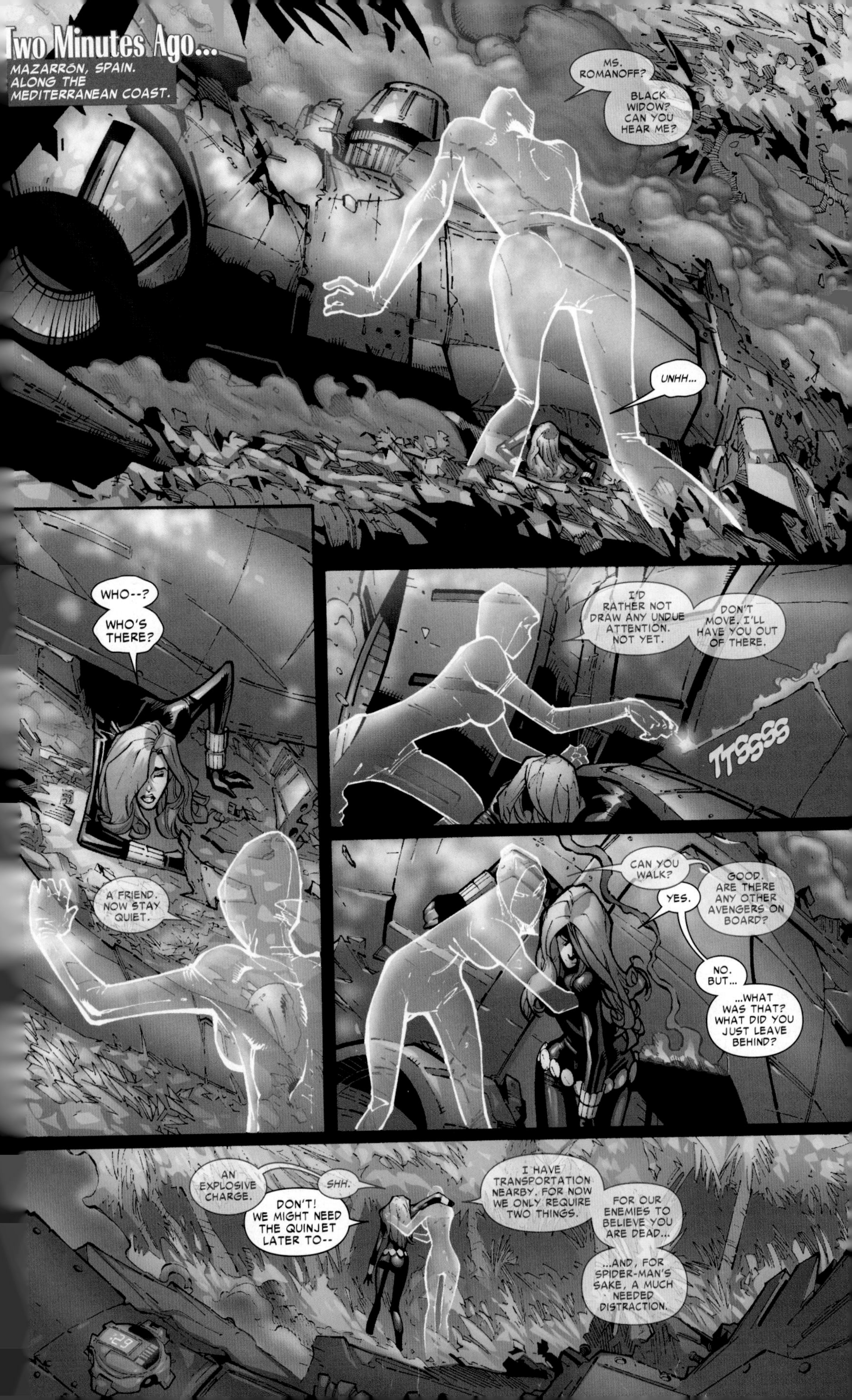

Two Minutes Ago...
MAZARRON, SPAIN. ALONG THE MEDITERRANEAN COAST.
MS. ROMANOFF?
BLACK WIDOW? CAN YOU HEAR ME?
UNHH...
WHO--?
WHO'S THERE?
A FRIEND. NOW STAY QUIET.
I'D RATHER NOT DRAW ANY UNDUE ATTENTION. NOT YET.
DON'T MOVE. I'LL HAVE YOU OUT OF THERE.
TTSSSS
CAN YOU WALK?
YES.
GOOD. ARE THERE ANY OTHER AVENGERS ON BOARD?
NO. BUT...
...WHAT WAS THAT? WHAT DID YOU JUST LEAVE BEHIND?
AN EXPLOSIVE CHARGE.
SHH.
DON'T! WE MIGHT NEED THE QUINJET LATER TO--
I HAVE TRANSPORTATION NEARBY. FOR NOW WE ONLY REQUIRE TWO THINGS.
FOR OUR ENEMIES TO BELIEVE YOU ARE DEAD...
...AND, FOR SPIDER-MAN'S SAKE, A MUCH NEEDED DISTRACTION.

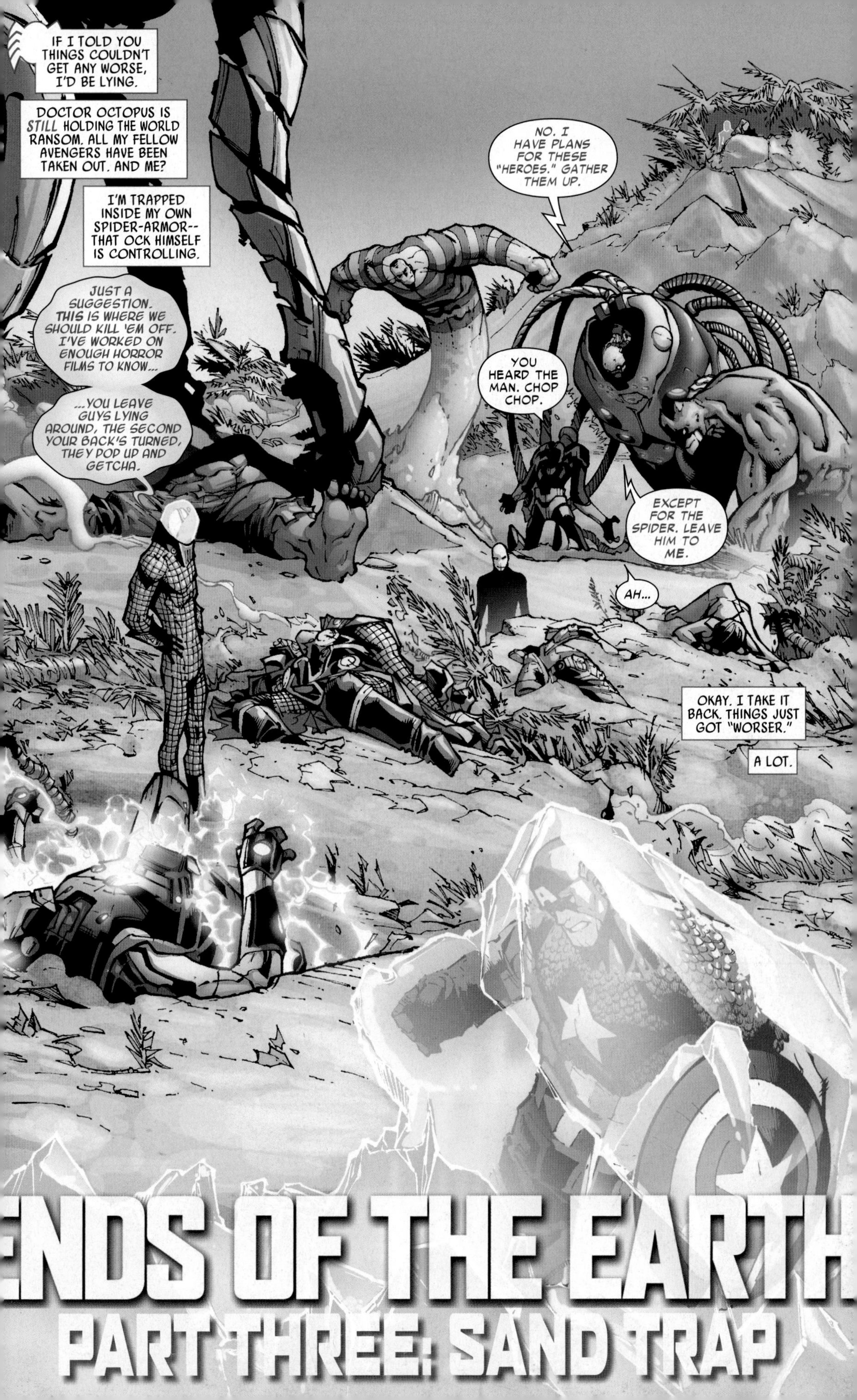

IF I TOLD YOU THINGS COULDN'T GET ANY WORSE, I'D BE LYING.
DOCTOR OCTOPUS IS STILL HOLDING THE WORLD RANSOM. ALL MY FELLOW AVENGERS HAVE BEEN TAKEN OUT. AND ME?
I'M TRAPPED INSIDE MY OWN SPIDER-ARMOR-- THAT OCK HIMSELF IS CONTROLLING.
JUST A SUGGESTION. THIS IS WHERE WE SHOULD KILL 'EM OFF. I'VE WORKED ON ENOUGH HORROR FILMS TO KNOW...
...YOU LEAVE GUYS LYING AROUND, THE SECOND YOUR BACK'S TURNED, THEY POP UP AND GETCHA.
NO. I HAVE PLANS FOR THESE "HEROES." GATHER THEM UP.
YOU HEARD THE MAN. CHOP CHOP.
EXCEPT FOR THE SPIDER. LEAVE HIM TO ME.
AH...
OKAY. I TAKE IT BACK. THINGS JUST GOT "WORSER."
A LOT.
ENDS OF THE EARTH
PART THREE: SAND TRAP

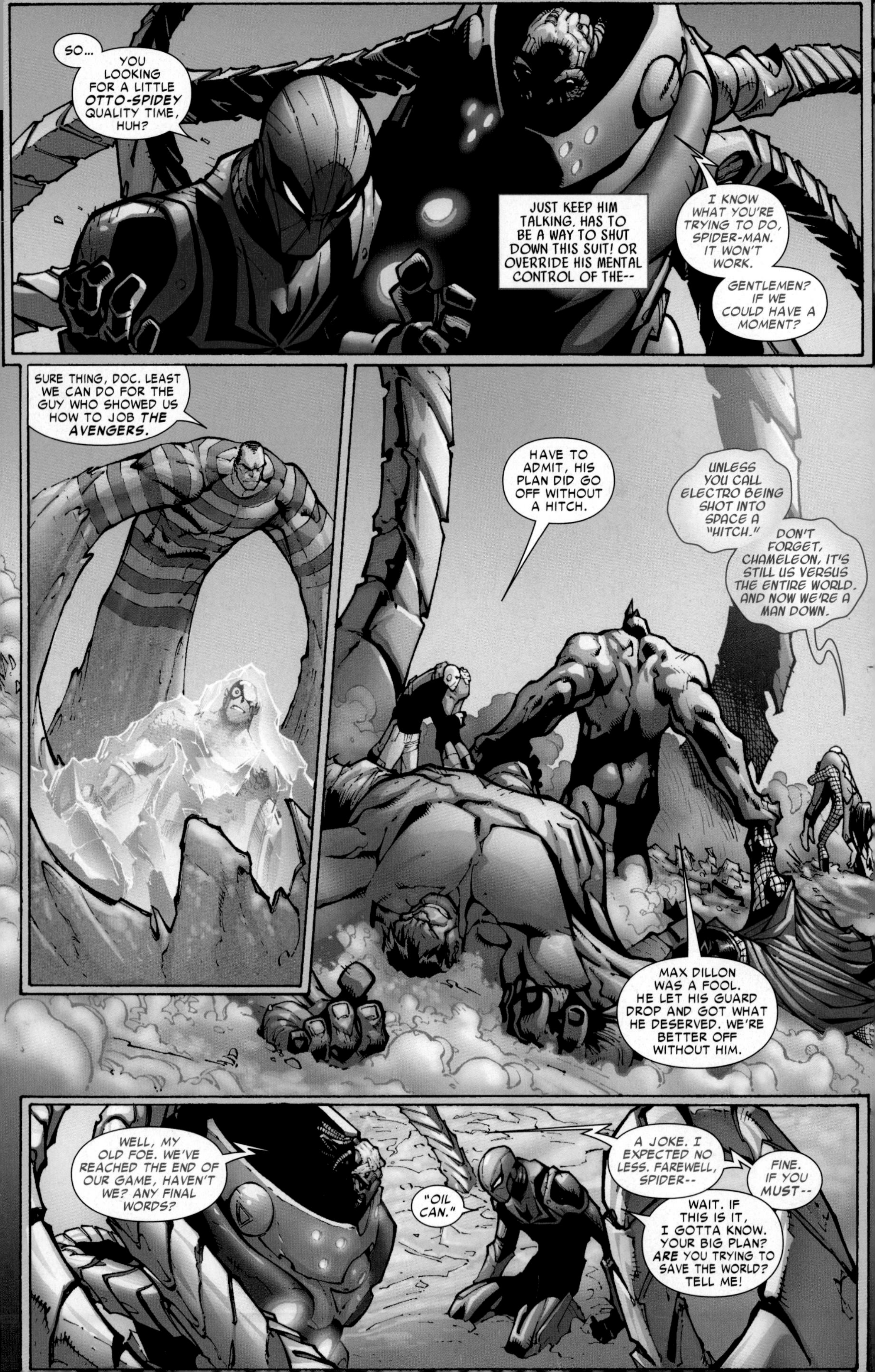
SO...
YOU LOOKING FOR A LITTLE OTTO-SPIDEY QUALITY TIME, HUH?
JUST KEEP HIM TALKING. HAS TO BE A WAY TO SHUT DOWN THIS SUIT! OR OVERRIDE HIS MENTAL CONTROL OF THE--
I KNOW WHAT YOU'RE TRYING TO DO, SPIDER-MAN. IT WON'T WORK.
GENTLEMEN? IF WE COULD HAVE A MOMENT?
SURE THING, DOC. LEAST WE CAN DO FOR THE GUY WHO SHOWED US HOW TO JOB THE AVENGERS.
HAVE TO ADMIT, HIS PLAN DID GO OFF WITHOUT A HITCH.
UNLESS YOU CALL ELECTRO BEING SHOT INTO SPACE A "HITCH."
DON'T FORGET, CHAMELEON, IT'S STILL US VERSUS THE ENTIRE WORLD. AND NOW WE'RE A MAN DOWN.
MAX DILLON WAS A FOOL. HE LET HIS GUARD DROP AND GOT WHAT HE DESERVED. WE'RE BETTER OFF WITHOUT HIM.
WELL, MY OLD FOE. WE'VE REACHED THE END OF OUR GAME, HAVEN'T WE? ANY FINAL WORDS?
"OIL CAN."
A JOKE. I EXPECTED NO LESS. FAREWELL, SPIDER--
WAIT. IF THIS IS IT, I GOTTA KNOW. YOUR BIG PLAN? ARE YOU TRYING TO SAVE THE WORLD? TELL ME!
FINE. IF YOU MUST--

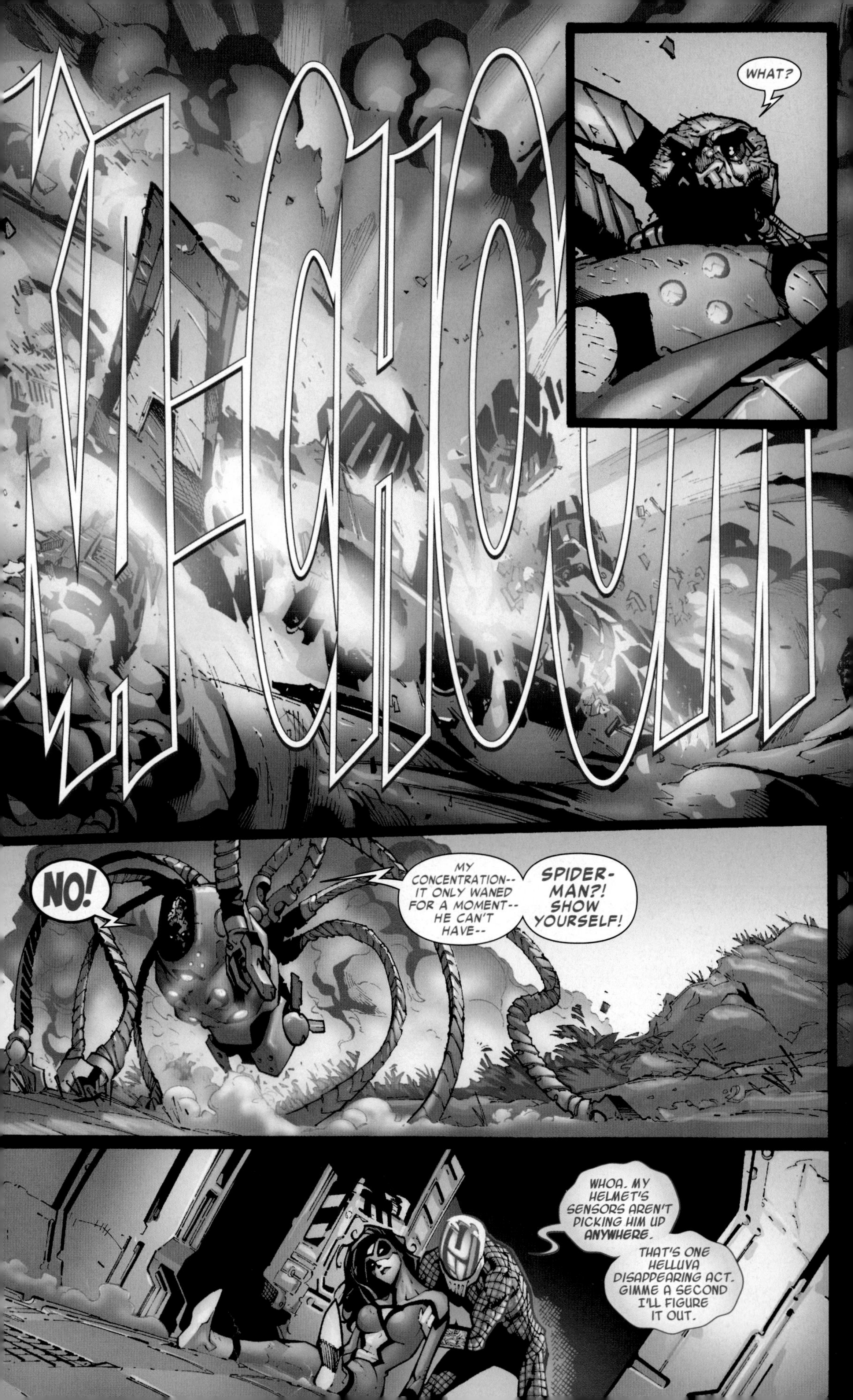
WHAT?
NO!
MY CONCENTRATION-- IT ONLY WANED FOR A MOMENT-- HE CAN'T HAVE--
SPIDER-MAN?! SHOW YOURSELF!
WHOA. MY HELMET'S SENSORS AREN'T PICKING HIM UP ANYWHERE.
THAT'S ONE HELLUVA DISAPPEARING ACT. GIMME A SECOND I'LL FIGURE IT OUT.

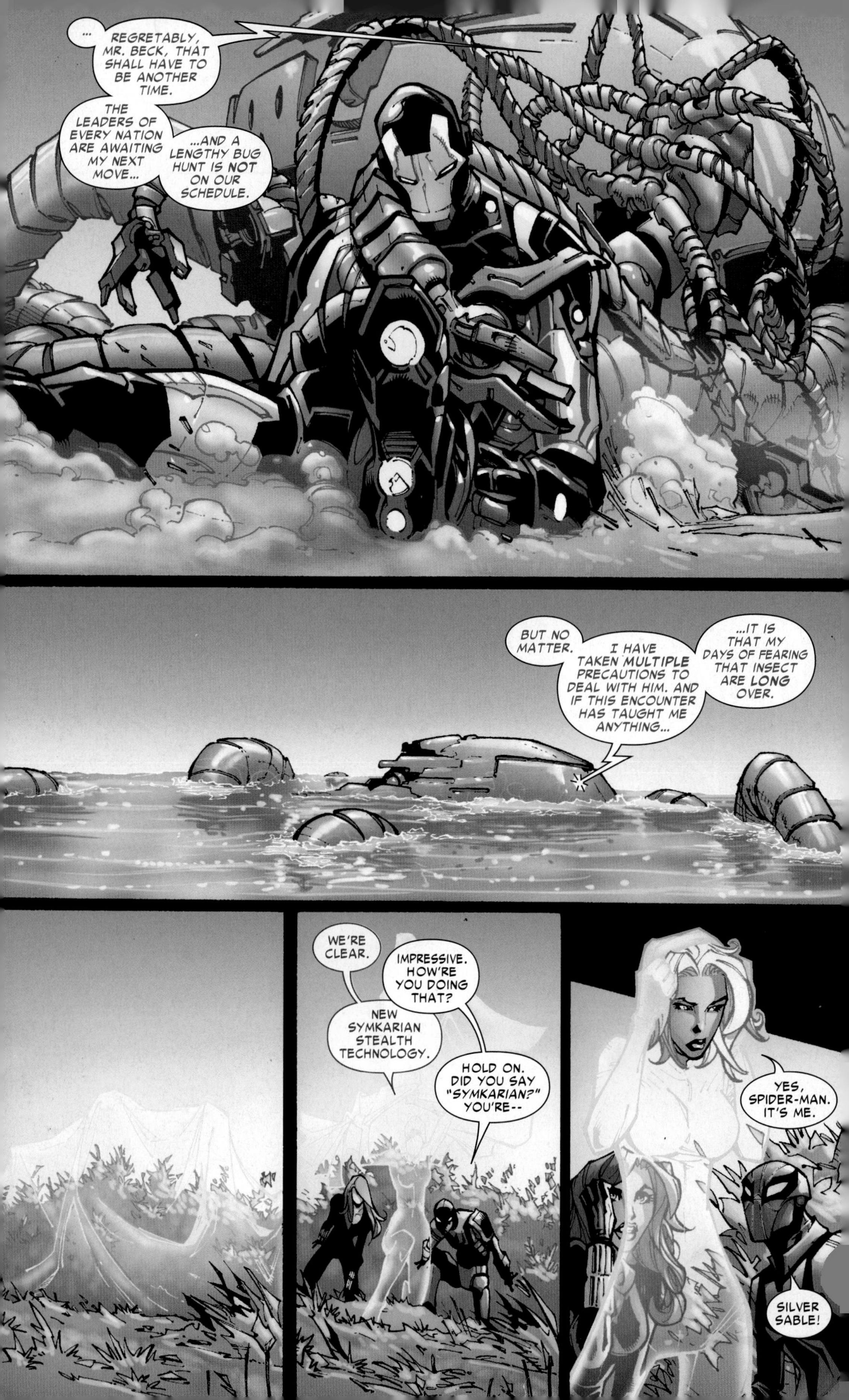
... REGRETABLY, MR. BECK, THAT SHALL HAVE TO BE ANOTHER TIME.
THE LEADERS OF EVERY NATION ARE AWAITING MY NEXT MOVE...
...AND A LENGTHY BUG HUNT IS NOT ON OUR SCHEDULE.
BUT NO MATTER.
I HAVE TAKEN MULTIPLE PRECAUTIONS TO DEAL WITH HIM. AND IF THIS ENCOUNTER HAS TAUGHT ME ANYTHING...
...IT IS THAT MY DAYS OF FEARING THAT INSECT ARE LONG OVER.
WE'RE CLEAR.
IMPRESSIVE. HOW'RE YOU DOING THAT?
NEW SYMKARIAN STEALTH TECHNOLOGY.
HOLD ON. DID YOU SAY "SYMKARIAN?" YOU'RE--
YES, SPIDER-MAN. IT'S ME.
SILVER SABLE!

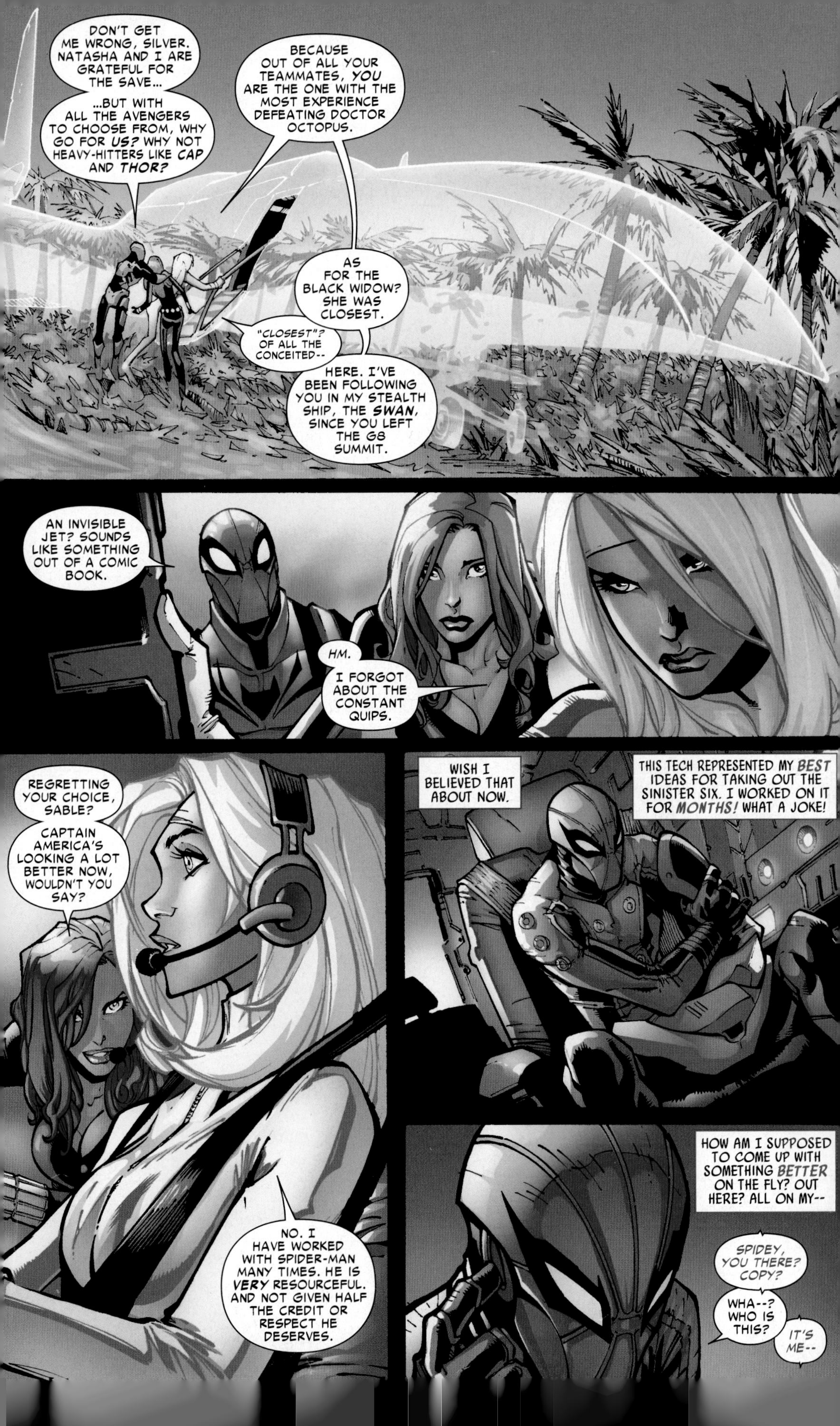
DON'T GET ME WRONG, SILVER. NATASHA AND I ARE GRATEFUL FOR THE SAVE...
...BUT WITH ALL THE AVENGERS TO CHOOSE FROM, WHY GO FOR US? WHY NOT HEAVY-HITTERS LIKE CAP AND THOR?
BECAUSE OUT OF ALL YOUR TEAMMATES, YOU ARE THE ONE WITH THE MOST EXPERIENCE DEFEATING DOCTOR OCTOPUS.
AS FOR THE BLACK WIDOW? SHE WAS CLOSEST.
"CLOSEST"? OF ALL THE CONCEITED--
HERE. I'VE BEEN FOLLOWING YOU IN MY STEALTH SHIP, THE SWAN, SINCE YOU LEFT THE G8 SUMMIT.
AN INVISIBLE JET? SOUNDS LIKE SOMETHING OUT OF A COMIC BOOK.
HM.
I FORGOT ABOUT THE CONSTANT QUIPS.
REGRETTING YOUR CHOICE, SABLE?
CAPTAIN AMERICA'S LOOKING A LOT BETTER NOW, WOULDN'T YOU SAY?
NO. I HAVE WORKED WITH SPIDER-MAN MANY TIMES. HE IS VERY RESOURCEFUL. AND NOT GIVEN HALF THE CREDIT OR RESPECT HE DESERVES.
WISH I BELIEVED THAT ABOUT NOW.
THIS TECH REPRESENTED MY BEST IDEAS FOR TAKING OUT THE SINISTER SIX. I WORKED ON IT FOR MONTHS! WHAT A JOKE!
HOW AM I SUPPOSED TO COME UP WITH SOMETHING BETTER ON THE FLY? OUT HERE? ALL ON MY--
SPIDEY, YOU THERE? COPY?
WHA--? WHO IS THIS?
IT'S ME--

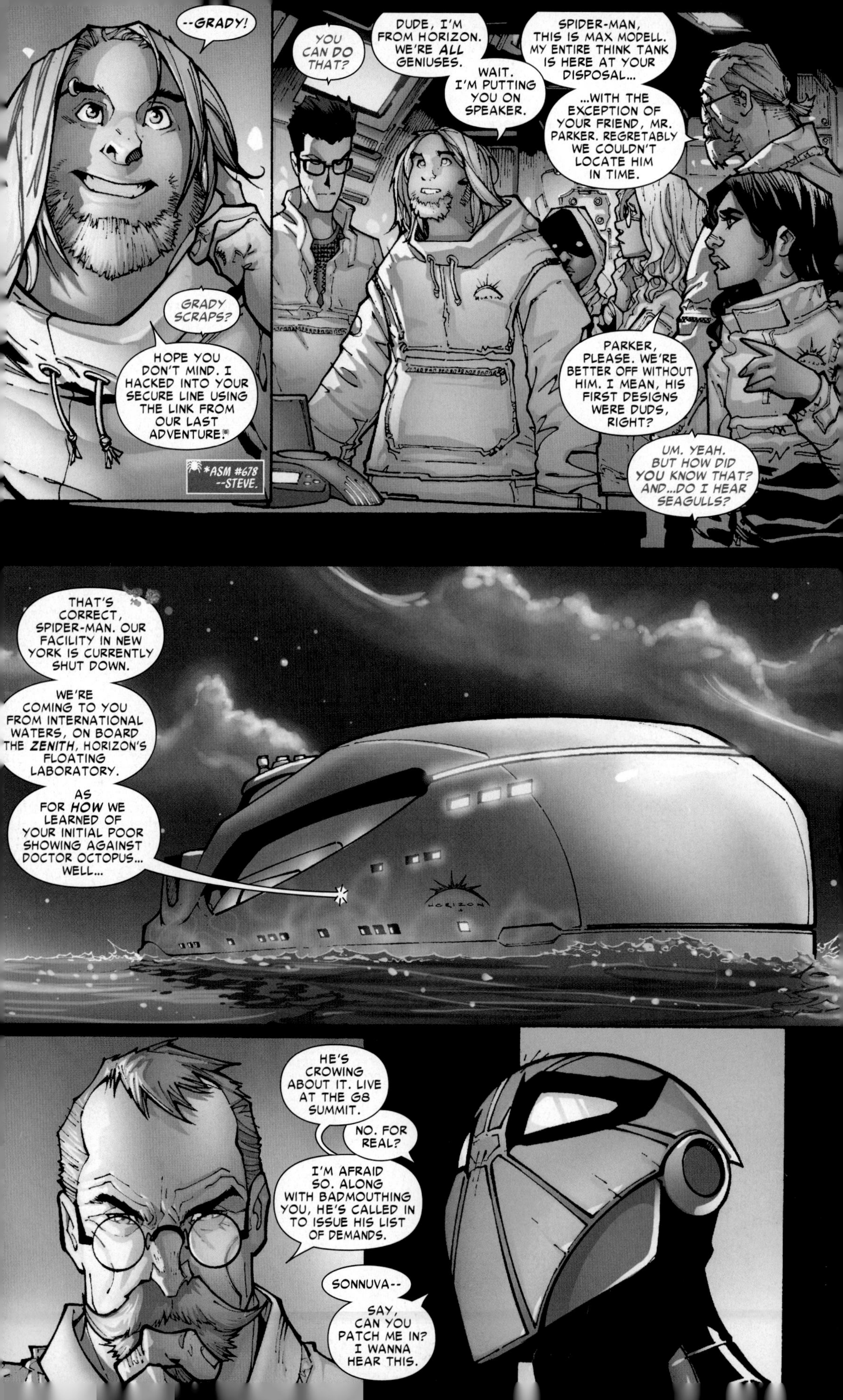
--GRADY!
GRADY SCRAPS?
HOPE YOU DON'T MIND. I HACKED INTO YOUR SECURE LINE USING THE LINK FROM OUR LAST ADVENTURE.*
*ASM #678 --STEVE.
YOU CAN DO THAT?
DUDE, I'M FROM HORIZON. WE'RE ALL GENIUSES.
WAIT. I'M PUTTING YOU ON SPEAKER.
SPIDER-MAN, THIS IS MAX MODELL. MY ENTIRE THINK TANK IS HERE AT YOUR DISPOSAL...
...WITH THE EXCEPTION OF YOUR FRIEND, MR. PARKER. REGRETABLY WE COULDN'T LOCATE HIM IN TIME.
PARKER, PLEASE. WE'RE BETTER OFF WITHOUT HIM. I MEAN, HIS FIRST DESIGNS WERE DUDS, RIGHT?
UM. YEAH. BUT HOW DID YOU KNOW THAT? AND...DO I HEAR SEAGULLS?
THAT'S CORRECT, SPIDER-MAN. OUR FACILITY IN NEW YORK IS CURRENTLY SHUT DOWN.
WE'RE COMING TO YOU FROM INTERNATIONAL WATERS, ON BOARD THE ZENITH, HORIZON'S FLOATING LABORATORY.
AS FOR HOW WE LEARNED OF YOUR INITIAL POOR SHOWING AGAINST DOCTOR OCTOPUS... WELL...
HE'S CROWING ABOUT IT. LIVE AT THE G8 SUMMIT.
NO. FOR REAL?
I'M AFRAID SO. ALONG WITH BADMOUTHING YOU, HE'S CALLED IN TO ISSUE HIS LIST OF DEMANDS.
SONNUVA--
SAY, CAN YOU PATCH ME IN? I WANNA HEAR THIS.

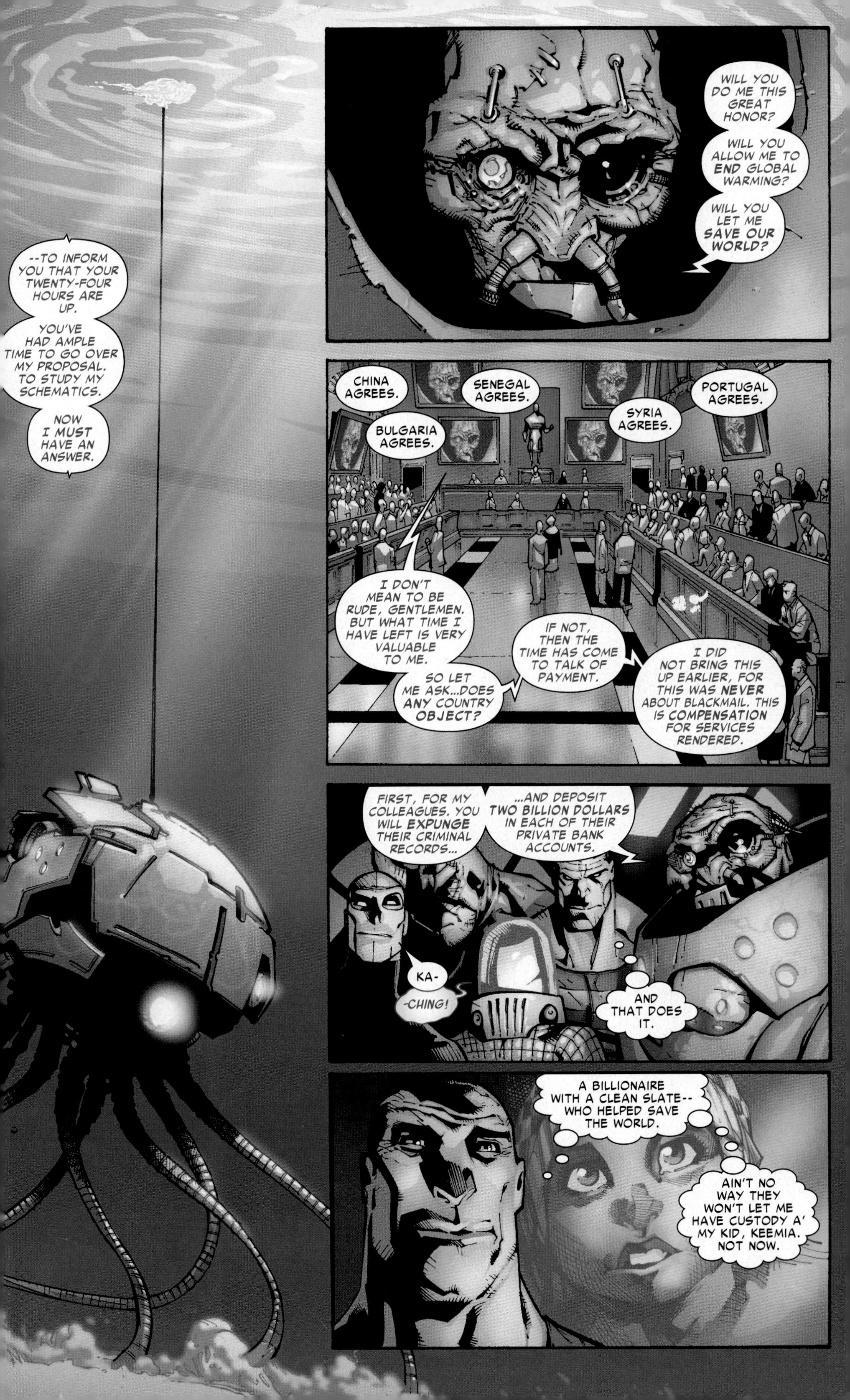
--TO INFORM YOU THAT YOUR TWENTY-FOUR HOURS ARE UP.
YOU'VE HAD AMPLE TIME TO GO OVER MY PROPOSAL. TO STUDY MY SCHEMATICS.
NOW I MUST HAVE AN ANSWER.
WILL YOU DO ME THIS GREAT HONOR?
WILL YOU ALLOW ME TO END GLOBAL WARMING?
WILL YOU LET ME SAVE OUR WORLD?
CHINA AGREES.
SENEGAL AGREES.
PORTUGAL AGREES.
BULGARIA AGREES.
SYRIA AGREES.
I DON'T MEAN TO BE RUDE, GENTLEMEN. BUT WHAT TIME I HAVE LEFT IS VERY VALUABLE TO ME.
SO LET ME ASK...DOES ANY COUNTRY OBJECT?
IF NOT, THEN THE TIME HAS COME TO TALK OF PAYMENT.
I DID NOT BRING THIS UP EARLIER, FOR THIS WAS NEVER ABOUT BLACKMAIL. THIS IS COMPENSATION FOR SERVICES RENDERED.
FIRST, FOR MY COLLEAGUES. YOU WILL EXPUNGE THEIR CRIMINAL RECORDS...
...AND DEPOSIT TWO BILLION DOLLARS IN EACH OF THEIR PRIVATE BANK ACCOUNTS.
KA-
-CHING!
AND THAT DOES IT.
A BILLIONAIRE WITH A CLEAN SLATE-- WHO HELPED SAVE THE WORLD.
AIN'T NO WAY THEY WON'T LET ME HAVE CUSTODY A' MY KID, KEEMIA. NOT NOW.

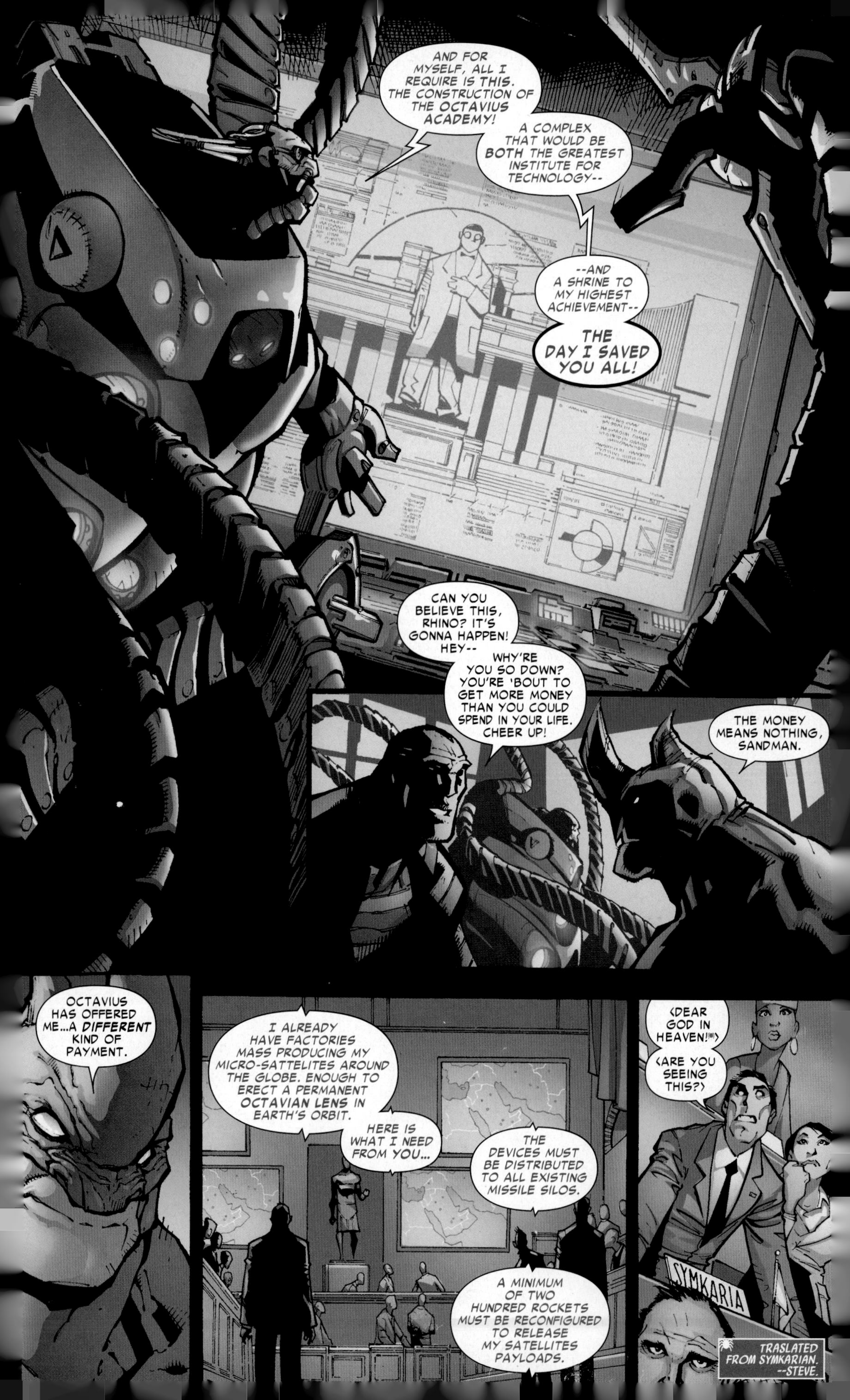
AND FOR MYSELF, ALL I REQUIRE IS THIS. THE CONSTRUCTION OF THE OCTAVIUS ACADEMY!
A COMPLEX THAT WOULD BE BOTH THE GREATEST INSTITUTE FOR TECHNOLOGY--
--AND A SHRINE TO MY HIGHEST ACHIEVEMENT--
THE DAY I SAVED YOU ALL!
CAN YOU BELIEVE THIS, RHINO? IT'S GONNA HAPPEN! HEY--
WHY'RE YOU SO DOWN? YOU'RE 'BOUT TO GET MORE MONEY THAN YOU COULD SPEND IN YOUR LIFE. CHEER UP!
THE MONEY MEANS NOTHING, SANDMAN.
OCTAVIUS HAS OFFERED ME...A DIFFERENT KIND OF PAYMENT.
I ALREADY HAVE FACTORIES MASS PRODUCING MY MICRO-SATTELITES AROUND THE GLOBE. ENOUGH TO ERECT A PERMANENT OCTAVIAN LENS IN EARTH'S ORBIT.
HERE IS WHAT I NEED FROM YOU...
THE DEVICES MUST BE DISTRIBUTED TO ALL EXISTING MISSILE SILOS.
A MINIMUM OF TWO HUNDRED ROCKETS MUST BE RECONFIGURED TO RELEASE MY SATELLITES PAYLOADS.
<DEAR GOD IN HEAVEN!>
<ARE YOU SEEING THIS?>
SYMKARIA
TRASLATED FROM SYMKARIAN. --STEVE.

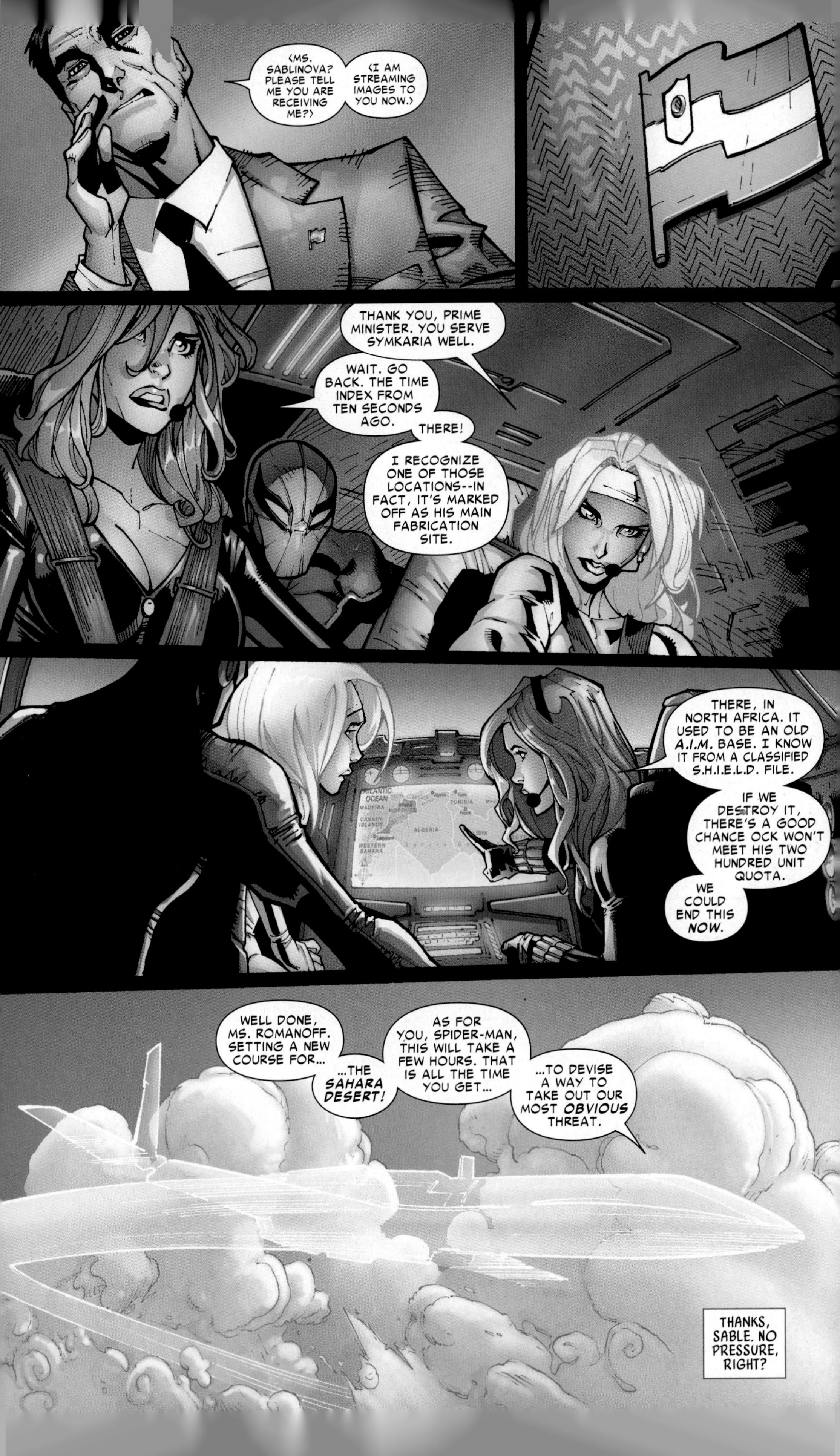

‹MS. SABLINOVA? PLEASE TELL ME YOU ARE RECEIVING ME?›
‹I AM STREAMING IMAGES TO YOU NOW.›
THANK YOU, PRIME MINISTER. YOU SERVE SYMKARIA WELL.
WAIT. GO BACK. THE TIME INDEX FROM TEN SECONDS AGO.
THERE!
I RECOGNIZE ONE OF THOSE LOCATIONS--IN FACT, IT'S MARKED OFF AS HIS MAIN FABRICATION SITE.
ATLANTIC OCEAN
MADEIRA
MOROCCO
CANARY ISLANDS
ALGERIA
TUNISIA
WESTERN SAHARA
THERE, IN NORTH AFRICA. IT USED TO BE AN OLD A.I.M. BASE. I KNOW IT FROM A CLASSIFIED S.H.I.E.L.D. FILE.
IF WE DESTROY IT, THERE'S A GOOD CHANCE OCK WON'T MEET HIS TWO HUNDRED UNIT QUOTA.
WE COULD END THIS NOW.
WELL DONE, MS. ROMANOFF. SETTING A NEW COURSE FOR...
...THE SAHARA DESERT!
AS FOR YOU, SPIDER-MAN, THIS WILL TAKE A FEW HOURS. THAT IS ALL THE TIME YOU GET...
...TO DEVISE A WAY TO TAKE OUT OUR MOST OBVIOUS THREAT.
THANKS, SABLE. NO PRESSURE, RIGHT?

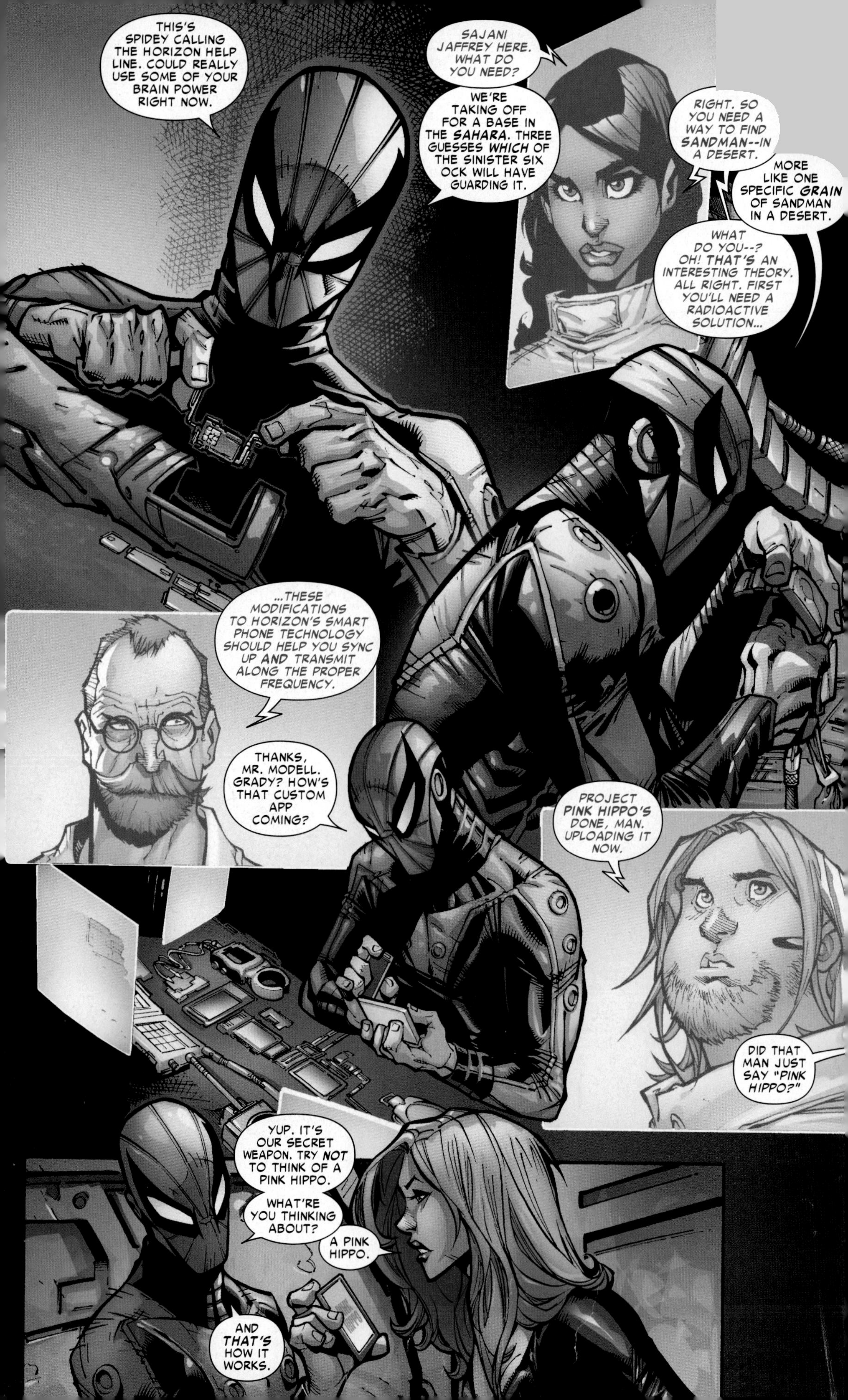
THIS'S SPIDEY CALLING THE HORIZON HELP LINE. COULD REALLY USE SOME OF YOUR BRAIN POWER RIGHT NOW.
SAJANI JAFFREY HERE. WHAT DO YOU NEED?
WE'RE TAKING OFF FOR A BASE IN THE SAHARA. THREE GUESSES WHICH OF THE SINISTER SIX OCK WILL HAVE GUARDING IT.
RIGHT. SO YOU NEED A WAY TO FIND SANDMAN--IN A DESERT.
MORE LIKE ONE SPECIFIC GRAIN OF SANDMAN IN A DESERT.
WHAT DO YOU--? OH! THAT'S AN INTERESTING THEORY. ALL RIGHT. FIRST YOU'LL NEED A RADIOACTIVE SOLUTION...
...THESE MODIFICATIONS TO HORIZON'S SMART PHONE TECHNOLOGY SHOULD HELP YOU SYNC UP AND TRANSMIT ALONG THE PROPER FREQUENCY.
THANKS, MR. MODELL. GRADY? HOW'S THAT CUSTOM APP COMING?
PROJECT PINK HIPPO'S DONE, MAN. UPLOADING IT NOW.
DID THAT MAN JUST SAY "PINK HIPPO?"
YUP. IT'S OUR SECRET WEAPON. TRY NOT TO THINK OF A PINK HIPPO.
WHAT'RE YOU THINKING ABOUT?
A PINK HIPPO.
AND THAT'S HOW IT WORKS.

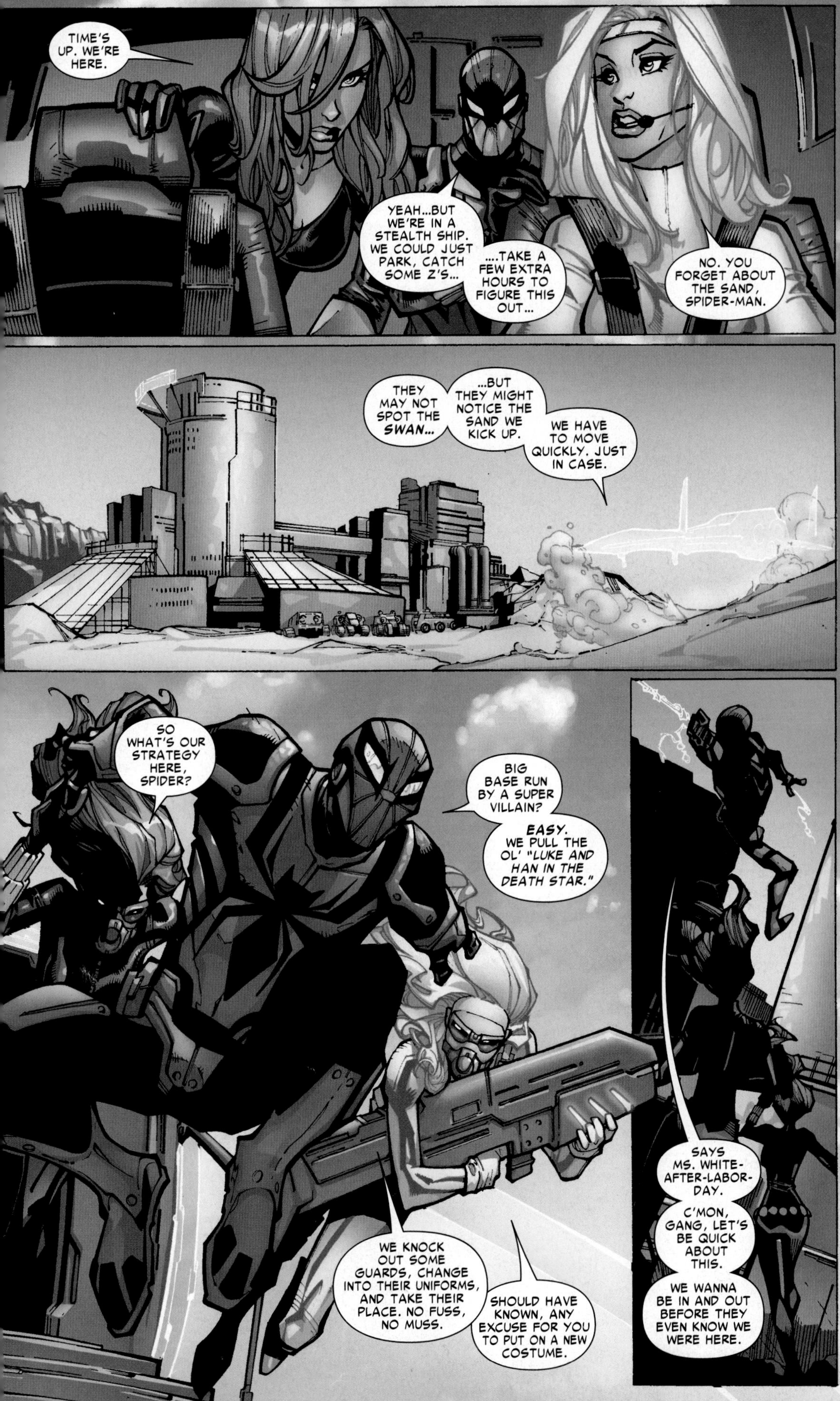
TIME'S UP. WE'RE HERE.
YEAH...BUT WE'RE IN A STEALTH SHIP. WE COULD JUST PARK, CATCH SOME Z'S...
....TAKE A FEW EXTRA HOURS TO FIGURE THIS OUT...
NO. YOU FORGET ABOUT THE SAND, SPIDER-MAN.
THEY MAY NOT SPOT THE SWAN...
...BUT THEY MIGHT NOTICE THE SAND WE KICK UP.
WE HAVE TO MOVE QUICKLY. JUST IN CASE.
SO WHAT'S OUR STRATEGY HERE, SPIDER?
BIG BASE RUN BY A SUPER VILLAIN?
EASY. WE PULL THE OL' "LUKE AND HAN IN THE DEATH STAR."
WE KNOCK OUT SOME GUARDS, CHANGE INTO THEIR UNIFORMS, AND TAKE THEIR PLACE. NO FUSS, NO MUSS.
SHOULD HAVE KNOWN, ANY EXCUSE FOR YOU TO PUT ON A NEW COSTUME.
SAYS MS. WHITE-AFTER-LABOR-DAY.
C'MON, GANG, LET'S BE QUICK ABOUT THIS.
WE WANNA BE IN AND OUT BEFORE THEY EVEN KNOW WE WERE HERE.

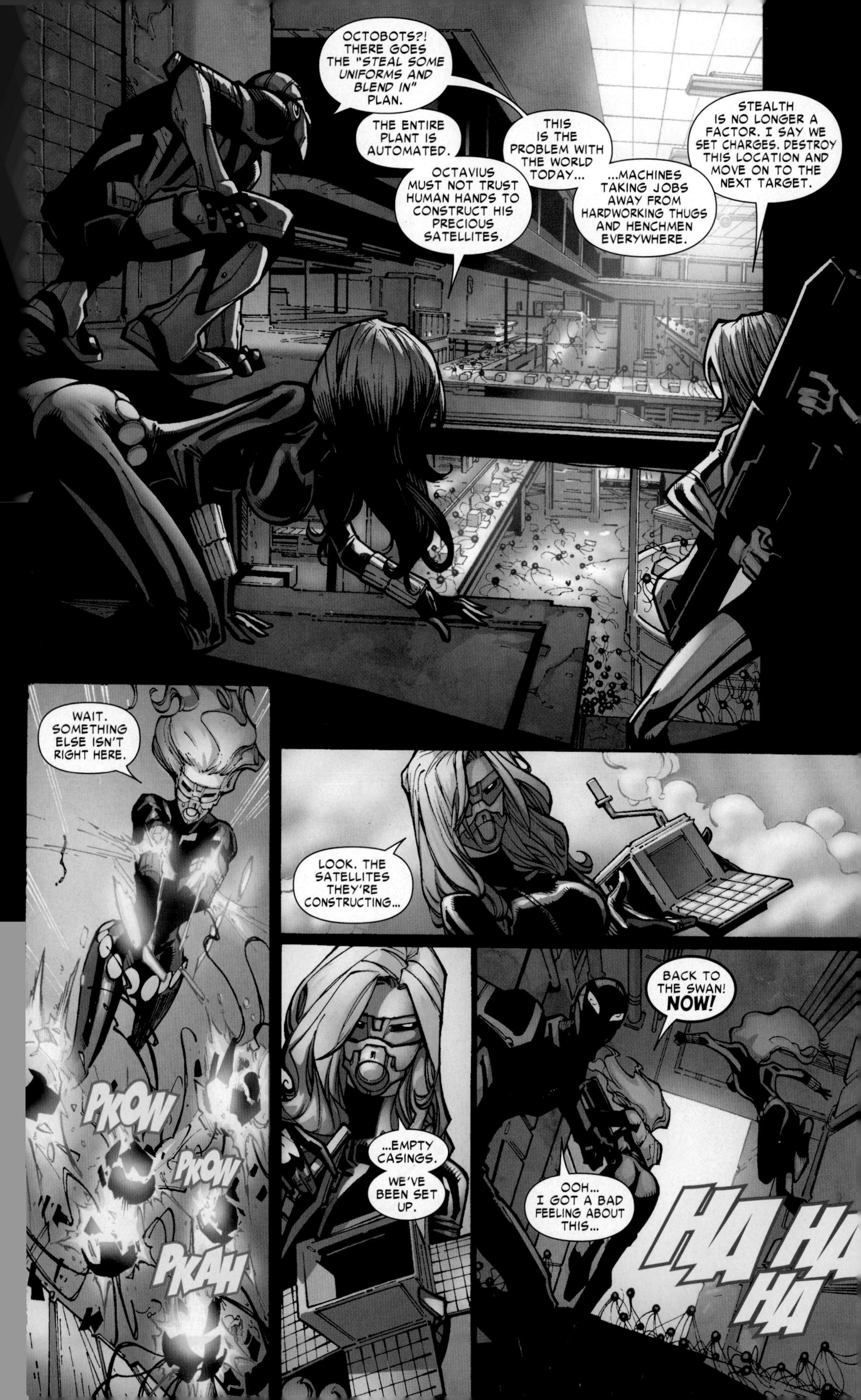
OCTOBOTS?! THERE GOES THE "STEAL SOME UNIFORMS AND BLEND IN" PLAN.
THE ENTIRE PLANT IS AUTOMATED.
OCTAVIUS MUST NOT TRUST HUMAN HANDS TO CONSTRUCT HIS PRECIOUS SATELLITES.
THIS IS THE PROBLEM WITH THE WORLD TODAY...
...MACHINES TAKING JOBS AWAY FROM HARDWORKING THUGS AND HENCHMEN EVERYWHERE.
STEALTH IS NO LONGER A FACTOR. I SAY WE SET CHARGES. DESTROY THIS LOCATION AND MOVE ON TO THE NEXT TARGET.
WAIT. SOMETHING ELSE ISN'T RIGHT HERE.
PKOW
PKOW
PKAH
LOOK. THE SATELLITES THEY'RE CONSTRUCTING...
...EMPTY CASINGS.
WE'VE BEEN SET UP.
BACK TO THE SWAN! **NOW!**
OOH... I GOT A BAD FEELING ABOUT THIS...
HA HA HA

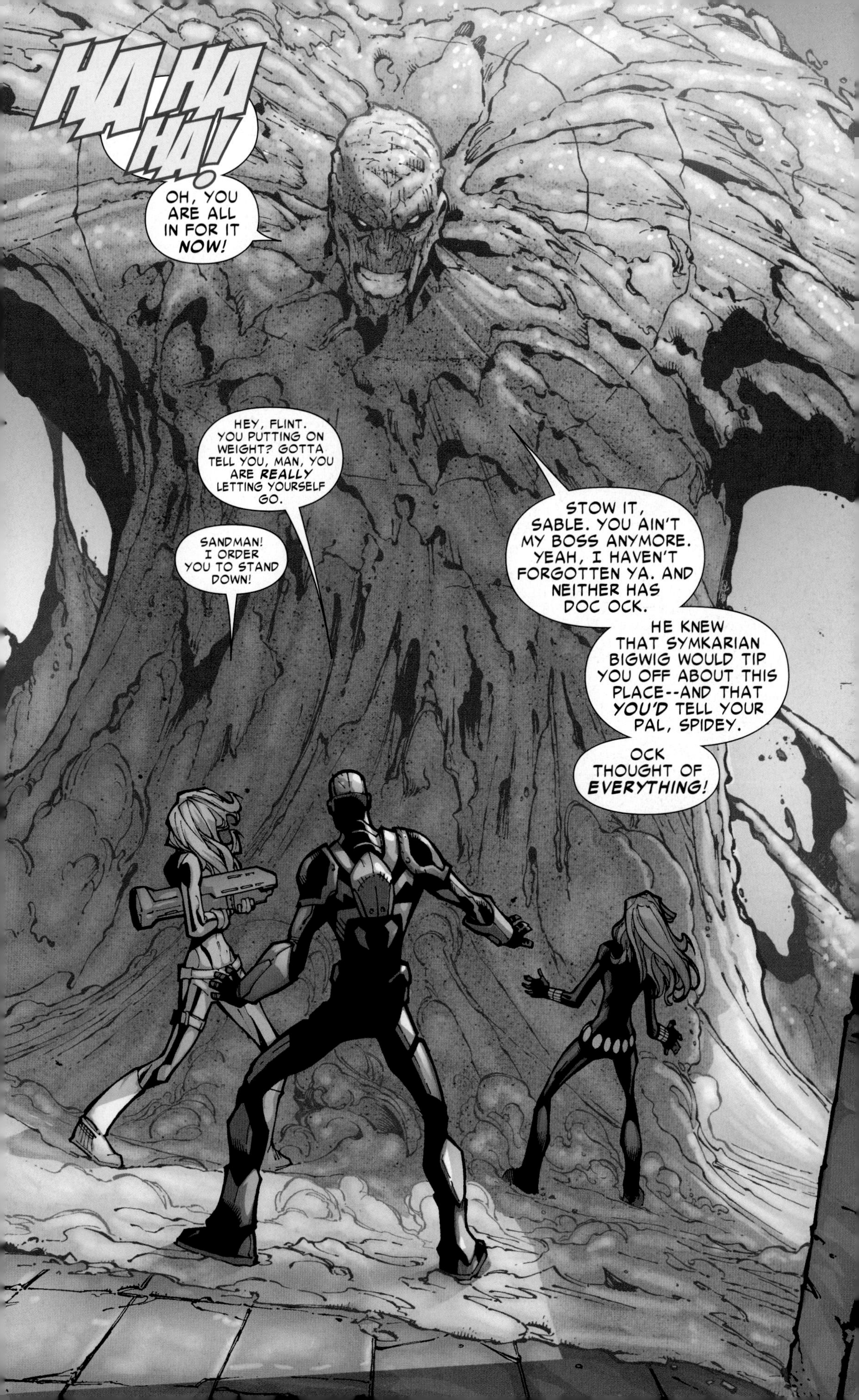
HA HA HA!
OH, YOU ARE ALL IN FOR IT NOW!
HEY, FLINT. YOU PUTTING ON WEIGHT? GOTTA TELL YOU, MAN, YOU ARE REALLY LETTING YOURSELF GO.
SANDMAN! I ORDER YOU TO STAND DOWN!
STOW IT, SABLE. YOU AIN'T MY BOSS ANYMORE. YEAH, I HAVEN'T FORGOTTEN YA. AND NEITHER HAS DOC OCK.
HE KNEW THAT SYMKARIAN BIGWIG WOULD TIP YOU OFF ABOUT THIS PLACE--AND THAT YOU'D TELL YOUR PAL, SPIDEY.
OCK THOUGHT OF EVERYTHING!

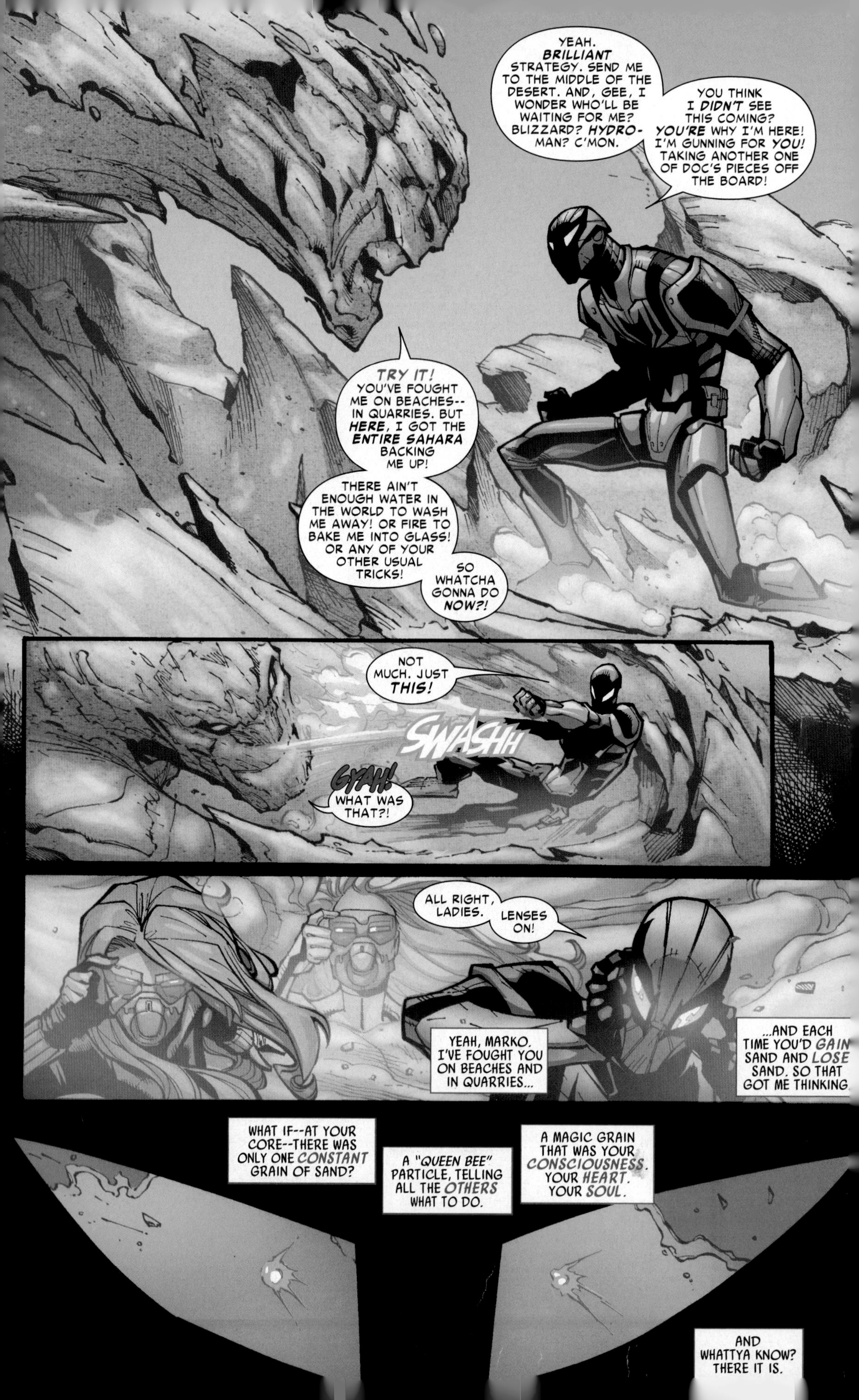
YEAH. BRILLIANT STRATEGY. SEND ME TO THE MIDDLE OF THE DESERT. AND, GEE, I WONDER WHO'LL BE WAITING FOR ME? BLIZZARD? HYDRO-MAN? C'MON.
YOU THINK I DIDN'T SEE THIS COMING? YOU'RE WHY I'M HERE! I'M GUNNING FOR YOU! TAKING ANOTHER ONE OF DOC'S PIECES OFF THE BOARD!
TRY IT! YOU'VE FOUGHT ME ON BEACHES-- IN QUARRIES. BUT HERE, I GOT THE ENTIRE SAHARA BACKING ME UP!
THERE AIN'T ENOUGH WATER IN THE WORLD TO WASH ME AWAY! OR FIRE TO BAKE ME INTO GLASS! OR ANY OF YOUR OTHER USUAL TRICKS!
SO WHATCHA GONNA DO NOW?!
NOT MUCH. JUST THIS!
SWASHH
GYAH! WHAT WAS THAT?!
ALL RIGHT, LADIES.
LENSES ON!
YEAH, MARKO. I'VE FOUGHT YOU ON BEACHES AND IN QUARRIES...
...AND EACH TIME YOU'D GAIN SAND AND LOSE SAND. SO THAT GOT ME THINKING.
WHAT IF--AT YOUR CORE--THERE WAS ONLY ONE CONSTANT GRAIN OF SAND?
A "QUEEN BEE" PARTICLE, TELLING ALL THE OTHERS WHAT TO DO.
A MAGIC GRAIN THAT WAS YOUR CONSCIOUSNESS. YOUR HEART. YOUR SOUL.
AND WHATTYA KNOW? THERE IT IS.

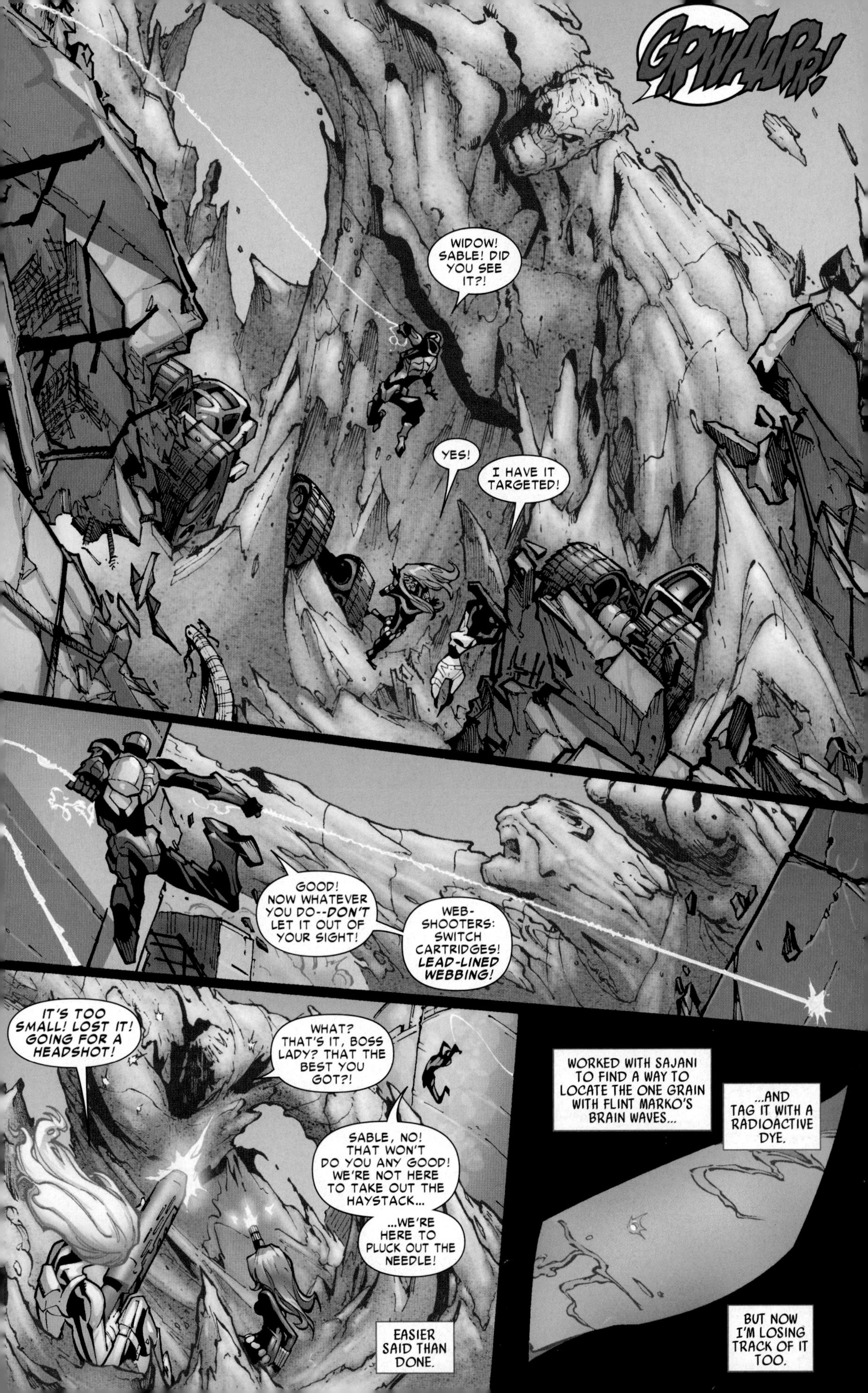
GRWAARRR!
WIDOW! SABLE! DID YOU SEE IT?!
YES!
I HAVE IT TARGETED!
GOOD! NOW WHATEVER YOU DO--DON'T LET IT OUT OF YOUR SIGHT!
WEB-SHOOTERS: SWITCH CARTRIDGES! LEAD-LINED WEBBING!
IT'S TOO SMALL! LOST IT! GOING FOR A HEADSHOT!
WHAT? THAT'S IT, BOSS LADY? THAT THE BEST YOU GOT?!
SABLE, NO! THAT WON'T DO YOU ANY GOOD! WE'RE NOT HERE TO TAKE OUT THE HAYSTACK...
...WE'RE HERE TO PLUCK OUT THE NEEDLE!
EASIER SAID THAN DONE.
WORKED WITH SAJANI TO FIND A WAY TO LOCATE THE ONE GRAIN WITH FLINT MARKO'S BRAIN WAVES...
...AND TAG IT WITH A RADIOACTIVE DYE.
BUT NOW I'M LOSING TRACK OF IT TOO.

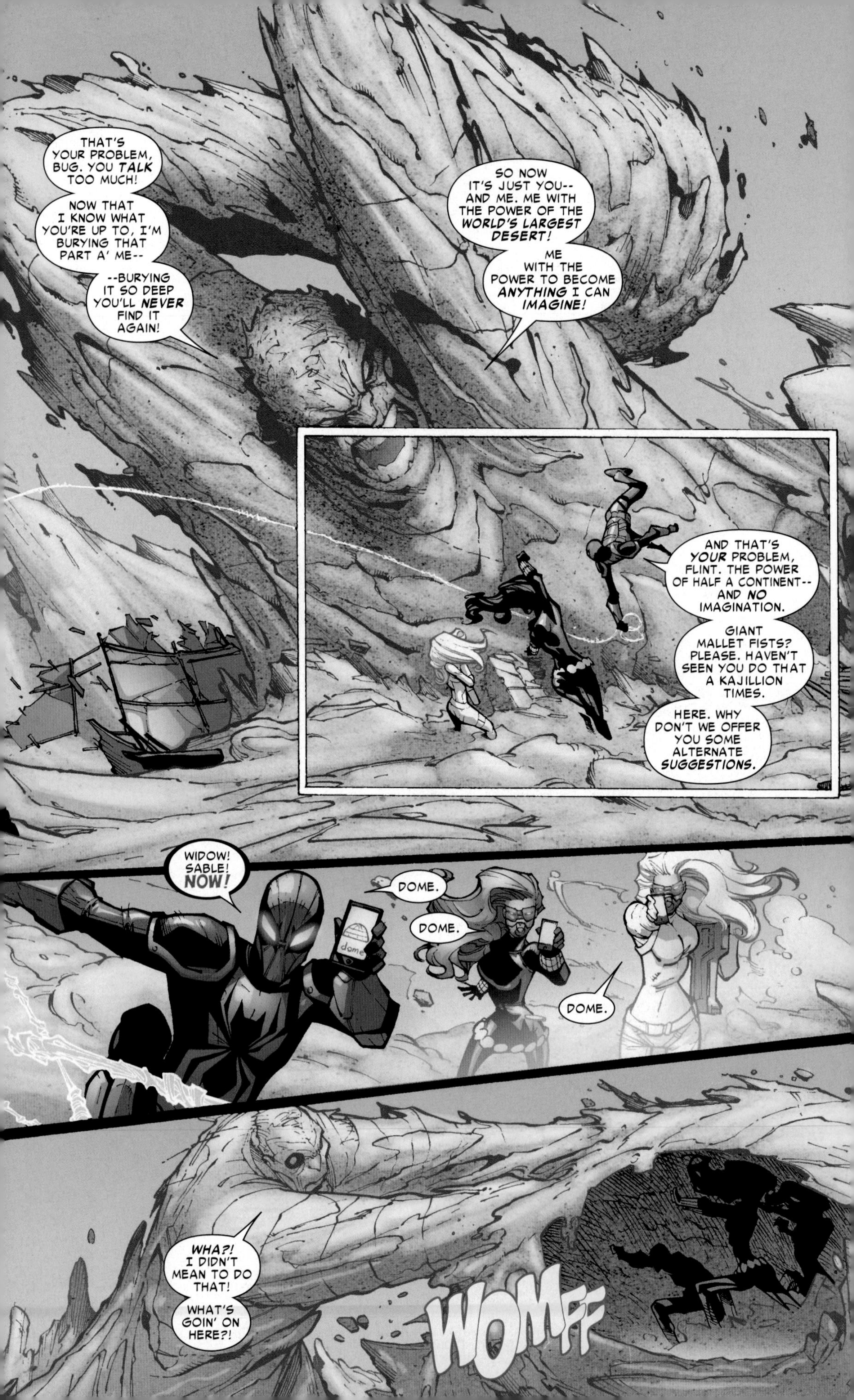
THAT'S YOUR PROBLEM, BUG. YOU TALK TOO MUCH!
NOW THAT I KNOW WHAT YOU'RE UP TO, I'M BURYING THAT PART A' ME--
--BURYING IT SO DEEP YOU'LL NEVER FIND IT AGAIN!
SO NOW IT'S JUST YOU-- AND ME. ME WITH THE POWER OF THE WORLD'S LARGEST DESERT!
ME WITH THE POWER TO BECOME ANYTHING I CAN IMAGINE!
AND THAT'S YOUR PROBLEM, FLINT. THE POWER OF HALF A CONTINENT-- AND NO IMAGINATION.
GIANT MALLET FISTS? PLEASE. HAVEN'T SEEN YOU DO THAT A KAJILLION TIMES.
HERE. WHY DON'T WE OFFER YOU SOME ALTERNATE SUGGESTIONS.
WIDOW! SABLE! NOW!
dome
DOME.
DOME.
DOME.
WHA?! I DIDN'T MEAN TO DO THAT!
WHAT'S GOIN' ON HERE?!
WOMFF

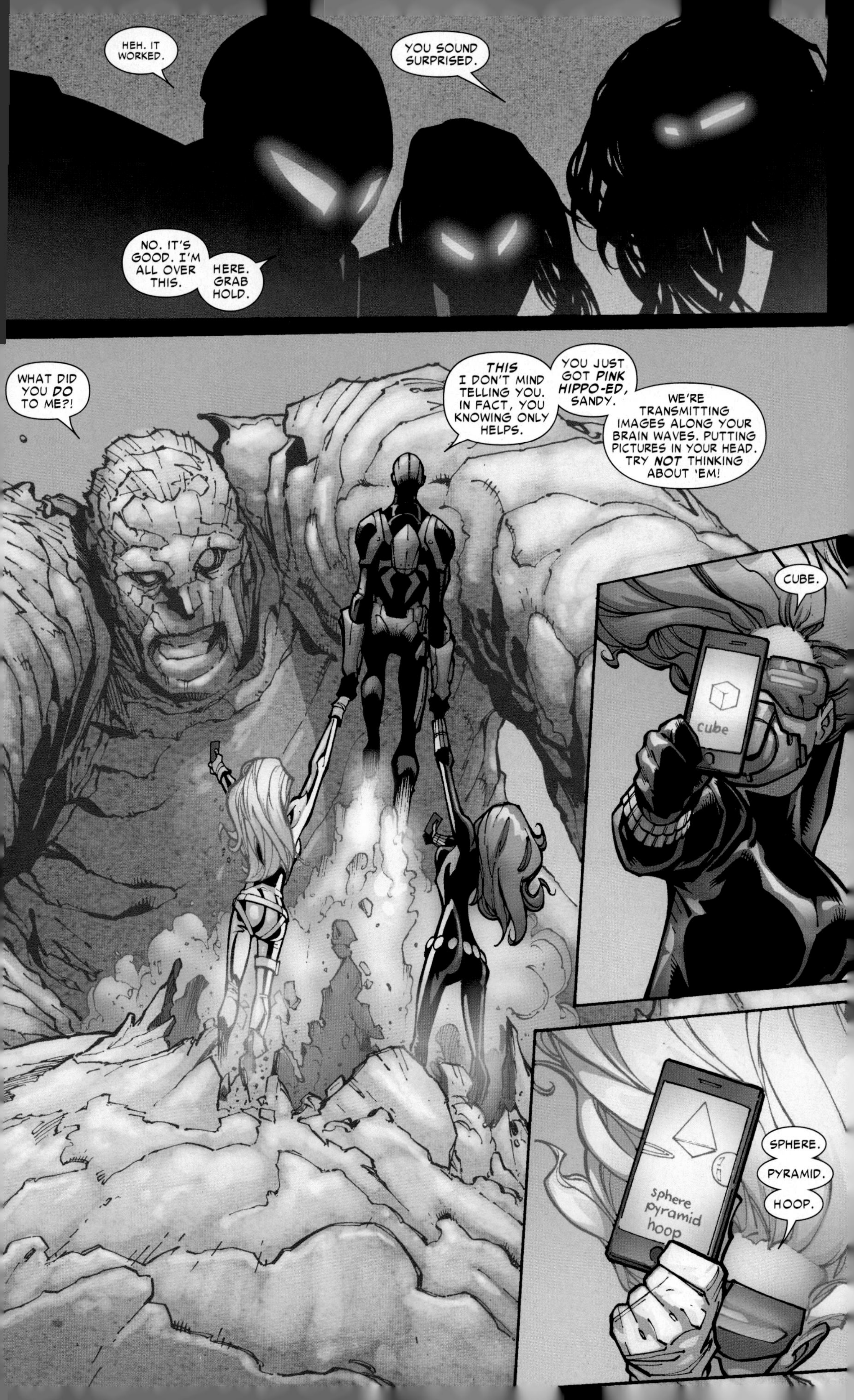
HEH. IT WORKED.
YOU SOUND SURPRISED.
NO. IT'S GOOD. I'M ALL OVER THIS.
HERE. GRAB HOLD.
WHAT DID YOU DO TO ME?!
THIS I DON'T MIND TELLING YOU. IN FACT, YOU KNOWING ONLY HELPS.
YOU JUST GOT PINK HIPPO-ED, SANDY.
WE'RE TRANSMITTING IMAGES ALONG YOUR BRAIN WAVES. PUTTING PICTURES IN YOUR HEAD. TRY NOT THINKING ABOUT 'EM!
CUBE.
cube
SPHERE.
PYRAMID.
HOOP.
sphere
pyramid
hoop

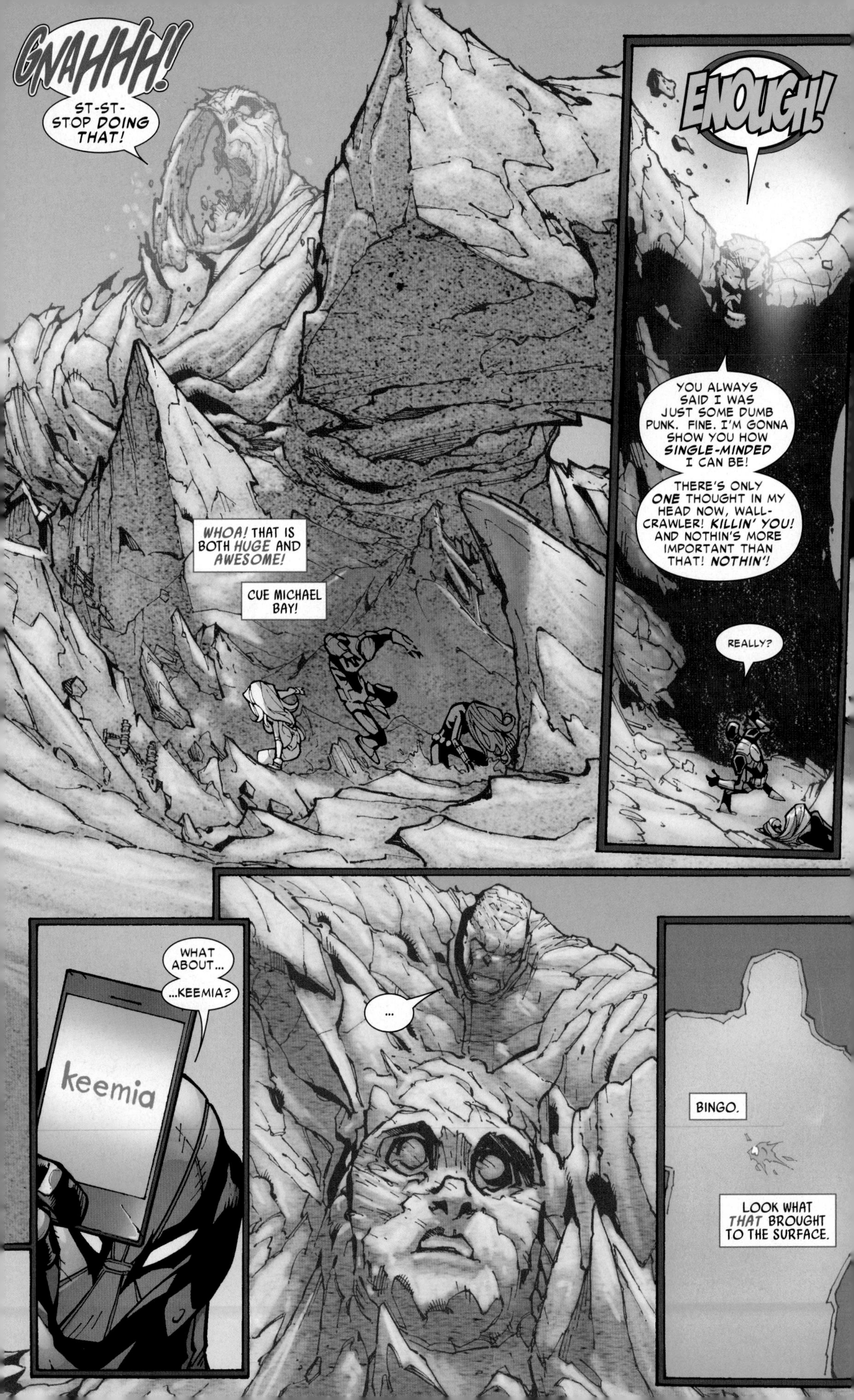
GNAHHH!
ST-ST-STOP DOING THAT!
WHOA! THAT IS BOTH HUGE AND AWESOME!
CUE MICHAEL BAY!
ENOUGH!
YOU ALWAYS SAID I WAS JUST SOME DUMB PUNK. FINE. I'M GONNA SHOW YOU HOW SINGLE-MINDED I CAN BE!
THERE'S ONLY ONE THOUGHT IN MY HEAD NOW, WALL-CRAWLER! KILLIN' YOU! AND NOTHIN'S MORE IMPORTANT THAN THAT! NOTHIN'!
REALLY?
WHAT ABOUT...
...KEEMIA?
keemia
...
BINGO.
LOOK WHAT THAT BROUGHT TO THE SURFACE.

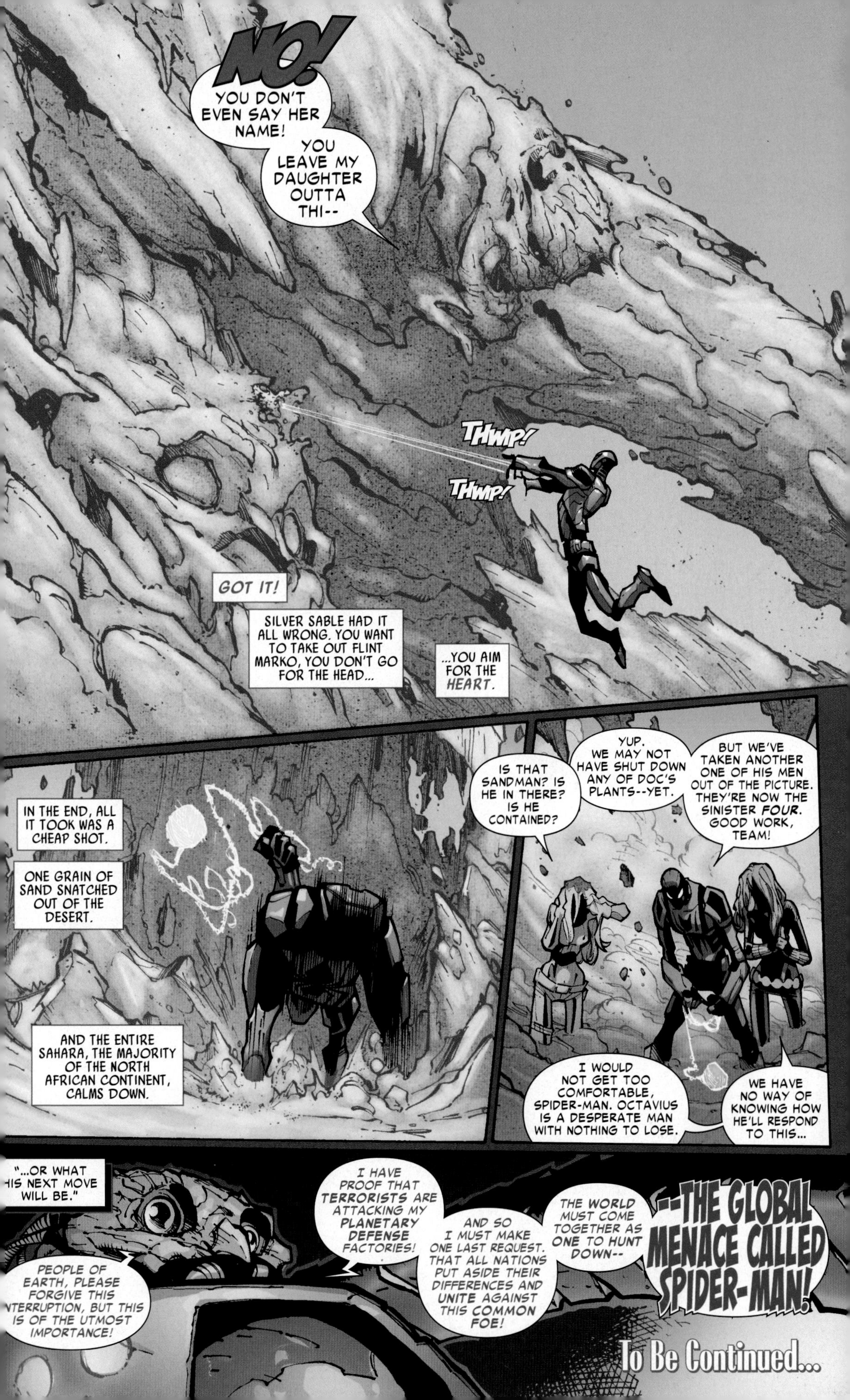
NO!
YOU DON'T EVEN SAY HER NAME!
YOU LEAVE MY DAUGHTER OUTTA THI--
THWP!
THWP!
GOT IT!
SILVER SABLE HAD IT ALL WRONG. YOU WANT TO TAKE OUT FLINT MARKO, YOU DON'T GO FOR THE HEAD...
...YOU AIM FOR THE HEART.
IN THE END, ALL IT TOOK WAS A CHEAP SHOT.
ONE GRAIN OF SAND SNATCHED OUT OF THE DESERT.
AND THE ENTIRE SAHARA, THE MAJORITY OF THE NORTH AFRICAN CONTINENT, CALMS DOWN.
IS THAT SANDMAN? IS HE IN THERE? IS HE CONTAINED?
YUP. WE MAY NOT HAVE SHUT DOWN ANY OF DOC'S PLANTS--YET.
BUT WE'VE TAKEN ANOTHER ONE OF HIS MEN OUT OF THE PICTURE. THEY'RE NOW THE SINISTER FOUR. GOOD WORK, TEAM!
I WOULD NOT GET TOO COMFORTABLE, SPIDER-MAN. OCTAVIUS IS A DESPERATE MAN WITH NOTHING TO LOSE.
WE HAVE NO WAY OF KNOWING HOW HE'LL RESPOND TO THIS...
"...OR WHAT HIS NEXT MOVE WILL BE."
PEOPLE OF EARTH, PLEASE FORGIVE THIS INTERRUPTION, BUT THIS IS OF THE UTMOST IMPORTANCE!
I HAVE PROOF THAT TERRORISTS ARE ATTACKING MY PLANETARY DEFENSE FACTORIES!
AND SO I MUST MAKE ONE LAST REQUEST. THAT ALL NATIONS PUT ASIDE THEIR DIFFERENCES AND UNITE AGAINST THIS COMMON FOE!
THE WORLD MUST COME TOGETHER AS ONE TO HUNT DOWN--
--THE GLOBAL MENACE CALLED SPIDER-MAN!
To Be Continued...

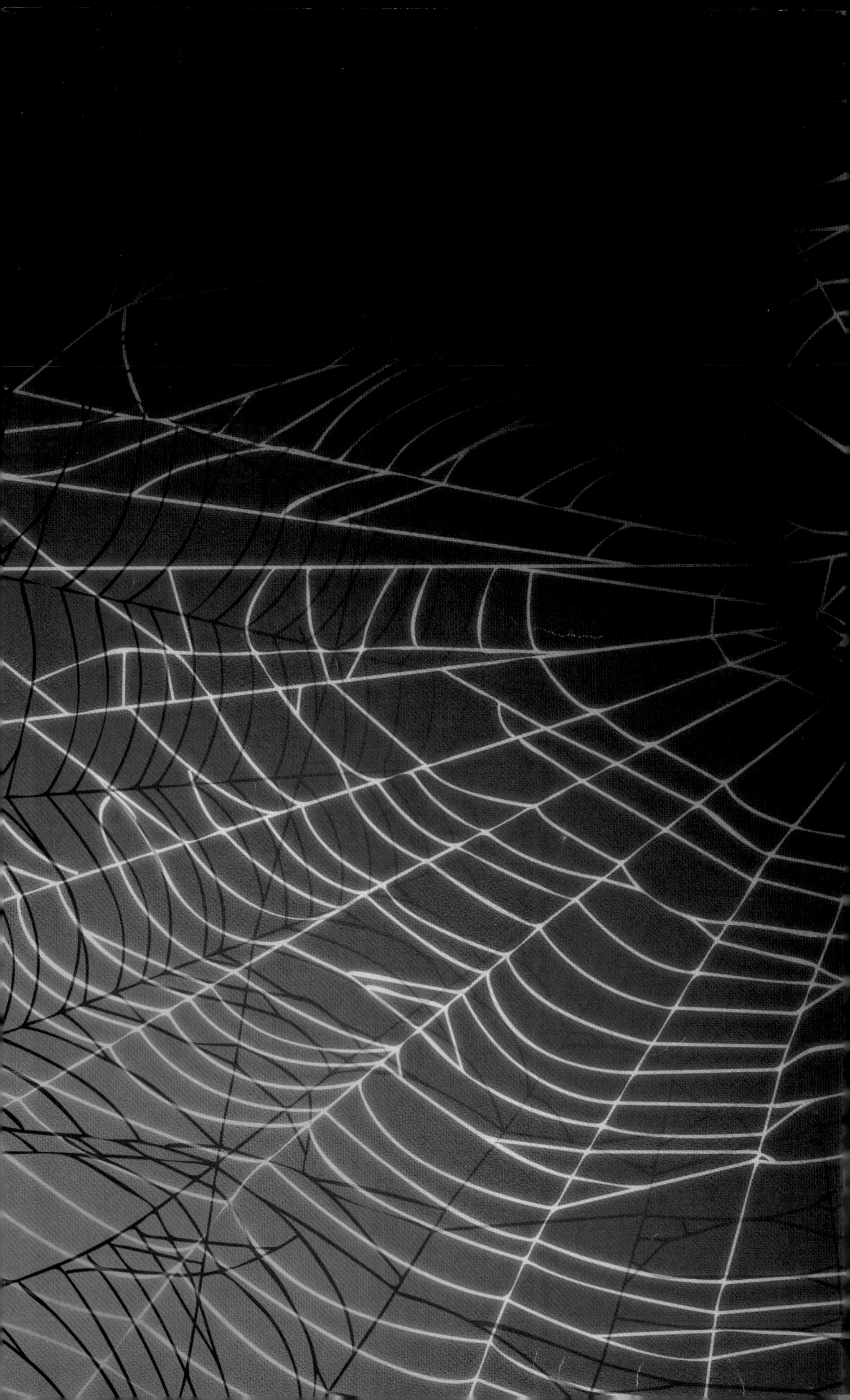

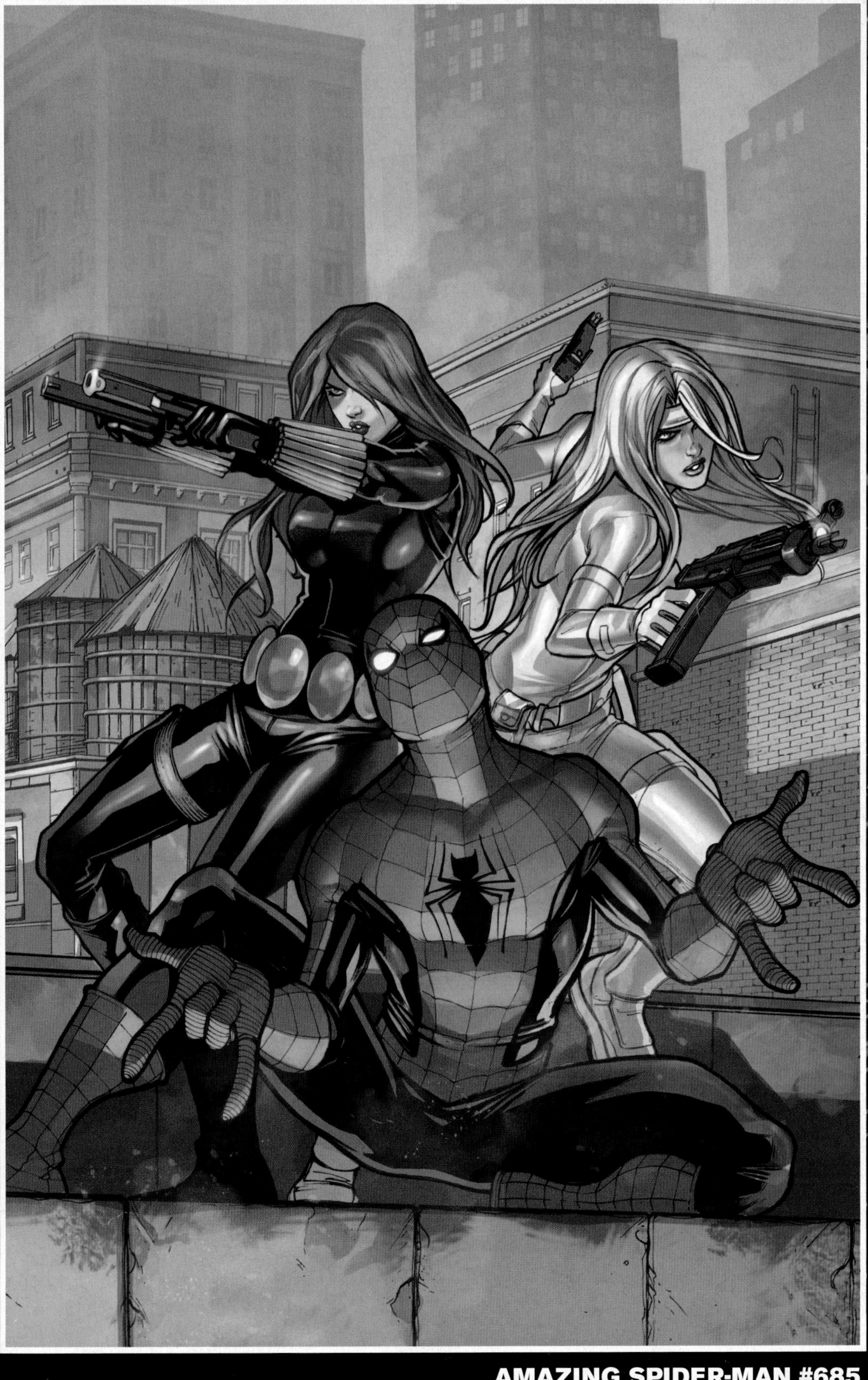

AMAZING SPIDER-MAN #685
COVER BY STEFANO CASELLI & LORENZO DE FELICI

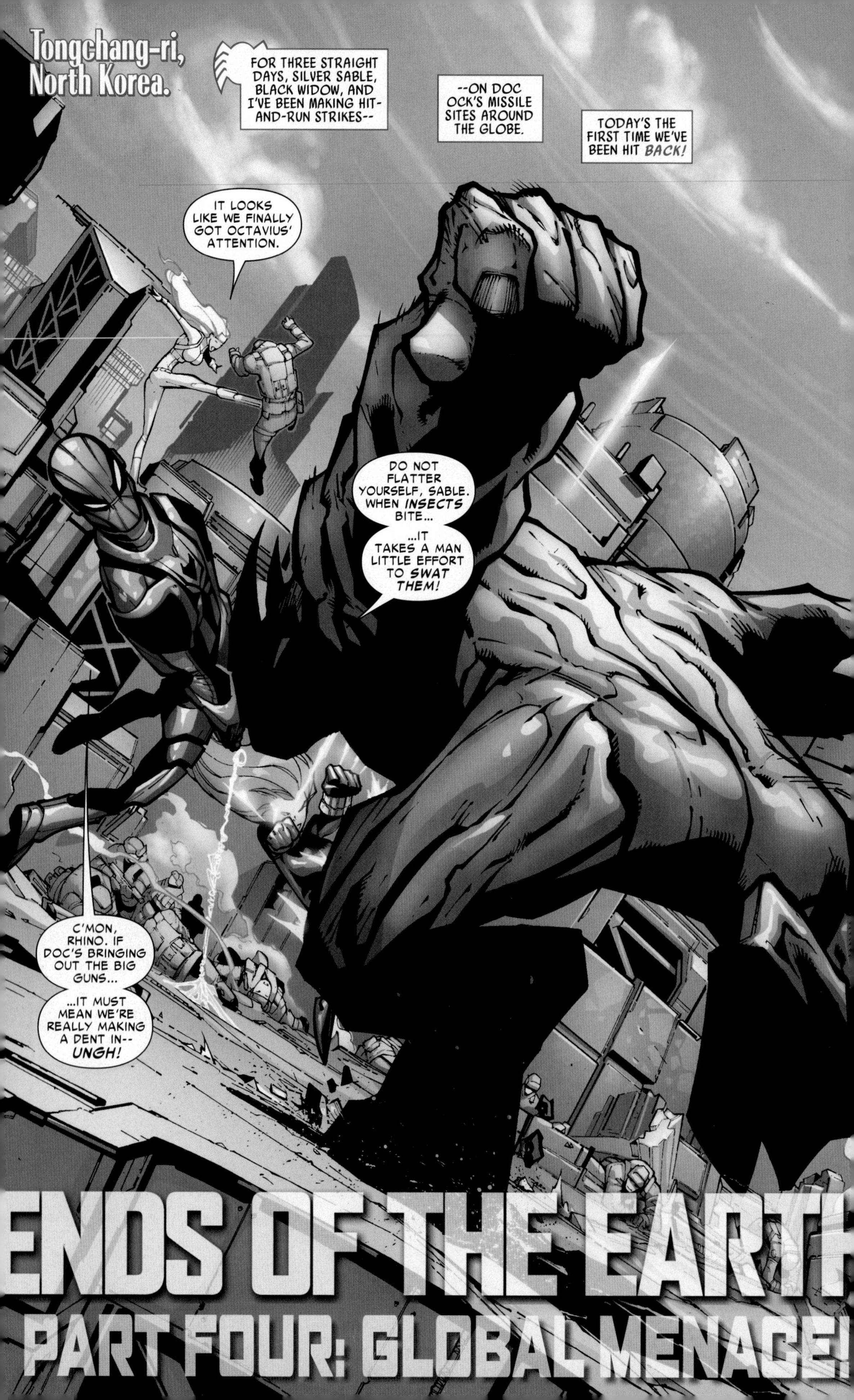

Tongchang-ri, North Korea.
FOR THREE STRAIGHT DAYS, SILVER SABLE, BLACK WIDOW, AND I'VE BEEN MAKING HIT-AND-RUN STRIKES--
--ON DOC OCK'S MISSILE SITES AROUND THE GLOBE.
TODAY'S THE FIRST TIME WE'VE BEEN HIT BACK!
IT LOOKS LIKE WE FINALLY GOT OCTAVIUS' ATTENTION.
DO NOT FLATTER YOURSELF, SABLE. WHEN INSECTS BITE...
...IT TAKES A MAN LITTLE EFFORT TO SWAT THEM!
C'MON, RHINO. IF DOC'S BRINGING OUT THE BIG GUNS...
...IT MUST MEAN WE'RE REALLY MAKING A DENT IN-- UNGH!
ENDS OF THE EARTH
PART FOUR: GLOBAL MENACE!

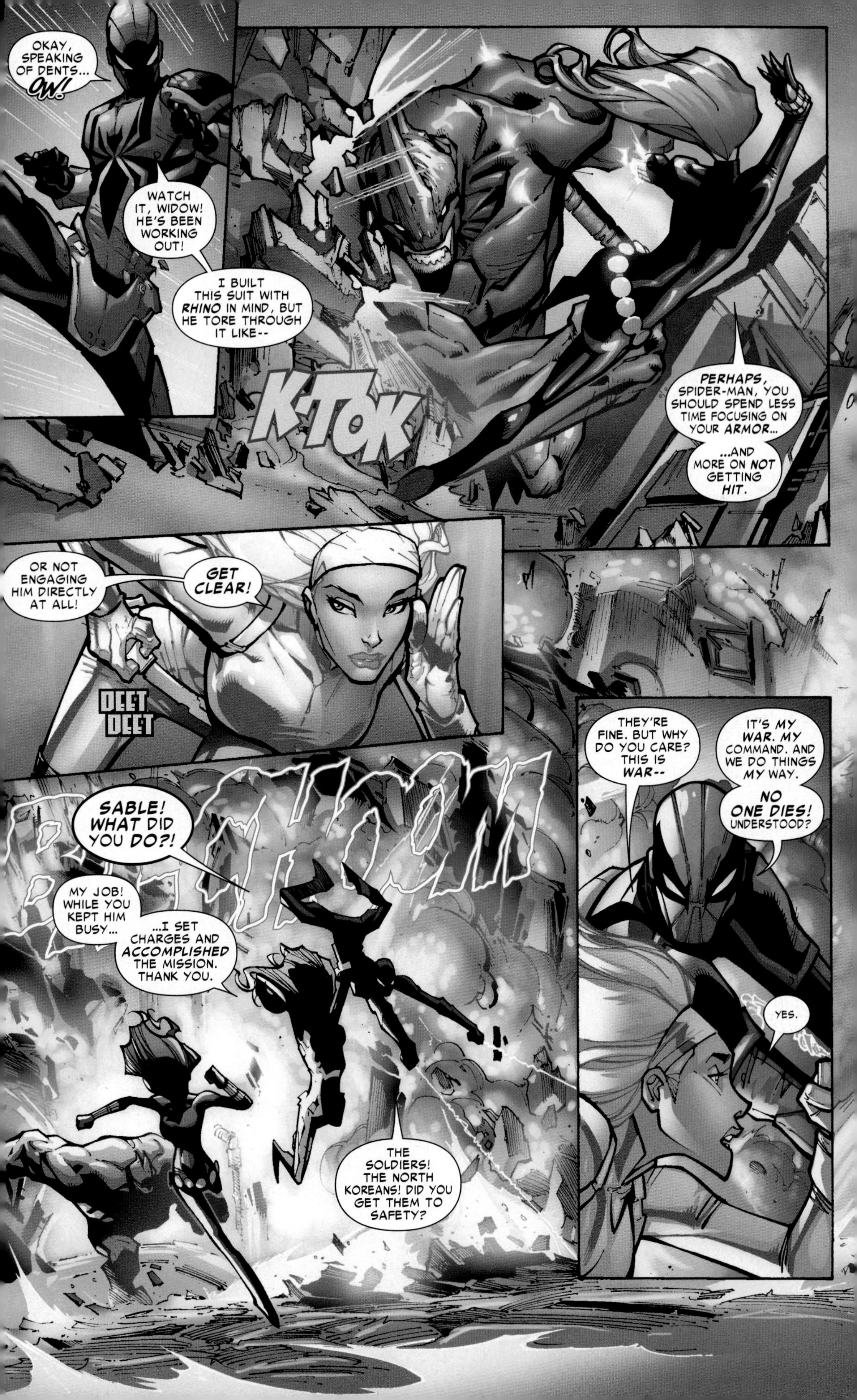
OKAY, SPEAKING OF DENTS... OW!
WATCH IT, WIDOW! HE'S BEEN WORKING OUT!
I BUILT THIS SUIT WITH RHINO IN MIND, BUT HE TORE THROUGH IT LIKE--
K-TOK
PERHAPS, SPIDER-MAN, YOU SHOULD SPEND LESS TIME FOCUSING ON YOUR ARMOR...
...AND MORE ON NOT GETTING HIT.
OR NOT ENGAGING HIM DIRECTLY AT ALL!
GET CLEAR!
DEET DEET
SABLE! WHAT DID YOU DO?!
MY JOB! WHILE YOU KEPT HIM BUSY...
...I SET CHARGES AND ACCOMPLISHED THE MISSION. THANK YOU.
THE SOLDIERS! THE NORTH KOREANS! DID YOU GET THEM TO SAFETY?
THEY'RE FINE. BUT WHY DO YOU CARE? THIS IS WAR--
IT'S MY WAR. MY COMMAND. AND WE DO THINGS MY WAY.
NO ONE DIES! UNDERSTOOD?
YES.

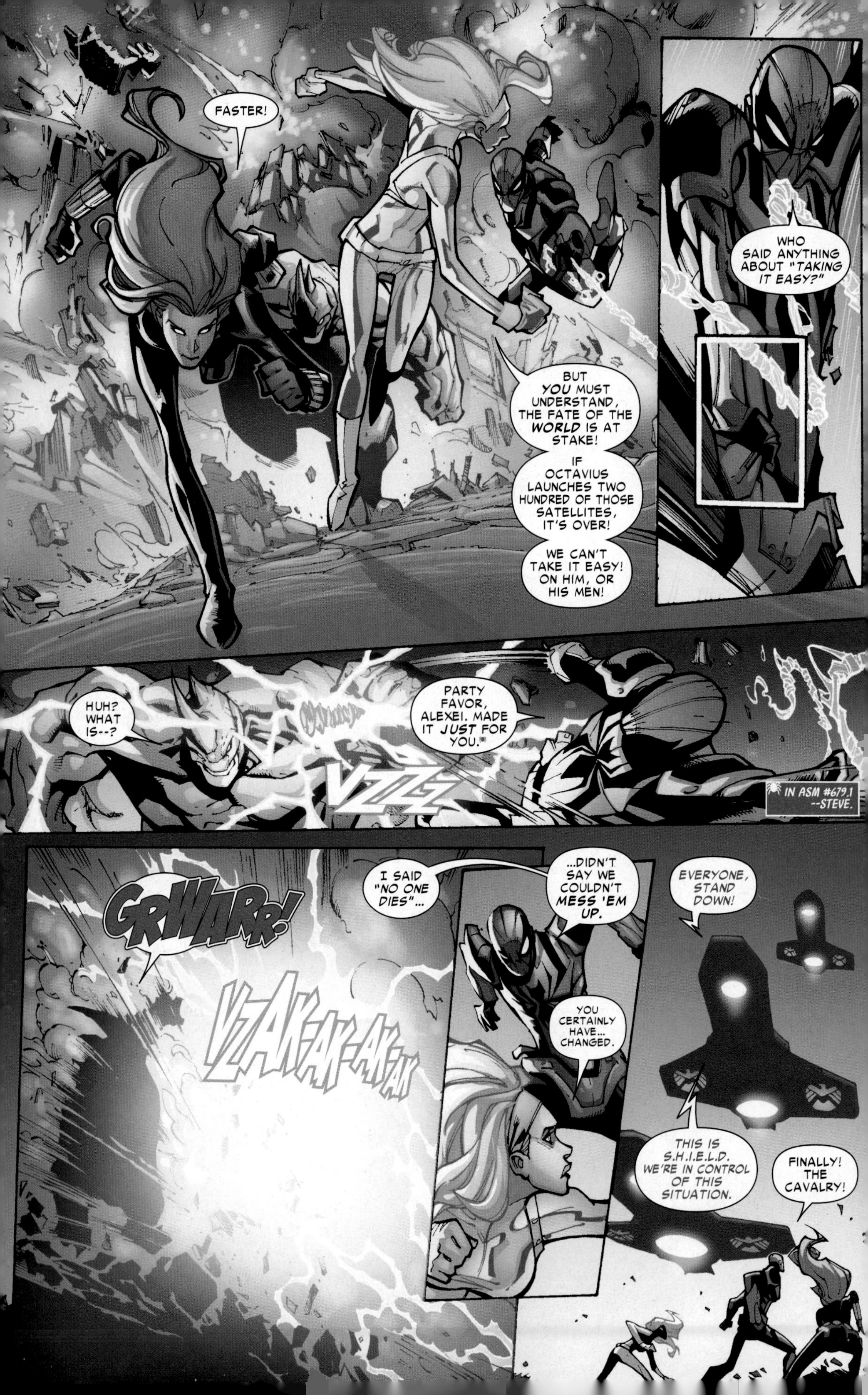
FASTER!
WHO SAID ANYTHING ABOUT "TAKING IT EASY?"
BUT YOU MUST UNDERSTAND, THE FATE OF THE WORLD IS AT STAKE!
IF OCTAVIUS LAUNCHES TWO HUNDRED OF THOSE SATELLITES, IT'S OVER!
WE CAN'T TAKE IT EASY! ON HIM, OR HIS MEN!
HUH? WHAT IS--?
PARTY FAVOR, ALEXEI. MADE IT JUST FOR YOU.*
VZZZ
*IN ASM #679.1 --STEVE.
GRWARR!
VZAK-AK-AK-AK
I SAID "NO ONE DIES"...
...DIDN'T SAY WE COULDN'T MESS 'EM UP.
YOU CERTAINLY HAVE... CHANGED.
EVERYONE, STAND DOWN!
THIS IS S.H.I.E.L.D. WE'RE IN CONTROL OF THIS SITUATION.
FINALLY! THE CAVALRY!

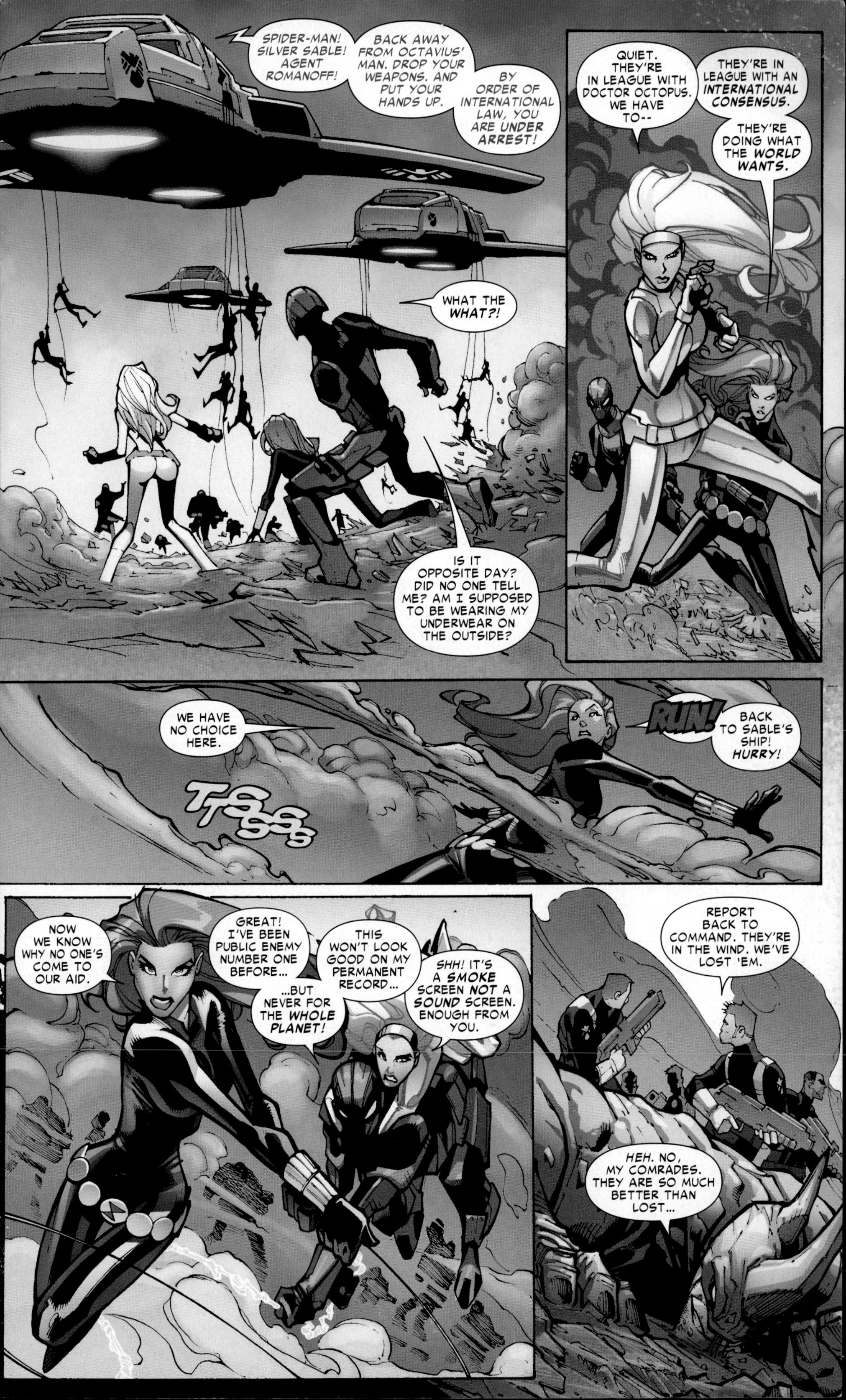
SPIDER-MAN! SILVER SABLE! AGENT ROMANOFF!
BACK AWAY FROM OCTAVIUS' MAN. DROP YOUR WEAPONS. AND PUT YOUR HANDS UP.
BY ORDER OF INTERNATIONAL LAW, YOU ARE UNDER ARREST!
WHAT THE WHAT?!
IS IT OPPOSITE DAY? DID NO ONE TELL ME? AM I SUPPOSED TO BE WEARING MY UNDERWEAR ON THE OUTSIDE?
QUIET. THEY'RE IN LEAGUE WITH DOCTOR OCTOPUS. WE HAVE TO--
THEY'RE IN LEAGUE WITH AN INTERNATIONAL CONSENSUS.
THEY'RE DOING WHAT THE WORLD WANTS.
WE HAVE NO CHOICE HERE.
TTSSSS
RUN!
BACK TO SABLE'S SHIP! HURRY!
NOW WE KNOW WHY NO ONE'S COME TO OUR AID.
GREAT! I'VE BEEN PUBLIC ENEMY NUMBER ONE BEFORE...
...BUT NEVER FOR THE WHOLE PLANET!
THIS WON'T LOOK GOOD ON MY PERMANENT RECORD...
SHH! IT'S A SMOKE SCREEN NOT A SOUND SCREEN. ENOUGH FROM YOU.
REPORT BACK TO COMMAND. THEY'RE IN THE WIND. WE'VE LOST 'EM.
HEH. NO, MY COMRADES. THEY ARE SO MUCH BETTER THAN LOST...

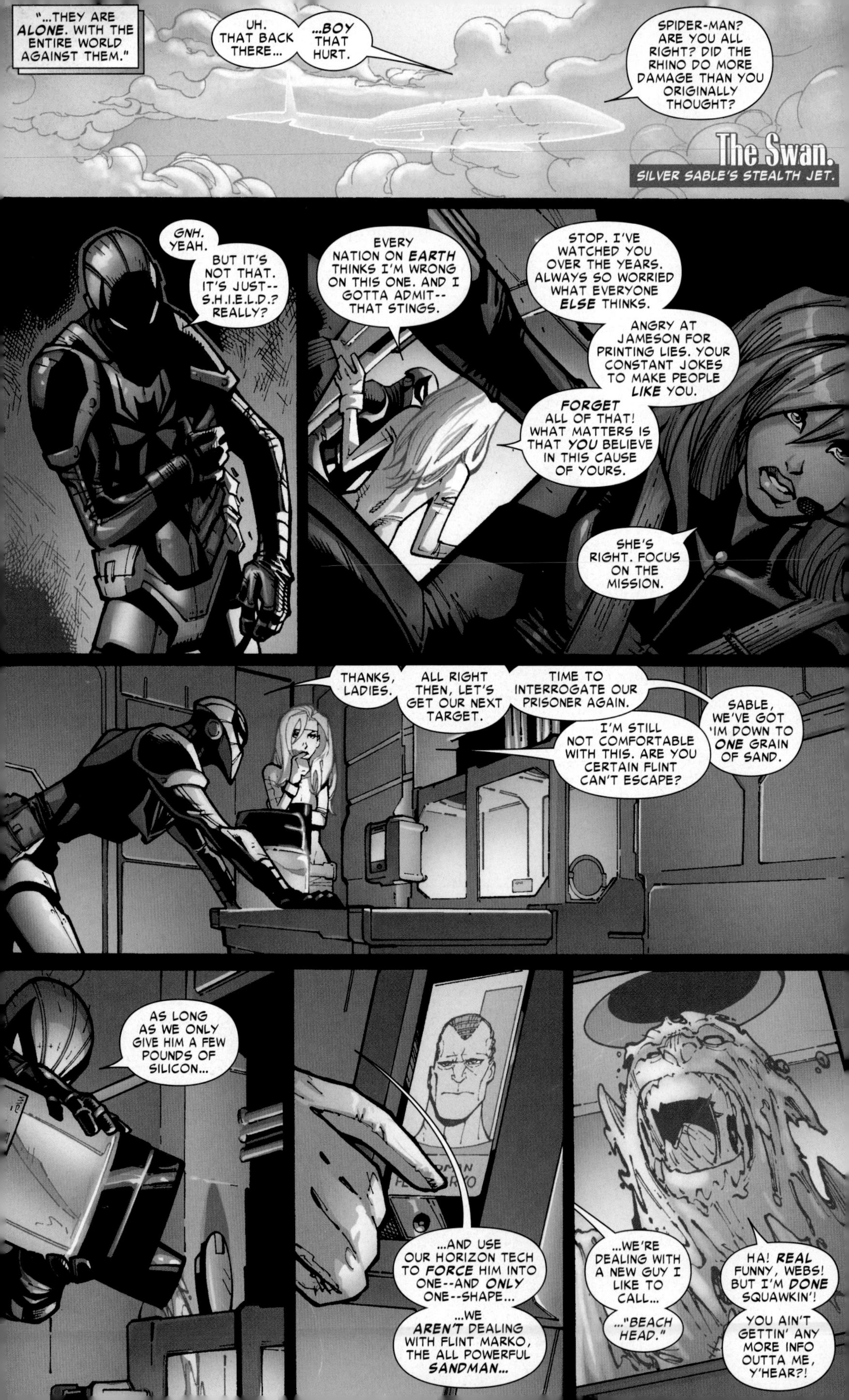
"...THEY ARE ALONE. WITH THE ENTIRE WORLD AGAINST THEM."
UH. THAT BACK THERE...
...BOY THAT HURT.
SPIDER-MAN? ARE YOU ALL RIGHT? DID THE RHINO DO MORE DAMAGE THAN YOU ORIGINALLY THOUGHT?
The Swan.
SILVER SABLE'S STEALTH JET.
GNH. YEAH.
BUT IT'S NOT THAT. IT'S JUST-- S.H.I.E.L.D.? REALLY?
EVERY NATION ON EARTH THINKS I'M WRONG ON THIS ONE. AND I GOTTA ADMIT-- THAT STINGS.
STOP. I'VE WATCHED YOU OVER THE YEARS. ALWAYS SO WORRIED WHAT EVERYONE ELSE THINKS.
ANGRY AT JAMESON FOR PRINTING LIES. YOUR CONSTANT JOKES TO MAKE PEOPLE LIKE YOU.
FORGET ALL OF THAT! WHAT MATTERS IS THAT YOU BELIEVE IN THIS CAUSE OF YOURS.
SHE'S RIGHT. FOCUS ON THE MISSION.
THANKS, LADIES.
ALL RIGHT THEN, LET'S GET OUR NEXT TARGET.
TIME TO INTERROGATE OUR PRISONER AGAIN.
SABLE, WE'VE GOT 'IM DOWN TO ONE GRAIN OF SAND.
I'M STILL NOT COMFORTABLE WITH THIS. ARE YOU CERTAIN FLINT CAN'T ESCAPE?
AS LONG AS WE ONLY GIVE HIM A FEW POUNDS OF SILICON...
...AND USE OUR HORIZON TECH TO FORCE HIM INTO ONE--AND ONLY ONE--SHAPE...
...WE AREN'T DEALING WITH FLINT MARKO, THE ALL POWERFUL SANDMAN...
...WE'RE DEALING WITH A NEW GUY I LIKE TO CALL...
..."BEACH HEAD."
HA! REAL FUNNY, WEBS! BUT I'M DONE SQUAWKIN'!
YOU AIN'T GETTIN' ANY MORE INFO OUTTA ME, Y'HEAR?!

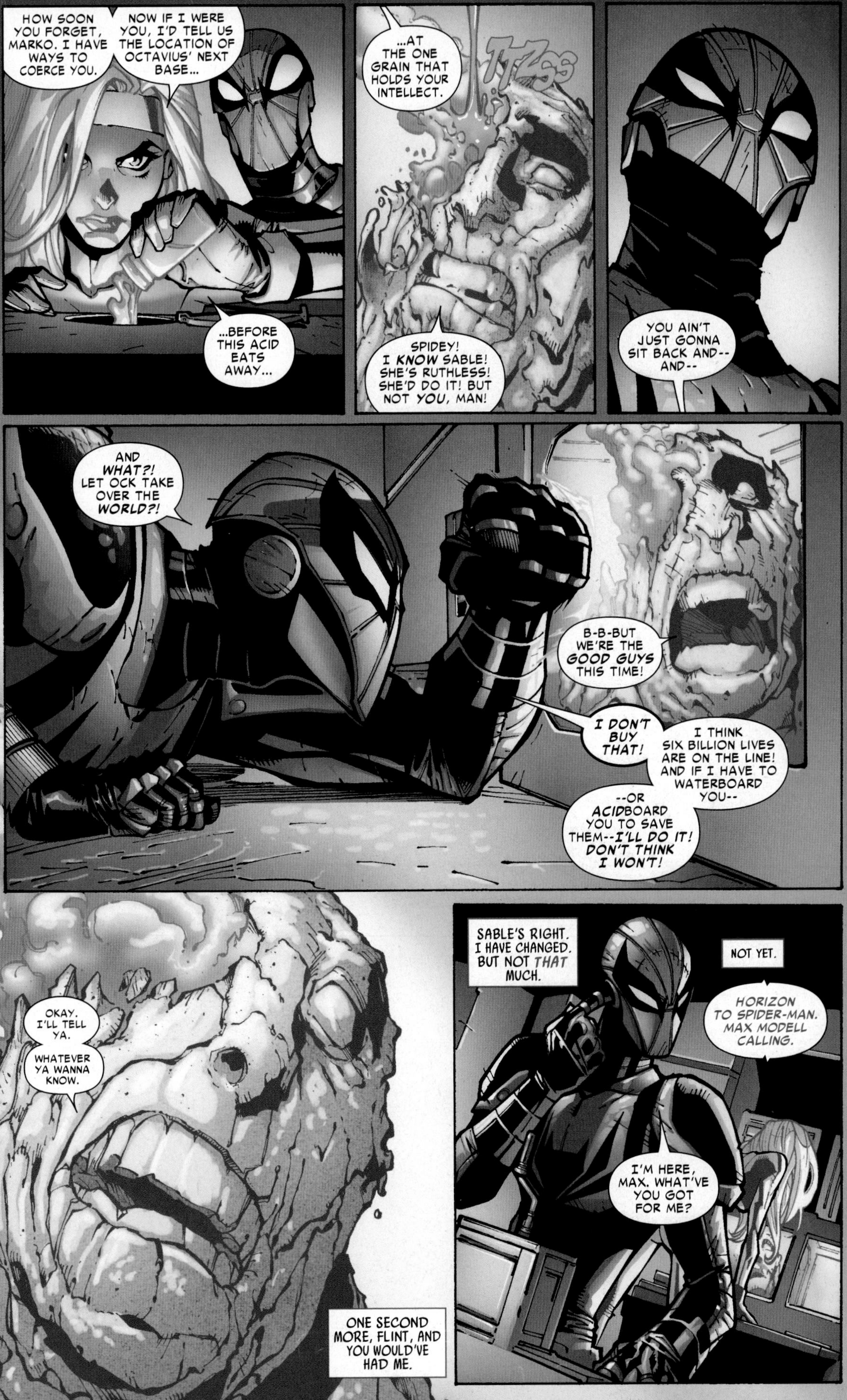
HOW SOON YOU FORGET, MARKO. I HAVE WAYS TO COERCE YOU.
NOW IF I WERE YOU, I'D TELL US THE LOCATION OF OCTAVIUS' NEXT BASE...
...BEFORE THIS ACID EATS AWAY...
...AT THE ONE GRAIN THAT HOLDS YOUR INTELLECT.
TTZSS
SPIDEY! I KNOW SABLE! SHE'S RUTHLESS! SHE'D DO IT! BUT NOT YOU, MAN!
YOU AIN'T JUST GONNA SIT BACK AND-- AND--
AND WHAT?! LET OCK TAKE OVER THE WORLD?!
B-B-BUT WE'RE THE GOOD GUYS THIS TIME!
I DON'T BUY THAT!
I THINK SIX BILLION LIVES ARE ON THE LINE! AND IF I HAVE TO WATERBOARD YOU--
--OR ACIDBOARD YOU TO SAVE THEM--I'LL DO IT! DON'T THINK I WON'T!
OKAY. I'LL TELL YA.
WHATEVER YA WANNA KNOW.
ONE SECOND MORE, FLINT, AND YOU WOULD'VE HAD ME.
SABLE'S RIGHT. I HAVE CHANGED. BUT NOT THAT MUCH.
NOT YET.
HORIZON TO SPIDER-MAN. MAX MODELL CALLING.
I'M HERE, MAX. WHAT'VE YOU GOT FOR ME?

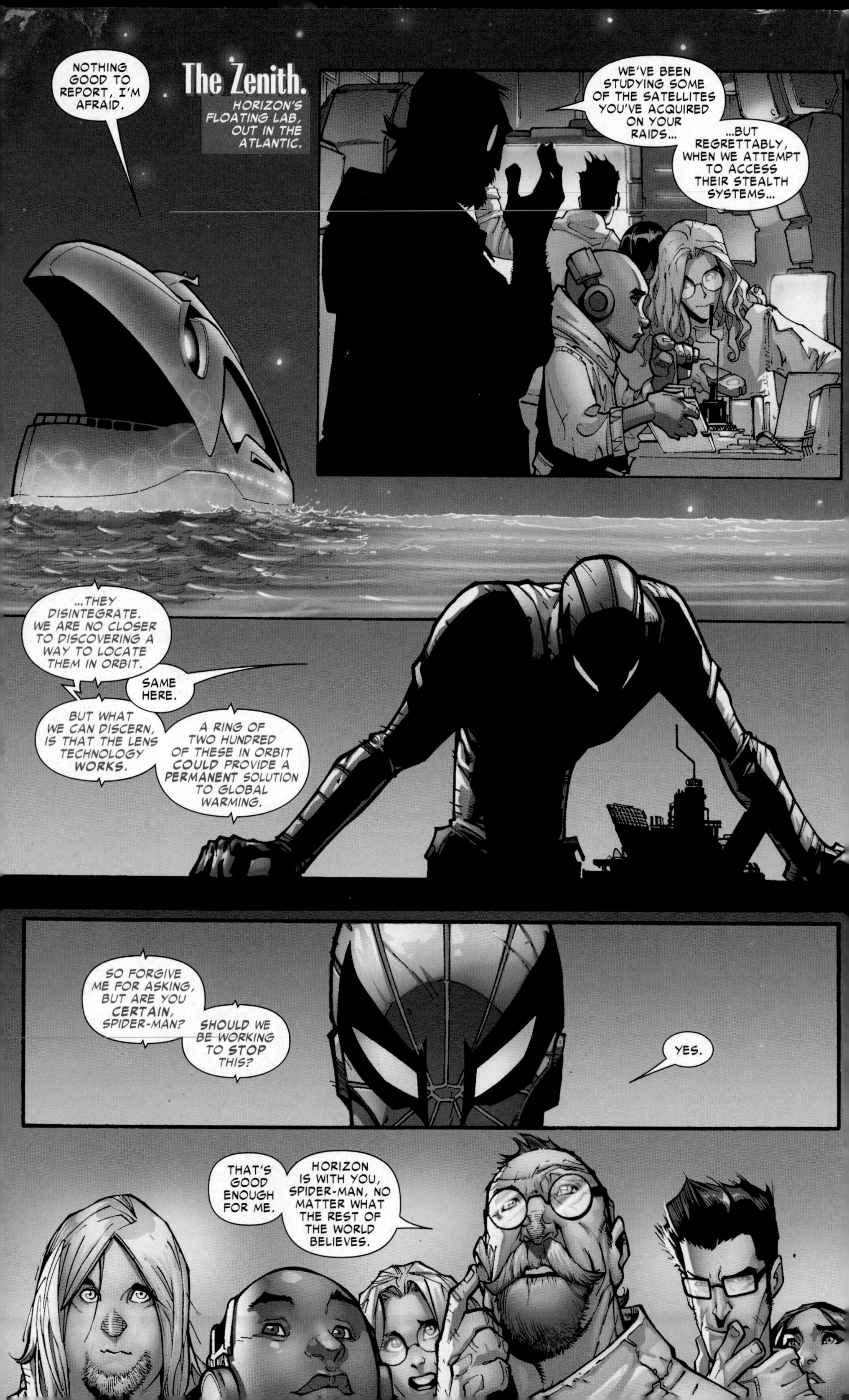
The Zenith.
HORIZON'S FLOATING LAB, OUT IN THE ATLANTIC.
NOTHING GOOD TO REPORT, I'M AFRAID.
WE'VE BEEN STUDYING SOME OF THE SATELLITES YOU'VE ACQUIRED ON YOUR RAIDS...
...BUT REGRETTABLY, WHEN WE ATTEMPT TO ACCESS THEIR STEALTH SYSTEMS...
...THEY DISINTEGRATE. WE ARE NO CLOSER TO DISCOVERING A WAY TO LOCATE THEM IN ORBIT.
SAME HERE.
BUT WHAT WE CAN DISCERN, IS THAT THE LENS TECHNOLOGY WORKS.
A RING OF TWO HUNDRED OF THESE IN ORBIT COULD PROVIDE A PERMANENT SOLUTION TO GLOBAL WARMING.
SO FORGIVE ME FOR ASKING, BUT ARE YOU CERTAIN, SPIDER-MAN?
SHOULD WE BE WORKING TO STOP THIS?
YES.
THAT'S GOOD ENOUGH FOR ME.
HORIZON IS WITH YOU, SPIDER-MAN, NO MATTER WHAT THE REST OF THE WORLD BELIEVES.

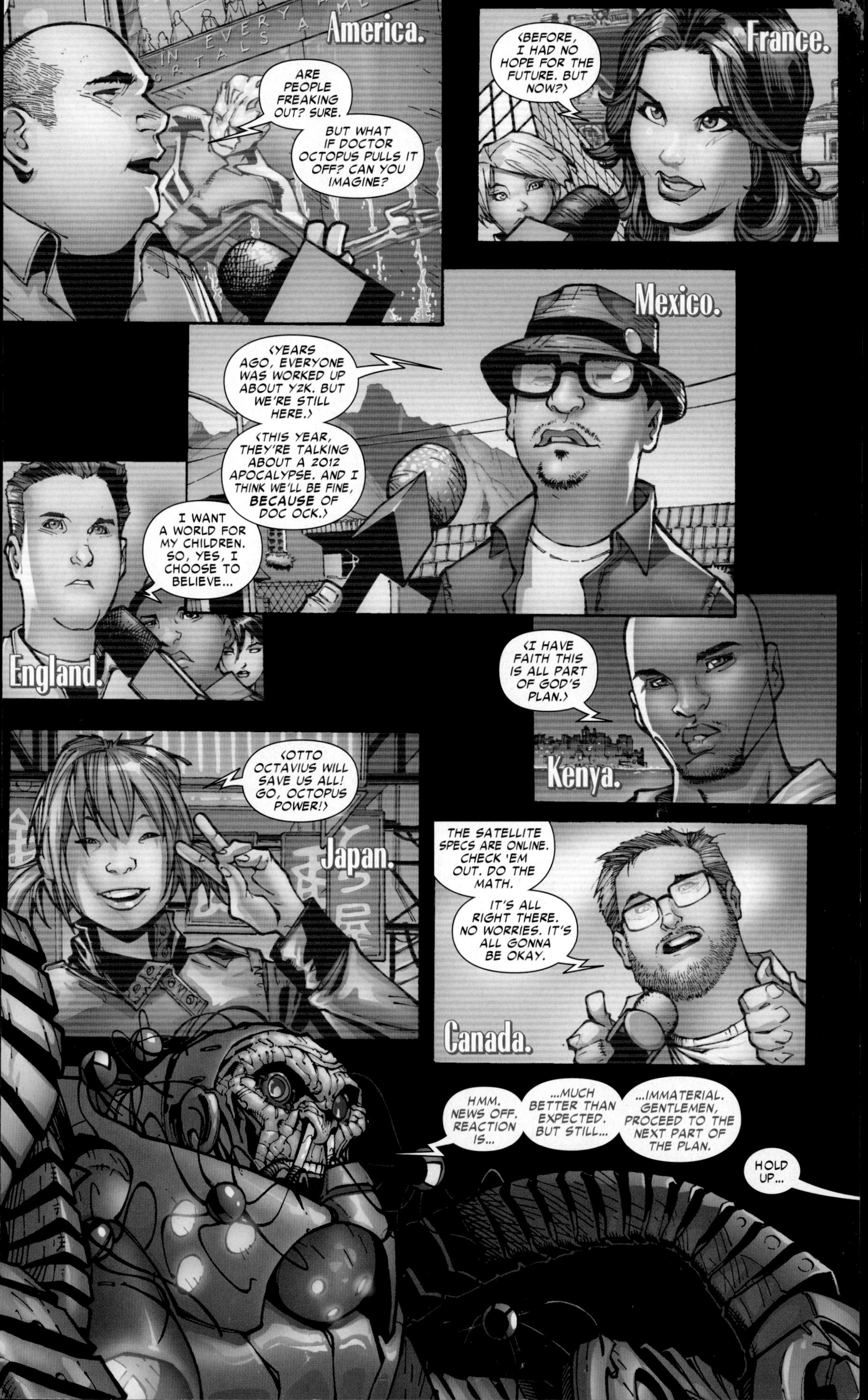

America.
ARE PEOPLE FREAKING OUT? SURE.
BUT WHAT IF DOCTOR OCTOPUS PULLS IT OFF? CAN YOU IMAGINE?
France.
‹BEFORE, I HAD NO HOPE FOR THE FUTURE. BUT NOW?›
Mexico.
‹YEARS AGO, EVERYONE WAS WORKED UP ABOUT Y2K. BUT WE'RE STILL HERE.›
‹THIS YEAR, THEY'RE TALKING ABOUT A 2012 APOCALYPSE. AND I THINK WE'LL BE FINE, BECAUSE OF DOC OCK.›
I WANT A WORLD FOR MY CHILDREN. SO, YES, I CHOOSE TO BELIEVE...
England.
‹I HAVE FAITH THIS IS ALL PART OF GOD'S PLAN.›
Kenya.
‹OTTO OCTAVIUS WILL SAVE US ALL! GO, OCTOPUS POWER!›
Japan.
THE SATELLITE SPECS ARE ONLINE. CHECK 'EM OUT. DO THE MATH.
IT'S ALL RIGHT THERE. NO WORRIES. IT'S ALL GONNA BE OKAY.
Canada.
HMM. NEWS OFF. REACTION IS...
...MUCH BETTER THAN EXPECTED. BUT STILL...
...IMMATERIAL. GENTLEMEN, PROCEED TO THE NEXT PART OF THE PLAN.
HOLD UP...

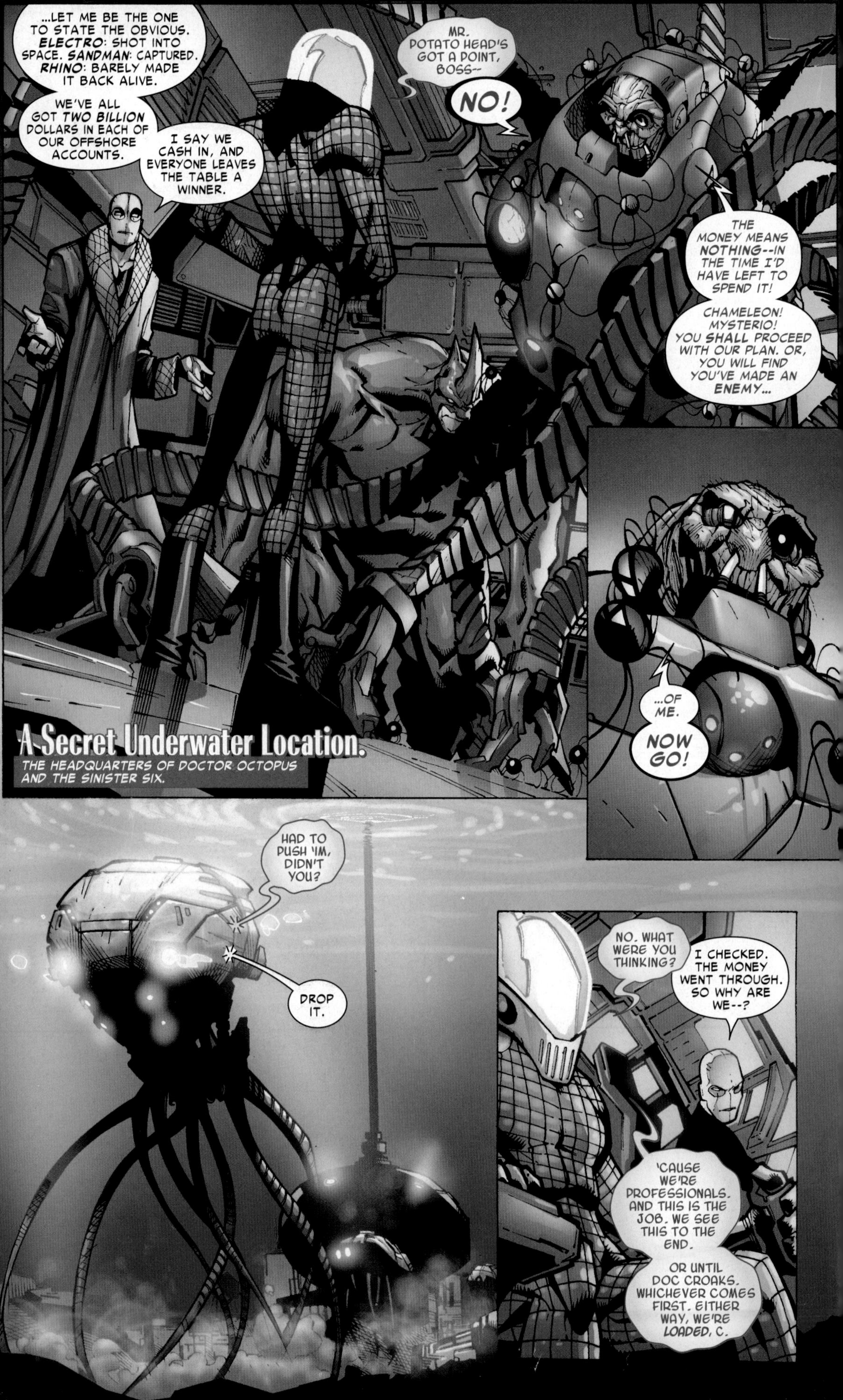

...LET ME BE THE ONE TO STATE THE OBVIOUS. ELECTRO: SHOT INTO SPACE. SANDMAN: CAPTURED. RHINO: BARELY MADE IT BACK ALIVE.
WE'VE ALL GOT TWO BILLION DOLLARS IN EACH OF OUR OFFSHORE ACCOUNTS.
I SAY WE CASH IN, AND EVERYONE LEAVES THE TABLE A WINNER.
MR. POTATO HEAD'S GOT A POINT, BOSS--
NO!
THE MONEY MEANS NOTHING--IN THE TIME I'D HAVE LEFT TO SPEND IT!
CHAMELEON! MYSTERIO! YOU SHALL PROCEED WITH OUR PLAN. OR, YOU WILL FIND YOU'VE MADE AN ENEMY...
A Secret Underwater Location.
THE HEADQUARTERS OF DOCTOR OCTOPUS AND THE SINISTER SIX.
...OF ME.
NOW GO!
HAD TO PUSH 'IM, DIDN'T YOU?
DROP IT.
NO. WHAT WERE YOU THINKING?
I CHECKED. THE MONEY WENT THROUGH. SO WHY ARE WE--?
'CAUSE WE'RE PROFESSIONALS. AND THIS IS THE JOB. WE SEE THIS TO THE END.
OR UNTIL DOC CROAKS. WHICHEVER COMES FIRST. EITHER WAY, WE'RE LOADED, C.

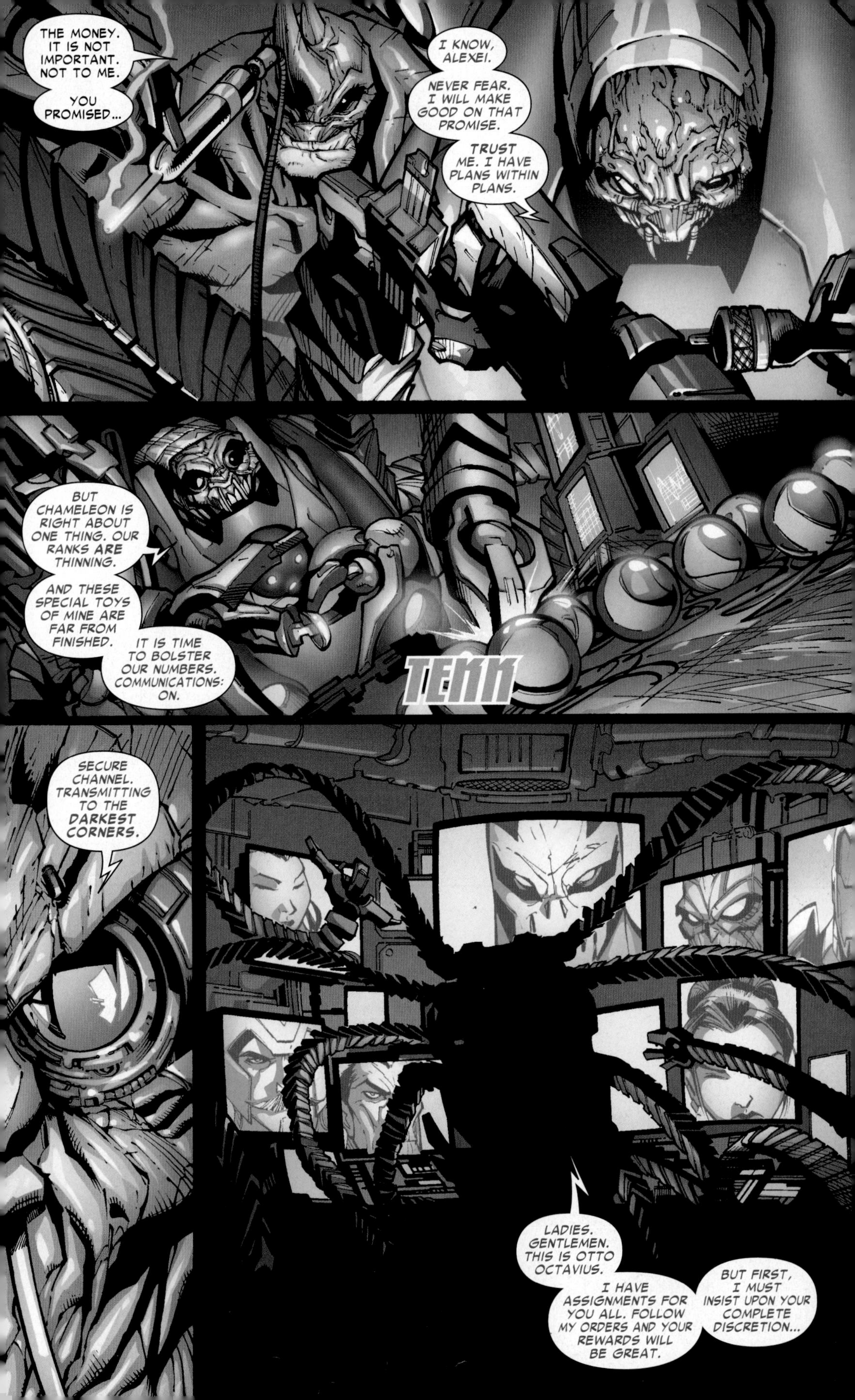
THE MONEY. IT IS NOT IMPORTANT. NOT TO ME.
YOU PROMISED...
I KNOW, ALEXEI.
NEVER FEAR. I WILL MAKE GOOD ON THAT PROMISE.
TRUST ME. I HAVE PLANS WITHIN PLANS.
BUT CHAMELEON IS RIGHT ABOUT ONE THING. OUR RANKS ARE THINNING.
AND THESE SPECIAL TOYS OF MINE ARE FAR FROM FINISHED.
IT IS TIME TO BOLSTER OUR NUMBERS. COMMUNICATIONS: ON.
TEKK
SECURE CHANNEL. TRANSMITTING TO THE DARKEST CORNERS.
LADIES. GENTLEMEN. THIS IS OTTO OCTAVIUS.
I HAVE ASSIGNMENTS FOR YOU ALL. FOLLOW MY ORDERS AND YOUR REWARDS WILL BE GREAT.
BUT FIRST, I MUST INSIST UPON YOUR COMPLETE DISCRETION...

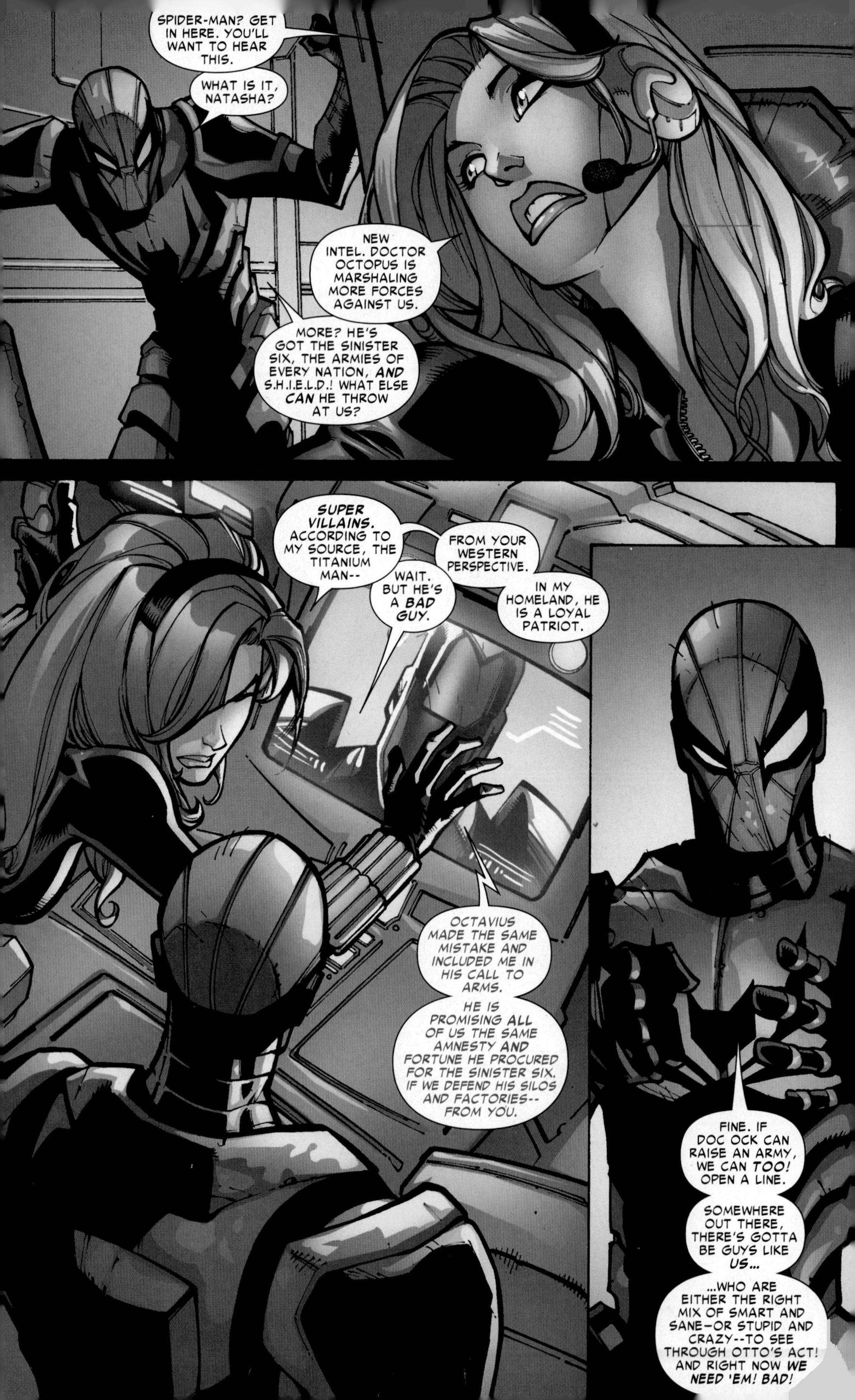

SPIDER-MAN? GET IN HERE. YOU'LL WANT TO HEAR THIS.
WHAT IS IT, NATASHA?
NEW INTEL. DOCTOR OCTOPUS IS MARSHALING MORE FORCES AGAINST US.
MORE? HE'S GOT THE SINISTER SIX, THE ARMIES OF EVERY NATION, *AND* S.H.I.E.L.D.! WHAT ELSE *CAN* HE THROW AT US?
SUPER VILLAINS. ACCORDING TO MY SOURCE, THE TITANIUM MAN--
WAIT. BUT HE'S A *BAD GUY.*
FROM YOUR WESTERN PERSPECTIVE.
IN MY HOMELAND, HE IS A LOYAL PATRIOT.
OCTAVIUS MADE THE SAME MISTAKE AND INCLUDED ME IN HIS CALL TO ARMS.
HE IS PROMISING *ALL* OF US THE SAME AMNESTY *AND* FORTUNE HE PROCURED FOR THE SINISTER SIX. IF WE DEFEND HIS SILOS AND FACTORIES-- FROM YOU.
FINE. IF DOC OCK CAN RAISE AN ARMY, WE CAN *TOO!* OPEN A LINE.
SOMEWHERE OUT THERE, THERE'S GOTTA BE GUYS LIKE *US...*
...WHO ARE EITHER THE RIGHT MIX OF SMART AND SANE--OR STUPID AND CRAZY--TO SEE THROUGH OTTO'S ACT! AND RIGHT NOW *WE NEED 'EM! BAD!*

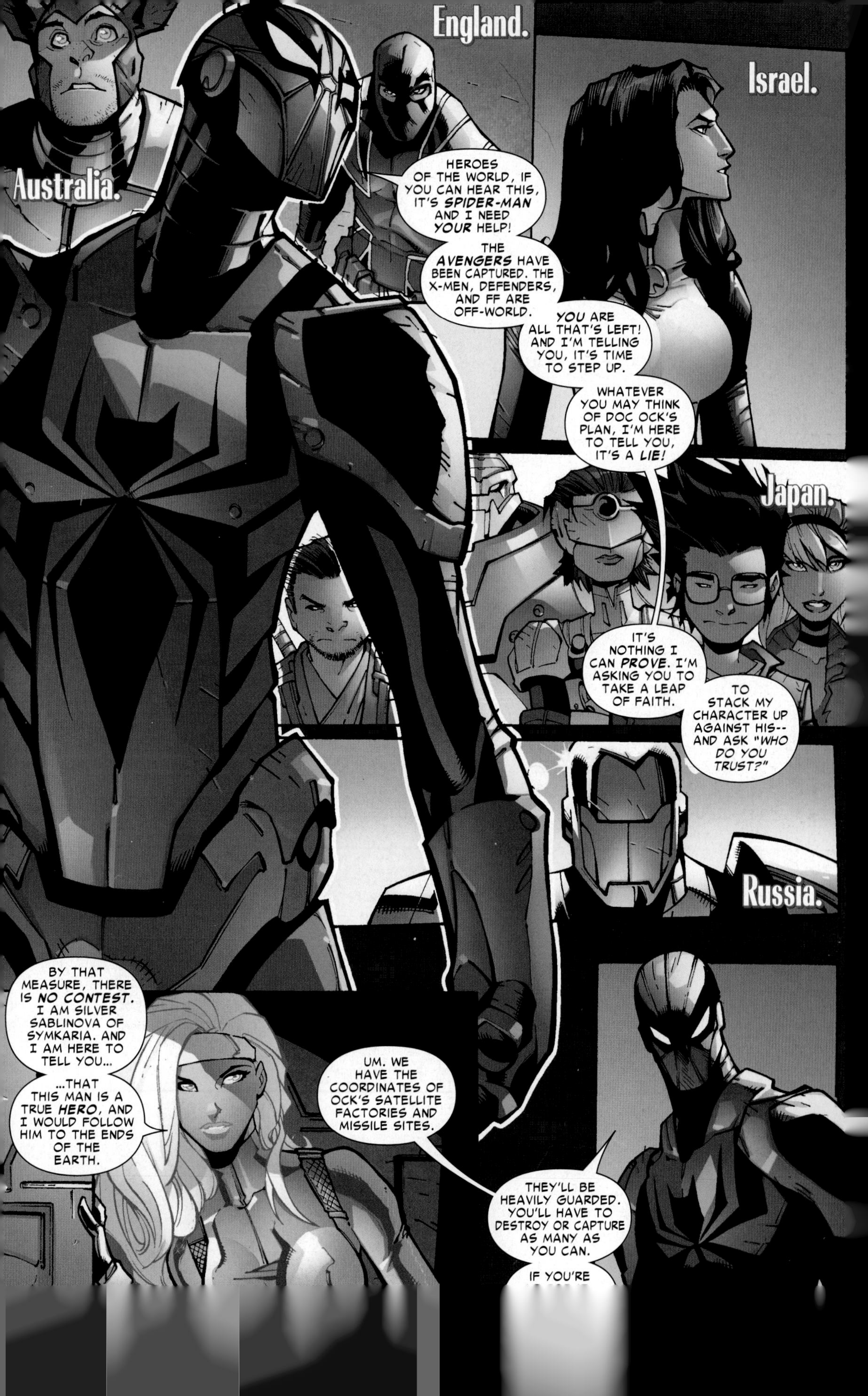
England.
Israel.
Australia.
HEROES OF THE WORLD, IF YOU CAN HEAR THIS, IT'S SPIDER-MAN AND I NEED YOUR HELP!
THE AVENGERS HAVE BEEN CAPTURED. THE X-MEN, DEFENDERS, AND FF ARE OFF-WORLD.
YOU ARE ALL THAT'S LEFT! AND I'M TELLING YOU, IT'S TIME TO STEP UP.
WHATEVER YOU MAY THINK OF DOC OCK'S PLAN, I'M HERE TO TELL YOU, IT'S A LIE!
Japan.
IT'S NOTHING I CAN PROVE. I'M ASKING YOU TO TAKE A LEAP OF FAITH.
TO STACK MY CHARACTER UP AGAINST HIS-- AND ASK "WHO DO YOU TRUST?"
Russia.
BY THAT MEASURE, THERE IS NO CONTEST. I AM SILVER SABLINOVA OF SYMKARIA. AND I AM HERE TO TELL YOU...
...THAT THIS MAN IS A TRUE HERO, AND I WOULD FOLLOW HIM TO THE ENDS OF THE EARTH.
UM. WE HAVE THE COORDINATES OF OCK'S SATELLITE FACTORIES AND MISSILE SITES.
THEY'LL BE HEAVILY GUARDED. YOU'LL HAVE TO DESTROY OR CAPTURE AS MANY AS YOU CAN.
IF YOU'RE

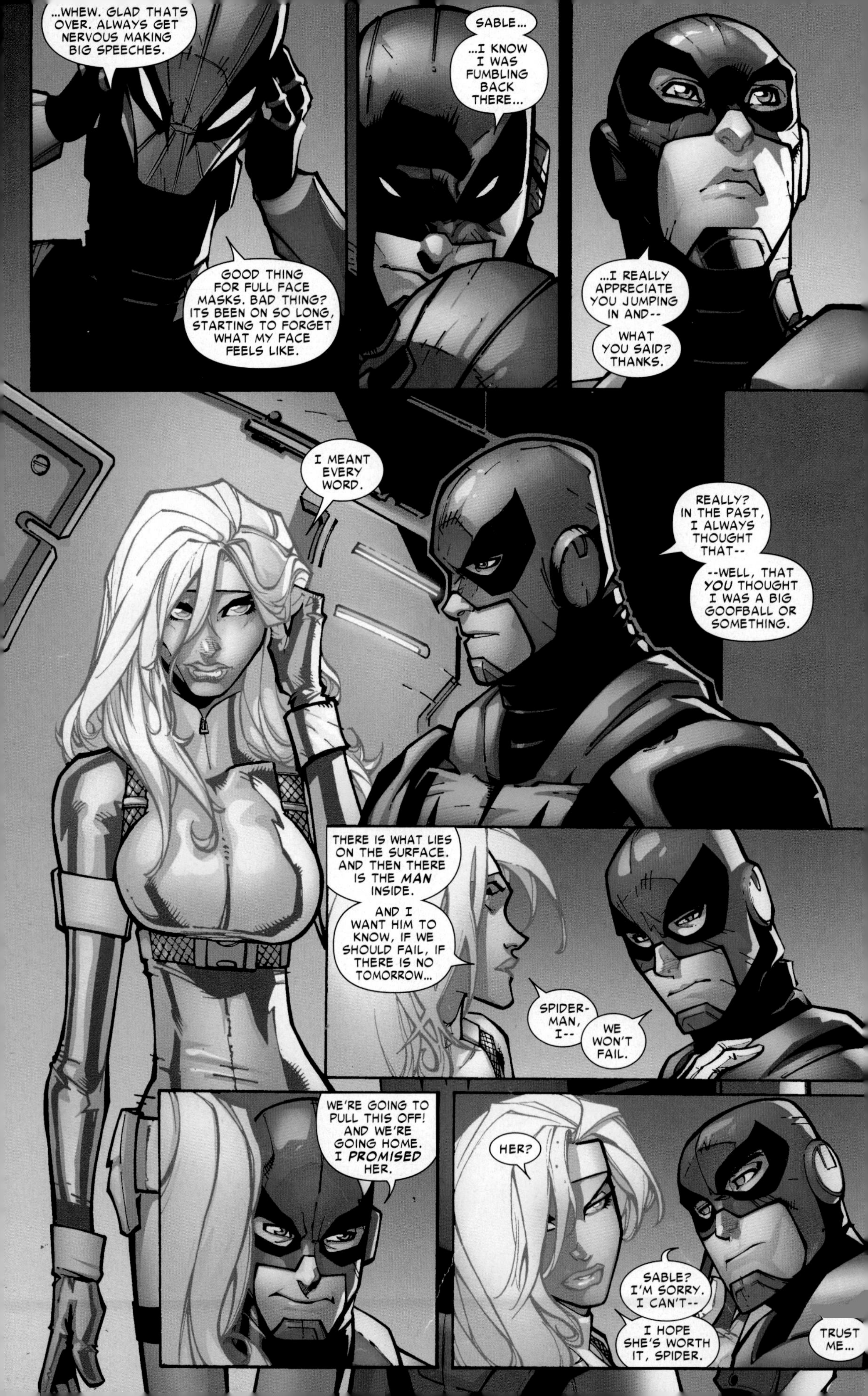
...WHEW. GLAD THATS OVER. ALWAYS GET NERVOUS MAKING BIG SPEECHES.
GOOD THING FOR FULL FACE MASKS. BAD THING? ITS BEEN ON SO LONG, STARTING TO FORGET WHAT MY FACE FEELS LIKE.
SABLE...
...I KNOW I WAS FUMBLING BACK THERE...
...I REALLY APPRECIATE YOU JUMPING IN AND--
WHAT YOU SAID? THANKS.
I MEANT EVERY WORD.
REALLY? IN THE PAST, I ALWAYS THOUGHT THAT--
--WELL, THAT YOU THOUGHT I WAS A BIG GOOFBALL OR SOMETHING.
THERE IS WHAT LIES ON THE SURFACE. AND THEN THERE IS THE MAN INSIDE.
AND I WANT HIM TO KNOW, IF WE SHOULD FAIL, IF THERE IS NO TOMORROW...
SPIDER-MAN, I--
WE WON'T FAIL.
WE'RE GOING TO PULL THIS OFF! AND WE'RE GOING HOME. I PROMISED HER.
HER?
SABLE? I'M SORRY. I CAN'T--
I HOPE SHE'S WORTH IT, SPIDER.
TRUST ME...

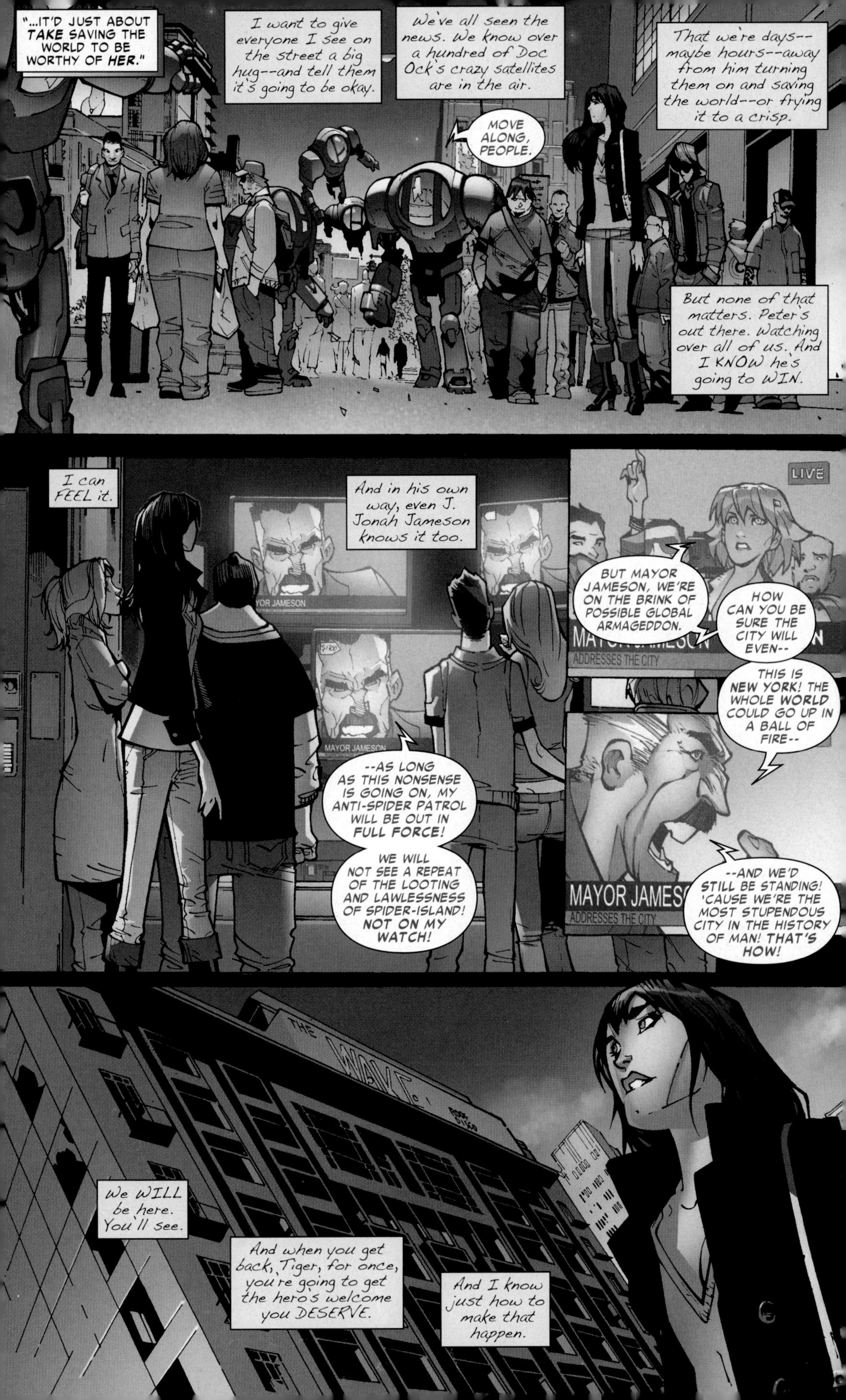
"...IT'D JUST ABOUT TAKE SAVING THE WORLD TO BE WORTHY OF HER."
I want to give everyone I see on the street a big hug--and tell them it's going to be okay.
We've all seen the news. We know over a hundred of Doc Ock's crazy satellites are in the air.
That we're days--maybe hours--away from him turning them on and saving the world--or frying it to a crisp.
MOVE ALONG, PEOPLE.
But none of that matters. Peter's out there. Watching over all of us. And I KNOW he's going to WIN.
I can FEEL it.
And in his own way, even J. Jonah Jameson knows it too.
MAYOR JAMESON
LIVE
MAYOR JAMESON
ADDRESSES THE CITY
BUT MAYOR JAMESON, WE'RE ON THE BRINK OF POSSIBLE GLOBAL ARMAGEDDON.
HOW CAN YOU BE SURE THE CITY WILL EVEN--
MAYOR JAMESON
--AS LONG AS THIS NONSENSE IS GOING ON, MY ANTI-SPIDER PATROL WILL BE OUT IN FULL FORCE!
WE WILL NOT SEE A REPEAT OF THE LOOTING AND LAWLESSNESS OF SPIDER-ISLAND! NOT ON MY WATCH!
THIS IS NEW YORK! THE WHOLE WORLD COULD GO UP IN A BALL OF FIRE--
--AND WE'D STILL BE STANDING! 'CAUSE WE'RE THE MOST STUPENDOUS CITY IN THE HISTORY OF MAN! THAT'S HOW!
ADDRESSES THE CITY
THE
We WILL be here. You'll see.
And when you get back, Tiger, for once, you're going to get the hero's welcome you DESERVE.
And I know just how to make that happen.

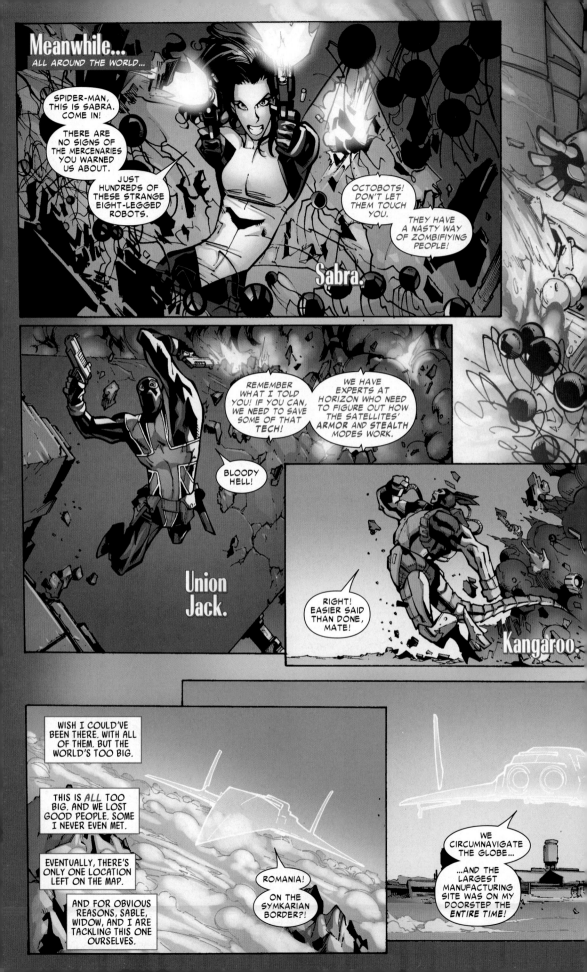

Meanwhile...
ALL AROUND THE WORLD...

SPIDER-MAN, THIS IS SABRA. COME IN!

THERE ARE NO SIGNS OF THE MERCENARIES YOU WARNED US ABOUT.

JUST HUNDREDS OF THESE STRANGE EIGHT-LEGGED ROBOTS.

OCTOBOTS! DON'T LET THEM TOUCH YOU.

THEY HAVE A NASTY WAY OF ZOMBIFIYING PEOPLE!

Sabra.

REMEMBER WHAT I TOLD YOU! IF YOU CAN, WE NEED TO SAVE SOME OF THAT TECH!

WE HAVE EXPERTS AT HORIZON WHO NEED TO FIGURE OUT HOW THE SATELLITES' ARMOR AND STEALTH MODES WORK.

BLOODY HELL!

Union Jack.

RIGHT! EASIER SAID THAN DONE, MATE!

Kangaroo.

WISH I COULD'VE BEEN THERE. WITH ALL OF THEM. BUT THE WORLD'S TOO BIG.

THIS IS ALL TOO BIG. AND WE LOST GOOD PEOPLE. SOME I NEVER EVEN MET.

EVENTUALLY, THERE'S ONLY ONE LOCATION LEFT ON THE MAP.

AND FOR OBVIOUS REASONS, SABLE, WIDOW, AND I ARE TACKLING THIS ONE OURSELVES.

ROMANIA! ON THE SYMKARIAN BORDER?!

WE CIRCUMNAVIGATE THE GLOBE...

...AND THE LARGEST MANUFACTURING SITE WAS ON MY DOORSTEP THE ENTIRE TIME!

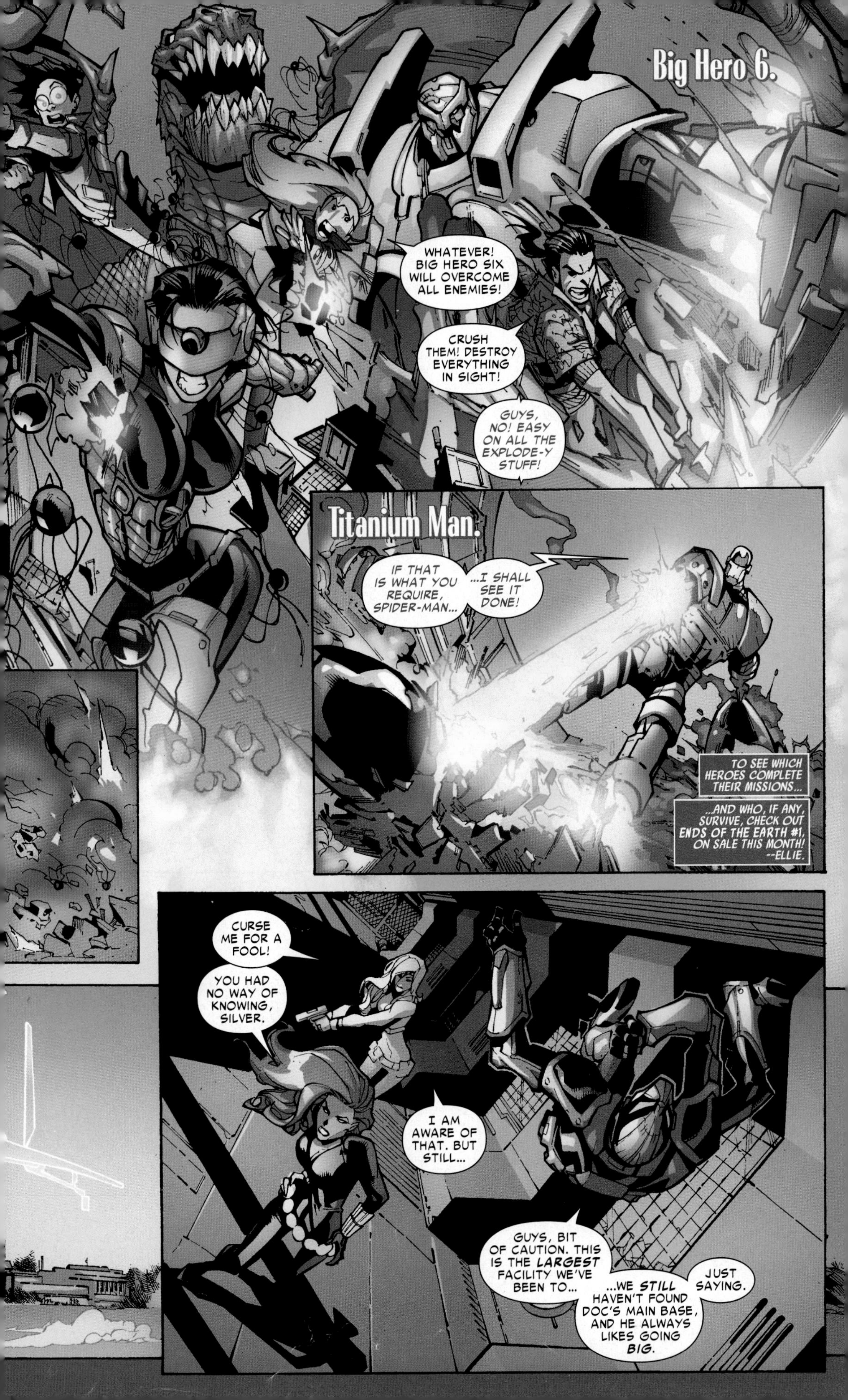

Big Hero 6.
WHATEVER! BIG HERO SIX WILL OVERCOME ALL ENEMIES!
CRUSH THEM! DESTROY EVERYTHING IN SIGHT!
GUYS, NO! EASY ON ALL THE EXPLODE-Y STUFF!
Titanium Man.
IF THAT IS WHAT YOU REQUIRE, SPIDER-MAN...
...I SHALL SEE IT DONE!
TO SEE WHICH HEROES COMPLETE THEIR MISSIONS...
...AND WHO, IF ANY, SURVIVE, CHECK OUT ENDS OF THE EARTH #1, ON SALE THIS MONTH! --ELLIE.
CURSE ME FOR A FOOL!
YOU HAD NO WAY OF KNOWING, SILVER.
I AM AWARE OF THAT. BUT STILL...
GUYS, BIT OF CAUTION. THIS IS THE LARGEST FACILITY WE'VE BEEN TO...
...WE STILL HAVEN'T FOUND DOC'S MAIN BASE, AND HE ALWAYS LIKES GOING BIG.
JUST SAYING.

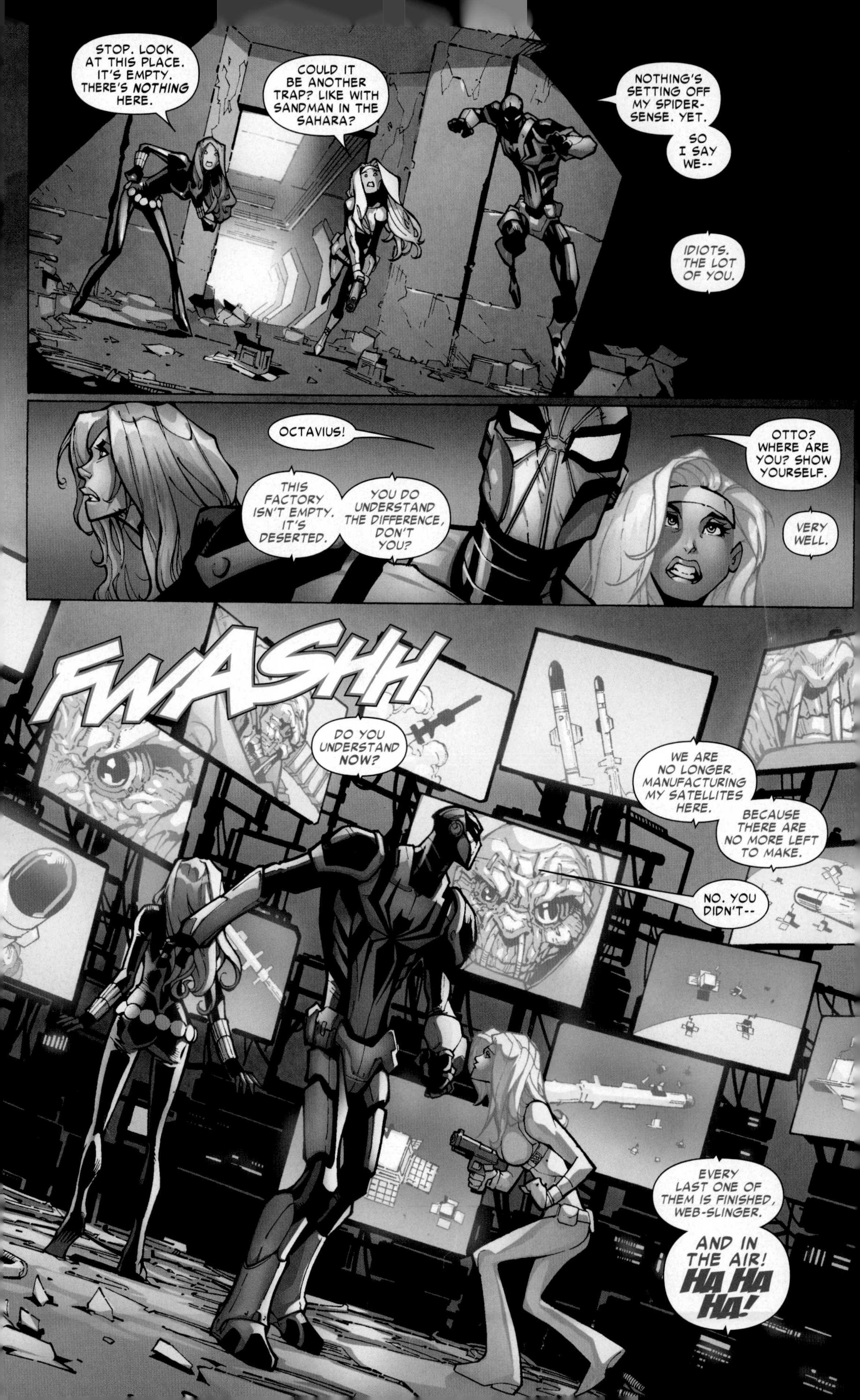
STOP. LOOK AT THIS PLACE. IT'S EMPTY. THERE'S NOTHING HERE.
COULD IT BE ANOTHER TRAP? LIKE WITH SANDMAN IN THE SAHARA?
NOTHING'S SETTING OFF MY SPIDER-SENSE. YET.
SO I SAY WE--
IDIOTS. THE LOT OF YOU.
OCTAVIUS!
OTTO? WHERE ARE YOU? SHOW YOURSELF.
THIS FACTORY ISN'T EMPTY. IT'S DESERTED.
YOU DO UNDERSTAND THE DIFFERENCE, DON'T YOU?
VERY WELL.
FWASHH
DO YOU UNDERSTAND NOW?
WE ARE NO LONGER MANUFACTURING MY SATELLITES HERE.
BECAUSE THERE ARE NO MORE LEFT TO MAKE.
NO. YOU DIDN'T--
EVERY LAST ONE OF THEM IS FINISHED, WEB-SLINGER.
AND IN THE AIR! HA HA HA!

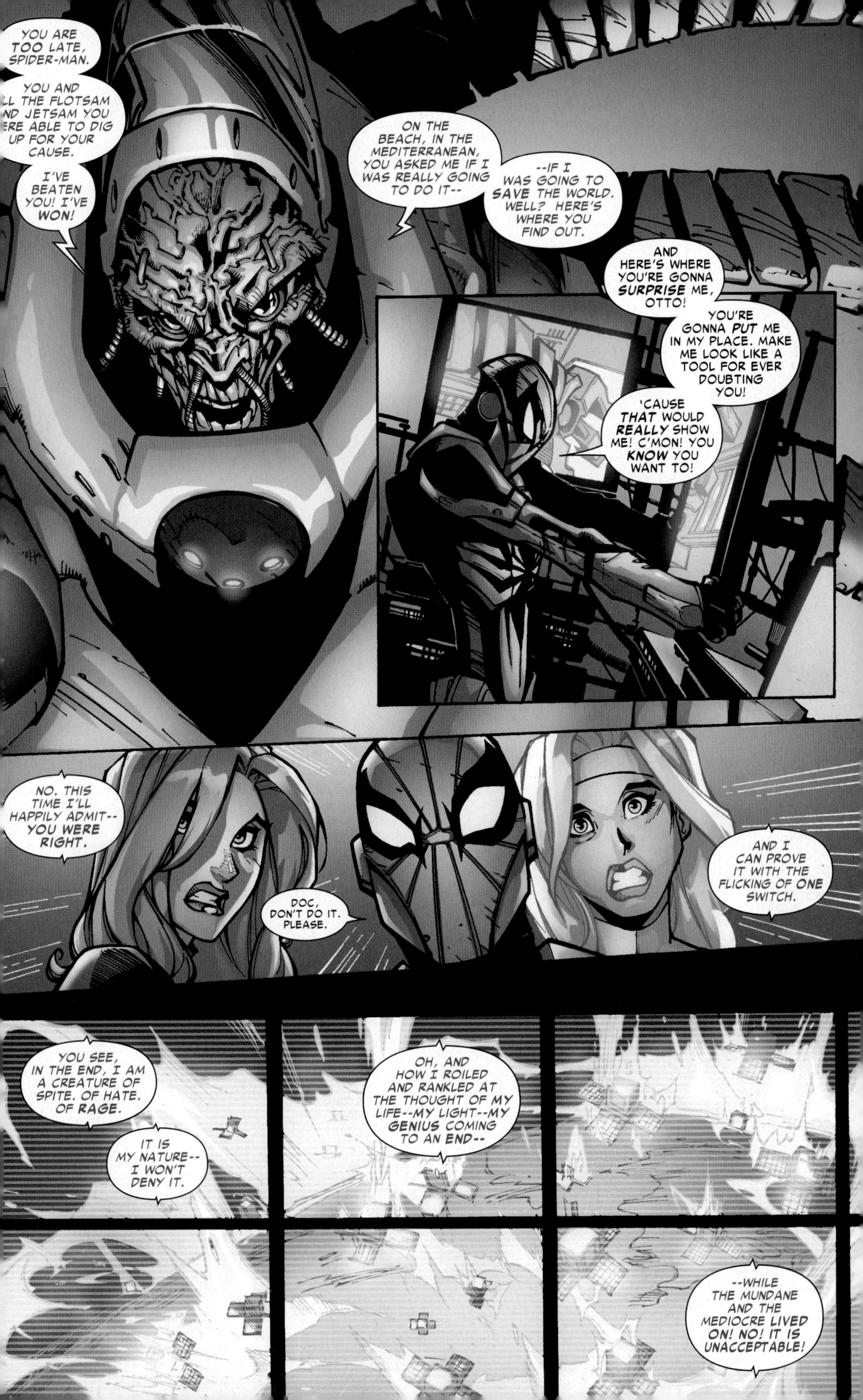

YOU ARE TOO LATE, SPIDER-MAN.
YOU AND LL THE FLOTSAM ND JETSAM YOU ERE ABLE TO DIG UP FOR YOUR CAUSE.
I'VE BEATEN YOU! I'VE WON!
ON THE BEACH, IN THE MEDITERRANEAN, YOU ASKED ME IF I WAS REALLY GOING TO DO IT--
--IF I WAS GOING TO SAVE THE WORLD. WELL? HERE'S WHERE YOU FIND OUT.
AND HERE'S WHERE YOU'RE GONNA SURPRISE ME, OTTO!
YOU'RE GONNA PUT ME IN MY PLACE. MAKE ME LOOK LIKE A TOOL FOR EVER DOUBTING YOU!
'CAUSE THAT WOULD REALLY SHOW ME! C'MON! YOU KNOW YOU WANT TO!
NO. THIS TIME I'LL HAPPILY ADMIT--YOU WERE RIGHT.
DOC, DON'T DO IT. PLEASE.
AND I CAN PROVE IT WITH THE FLICKING OF ONE SWITCH.
YOU SEE, IN THE END, I AM A CREATURE OF SPITE. OF HATE. OF RAGE.
IT IS MY NATURE--I WON'T DENY IT.
OH, AND HOW I ROILED AND RANKLED AT THE THOUGHT OF MY LIFE--MY LIGHT--MY GENIUS COMING TO AN END--
--WHILE THE MUNDANE AND THE MEDIOCRE LIVED ON! NO! IT IS UNACCEPTABLE!

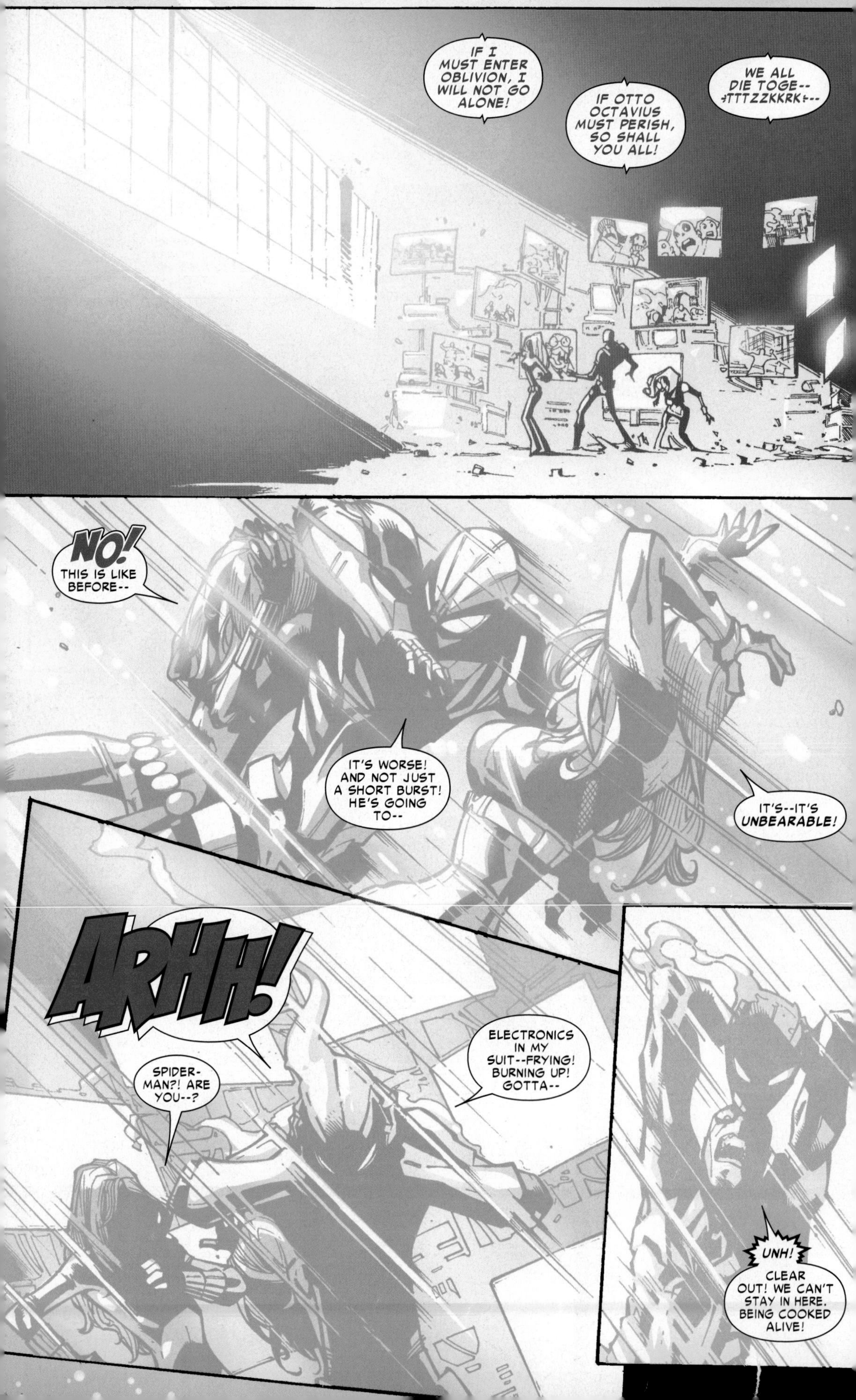
IF I MUST ENTER OBLIVION, I WILL NOT GO ALONE!
IF OTTO OCTAVIUS MUST PERISH, SO SHALL YOU ALL!
WE ALL DIE TOGE-- -TTTZZKKRK--
NO! THIS IS LIKE BEFORE--
IT'S WORSE! AND NOT JUST A SHORT BURST! HE'S GOING TO--
IT'S--IT'S UNBEARABLE!
ARHH!
SPIDER-MAN?! ARE YOU--?
ELECTRONICS IN MY SUIT--FRYING! BURNING UP! GOTTA--
UNH! CLEAR OUT! WE CAN'T STAY IN HERE. BEING COOKED ALIVE!

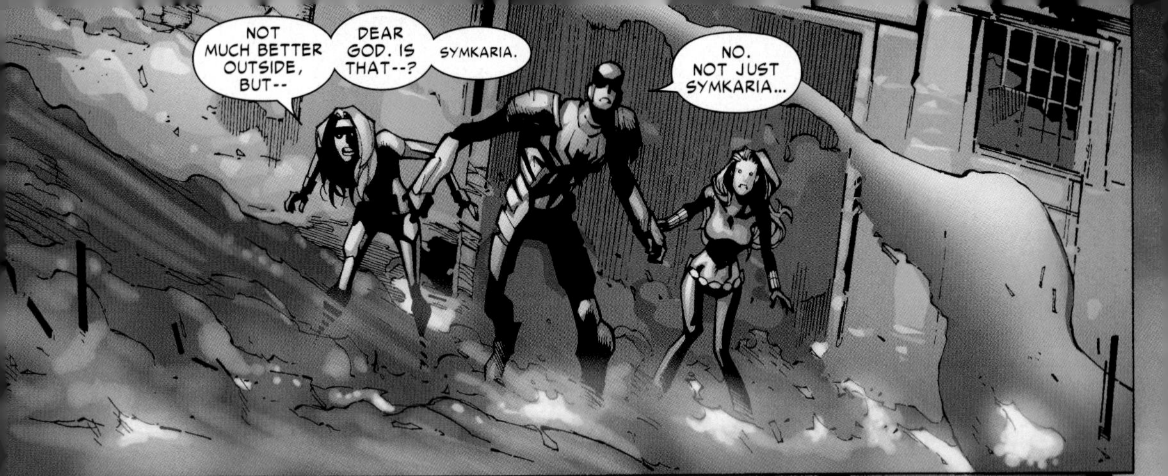
NOT MUCH BETTER OUTSIDE, BUT--
DEAR GOD. IS THAT--?
SYMKARIA.
NO. NOT JUST SYMKARIA...

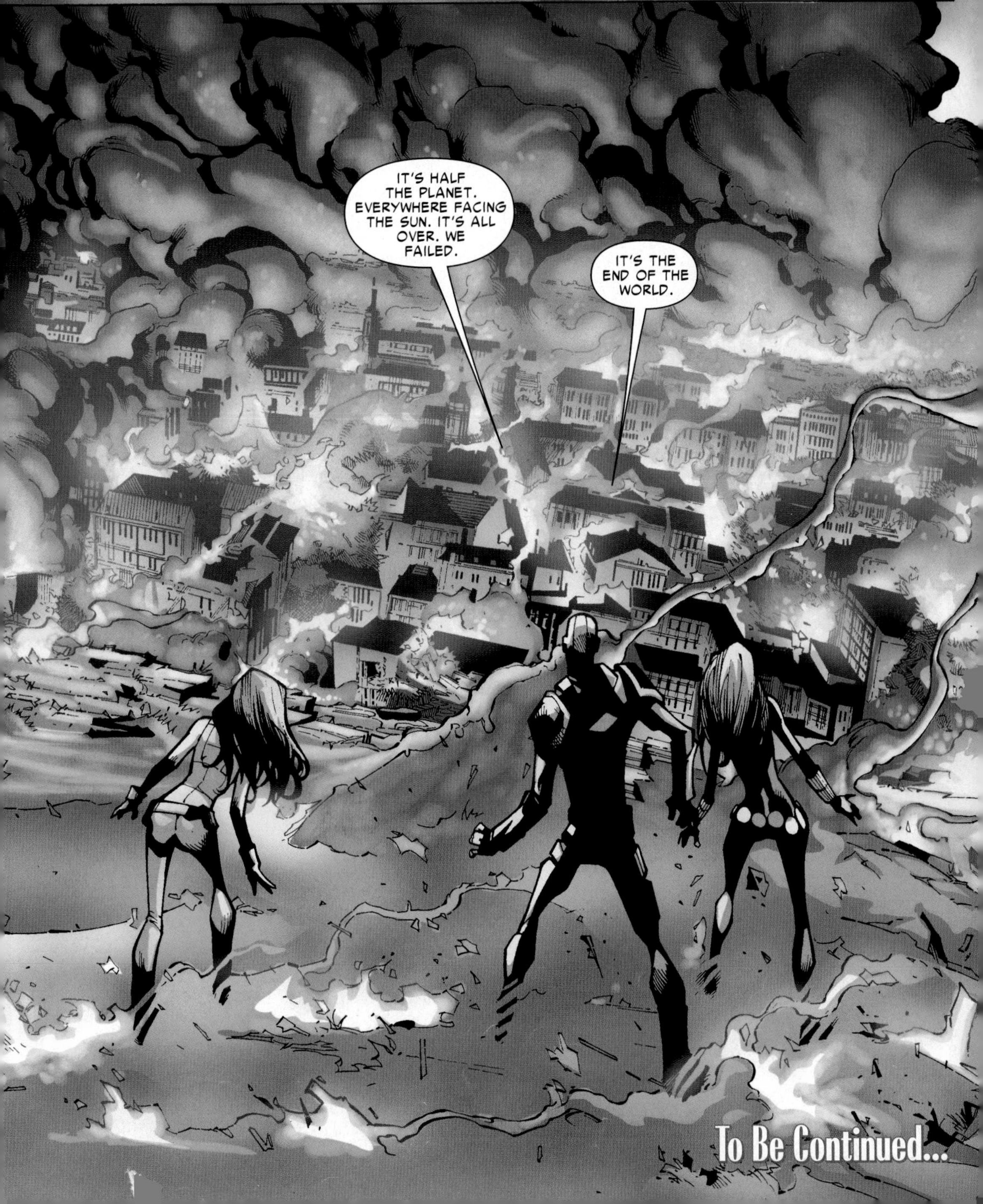
IT'S HALF THE PLANET. EVERYWHERE FACING THE SUN. IT'S ALL OVER. WE FAILED.
IT'S THE END OF THE WORLD.
To Be Continued...

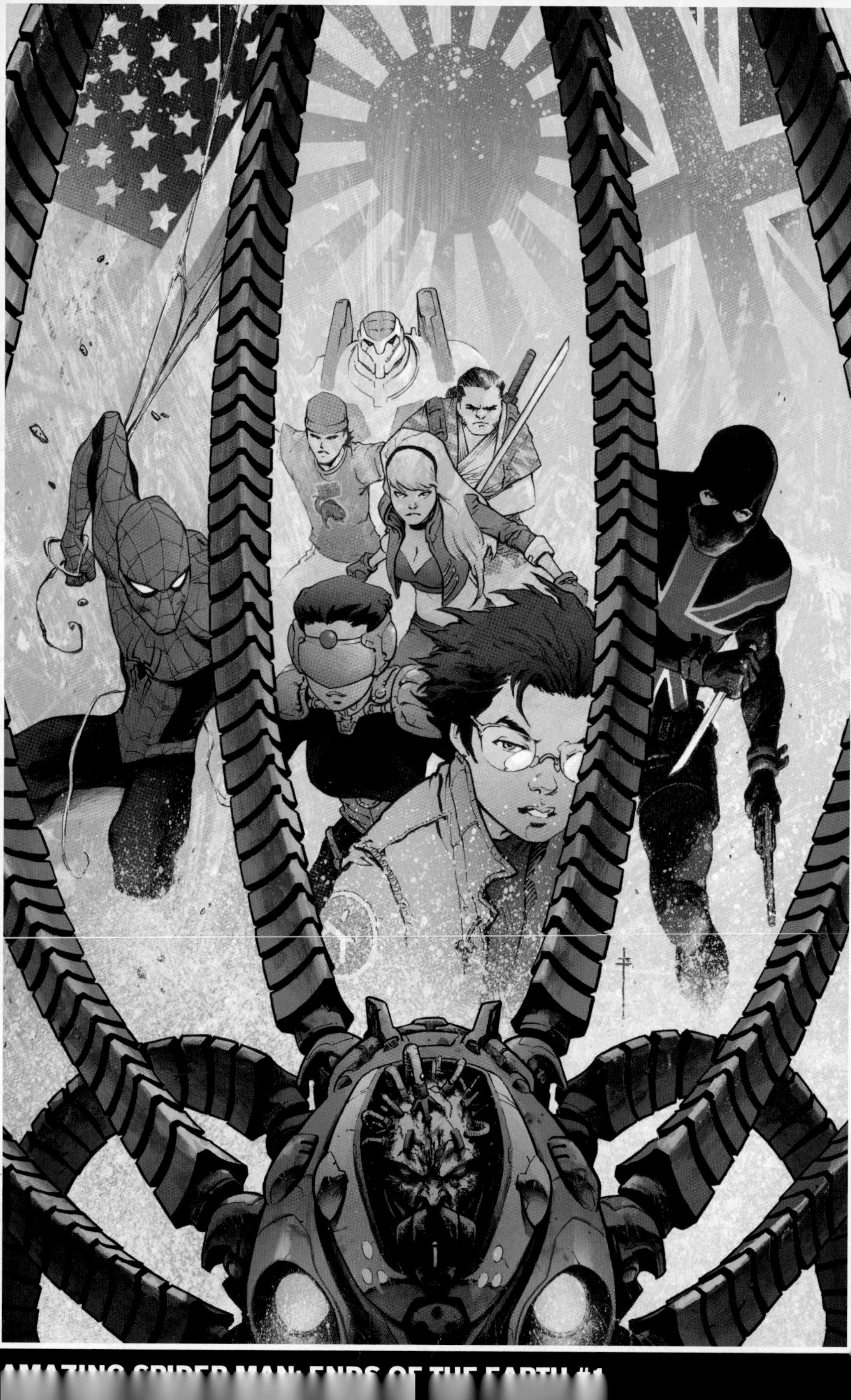

AMAZING SPIDER-MAN: ENDS OF THE EARTH #1

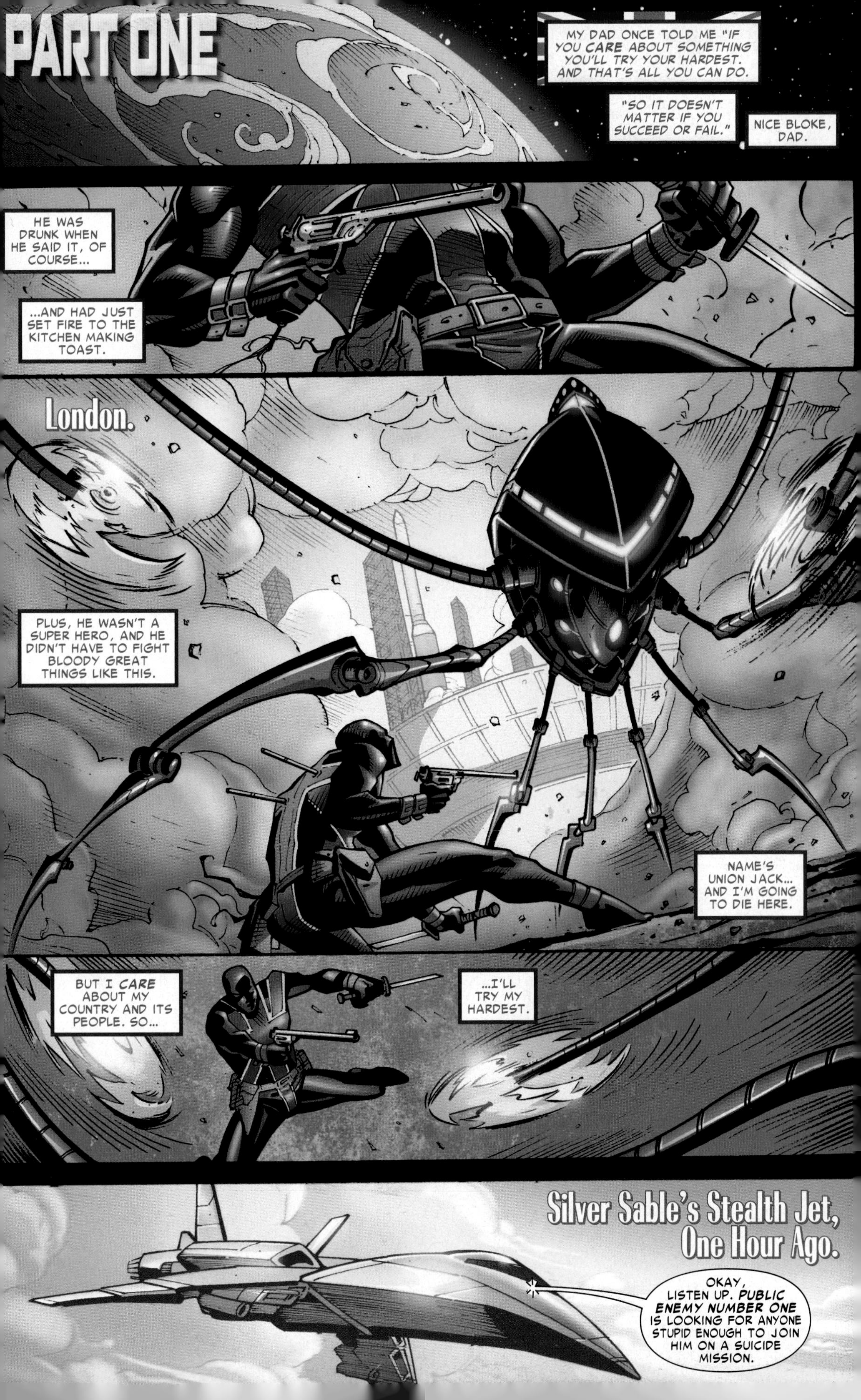
PART ONE
MY DAD ONCE TOLD ME "IF YOU CARE ABOUT SOMETHING YOU'LL TRY YOUR HARDEST. AND THAT'S ALL YOU CAN DO.
"SO IT DOESN'T MATTER IF YOU SUCCEED OR FAIL."
NICE BLOKE, DAD.
HE WAS DRUNK WHEN HE SAID IT, OF COURSE...
...AND HAD JUST SET FIRE TO THE KITCHEN MAKING TOAST.
London.
PLUS, HE WASN'T A SUPER HERO, AND HE DIDN'T HAVE TO FIGHT BLOODY GREAT THINGS LIKE THIS.
NAME'S UNION JACK... AND I'M GOING TO DIE HERE.
BUT I CARE ABOUT MY COUNTRY AND ITS PEOPLE. SO...
...I'LL TRY MY HARDEST.
Silver Sable's Stealth Jet, One Hour Ago.
OKAY, LISTEN UP. PUBLIC ENEMY NUMBER ONE IS LOOKING FOR ANYONE STUPID ENOUGH TO JOIN HIM ON A SUICIDE MISSION.

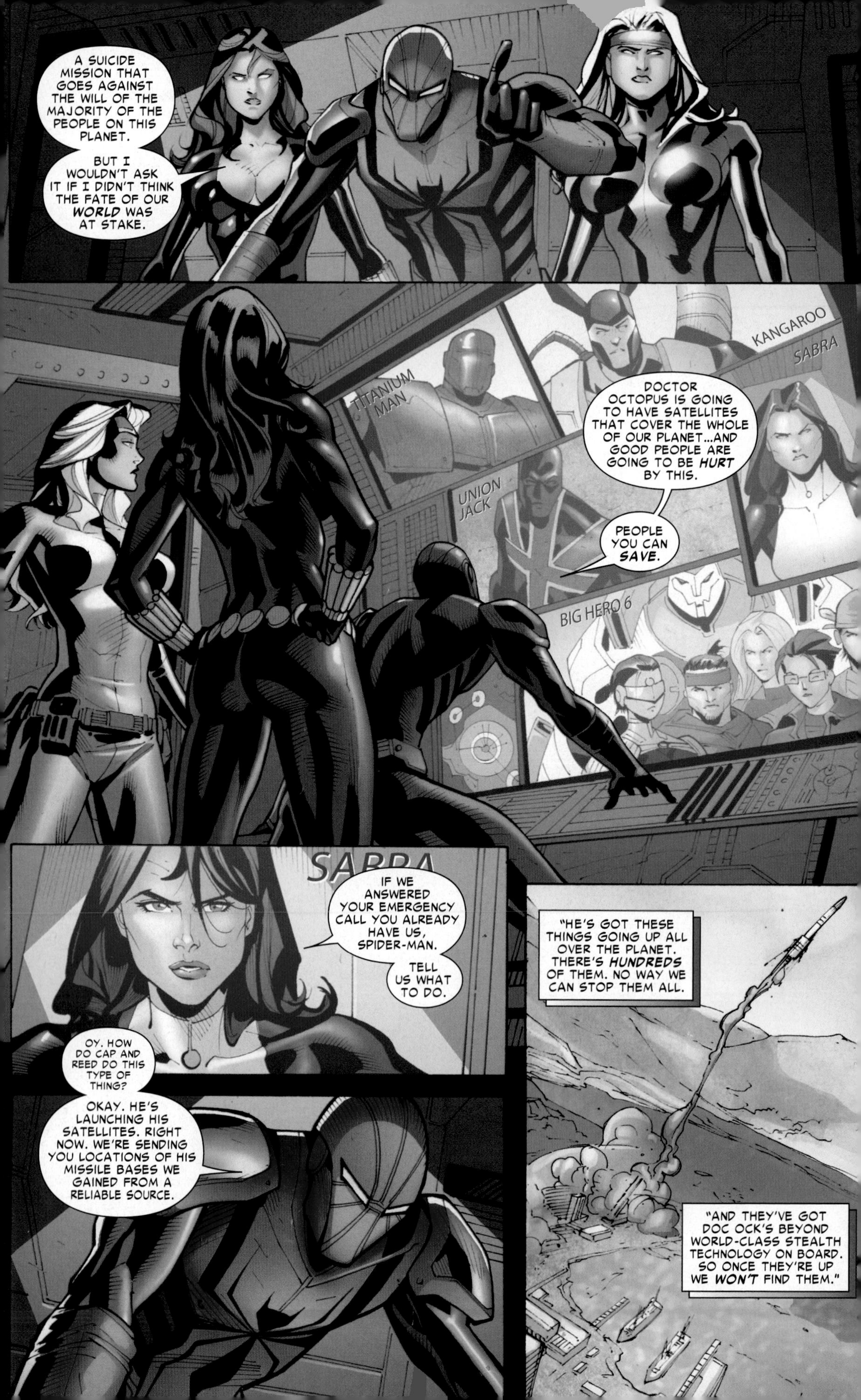
A SUICIDE MISSION THAT GOES AGAINST THE WILL OF THE MAJORITY OF THE PEOPLE ON THIS PLANET.
BUT I WOULDN'T ASK IT IF I DIDN'T THINK THE FATE OF OUR WORLD WAS AT STAKE.
KANGAROO
SABRA
TITANIUM MAN
UNION JACK
BIG HERO 6
DOCTOR OCTOPUS IS GOING TO HAVE SATELLITES THAT COVER THE WHOLE OF OUR PLANET...AND GOOD PEOPLE ARE GOING TO BE HURT BY THIS.
PEOPLE YOU CAN SAVE.
SABRA
IF WE ANSWERED YOUR EMERGENCY CALL YOU ALREADY HAVE US, SPIDER-MAN.
TELL US WHAT TO DO.
OY. HOW DO CAP AND REED DO THIS TYPE OF THING?
OKAY. HE'S LAUNCHING HIS SATELLITES. RIGHT NOW. WE'RE SENDING YOU LOCATIONS OF HIS MISSILE BASES WE GAINED FROM A RELIABLE SOURCE.
"HE'S GOT THESE THINGS GOING UP ALL OVER THE PLANET. THERE'S HUNDREDS OF THEM. NO WAY WE CAN STOP THEM ALL.
"AND THEY'VE GOT DOC OCK'S BEYOND WORLD-CLASS STEALTH TECHNOLOGY ON BOARD. SO ONCE THEY'RE UP WE WON'T FIND THEM."

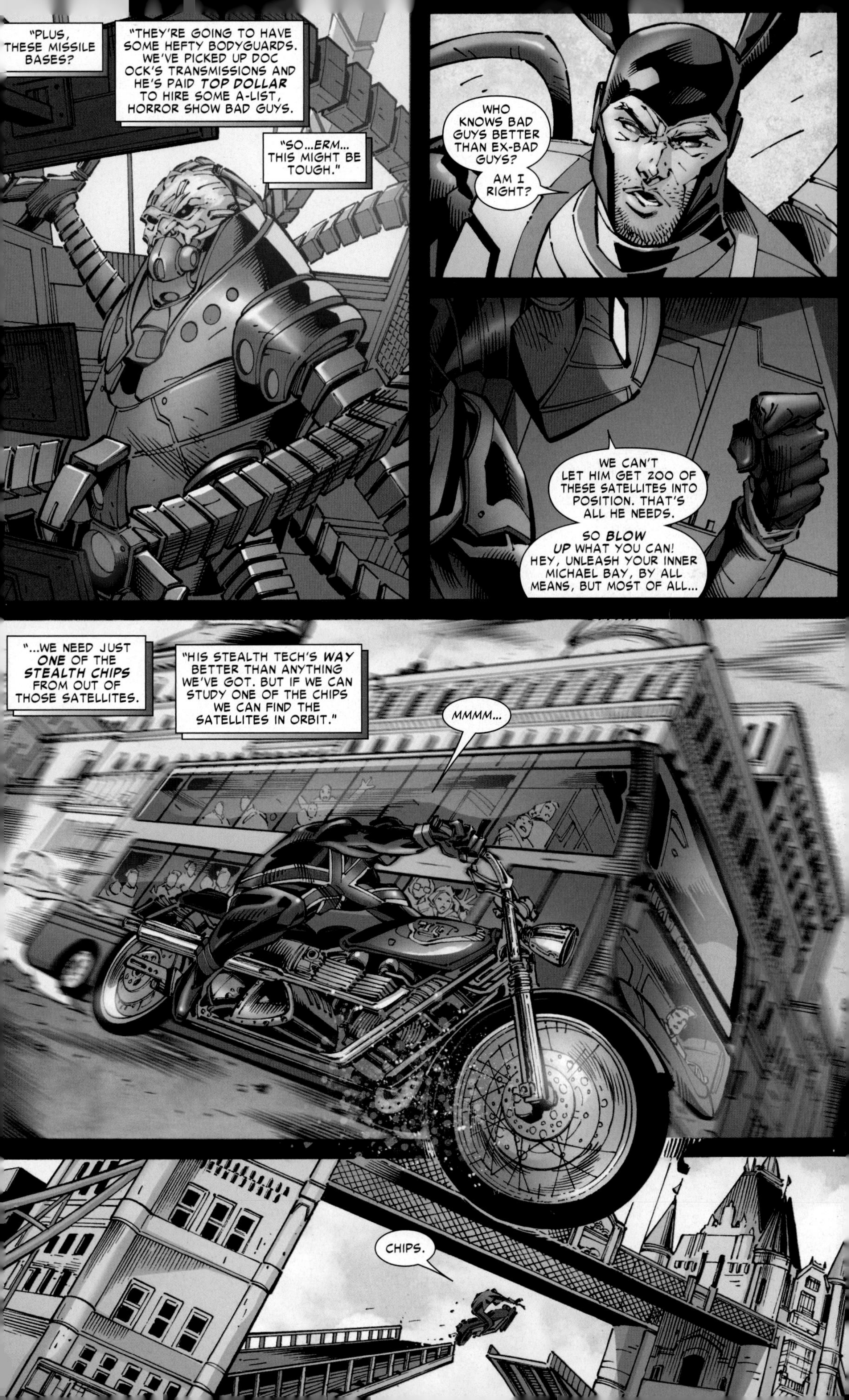
"PLUS, THESE MISSILE BASES?
"THEY'RE GOING TO HAVE SOME HEFTY BODYGUARDS. WE'VE PICKED UP DOC OCK'S TRANSMISSIONS AND HE'S PAID *TOP DOLLAR* TO HIRE SOME A-LIST, HORROR SHOW BAD GUYS.
"SO...*ERM*... THIS MIGHT BE TOUGH."
WHO KNOWS BAD GUYS BETTER THAN EX-BAD GUYS?
AM I RIGHT?
WE CAN'T LET HIM GET 200 OF THESE SATELLITES INTO POSITION. THAT'S ALL HE NEEDS.
SO *BLOW UP* WHAT YOU CAN! HEY, UNLEASH YOUR INNER MICHAEL BAY, BY ALL MEANS, BUT MOST OF ALL...
"...WE NEED JUST *ONE* OF THE *STEALTH CHIPS* FROM OUT OF THOSE SATELLITES.
"HIS STEALTH TECH'S *WAY* BETTER THAN ANYTHING WE'VE GOT. BUT IF WE CAN STUDY ONE OF THE CHIPS WE CAN FIND THE SATELLITES IN ORBIT."
MMMM...
CHIPS.

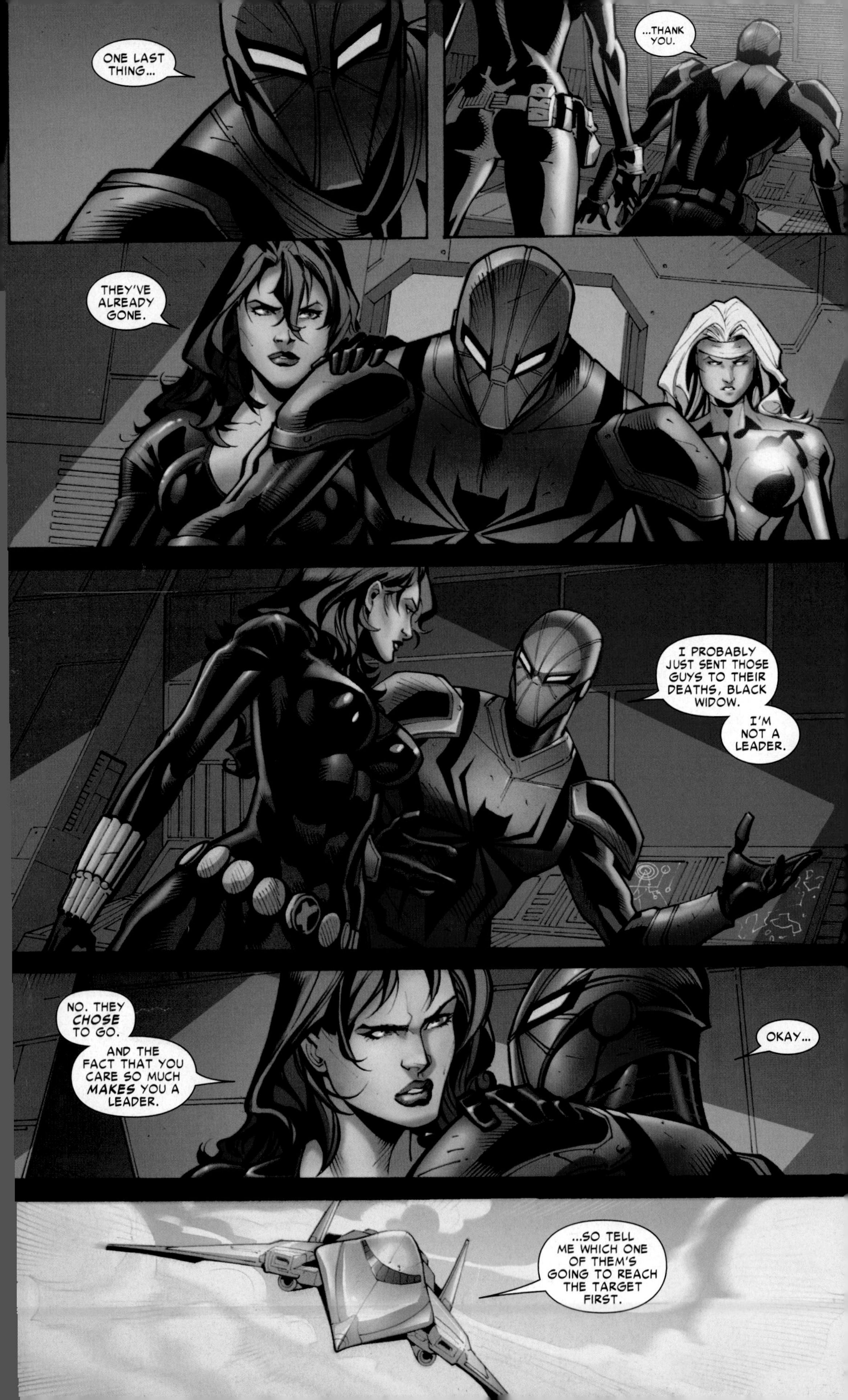
ONE LAST THING...
...THANK YOU.
THEY'VE ALREADY GONE.
I PROBABLY JUST SENT THOSE GUYS TO THEIR DEATHS, BLACK WIDOW.
I'M NOT A LEADER.
NO. THEY *CHOSE* TO GO.
AND THE FACT THAT YOU CARE SO MUCH *MAKES* YOU A LEADER.
OKAY...
...SO TELL ME WHICH ONE OF THEM'S GOING TO REACH THE TARGET FIRST.

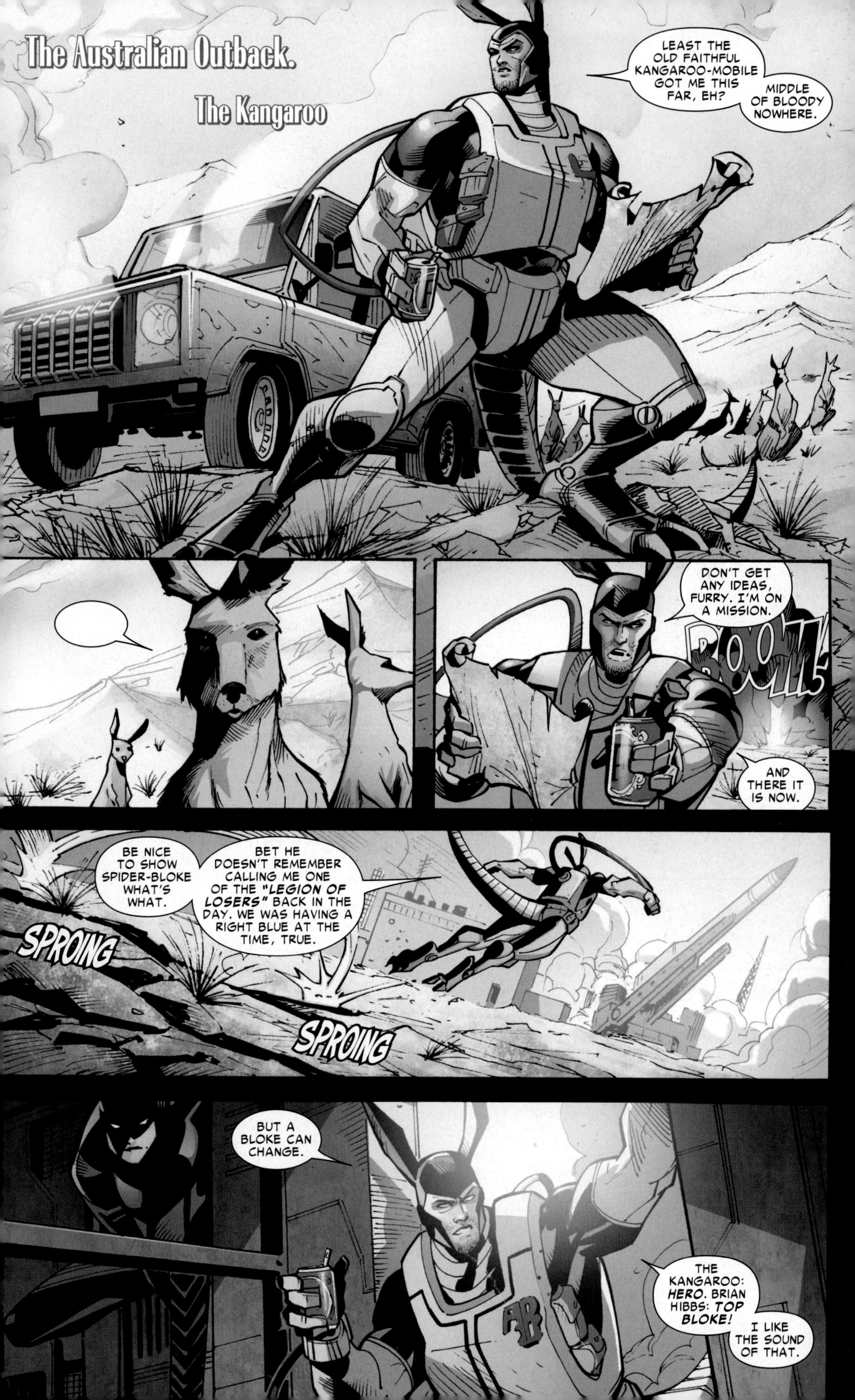
The Australian Outback.
The Kangaroo
LEAST THE OLD FAITHFUL KANGAROO-MOBILE GOT ME THIS FAR, EH?
MIDDLE OF BLOODY NOWHERE.
DON'T GET ANY IDEAS, FURRY. I'M ON A MISSION.
BOOM!
AND THERE IT IS NOW.
BE NICE TO SHOW SPIDER-BLOKE WHAT'S WHAT.
BET HE DOESN'T REMEMBER CALLING ME ONE OF THE "LEGION OF LOSERS" BACK IN THE DAY. WE WAS HAVING A RIGHT BLUE AT THE TIME, TRUE.
SPROING
SPROING
BUT A BLOKE CAN CHANGE.
THE KANGAROO: HERO. BRIAN HIBBS: TOP BLOKE!
I LIKE THE SOUND OF THAT.

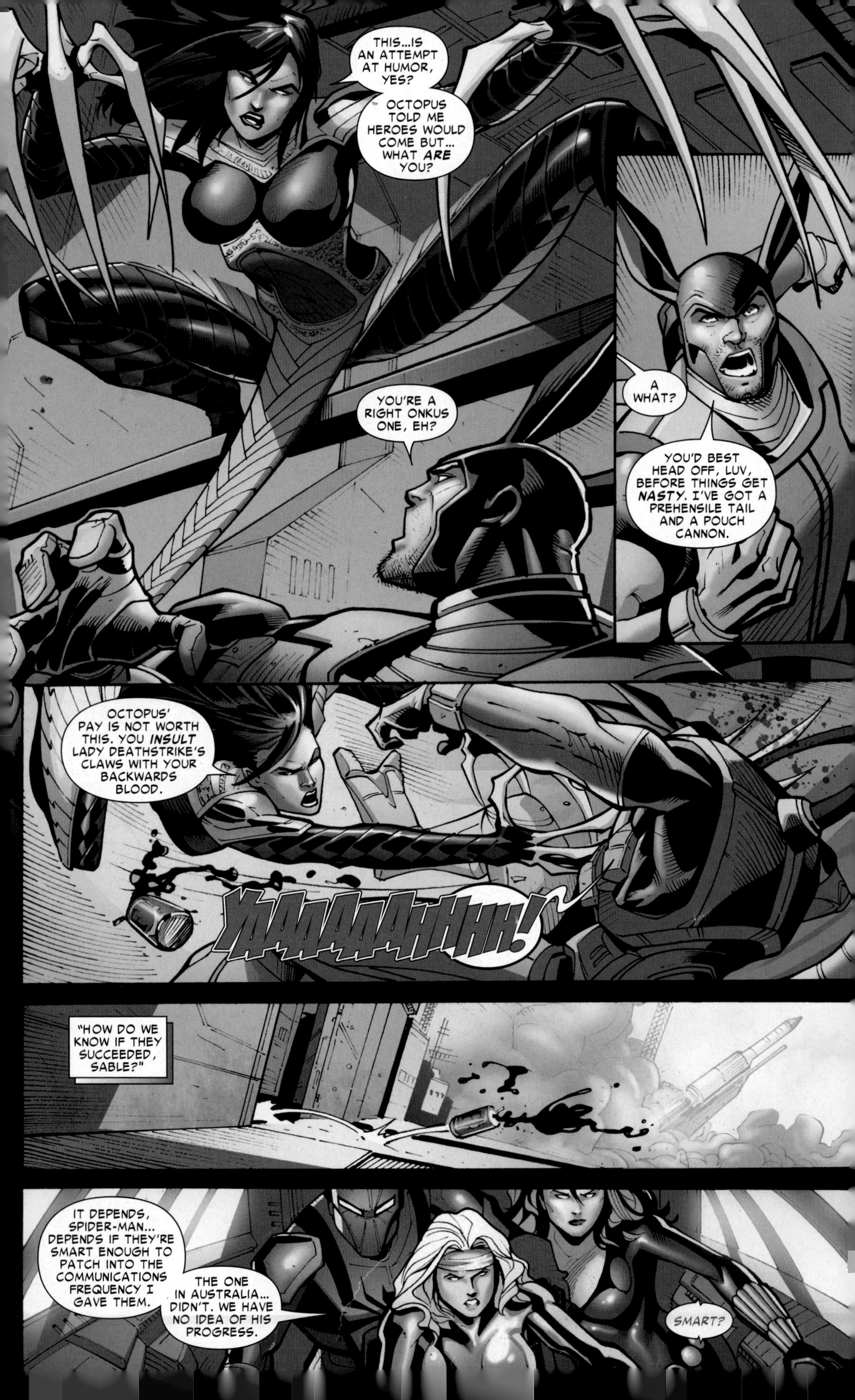
THIS...IS AN ATTEMPT AT HUMOR, YES?
OCTOPUS TOLD ME HEROES WOULD COME BUT... WHAT ARE YOU?
YOU'RE A RIGHT ONKUS ONE, EH?
A WHAT?
YOU'D BEST HEAD OFF, LUV, BEFORE THINGS GET NASTY. I'VE GOT A PREHENSILE TAIL AND A POUCH CANNON.
OCTOPUS' PAY IS NOT WORTH THIS. YOU INSULT LADY DEATHSTRIKE'S CLAWS WITH YOUR BACKWARDS BLOOD.
YAAAAAAHHHH!
"HOW DO WE KNOW IF THEY SUCCEEDED, SABLE?"
IT DEPENDS, SPIDER-MAN... DEPENDS IF THEY'RE SMART ENOUGH TO PATCH INTO THE COMMUNICATIONS FREQUENCY I GAVE THEM.
THE ONE IN AUSTRALIA... DIDN'T. WE HAVE NO IDEA OF HIS PROGRESS.
SMART?

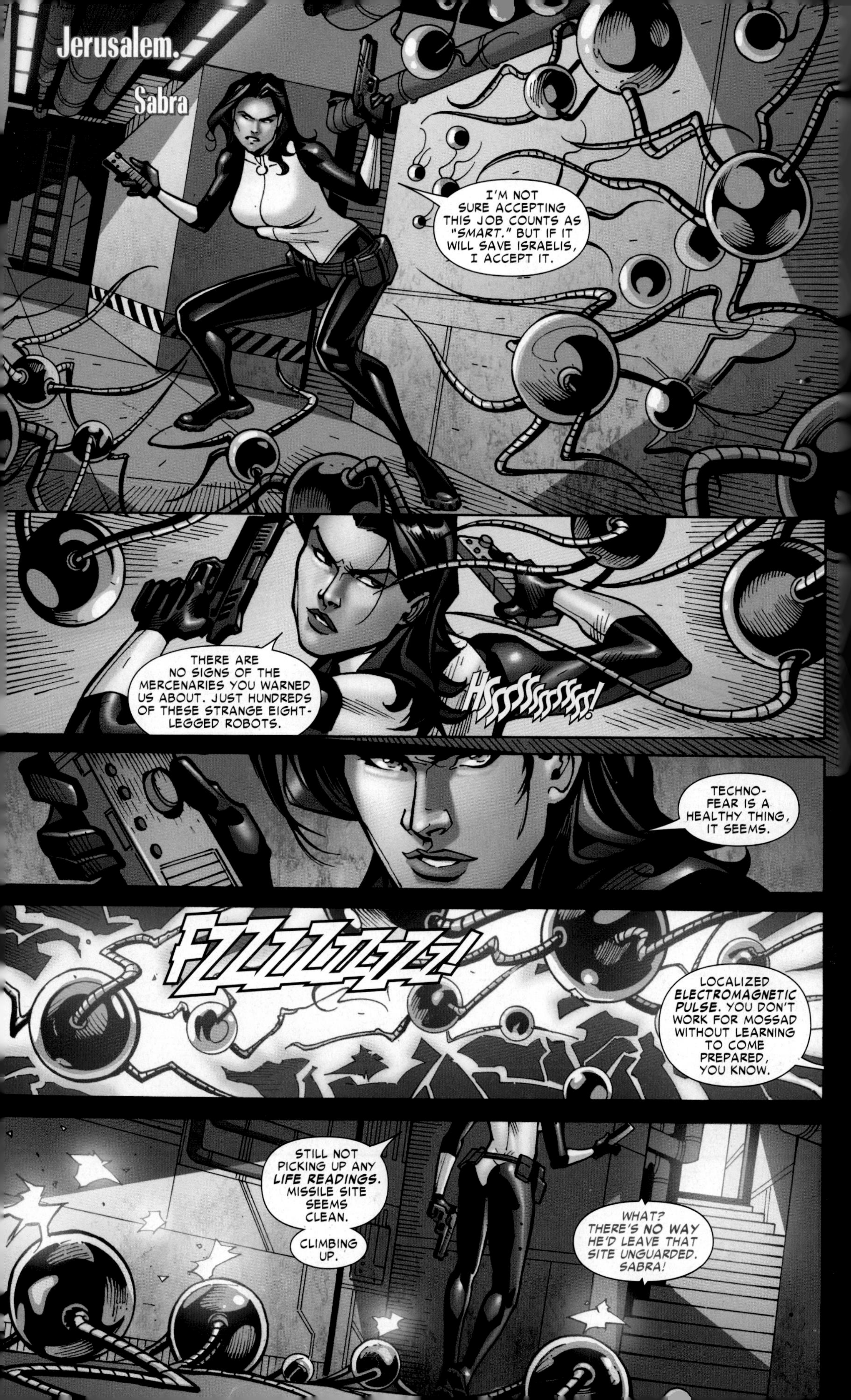
Jerusalem.
Sabra
I'M NOT SURE ACCEPTING THIS JOB COUNTS AS "SMART." BUT IF IT WILL SAVE ISRAELIS, I ACCEPT IT.
THERE ARE NO SIGNS OF THE MERCENARIES YOU WARNED US ABOUT. JUST HUNDREDS OF THESE STRANGE EIGHT-LEGGED ROBOTS.
HSSSSSSSSSS!
TECHNO-FEAR IS A HEALTHY THING, IT SEEMS.
FZZZZZZZZZ!
LOCALIZED ELECTROMAGNETIC PULSE. YOU DON'T WORK FOR MOSSAD WITHOUT LEARNING TO COME PREPARED, YOU KNOW.
STILL NOT PICKING UP ANY LIFE READINGS. MISSILE SITE SEEMS CLEAN.
CLIMBING UP.
WHAT? THERE'S NO WAY HE'D LEAVE THAT SITE UNGUARDED. SABRA!

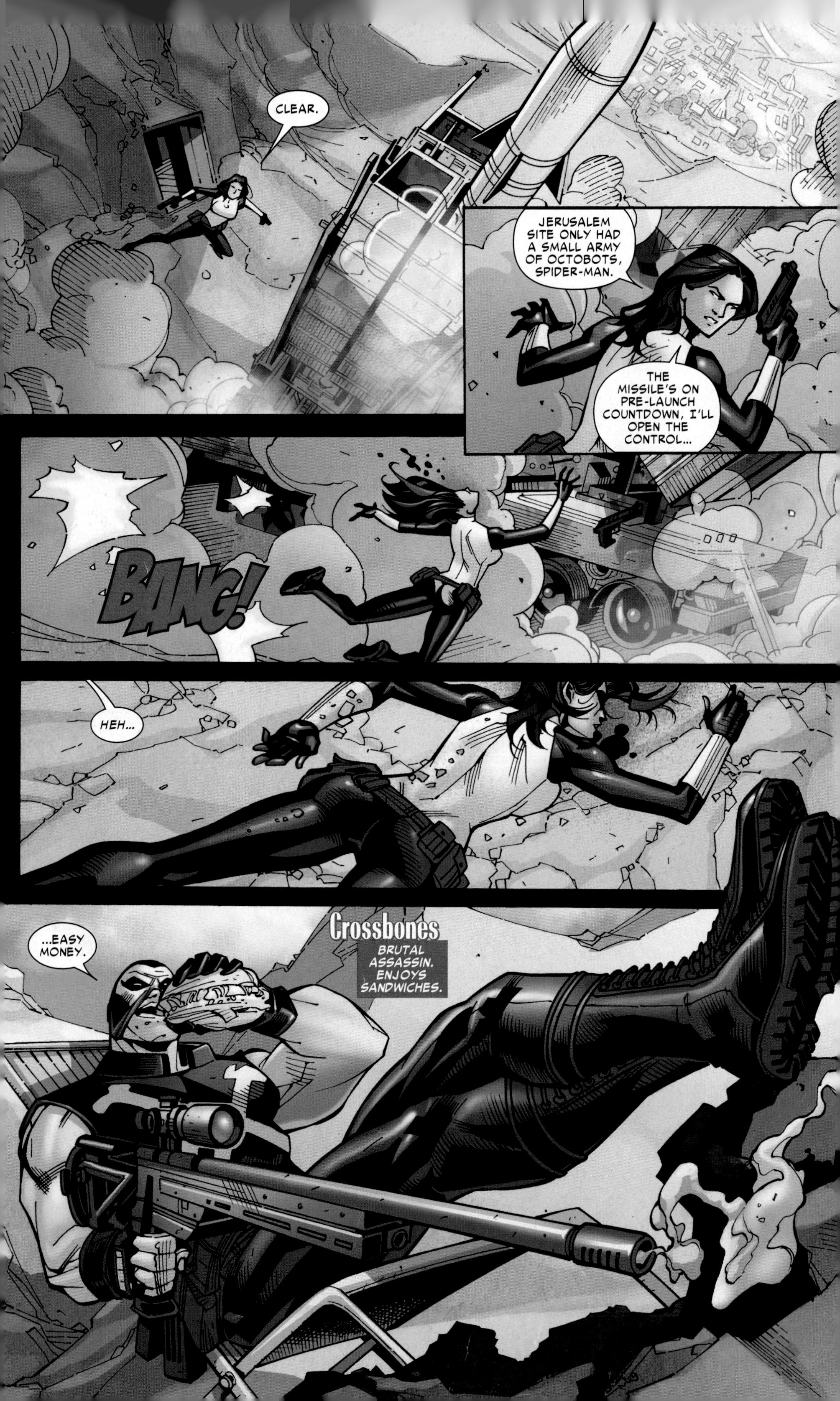
CLEAR.
JERUSALEM SITE ONLY HAD A SMALL ARMY OF OCTOBOTS, SPIDER-MAN.
THE MISSILE'S ON PRE-LAUNCH COUNTDOWN, I'LL OPEN THE CONTROL...
BANG!
HEH...
...EASY MONEY.
Crossbones
BRUTAL ASSASSIN. ENJOYS SANDWICHES.

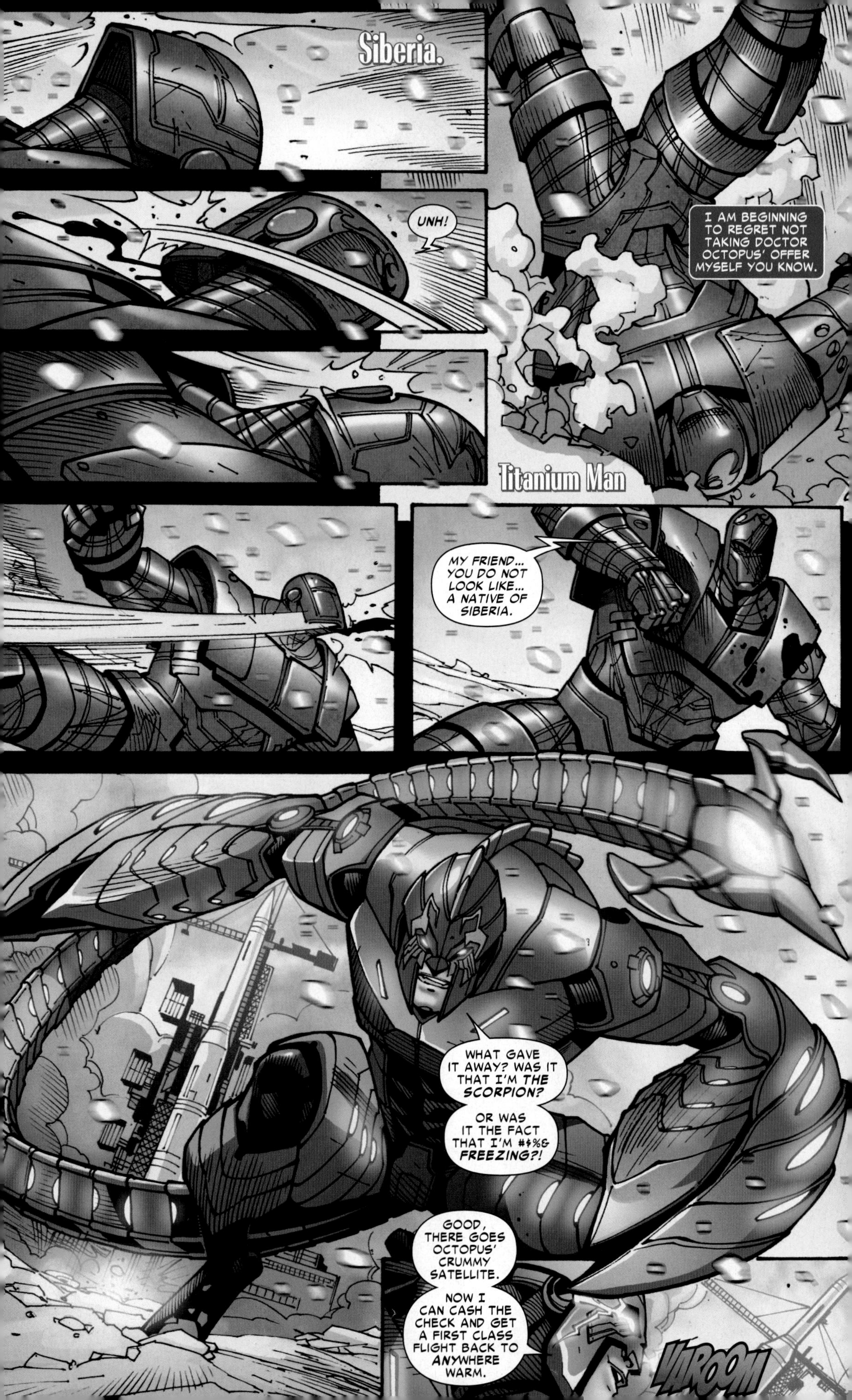
Siberia.
UNH!
I AM BEGINNING TO REGRET NOT TAKING DOCTOR OCTOPUS' OFFER MYSELF YOU KNOW.
Titanium Man
MY FRIEND... YOU DO NOT LOOK LIKE... A NATIVE OF SIBERIA.
WHAT GAVE IT AWAY? WAS IT THAT I'M THE SCORPION?
OR WAS IT THE FACT THAT I'M #$%& FREEZING?!
GOOD, THERE GOES OCTOPUS' CRUMMY SATELLITE.
NOW I CAN CASH THE CHECK AND GET A FIRST CLASS FLIGHT BACK TO ANYWHERE WARM.
VAROOM

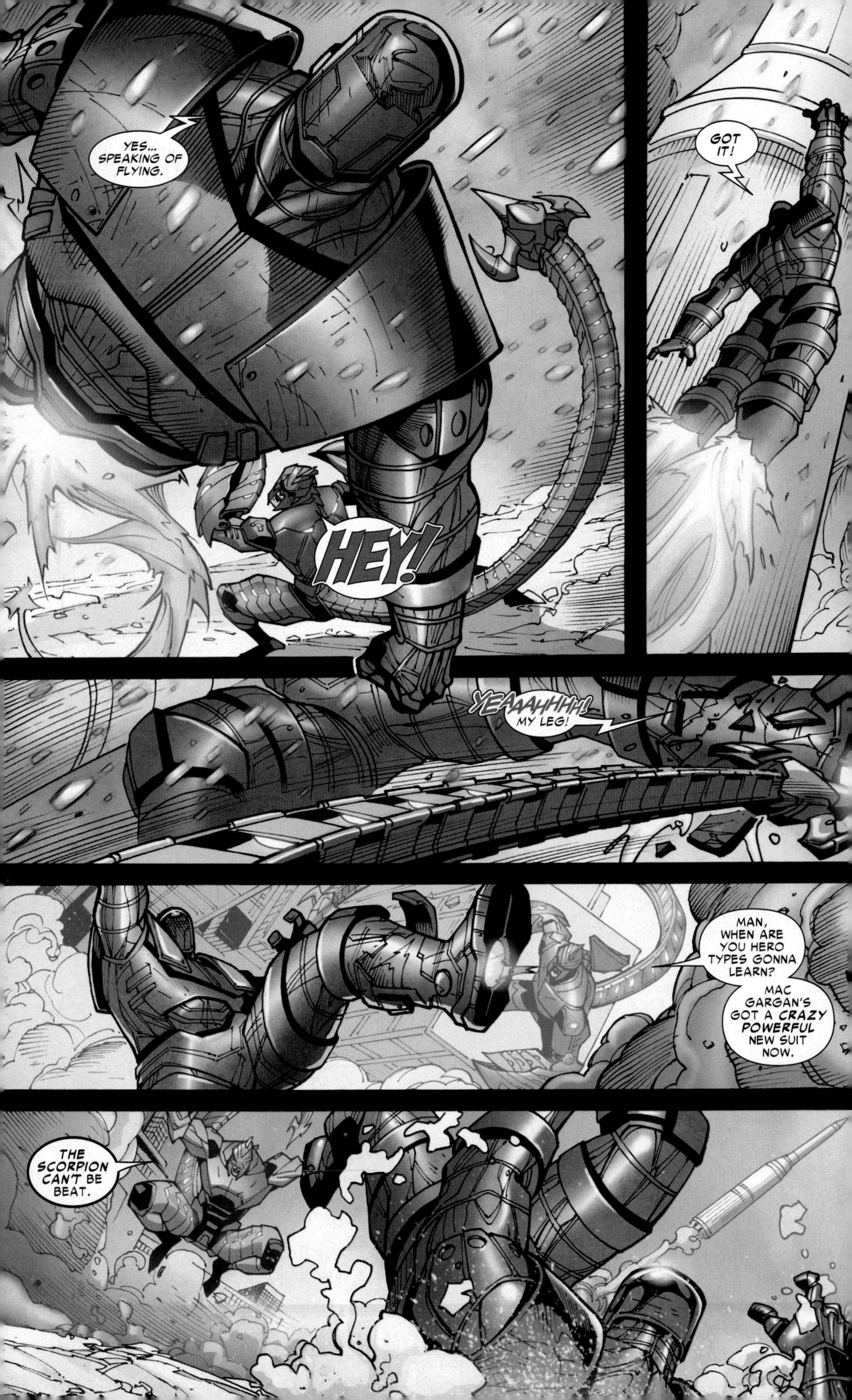

YES... SPEAKING OF FLYING.
GOT IT!
HEY!
YEAAAHHHH! MY LEG!
MAN, WHEN ARE YOU HERO TYPES GONNA LEARN?
MAC GARGAN'S GOT A CRAZY POWERFUL NEW SUIT NOW.
THE SCORPION CAN'T BE BEAT.

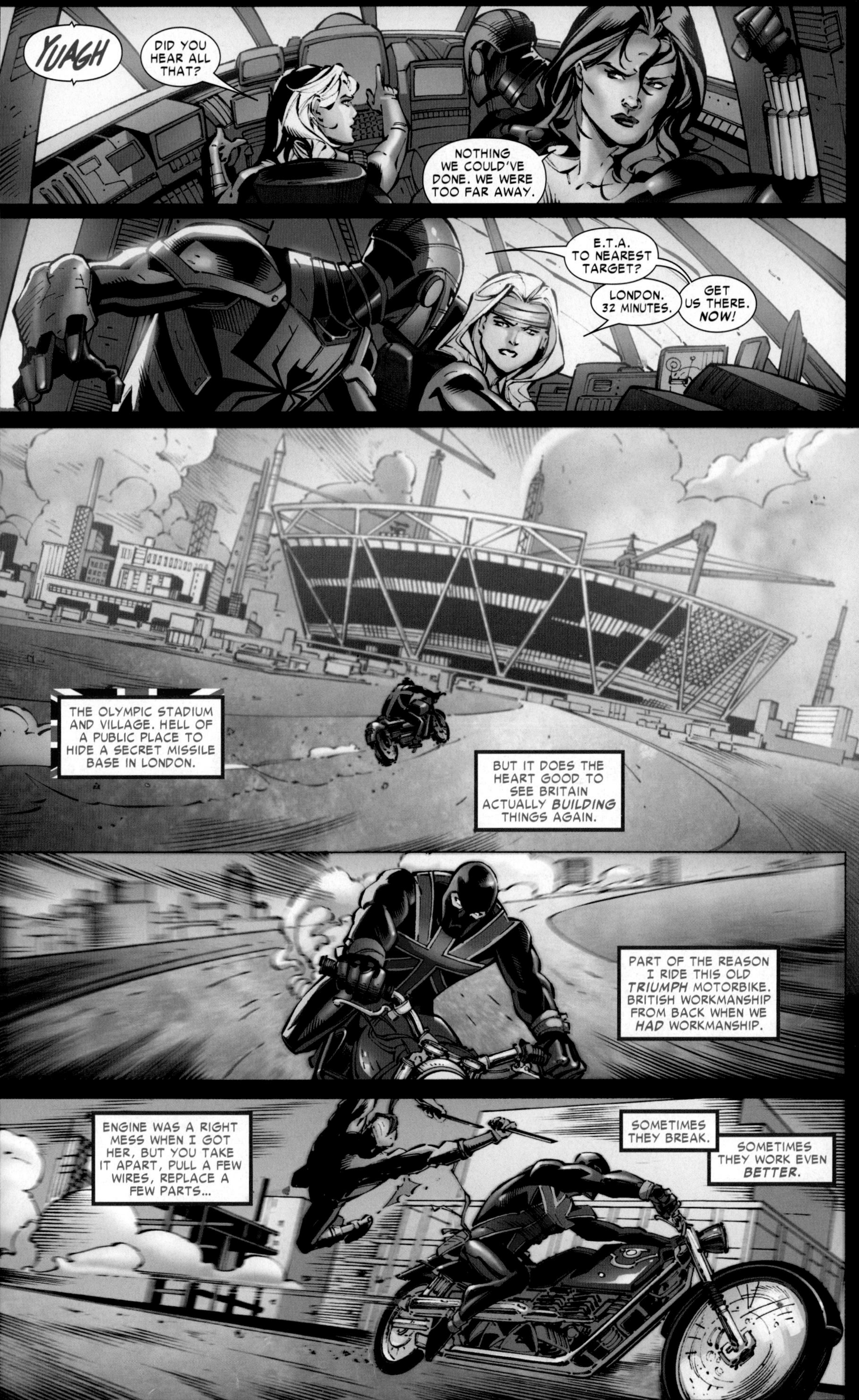
YUAGH
DID YOU HEAR ALL THAT?
NOTHING WE COULD'VE DONE. WE WERE TOO FAR AWAY.
E.T.A. TO NEAREST TARGET?
LONDON. 32 MINUTES.
GET US THERE. NOW!
THE OLYMPIC STADIUM AND VILLAGE. HELL OF A PUBLIC PLACE TO HIDE A SECRET MISSILE BASE IN LONDON.
BUT IT DOES THE HEART GOOD TO SEE BRITAIN ACTUALLY BUILDING THINGS AGAIN.
PART OF THE REASON I RIDE THIS OLD TRIUMPH MOTORBIKE. BRITISH WORKMANSHIP FROM BACK WHEN WE HAD WORKMANSHIP.
ENGINE WAS A RIGHT MESS WHEN I GOT HER, BUT YOU TAKE IT APART, PULL A FEW WIRES, REPLACE A FEW PARTS...
SOMETIMES THEY BREAK.
SOMETIMES THEY WORK EVEN BETTER.

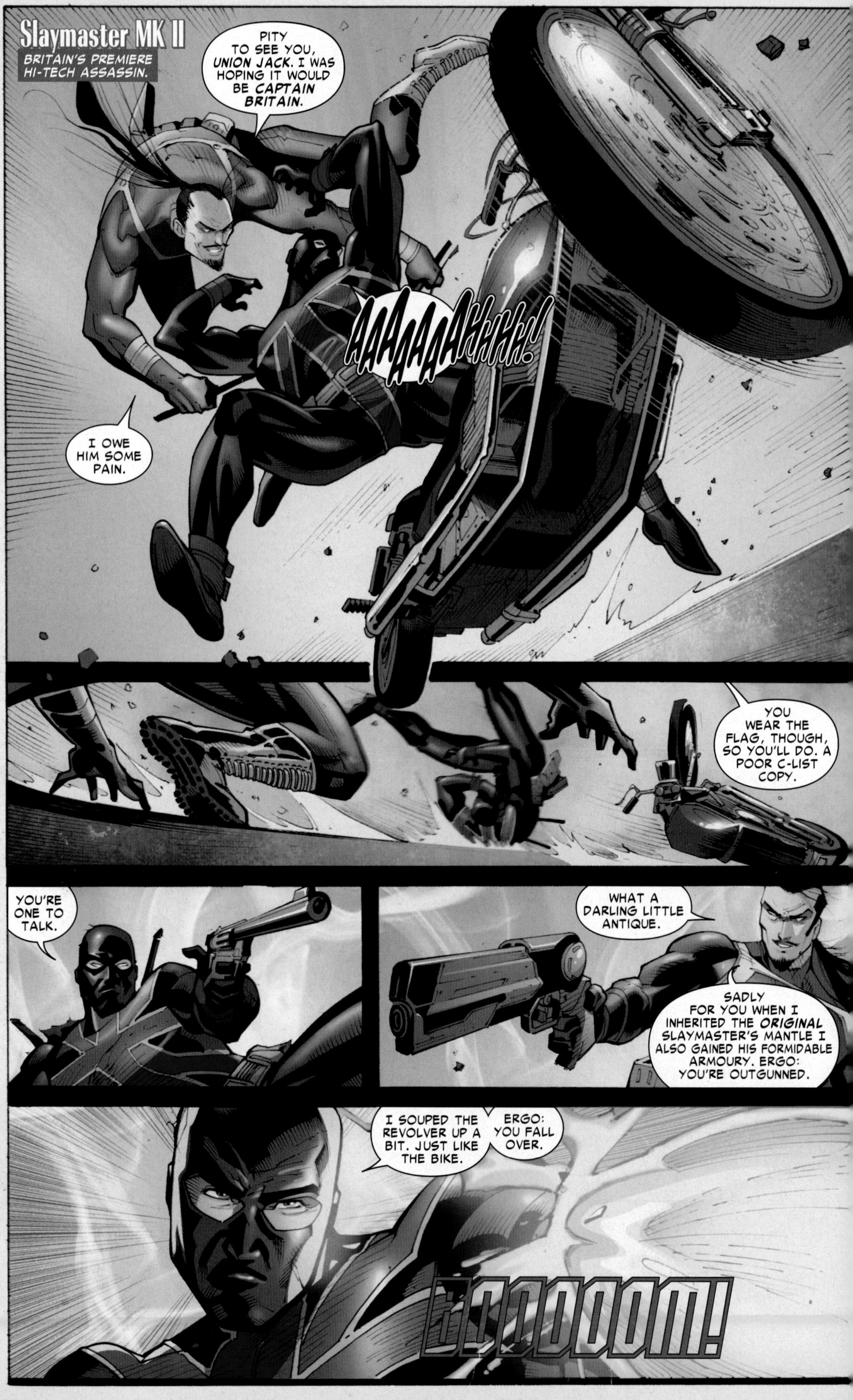
Slaymaster MK II
BRITAIN'S PREMIERE HI-TECH ASSASSIN.
PITY TO SEE YOU, UNION JACK. I WAS HOPING IT WOULD BE CAPTAIN BRITAIN.
I OWE HIM SOME PAIN.
AAAAAAAAHHHH!
YOU WEAR THE FLAG, THOUGH, SO YOU'LL DO. A POOR C-LIST COPY.
YOU'RE ONE TO TALK.
WHAT A DARLING LITTLE ANTIQUE.
SADLY FOR YOU WHEN I INHERITED THE ORIGINAL SLAYMASTER'S MANTLE I ALSO GAINED HIS FORMIDABLE ARMOURY. ERGO: YOU'RE OUTGUNNED.
I SOUPED THE REVOLVER UP A BIT. JUST LIKE THE BIKE.
ERGO: YOU FALL OVER.

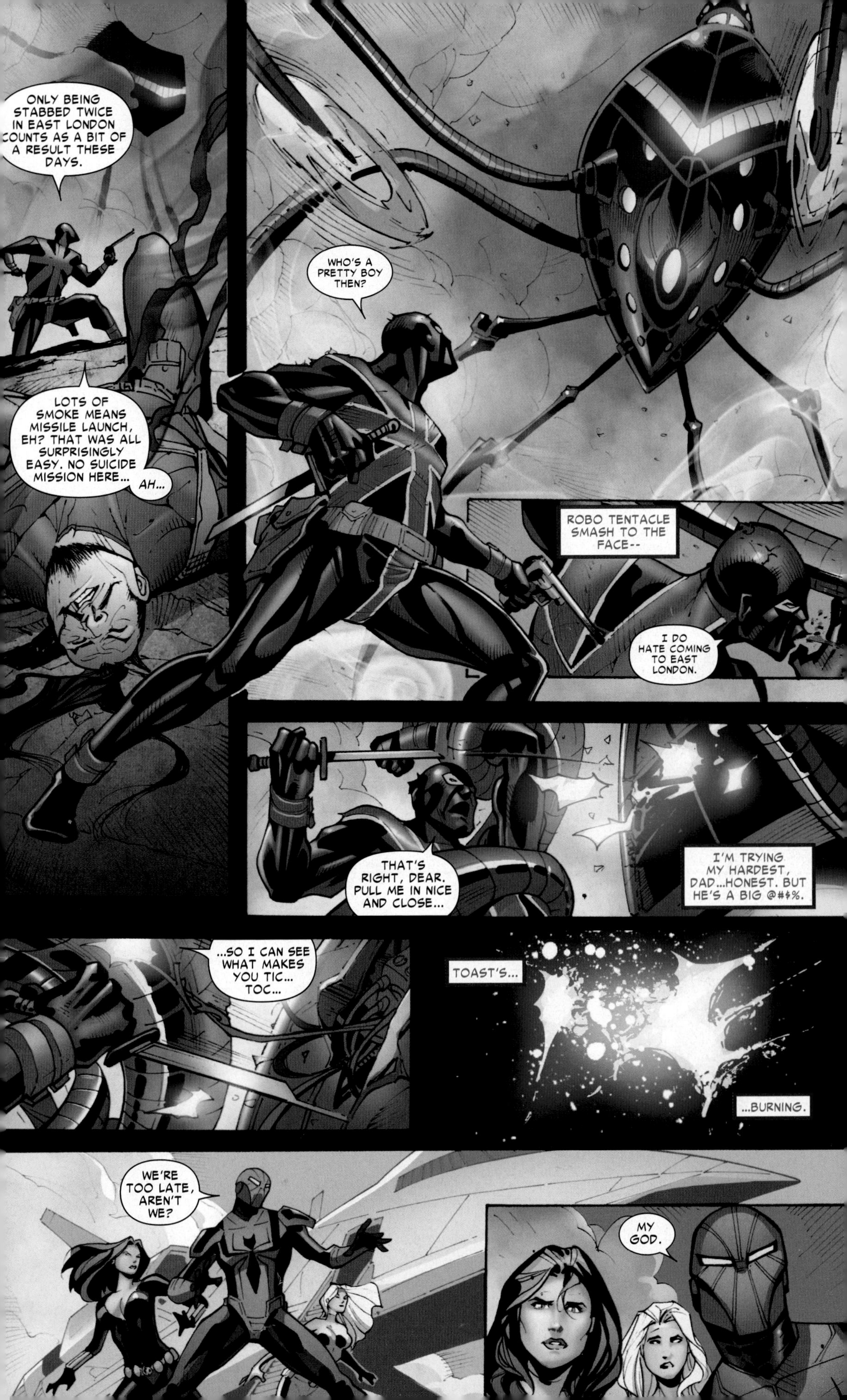
ONLY BEING STABBED TWICE IN EAST LONDON COUNTS AS A BIT OF A RESULT THESE DAYS.
LOTS OF SMOKE MEANS MISSILE LAUNCH, EH? THAT WAS ALL SURPRISINGLY EASY. NO SUICIDE MISSION HERE...
AH...
WHO'S A PRETTY BOY THEN?
ROBO TENTACLE SMASH TO THE FACE--
I DO HATE COMING TO EAST LONDON.
THAT'S RIGHT, DEAR. PULL ME IN NICE AND CLOSE...
I'M TRYING MY HARDEST, DAD...HONEST. BUT HE'S A BIG @#$%.
...SO I CAN SEE WHAT MAKES YOU TIC... TOC...
TOAST'S...
...BURNING.
WE'RE TOO LATE, AREN'T WE?
MY GOD.

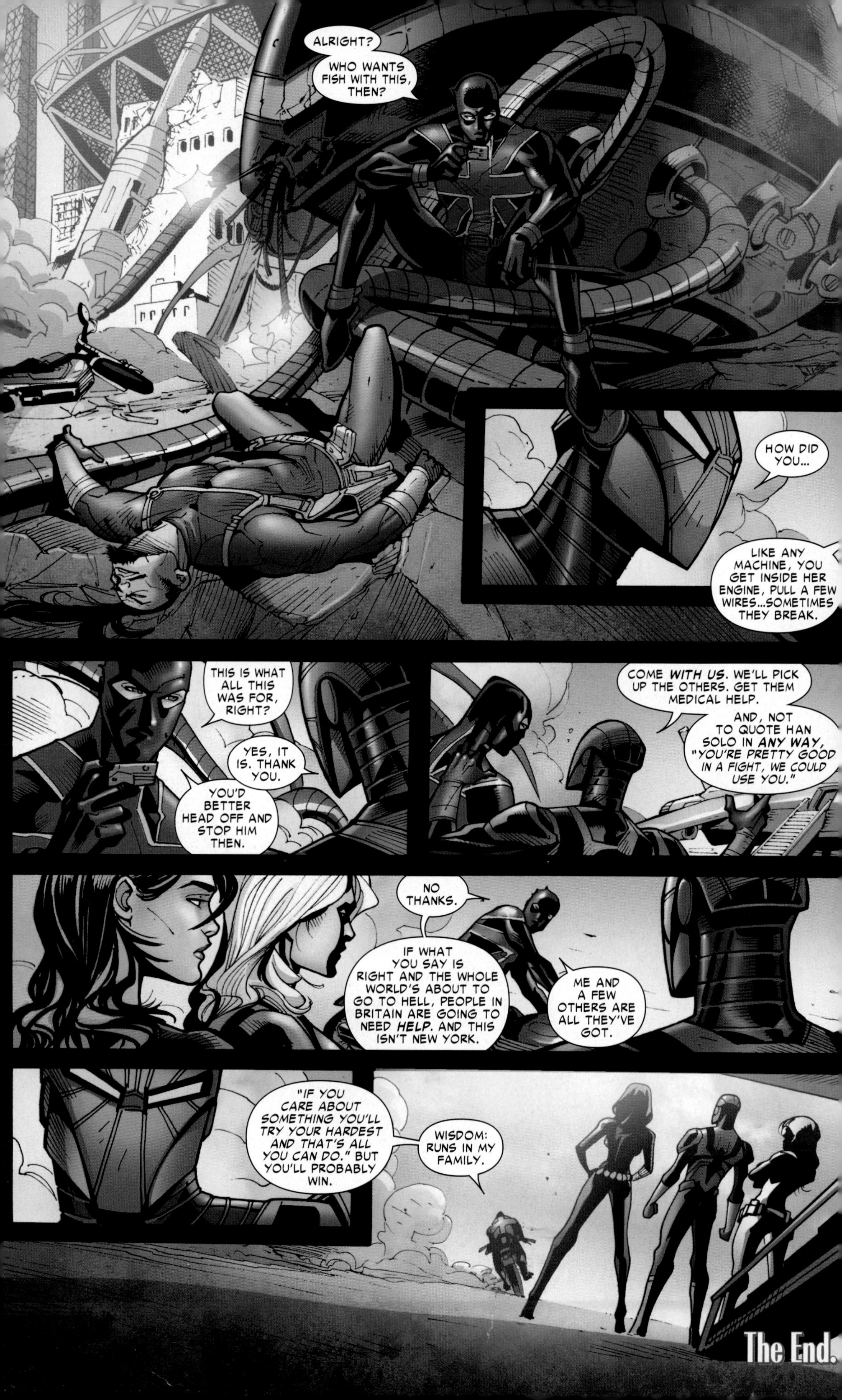

ALRIGHT?
WHO WANTS FISH WITH THIS, THEN?
HOW DID YOU...
LIKE ANY MACHINE, YOU GET INSIDE HER ENGINE, PULL A FEW WIRES...SOMETIMES THEY BREAK.
THIS IS WHAT ALL THIS WAS FOR, RIGHT?
YES, IT IS. THANK YOU.
YOU'D BETTER HEAD OFF AND STOP HIM THEN.
COME WITH US. WE'LL PICK UP THE OTHERS. GET THEM MEDICAL HELP.
AND, NOT TO QUOTE HAN SOLO IN ANY WAY, "YOU'RE PRETTY GOOD IN A FIGHT, WE COULD USE YOU."
NO THANKS.
IF WHAT YOU SAY IS RIGHT AND THE WHOLE WORLD'S ABOUT TO GO TO HELL, PEOPLE IN BRITAIN ARE GOING TO NEED HELP. AND THIS ISN'T NEW YORK.
ME AND A FEW OTHERS ARE ALL THEY'VE GOT.
"IF YOU CARE ABOUT SOMETHING YOU'LL TRY YOUR HARDEST AND THAT'S ALL YOU CAN DO." BUT YOU'LL PROBABLY WIN.
WISDOM: RUNS IN MY FAMILY.
The End.

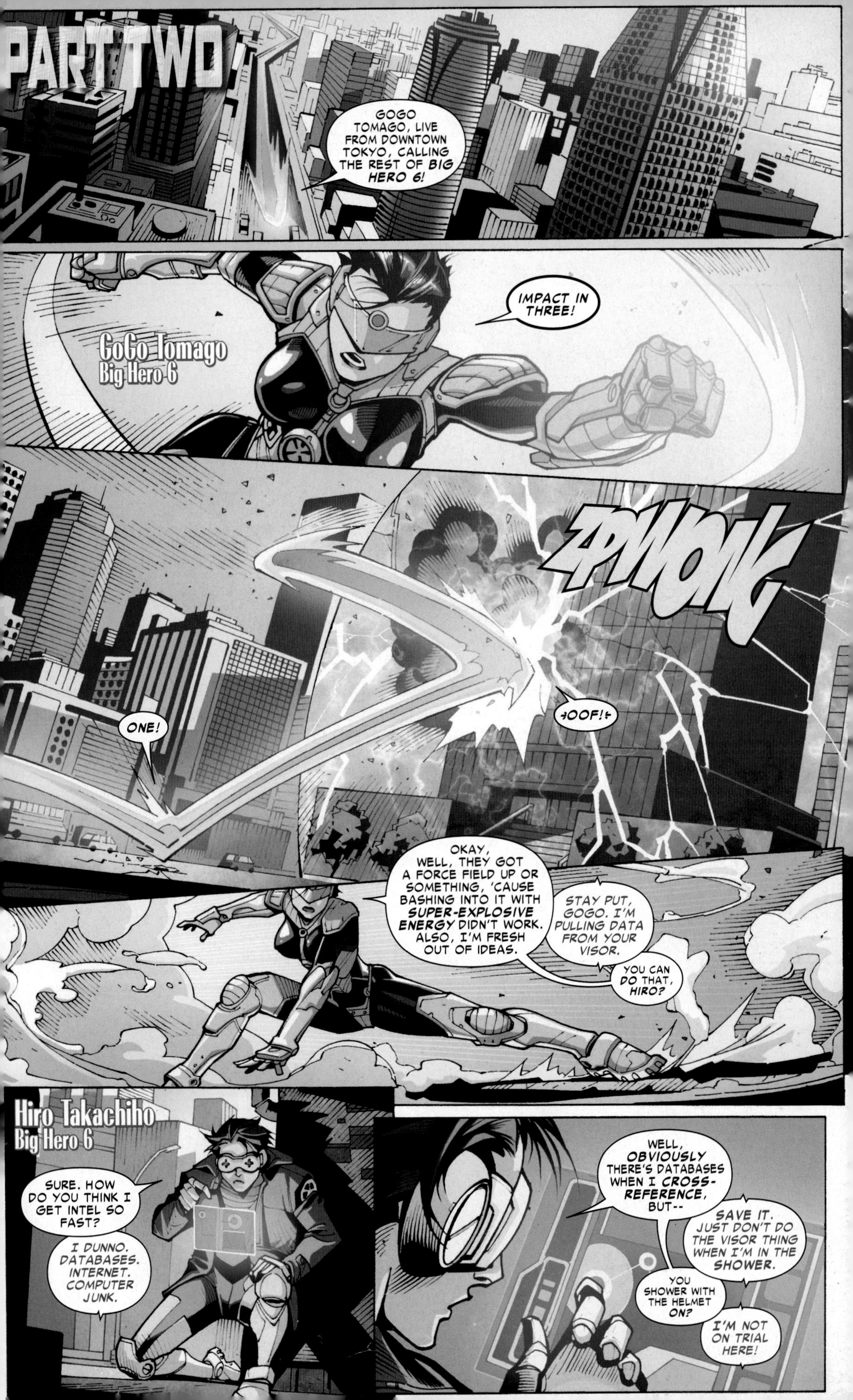
PART TWO
GOGO TOMAGO, LIVE FROM DOWNTOWN TOKYO, CALLING THE REST OF BIG HERO 6!
IMPACT IN THREE!
GoGo Tomago
Big Hero 6
ZAVWOM
ONE!
OOF!
OKAY, WELL, THEY GOT A FORCE FIELD UP OR SOMETHING, 'CAUSE BASHING INTO IT WITH SUPER-EXPLOSIVE ENERGY DIDN'T WORK. ALSO, I'M FRESH OUT OF IDEAS.
STAY PUT, GOGO. I'M PULLING DATA FROM YOUR VISOR.
YOU CAN DO THAT, HIRO?
Hiro Takachiho
Big Hero 6
SURE. HOW DO YOU THINK I GET INTEL SO FAST?
I DUNNO. DATABASES. INTERNET. COMPUTER JUNK.
WELL, OBVIOUSLY THERE'S DATABASES WHEN I CROSS-REFERENCE, BUT--
SAVE IT. JUST DON'T DO THE VISOR THING WHEN I'M IN THE SHOWER.
YOU SHOWER WITH THE HELMET ON?
I'M NOT ON TRIAL HERE!

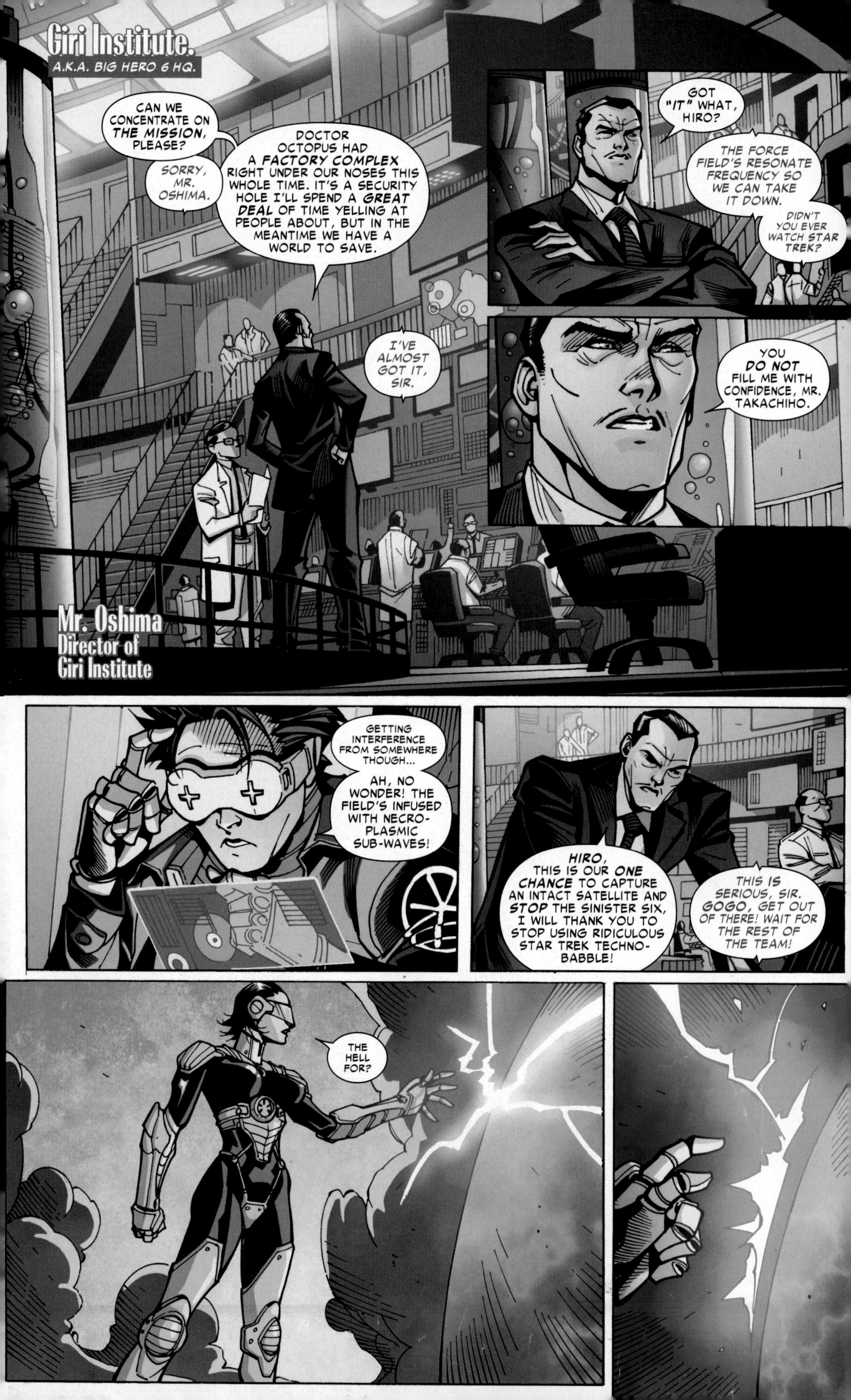
Giri Institute.
A.K.A. BIG HERO 6 HQ.
CAN WE CONCENTRATE ON THE MISSION, PLEASE?
SORRY, MR. OSHIMA.
DOCTOR OCTOPUS HAD A FACTORY COMPLEX RIGHT UNDER OUR NOSES THIS WHOLE TIME. IT'S A SECURITY HOLE I'LL SPEND A GREAT DEAL OF TIME YELLING AT PEOPLE ABOUT, BUT IN THE MEANTIME WE HAVE A WORLD TO SAVE.
I'VE ALMOST GOT IT, SIR.
Mr. Oshima
Director of Giri Institute
GOT "IT" WHAT, HIRO?
THE FORCE FIELD'S RESONATE FREQUENCY SO WE CAN TAKE IT DOWN.
DIDN'T YOU EVER WATCH STAR TREK?
YOU DO NOT FILL ME WITH CONFIDENCE, MR. TAKACHIHO.
GETTING INTERFERENCE FROM SOMEWHERE THOUGH...
AH, NO WONDER! THE FIELD'S INFUSED WITH NECRO-PLASMIC SUB-WAVES!
HIRO, THIS IS OUR ONE CHANCE TO CAPTURE AN INTACT SATELLITE AND STOP THE SINISTER SIX, I WILL THANK YOU TO STOP USING RIDICULOUS STAR TREK TECHNO-BABBLE!
THIS IS SERIOUS, SIR. GOGO, GET OUT OF THERE! WAIT FOR THE REST OF THE TEAM!
THE HELL FOR?

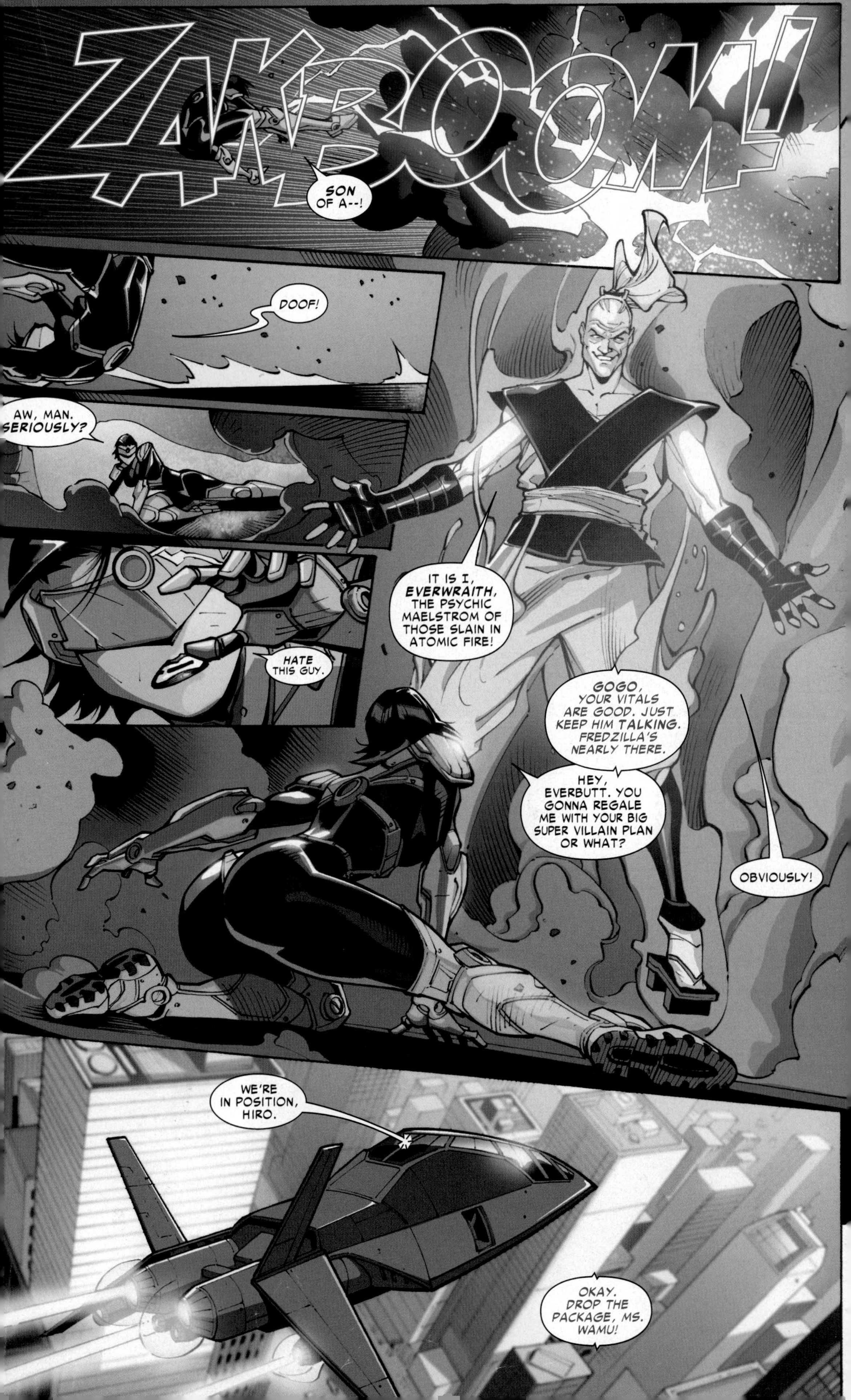
ZAKROOM!
SON OF A--!
DOOF!
AW, MAN. SERIOUSLY?
HATE THIS GUY.
IT IS I, EVERWRAITH, THE PSYCHIC MAELSTROM OF THOSE SLAIN IN ATOMIC FIRE!
GOGO, YOUR VITALS ARE GOOD. JUST KEEP HIM TALKING. FREDZILLA'S NEARLY THERE.
HEY, EVERBUTT. YOU GONNA REGALE ME WITH YOUR BIG SUPER VILLAIN PLAN OR WHAT?
OBVIOUSLY!
WE'RE IN POSITION, HIRO.
OKAY. DROP THE PACKAGE, MS. WAMU!

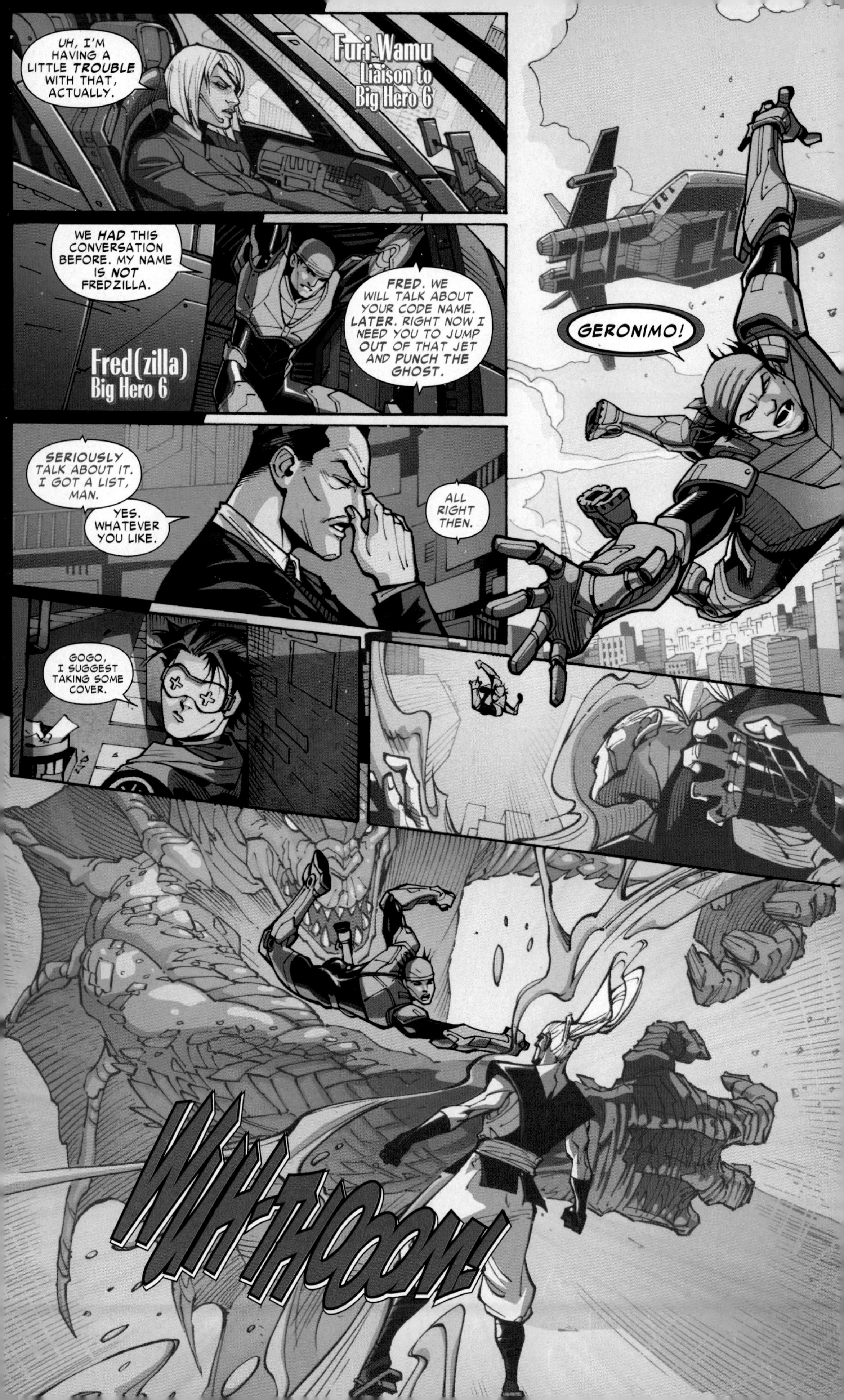

UH, I'M HAVING A LITTLE TROUBLE WITH THAT, ACTUALLY.
Furi Wamu
Liaison to Big Hero 6
WE HAD THIS CONVERSATION BEFORE. MY NAME IS NOT FREDZILLA.
Fred(zilla)
Big Hero 6
FRED. WE WILL TALK ABOUT YOUR CODE NAME. LATER. RIGHT NOW I NEED YOU TO JUMP OUT OF THAT JET AND PUNCH THE GHOST.
SERIOUSLY TALK ABOUT IT. I GOT A LIST, MAN.
YES. WHATEVER YOU LIKE.
ALL RIGHT THEN.
GERONIMO!
GOGO, I SUGGEST TAKING SOME COVER.
WHHOOOM!

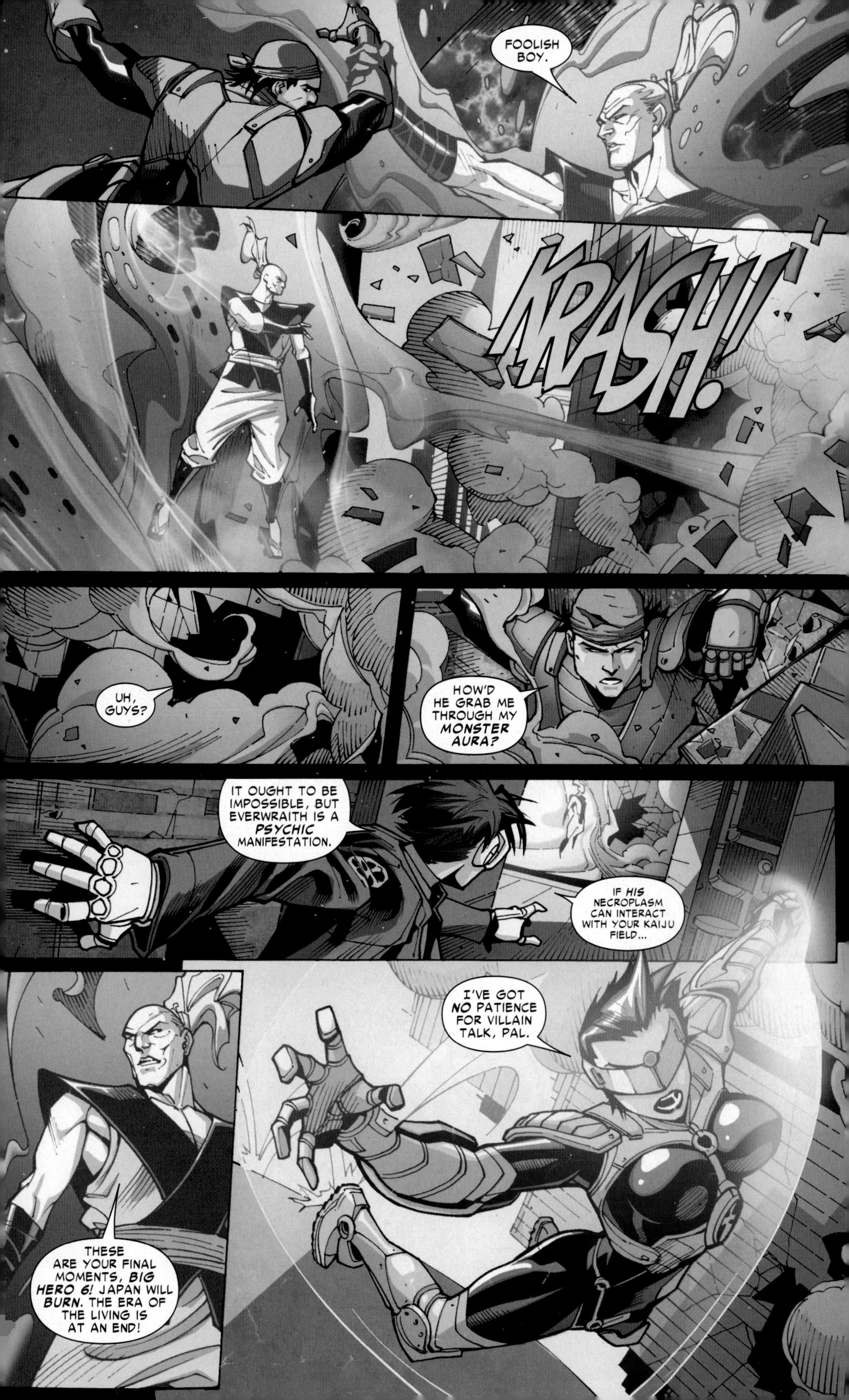
FOOLISH BOY.
KRASH!
UH, GUYS?
HOW'D HE GRAB ME THROUGH MY MONSTER AURA?
IT OUGHT TO BE IMPOSSIBLE, BUT EVERWRAITH IS A PSYCHIC MANIFESTATION.
IF HIS NECROPLASM CAN INTERACT WITH YOUR KAIJU FIELD...
I'VE GOT NO PATIENCE FOR VILLAIN TALK, PAL.
THESE ARE YOUR FINAL MOMENTS, BIG HERO 6! JAPAN WILL BURN. THE ERA OF THE LIVING IS AT AN END!

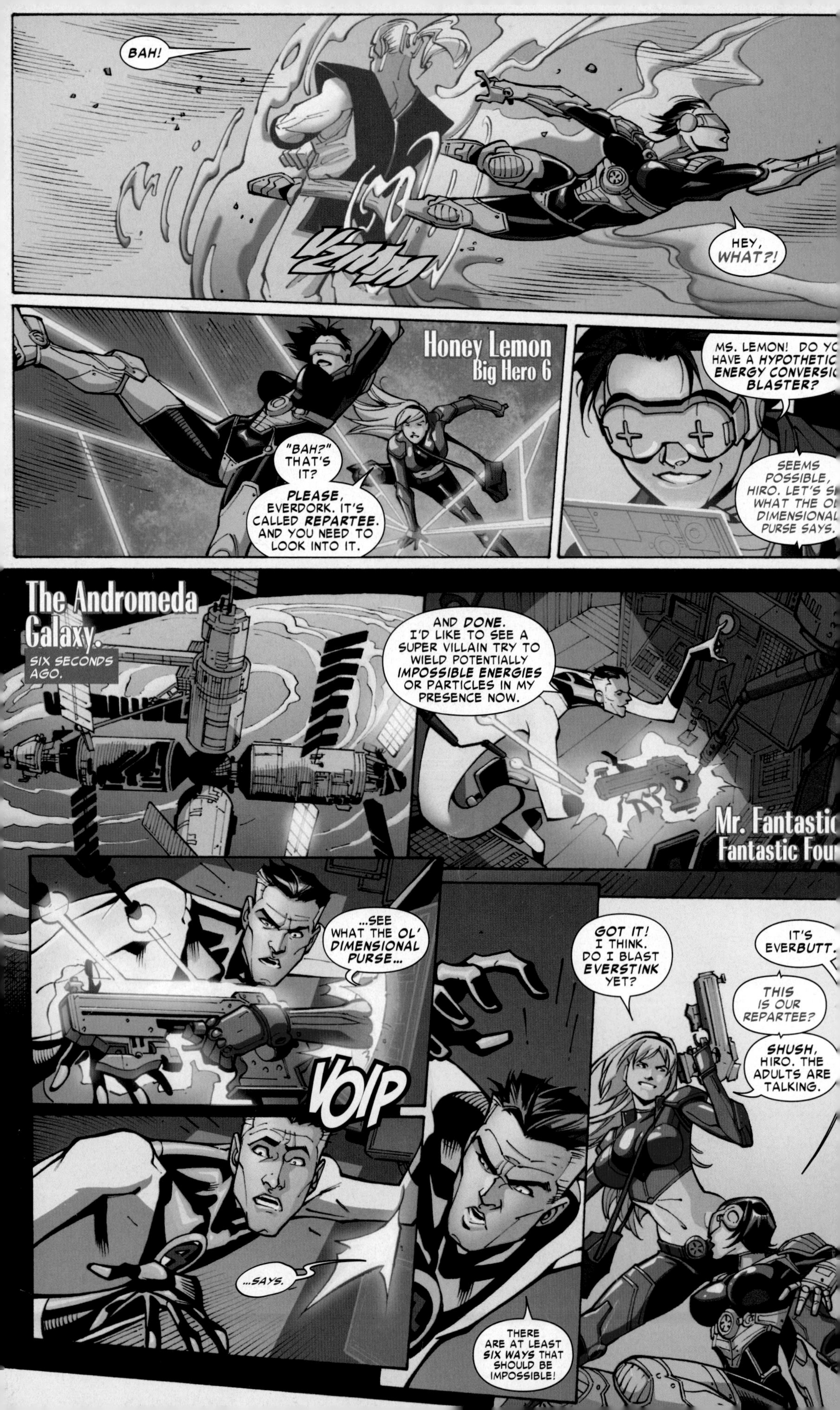
BAH!
VZMM
HEY, WHAT?!
Honey Lemon
Big Hero 6
"BAH?" THAT'S IT?
PLEASE, EVERDORK. IT'S CALLED REPARTEE. AND YOU NEED TO LOOK INTO IT.
MS. LEMON! DO YO HAVE A HYPOTHETIC ENERGY CONVERSI BLASTER?
SEEMS POSSIBLE, HIRO. LET'S S WHAT THE OL DIMENSIONAL PURSE SAYS.
The Andromeda Galaxy.
SIX SECONDS AGO.
AND DONE. I'D LIKE TO SEE A SUPER VILLAIN TRY TO WIELD POTENTIALLY IMPOSSIBLE ENERGIES OR PARTICLES IN MY PRESENCE NOW.
Mr. Fantastic
Fantastic Four
...SEE WHAT THE OL' DIMENSIONAL PURSE...
VOIP
...SAYS.
THERE ARE AT LEAST SIX WAYS THAT SHOULD BE IMPOSSIBLE!
GOT IT! I THINK. DO I BLAST EVERSTINK YET?
IT'S EVERBUTT.
THIS IS OUR REPARTEE?
SHUSH, HIRO. THE ADULTS ARE TALKING.

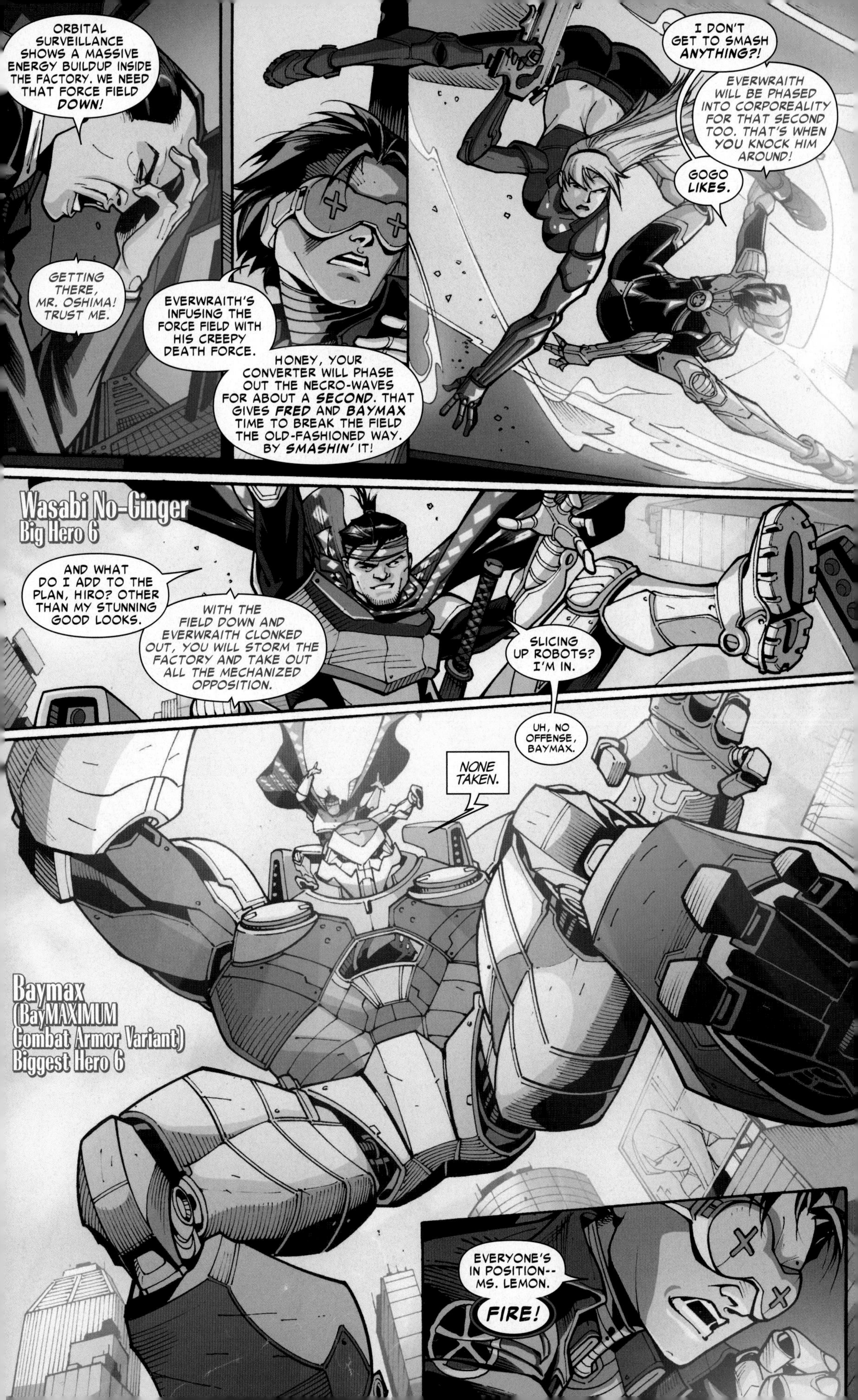
ORBITAL SURVEILLANCE SHOWS A MASSIVE ENERGY BUILDUP INSIDE THE FACTORY. WE NEED THAT FORCE FIELD DOWN!
GETTING THERE, MR. OSHIMA! TRUST ME.
EVERWRAITH'S INFUSING THE FORCE FIELD WITH HIS CREEPY DEATH FORCE.
HONEY, YOUR CONVERTER WILL PHASE OUT THE NECRO-WAVES FOR ABOUT A SECOND. THAT GIVES FRED AND BAYMAX TIME TO BREAK THE FIELD THE OLD-FASHIONED WAY. BY SMASHIN' IT!
I DON'T GET TO SMASH ANYTHING?!
EVERWRAITH WILL BE PHASED INTO CORPOREALITY FOR THAT SECOND TOO. THAT'S WHEN YOU KNOCK HIM AROUND!
GOGO LIKES.
Wasabi No-Ginger
Big Hero 6
AND WHAT DO I ADD TO THE PLAN, HIRO? OTHER THAN MY STUNNING GOOD LOOKS.
WITH THE FIELD DOWN AND EVERWRAITH CLONKED OUT, YOU WILL STORM THE FACTORY AND TAKE OUT ALL THE MECHANIZED OPPOSITION.
SLICING UP ROBOTS? I'M IN.
UH, NO OFFENSE, BAYMAX.
NONE TAKEN.
Baymax
(BayMAXIMUM
Combat Armor Variant)
Biggest Hero 6
EVERYONE'S IN POSITION-- MS. LEMON.
FIRE!

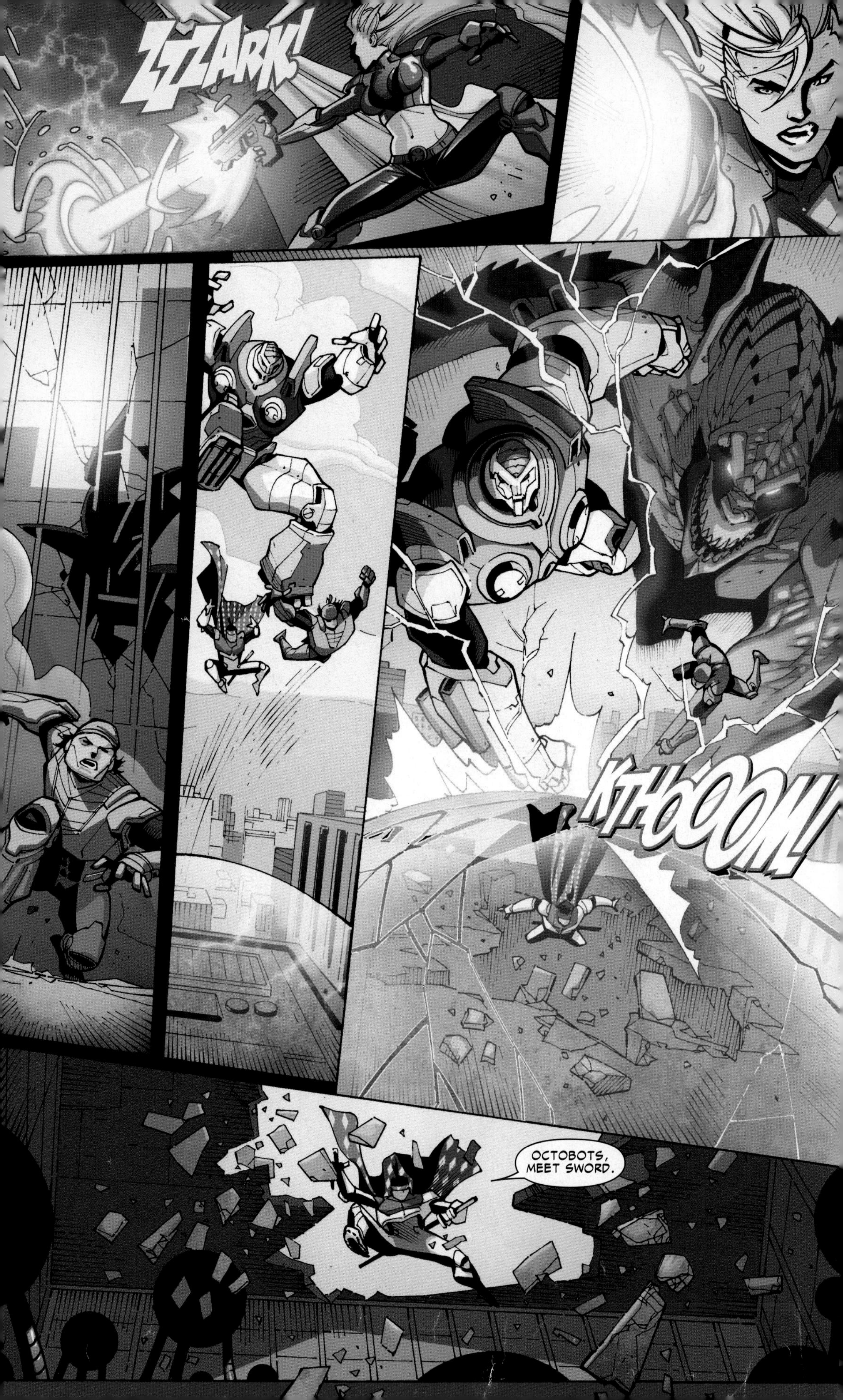
ZZZARK!
KT-BOOOM!
OCTOBOTS,
MEET SWORD.

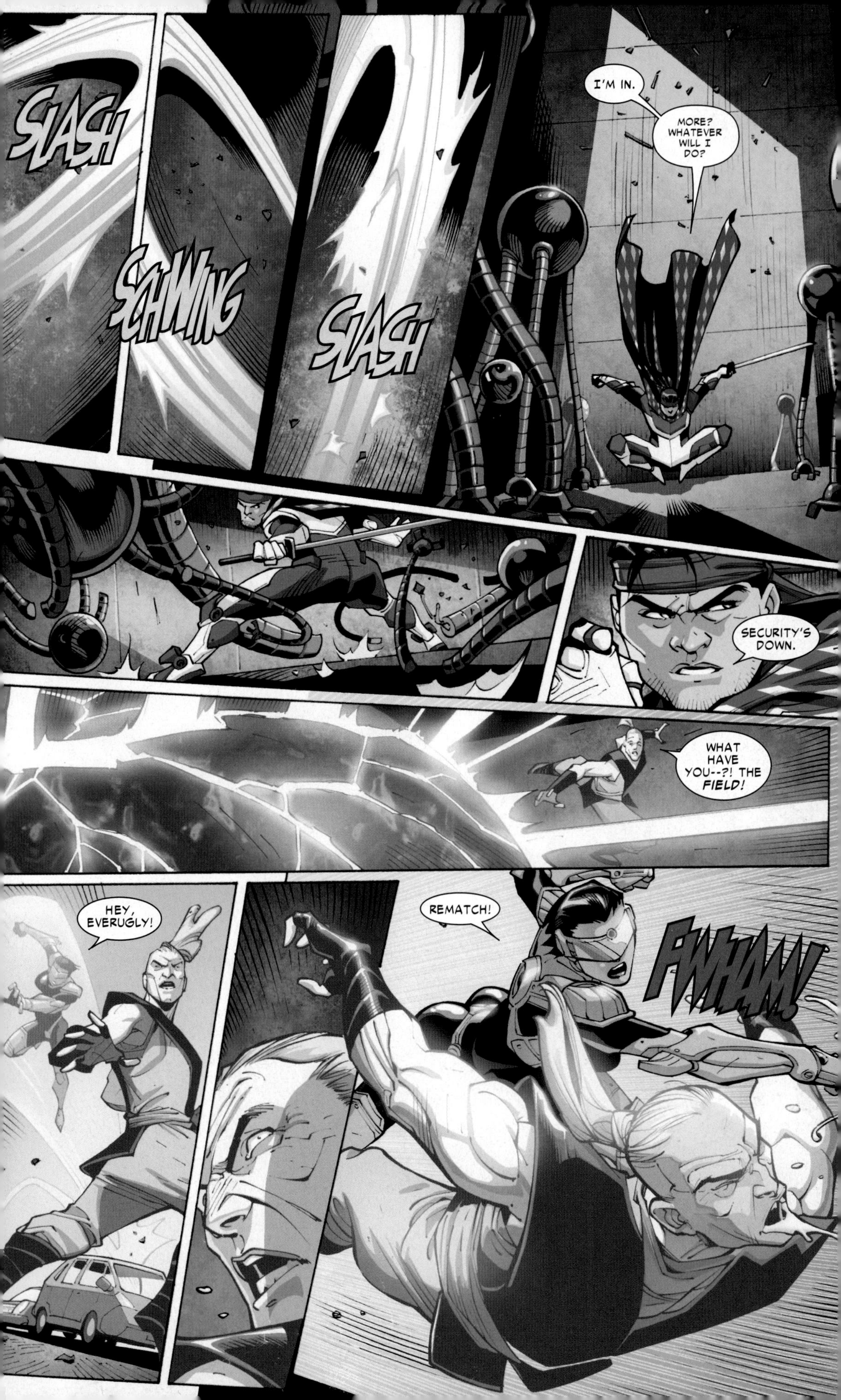
SLASH
SCHWING
SLASH
I'M IN.
MORE? WHATEVER WILL I DO?
SECURITY'S DOWN.
WHAT HAVE YOU--?! THE FIELD!
HEY, EVERUGLY!
REMATCH!
FWHAM!

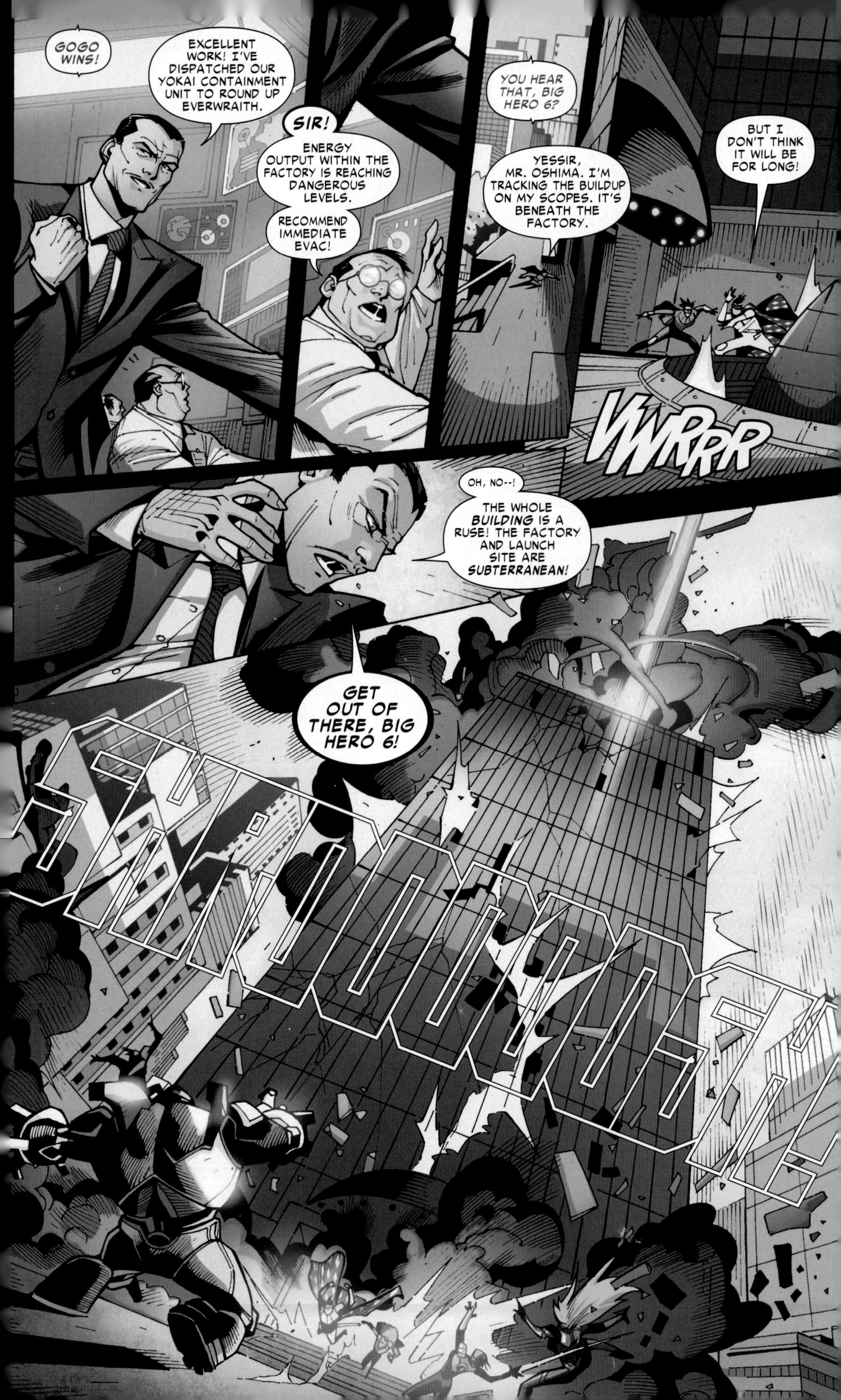
GOGO WINS!
EXCELLENT WORK! I'VE DISPATCHED OUR YOKAI CONTAINMENT UNIT TO ROUND UP EVERWRAITH.
SIR!
ENERGY OUTPUT WITHIN THE FACTORY IS REACHING DANGEROUS LEVELS.
RECOMMEND IMMEDIATE EVAC!
YOU HEAR THAT, BIG HERO 6?
YESSIR, MR. OSHIMA. I'M TRACKING THE BUILDUP ON MY SCOPES. IT'S BENEATH THE FACTORY.
BUT I DON'T THINK IT WILL BE FOR LONG!
VWRRR
OH, NO--!
THE WHOLE BUILDING IS A RUSE! THE FACTORY AND LAUNCH SITE ARE SUBTERRANEAN!
GET OUT OF THERE, BIG HERO 6!

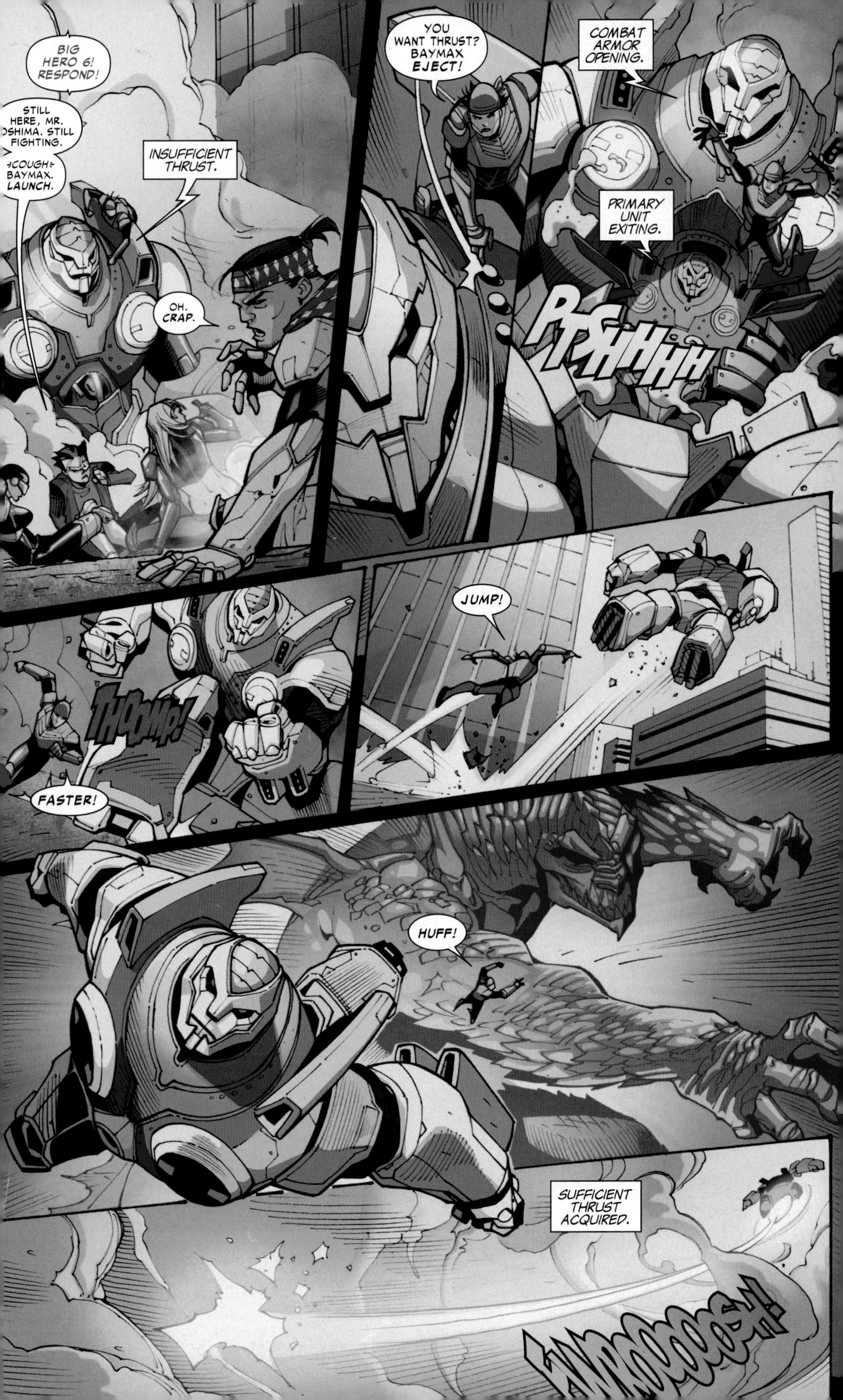
BIG HERO 6! RESPOND!
STILL HERE, MR. OSHIMA. STILL FIGHTING.
≠COUGH≠ BAYMAX. LAUNCH.
INSUFFICIENT THRUST.
OH. CRAP.
YOU WANT THRUST? BAYMAX EJECT!
COMBAT ARMOR OPENING.
PRIMARY UNIT EXITING.
PTSHHHH
THOOMP!
FASTER!
JUMP!
HUFF!
SUFFICIENT THRUST ACQUIRED.
WHOOOOOSH!

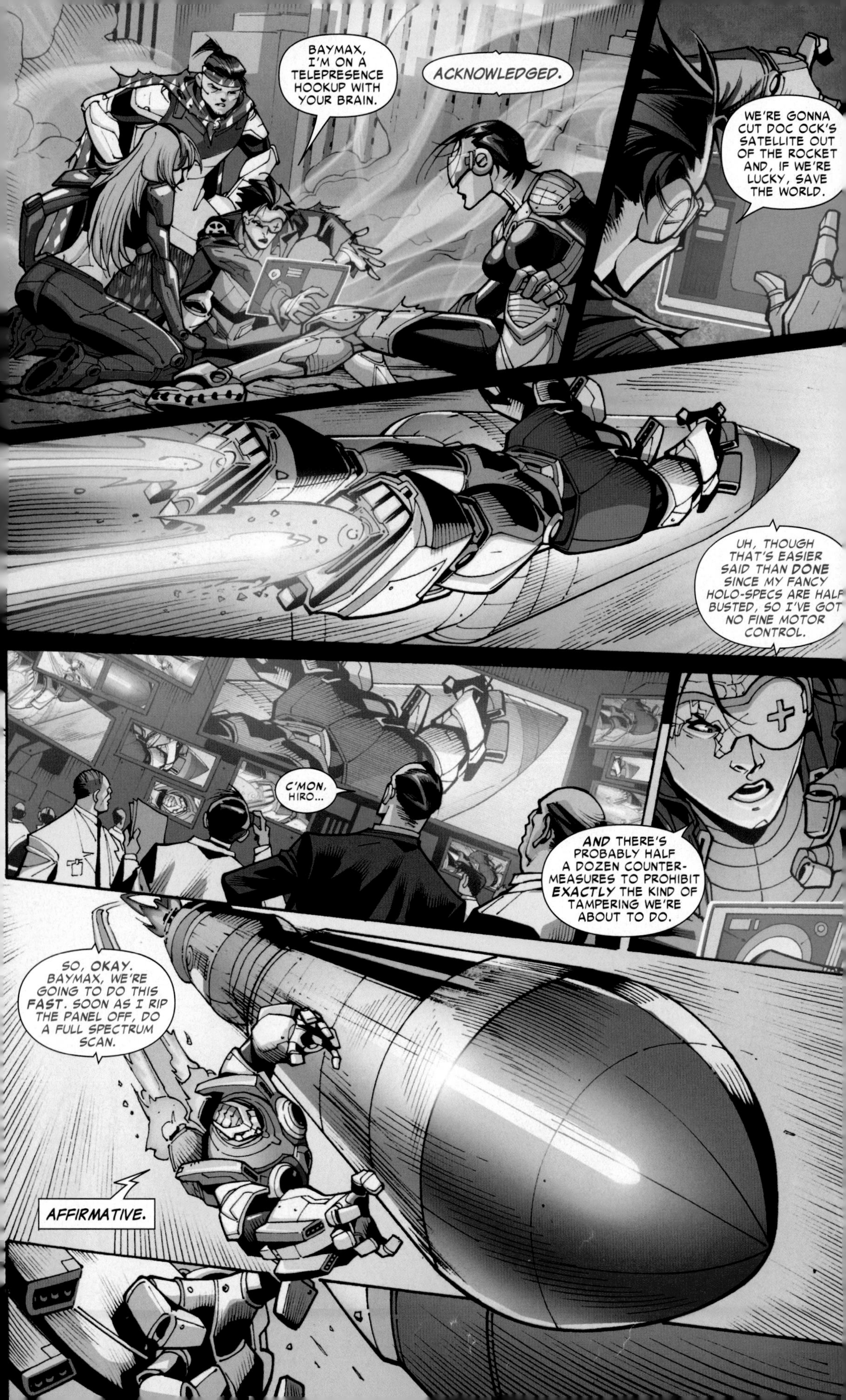
BAYMAX, I'M ON A TELEPRESENCE HOOKUP WITH YOUR BRAIN.
ACKNOWLEDGED.
WE'RE GONNA CUT DOC OCK'S SATELLITE OUT OF THE ROCKET AND, IF WE'RE LUCKY, SAVE THE WORLD.
UH, THOUGH THAT'S EASIER SAID THAN DONE SINCE MY FANCY HOLO-SPECS ARE HALF BUSTED, SO I'VE GOT NO FINE MOTOR CONTROL.
C'MON, HIRO...
AND THERE'S PROBABLY HALF A DOZEN COUNTER-MEASURES TO PROHIBIT EXACTLY THE KIND OF TAMPERING WE'RE ABOUT TO DO.
SO, OKAY. BAYMAX, WE'RE GOING TO DO THIS FAST. SOON AS I RIP THE PANEL OFF, DO A FULL SPECTRUM SCAN.
AFFIRMATIVE.

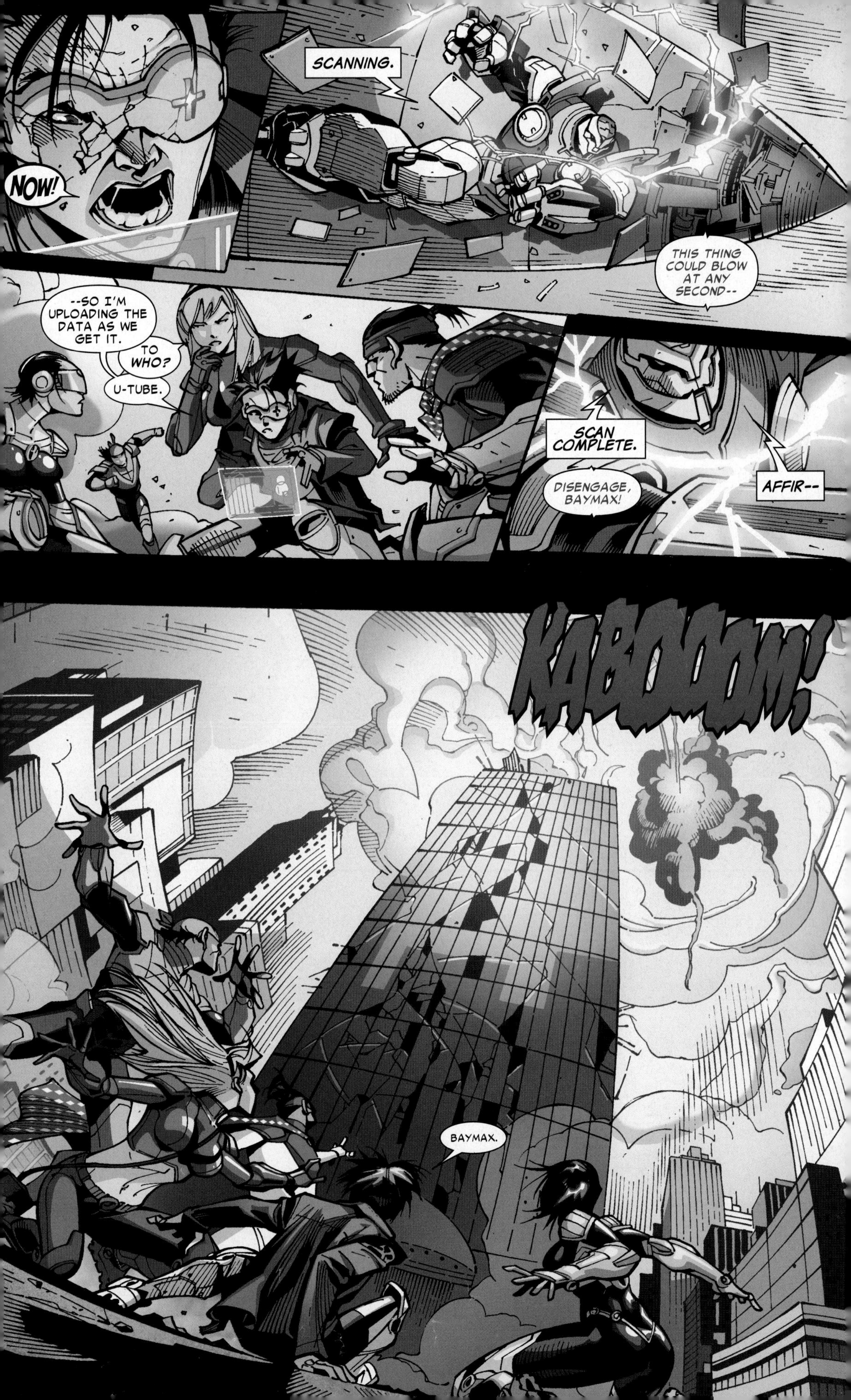
NOW!
SCANNING.
THIS THING COULD BLOW AT ANY SECOND--
--SO I'M UPLOADING THE DATA AS WE GET IT.
TO WHO?
U-TUBE.
SCAN COMPLETE.
DISENGAGE, BAYMAX!
AFFIR--
KABOOOM!
BAYMAX.

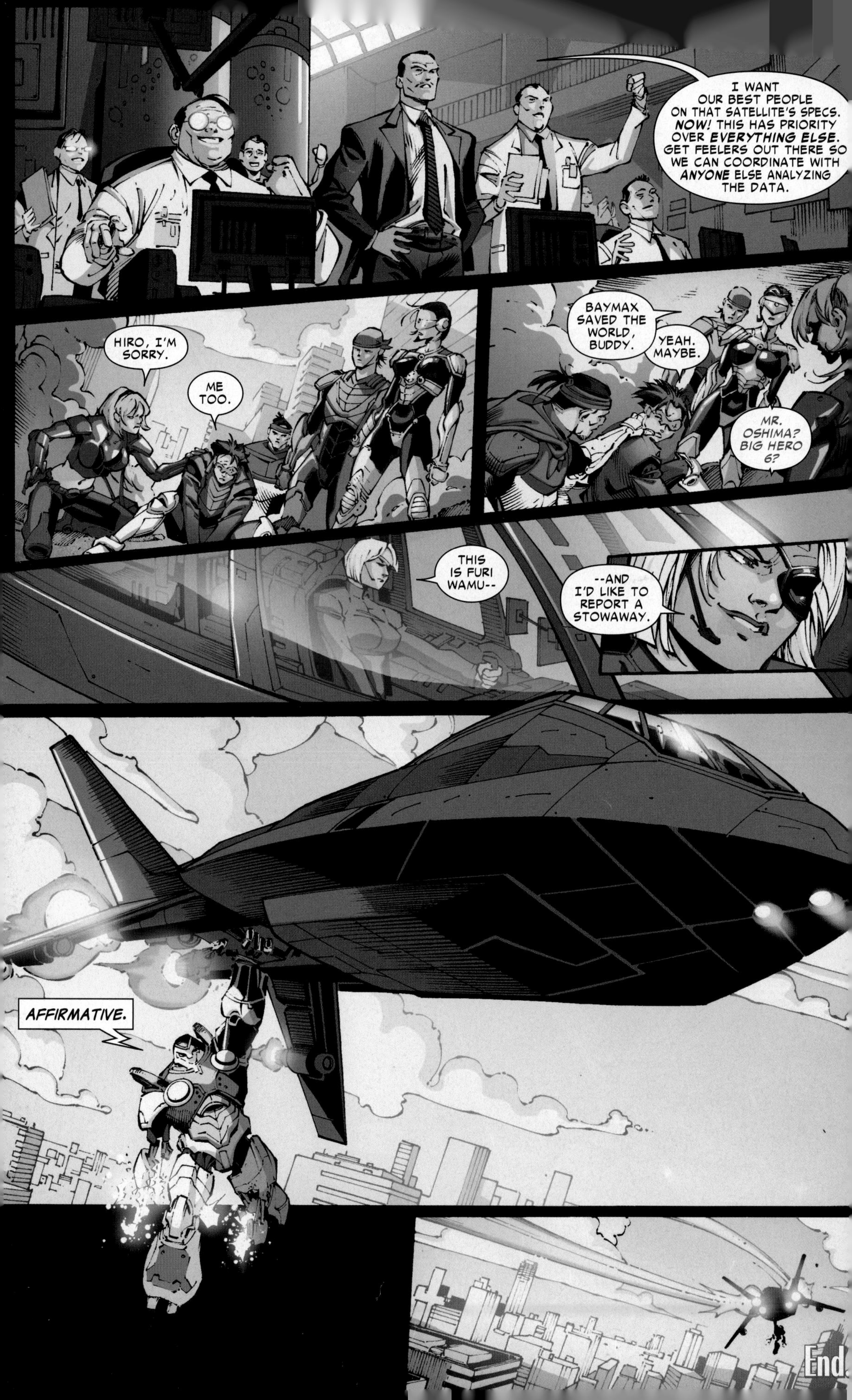

I WANT OUR BEST PEOPLE ON THAT SATELLITE'S SPECS. ***NOW!*** THIS HAS PRIORITY OVER ***EVERYTHING ELSE***. GET FEELERS OUT THERE SO WE CAN COORDINATE WITH ***ANYONE*** ELSE ANALYZING THE DATA.
HIRO, I'M SORRY.
ME TOO.
BAYMAX SAVED THE WORLD, BUDDY.
YEAH. MAYBE.
MR. OSHIMA? BIG HERO 6?
THIS IS FURI WAMU--
--AND I'D LIKE TO REPORT A STOWAWAY.
AFFIRMATIVE.
End.

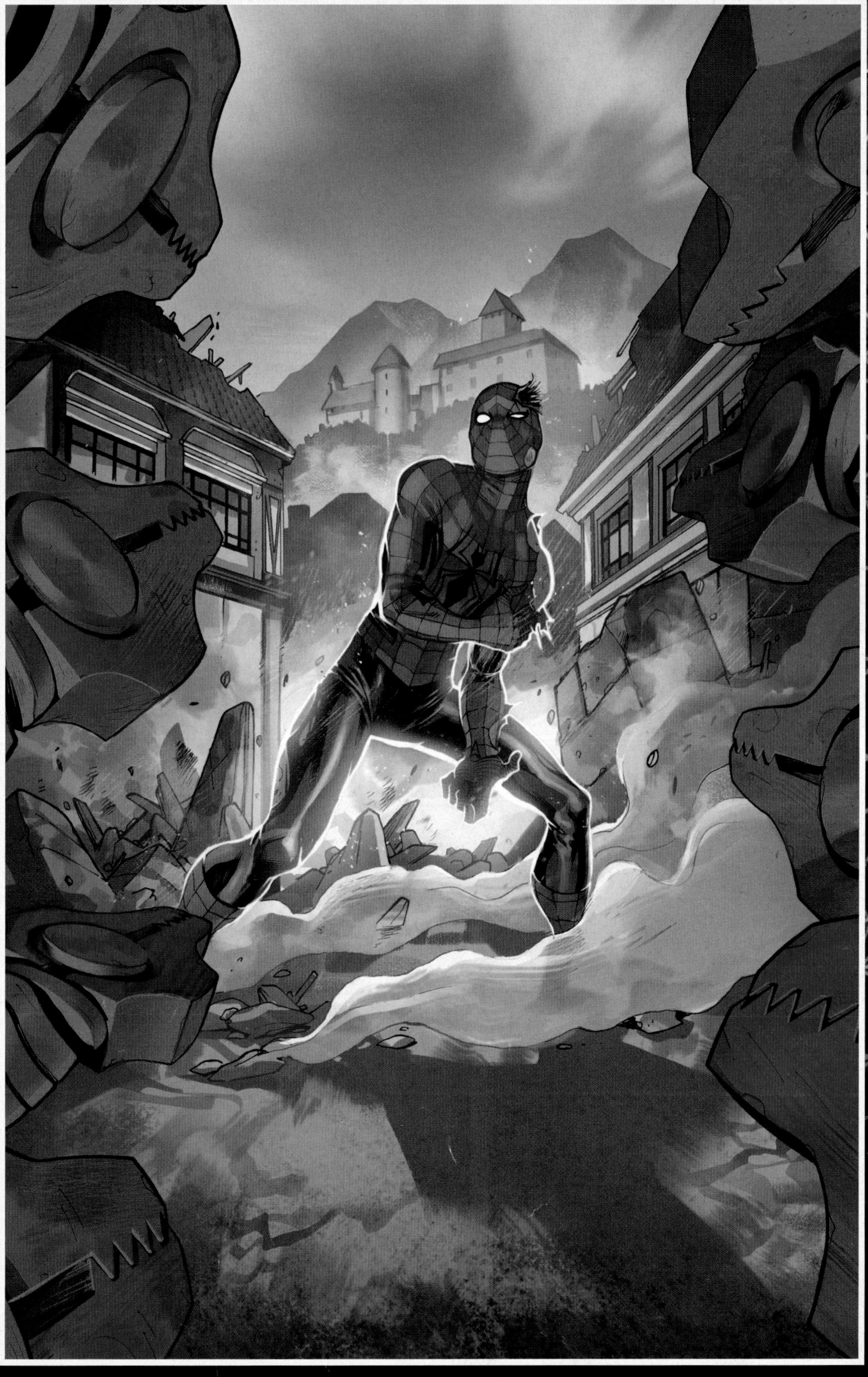

AMAZING SPIDER-MAN #686
COVER BY STEFANO CASELLI & LORENZO DE FELICI

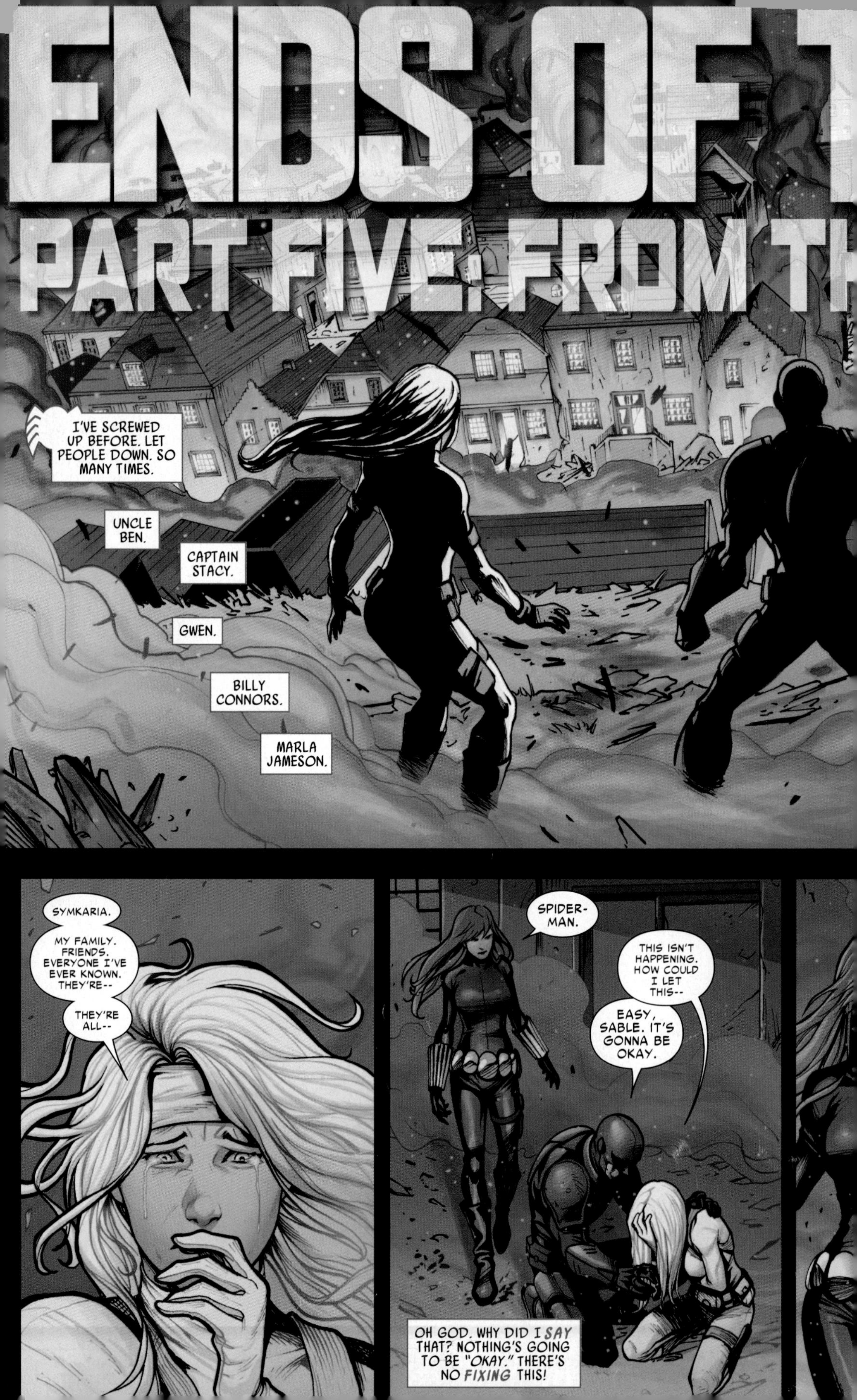
ENDS OF T
PART FIVE: FROM TH
I'VE SCREWED UP BEFORE. LET PEOPLE DOWN. SO MANY TIMES.
UNCLE BEN.
CAPTAIN STACY.
GWEN.
BILLY CONNORS.
MARLA JAMESON.
SYMKARIA.
MY FAMILY. FRIENDS. EVERYONE I'VE EVER KNOWN. THEY'RE--
THEY'RE ALL--
SPIDER-MAN.
THIS ISN'T HAPPENING. HOW COULD I LET THIS--
EASY, SABLE. IT'S GONNA BE OKAY.
OH GOD. WHY DID I SAY THAT? NOTHING'S GOING TO BE "OKAY." THERE'S NO FIXING THIS!

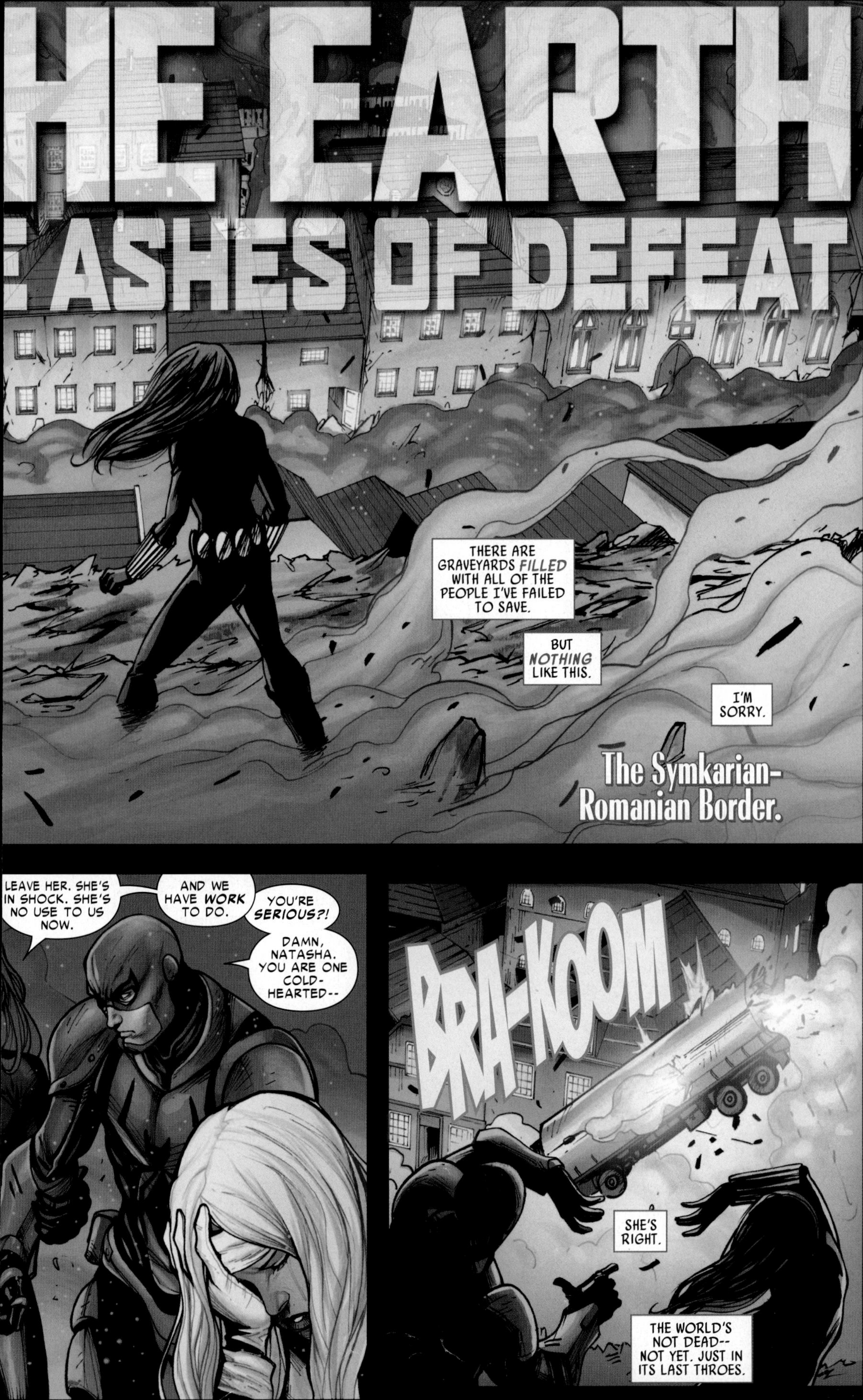

HE EARTH
E ASHES OF DEFEAT
THERE ARE GRAVEYARDS FILLED WITH ALL OF THE PEOPLE I'VE FAILED TO SAVE.
BUT NOTHING LIKE THIS.
I'M SORRY.
The Symkarian-Romanian Border.
LEAVE HER. SHE'S IN SHOCK. SHE'S NO USE TO US NOW.
AND WE HAVE WORK TO DO.
YOU'RE SERIOUS?!
DAMN, NATASHA. YOU ARE ONE COLD-HEARTED--
BRA-KOOM
SHE'S RIGHT.
THE WORLD'S NOT DEAD-- NOT YET. JUST IN ITS LAST THROES.

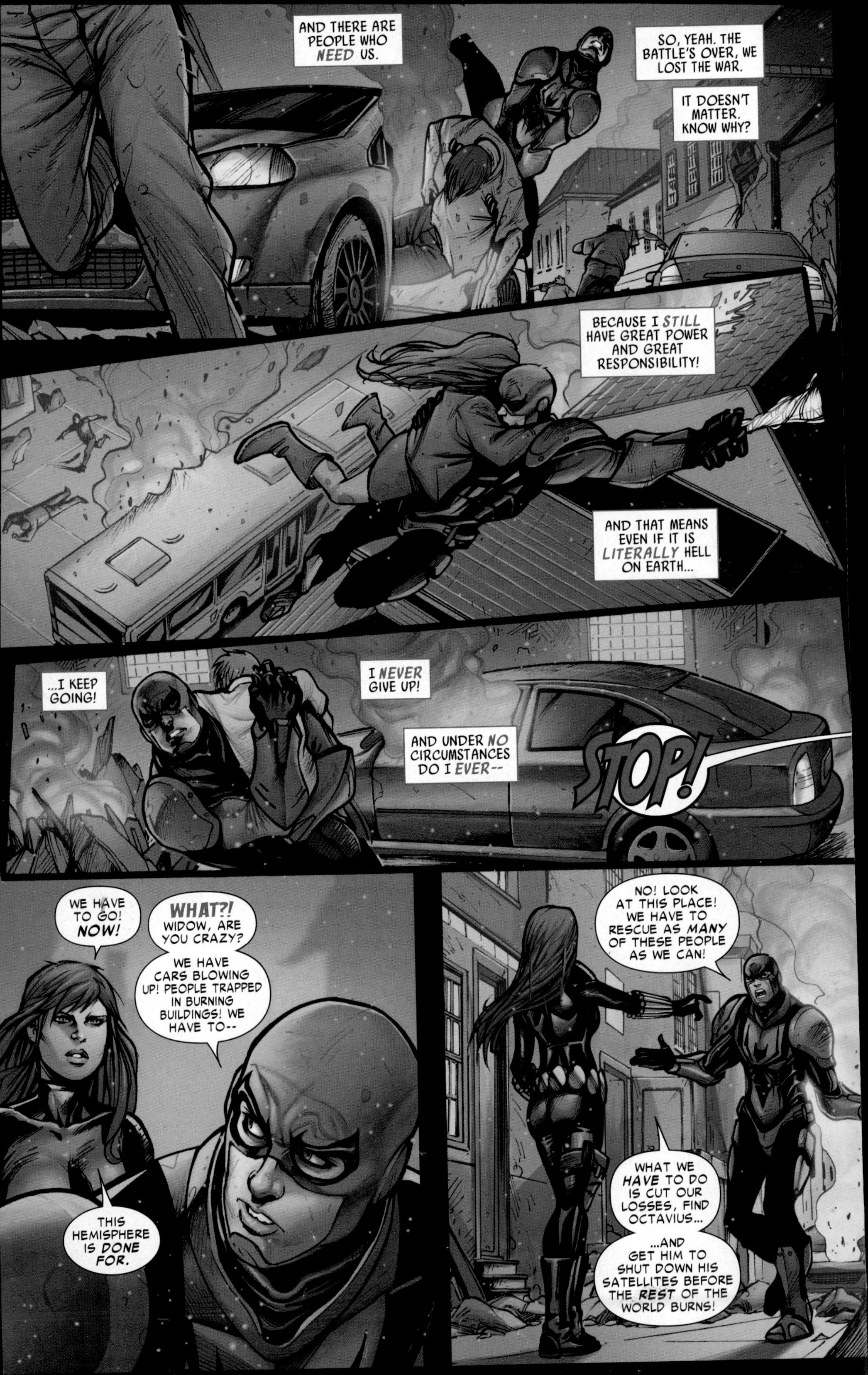
AND THERE ARE PEOPLE WHO NEED US.
SO, YEAH. THE BATTLE'S OVER, WE LOST THE WAR.
IT DOESN'T MATTER. KNOW WHY?
BECAUSE I STILL HAVE GREAT POWER AND GREAT RESPONSIBILITY!
AND THAT MEANS EVEN IF IT IS LITERALLY HELL ON EARTH...
...I KEEP GOING!
I NEVER GIVE UP!
AND UNDER NO CIRCUMSTANCES DO I EVER--
STOP!
WE HAVE TO GO! NOW!
WHAT?! WIDOW, ARE YOU CRAZY?
WE HAVE CARS BLOWING UP! PEOPLE TRAPPED IN BURNING BUILDINGS! WE HAVE TO--
THIS HEMISPHERE IS DONE FOR.
NO! LOOK AT THIS PLACE! WE HAVE TO RESCUE AS MANY OF THESE PEOPLE AS WE CAN!
WHAT WE HAVE TO DO IS CUT OUR LOSSES, FIND OCTAVIUS...
...AND GET HIM TO SHUT DOWN HIS SATELLITES BEFORE THE REST OF THE WORLD BURNS!

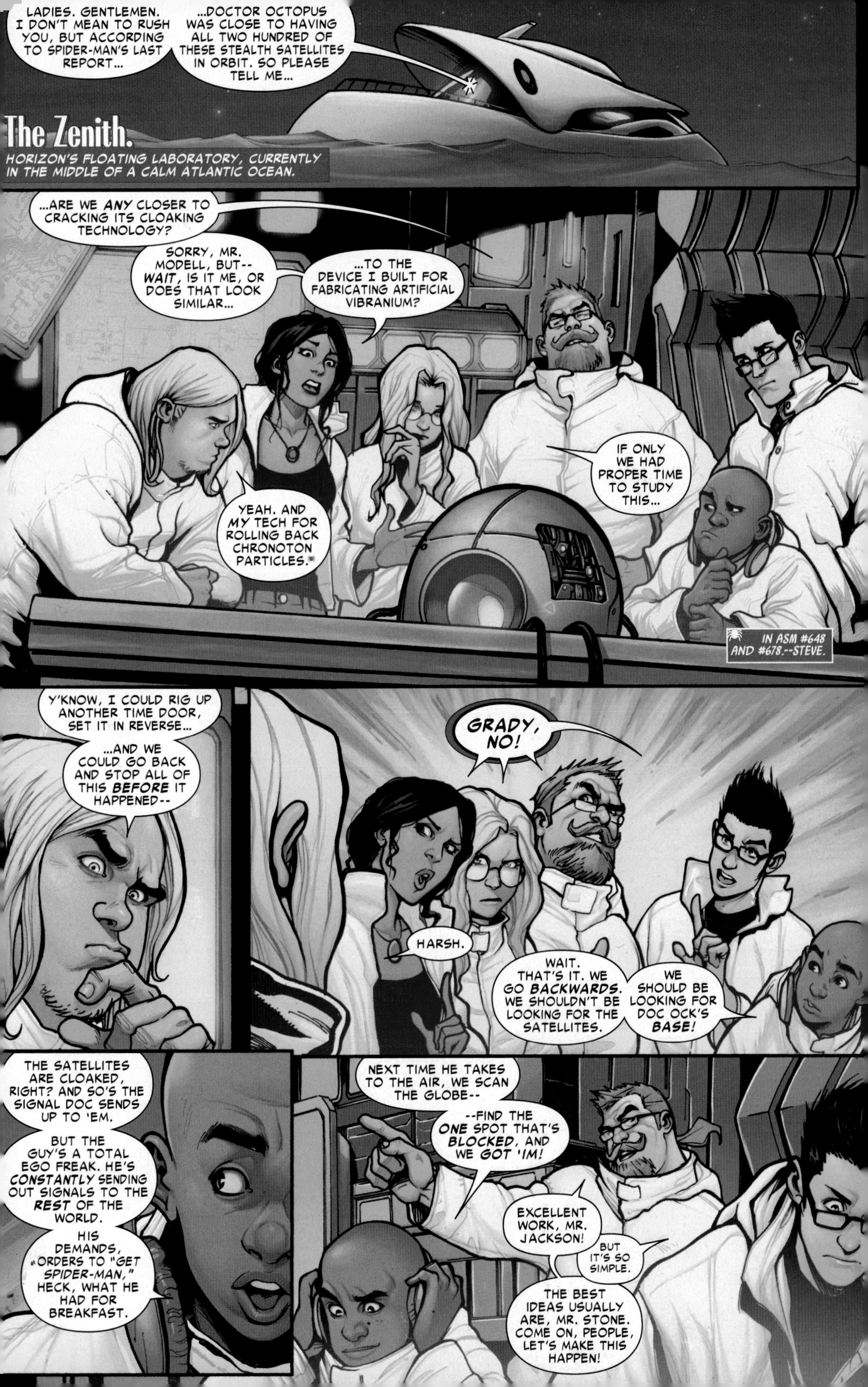
LADIES. GENTLEMEN. I DON'T MEAN TO RUSH YOU, BUT ACCORDING TO SPIDER-MAN'S LAST REPORT...
...DOCTOR OCTOPUS WAS CLOSE TO HAVING ALL TWO HUNDRED OF THESE STEALTH SATELLITES IN ORBIT. SO PLEASE TELL ME...
The Zenith.
HORIZON'S FLOATING LABORATORY, CURRENTLY IN THE MIDDLE OF A CALM ATLANTIC OCEAN.
...ARE WE ANY CLOSER TO CRACKING ITS CLOAKING TECHNOLOGY?
SORRY, MR. MODELL, BUT-- WAIT, IS IT ME, OR DOES THAT LOOK SIMILAR...
...TO THE DEVICE I BUILT FOR FABRICATING ARTIFICIAL VIBRANIUM?
YEAH. AND MY TECH FOR ROLLING BACK CHRONOTON PARTICLES.*
IF ONLY WE HAD PROPER TIME TO STUDY THIS...
*IN ASM #648 AND #678.--STEVE.
Y'KNOW, I COULD RIG UP ANOTHER TIME DOOR, SET IT IN REVERSE...
...AND WE COULD GO BACK AND STOP ALL OF THIS BEFORE IT HAPPENED--
GRADY, NO!
HARSH.
WAIT. THAT'S IT. WE GO BACKWARDS. WE SHOULDN'T BE LOOKING FOR THE SATELLITES.
WE SHOULD BE LOOKING FOR DOC OCK'S BASE!
THE SATELLITES ARE CLOAKED, RIGHT? AND SO'S THE SIGNAL DOC SENDS UP TO 'EM.
BUT THE GUY'S A TOTAL EGO FREAK. HE'S CONSTANTLY SENDING OUT SIGNALS TO THE REST OF THE WORLD.
HIS DEMANDS, "ORDERS TO "GET SPIDER-MAN," HECK, WHAT HE HAD FOR BREAKFAST.
NEXT TIME HE TAKES TO THE AIR, WE SCAN THE GLOBE--
--FIND THE ONE SPOT THAT'S BLOCKED, AND WE GOT 'IM!
EXCELLENT WORK, MR. JACKSON!
BUT IT'S SO SIMPLE.
THE BEST IDEAS USUALLY ARE, MR. STONE. COME ON, PEOPLE, LET'S MAKE THIS HAPPEN!

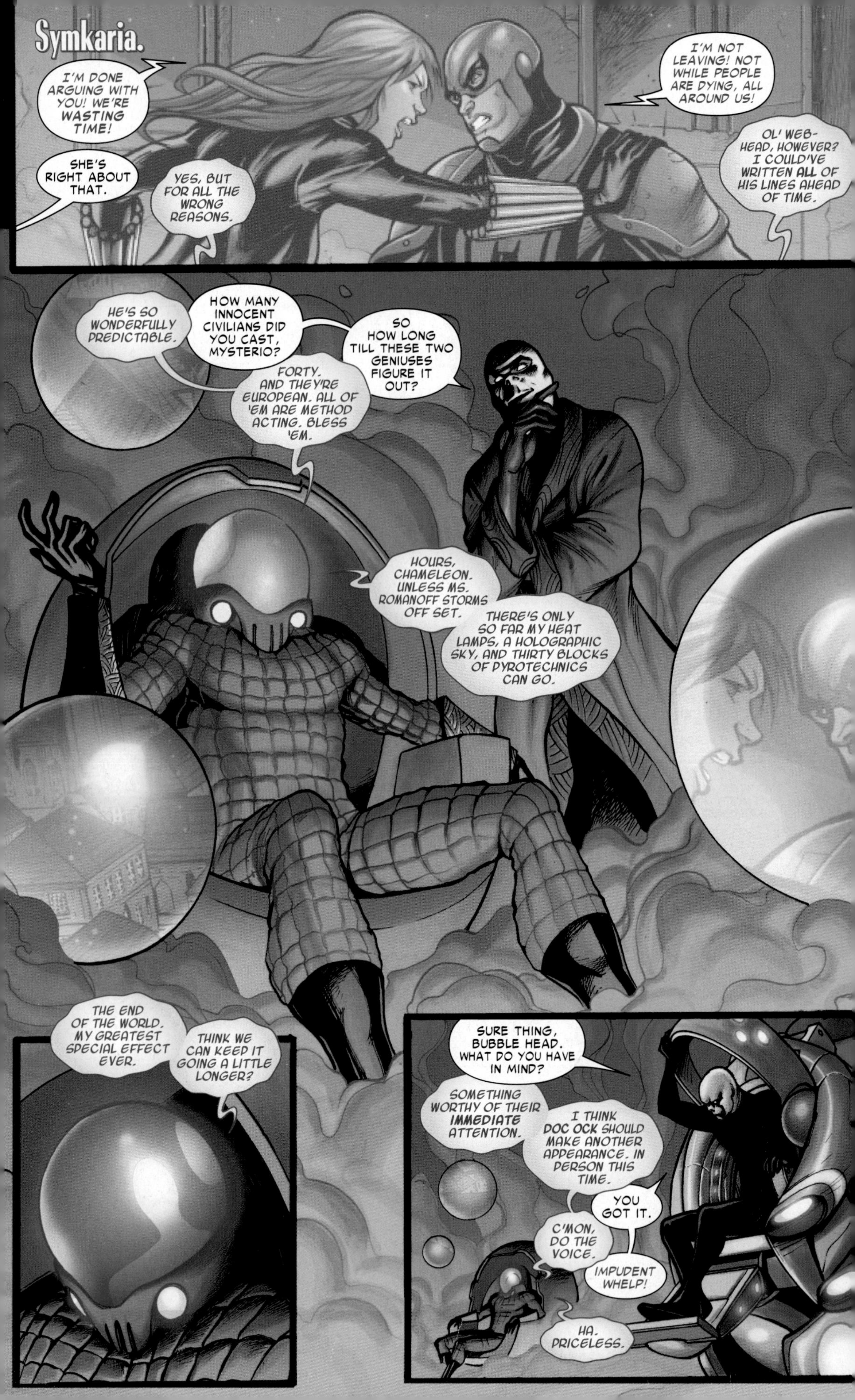
Symkaria.
I'M DONE ARGUING WITH YOU! WE'RE WASTING TIME!
I'M NOT LEAVING! NOT WHILE PEOPLE ARE DYING, ALL AROUND US!
SHE'S RIGHT ABOUT THAT.
YES, BUT FOR ALL THE WRONG REASONS.
OL' WEB-HEAD, HOWEVER? I COULD'VE WRITTEN ALL OF HIS LINES AHEAD OF TIME.
HE'S SO WONDERFULLY PREDICTABLE.
HOW MANY INNOCENT CIVILIANS DID YOU CAST, MYSTERIO?
FORTY. AND THEY'RE EUROPEAN. ALL OF 'EM ARE METHOD ACTING. BLESS 'EM.
SO HOW LONG TILL THESE TWO GENIUSES FIGURE IT OUT?
HOURS, CHAMELEON. UNLESS MS. ROMANOFF STORMS OFF SET.
THERE'S ONLY SO FAR MY HEAT LAMPS, A HOLOGRAPHIC SKY, AND THIRTY BLOCKS OF PYROTECHNICS CAN GO.
THE END OF THE WORLD. MY GREATEST SPECIAL EFFECT EVER.
THINK WE CAN KEEP IT GOING A LITTLE LONGER?
SURE THING, BUBBLE HEAD. WHAT DO YOU HAVE IN MIND?
SOMETHING WORTHY OF THEIR IMMEDIATE ATTENTION.
I THINK DOC OCK SHOULD MAKE ANOTHER APPEARANCE. IN PERSON THIS TIME.
YOU GOT IT.
C'MON, DO THE VOICE.
IMPUDENT WHELP!
HA. PRICELESS.

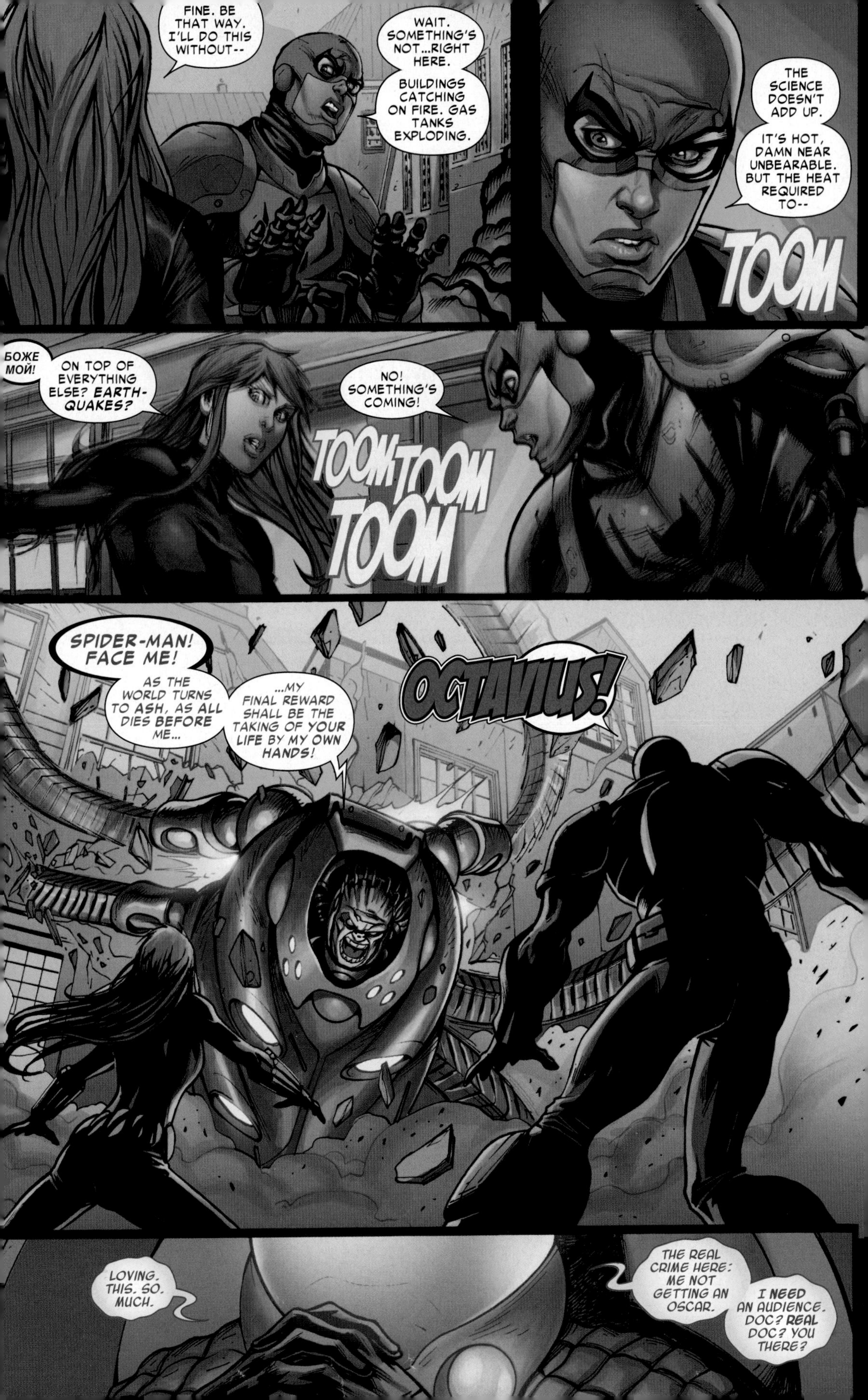
FINE. BE THAT WAY. I'LL DO THIS WITHOUT--
WAIT. SOMETHING'S NOT...RIGHT HERE.
BUILDINGS CATCHING ON FIRE. GAS TANKS EXPLODING.
THE SCIENCE DOESN'T ADD UP.
IT'S HOT, DAMN NEAR UNBEARABLE. BUT THE HEAT REQUIRED TO--
TOOM
БОЖЕ МОЙ!
ON TOP OF EVERYTHING ELSE? EARTH-QUAKES?
NO! SOMETHING'S COMING!
TOOM TOOM
TOOM
SPIDER-MAN! FACE ME!
AS THE WORLD TURNS TO ASH, AS ALL DIES BEFORE ME...
...MY FINAL REWARD SHALL BE THE TAKING OF YOUR LIFE BY MY OWN HANDS!
OCTAVIUS!
LOVING. THIS. SO. MUCH.
THE REAL CRIME HERE: ME NOT GETTING AN OSCAR.
I NEED AN AUDIENCE. DOC? REAL DOC? YOU THERE?

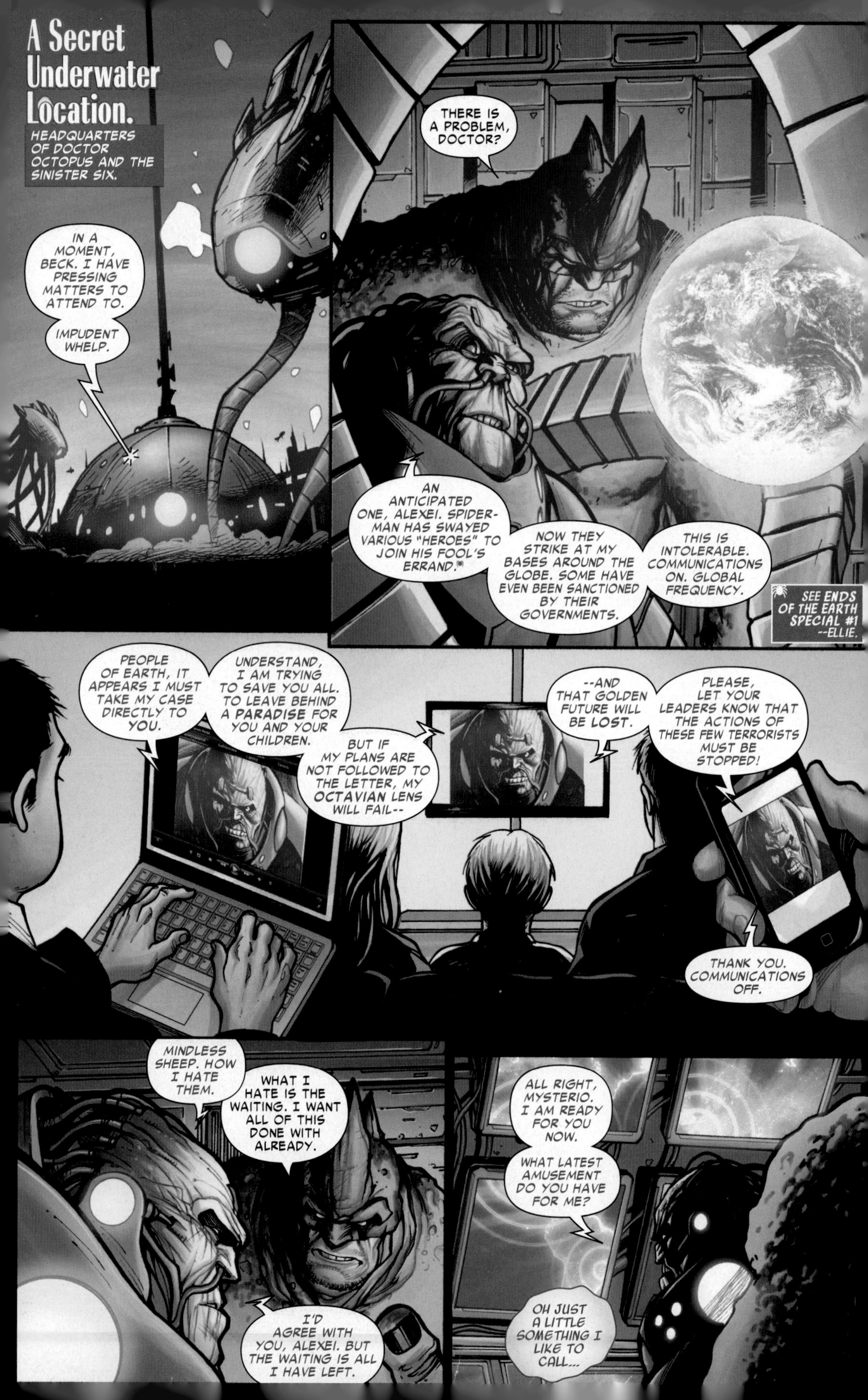
A Secret Underwater Location.
HEADQUARTERS OF DOCTOR OCTOPUS AND THE SINISTER SIX.
IN A MOMENT, BECK. I HAVE PRESSING MATTERS TO ATTEND TO.
IMPUDENT WHELP.
THERE IS A PROBLEM, DOCTOR?
AN ANTICIPATED ONE, ALEXEI. SPIDER-MAN HAS SWAYED VARIOUS "HEROES" TO JOIN HIS FOOL'S ERRAND.*
NOW THEY STRIKE AT MY BASES AROUND THE GLOBE. SOME HAVE EVEN BEEN SANCTIONED BY THEIR GOVERNMENTS.
THIS IS INTOLERABLE. COMMUNICATIONS ON. GLOBAL FREQUENCY.
*SEE ENDS OF THE EARTH SPECIAL #1 --ELLIE.
PEOPLE OF EARTH, IT APPEARS I MUST TAKE MY CASE DIRECTLY TO YOU.
UNDERSTAND, I AM TRYING TO SAVE YOU ALL. TO LEAVE BEHIND A PARADISE FOR YOU AND YOUR CHILDREN.
BUT IF MY PLANS ARE NOT FOLLOWED TO THE LETTER, MY OCTAVIAN LENS WILL FAIL--
--AND THAT GOLDEN FUTURE WILL BE LOST.
PLEASE, LET YOUR LEADERS KNOW THAT THE ACTIONS OF THESE FEW TERRORISTS MUST BE STOPPED!
THANK YOU. COMMUNICATIONS OFF.
MINDLESS SHEEP. HOW I HATE THEM.
WHAT I HATE IS THE WAITING. I WANT ALL OF THIS DONE WITH ALREADY.
I'D AGREE WITH YOU, ALEXEI. BUT THE WAITING IS ALL I HAVE LEFT.
ALL RIGHT, MYSTERIO. I AM READY FOR YOU NOW.
WHAT LATEST AMUSEMENT DO YOU HAVE FOR ME?
OH JUST A LITTLE SOMETHING I LIKE TO CALL...

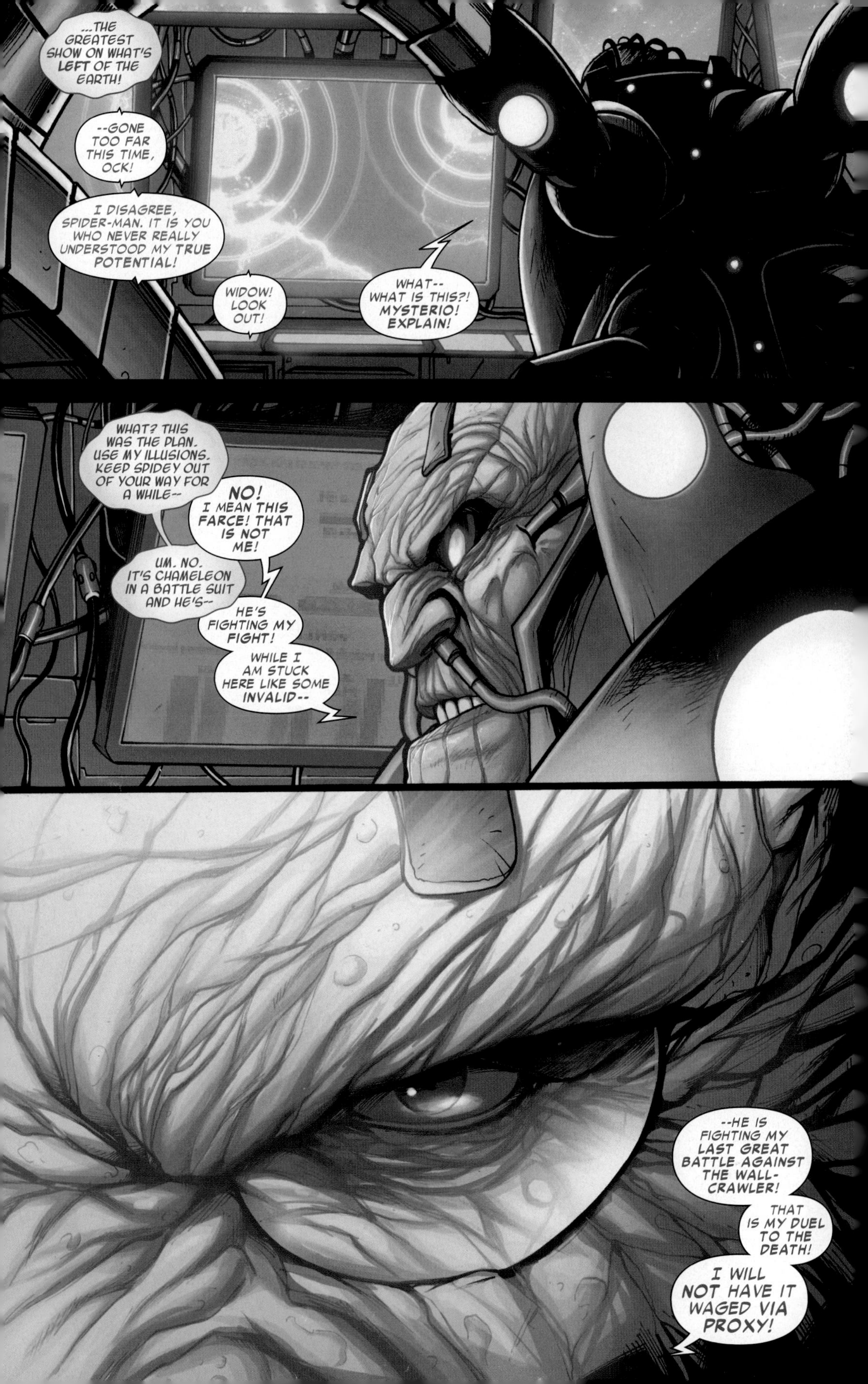
...THE GREATEST SHOW ON WHAT'S LEFT OF THE EARTH!
--GONE TOO FAR THIS TIME, OCK!
I DISAGREE, SPIDER-MAN. IT IS YOU WHO NEVER REALLY UNDERSTOOD MY TRUE POTENTIAL!
WIDOW! LOOK OUT!
WHAT-- WHAT IS THIS?! MYSTERIO! EXPLAIN!
WHAT? THIS WAS THE PLAN. USE MY ILLUSIONS. KEEP SPIDEY OUT OF YOUR WAY FOR A WHILE--
NO! I MEAN THIS FARCE! THAT IS NOT ME!
UM. NO. IT'S CHAMELEON IN A BATTLE SUIT AND HE'S--
HE'S FIGHTING MY FIGHT!
WHILE I AM STUCK HERE LIKE SOME INVALID--
--HE IS FIGHTING MY LAST GREAT BATTLE AGAINST THE WALL-CRAWLER!
THAT IS MY DUEL TO THE DEATH!
I WILL NOT HAVE IT WAGED VIA PROXY!

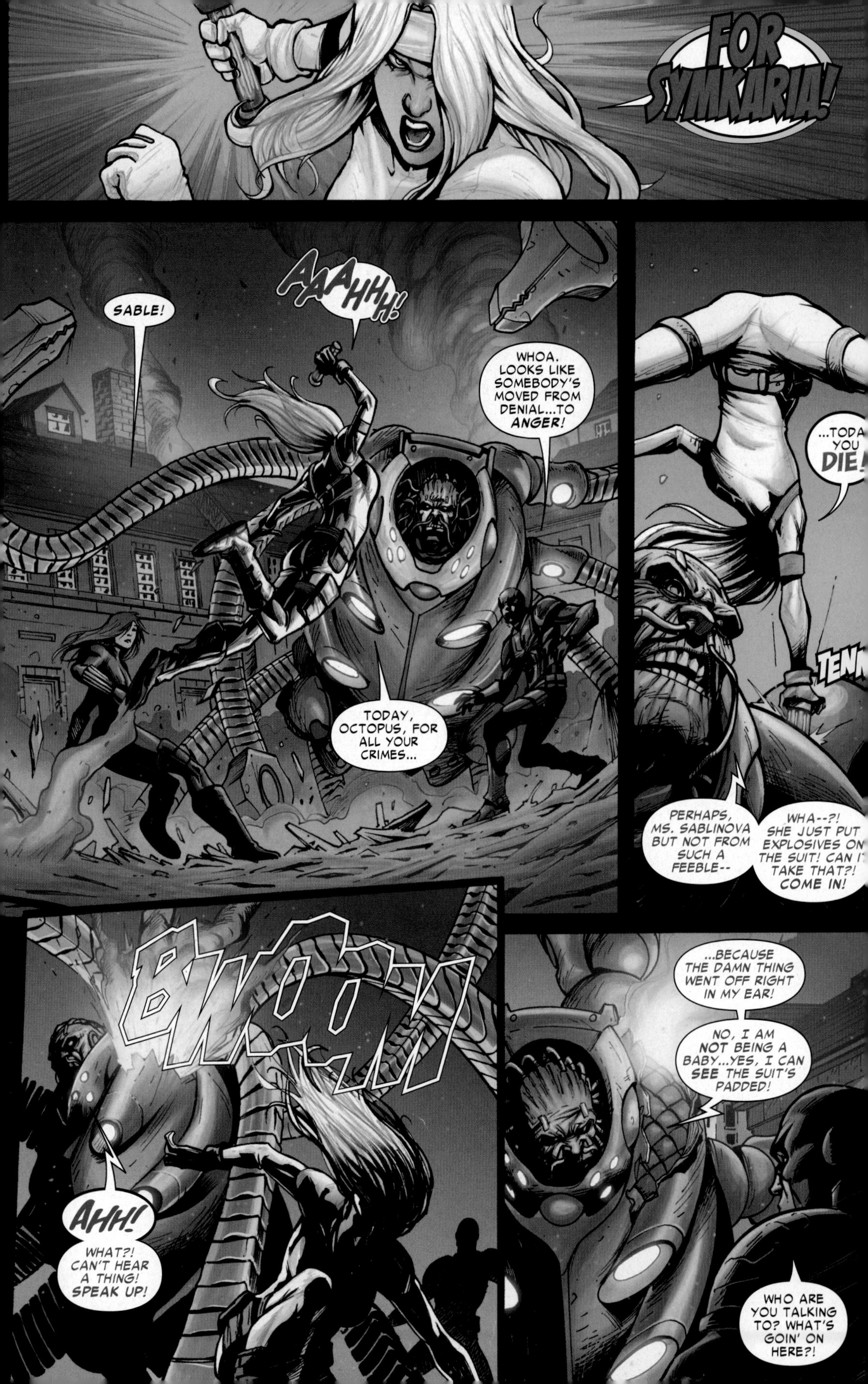
FOR SYMKARIA!
SABLE!
AAAHHH!
WHOA. LOOKS LIKE SOMEBODY'S MOVED FROM DENIAL...TO ANGER!
TODAY, OCTOPUS, FOR ALL YOUR CRIMES...
...TODA YOU DIE!
TENN
PERHAPS, MS. SABLINOVA BUT NOT FROM SUCH A FEEBLE--
WHA--?! SHE JUST PUT EXPLOSIVES ON THE SUIT! CAN I TAKE THAT?! COME IN!
BWOOM
AHH!
WHAT?! CAN'T HEAR A THING! SPEAK UP!
...BECAUSE THE DAMN THING WENT OFF RIGHT IN MY EAR!
NO, I AM NOT BEING A BABY...YES, I CAN SEE THE SUIT'S PADDED!
WHO ARE YOU TALKING TO? WHAT'S GOIN' ON HERE?!

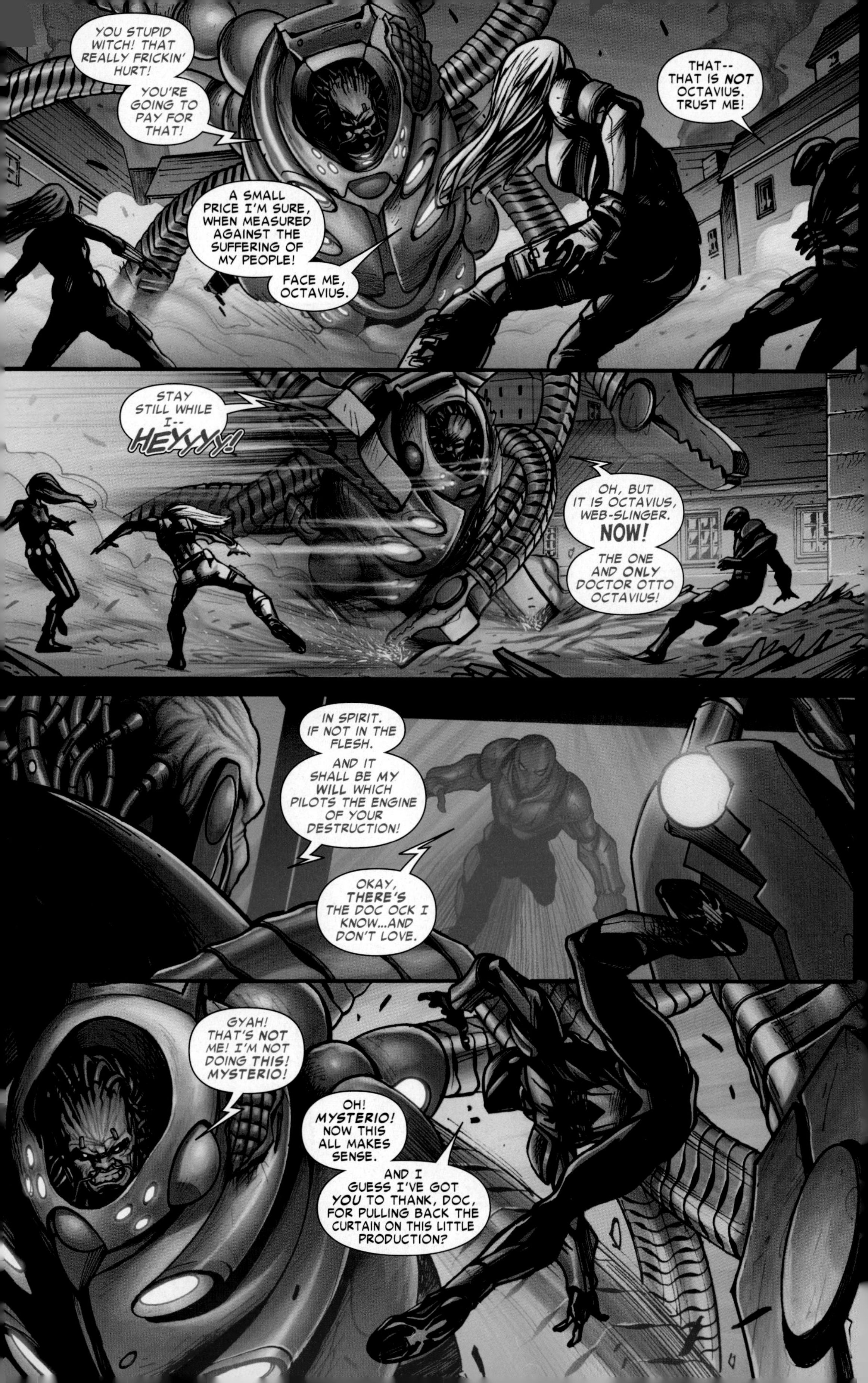
YOU STUPID WITCH! THAT REALLY FRICKIN' HURT!
YOU'RE GOING TO PAY FOR THAT!
THAT-- THAT IS NOT OCTAVIUS. TRUST ME!
A SMALL PRICE I'M SURE, WHEN MEASURED AGAINST THE SUFFERING OF MY PEOPLE!
FACE ME, OCTAVIUS.
STAY STILL WHILE I--
HEYYYY!
OH, BUT IT IS OCTAVIUS, WEB-SLINGER. NOW!
THE ONE AND ONLY DOCTOR OTTO OCTAVIUS!
IN SPIRIT. IF NOT IN THE FLESH.
AND IT SHALL BE MY WILL WHICH PILOTS THE ENGINE OF YOUR DESTRUCTION!
OKAY, THERE'S THE DOC OCK I KNOW...AND DON'T LOVE.
GYAH! THAT'S NOT ME! I'M NOT DOING THIS! MYSTERIO!
OH! MYSTERIO! NOW THIS ALL MAKES SENSE.
AND I GUESS I'VE GOT YOU TO THANK, DOC, FOR PULLING BACK THE CURTAIN ON THIS LITTLE PRODUCTION?

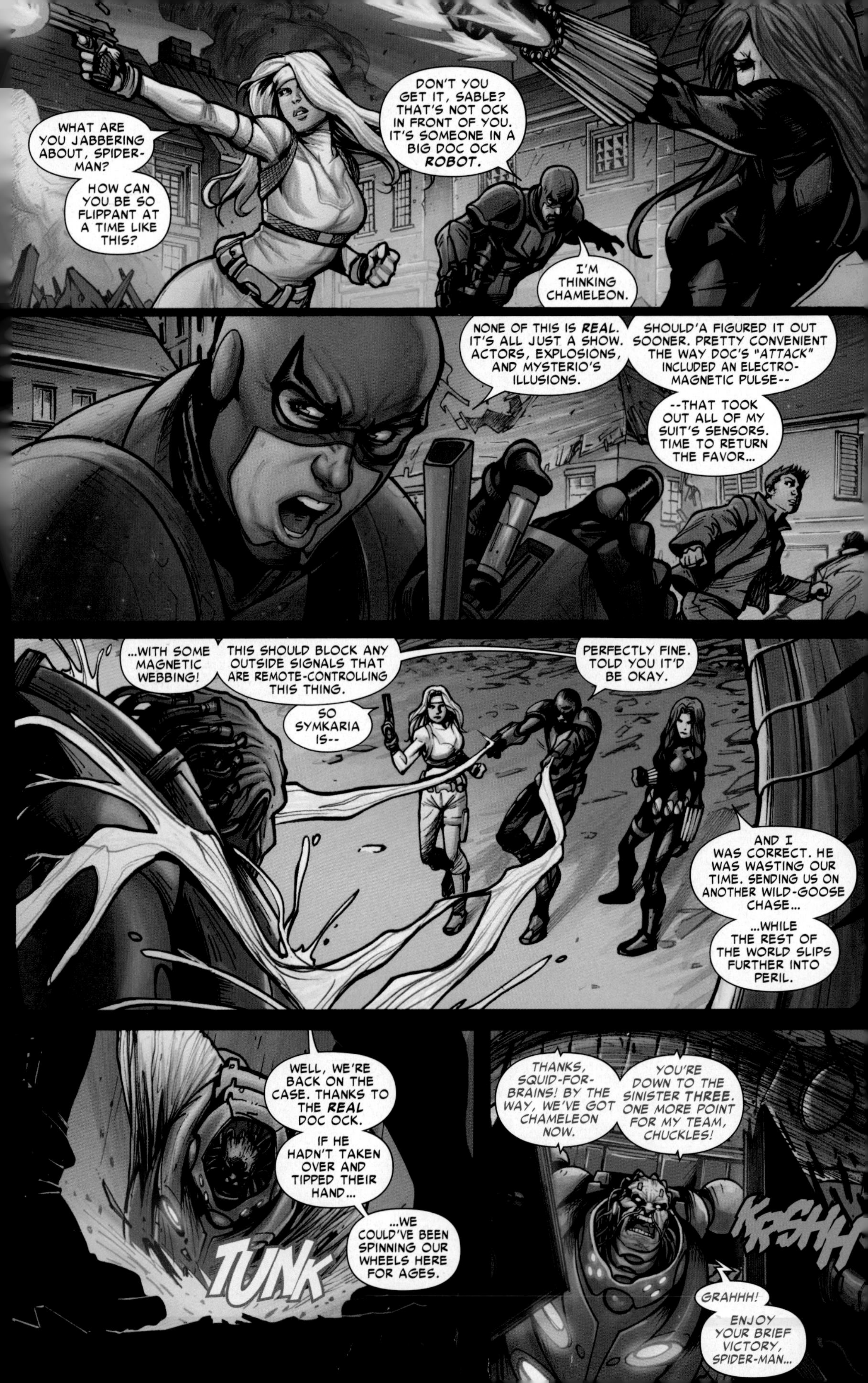
WHAT ARE YOU JABBERING ABOUT, SPIDER-MAN?
HOW CAN YOU BE SO FLIPPANT AT A TIME LIKE THIS?
DON'T YOU GET IT, SABLE? THAT'S NOT OCK IN FRONT OF YOU. IT'S SOMEONE IN A BIG DOC OCK ROBOT.
I'M THINKING CHAMELEON.
NONE OF THIS IS REAL. IT'S ALL JUST A SHOW. ACTORS, EXPLOSIONS, AND MYSTERIO'S ILLUSIONS.
SHOULD'A FIGURED IT OUT SOONER. PRETTY CONVENIENT THE WAY DOC'S "ATTACK" INCLUDED AN ELECTRO-MAGNETIC PULSE--
--THAT TOOK OUT ALL OF MY SUIT'S SENSORS. TIME TO RETURN THE FAVOR...
...WITH SOME MAGNETIC WEBBING!
THIS SHOULD BLOCK ANY OUTSIDE SIGNALS THAT ARE REMOTE-CONTROLLING THIS THING.
SO SYMKARIA IS--
PERFECTLY FINE. TOLD YOU IT'D BE OKAY.
AND I WAS CORRECT. HE WAS WASTING OUR TIME. SENDING US ON ANOTHER WILD-GOOSE CHASE...
...WHILE THE REST OF THE WORLD SLIPS FURTHER INTO PERIL.
WELL, WE'RE BACK ON THE CASE. THANKS TO THE REAL DOC OCK.
IF HE HADN'T TAKEN OVER AND TIPPED THEIR HAND...
...WE COULD'VE BEEN SPINNING OUR WHEELS HERE FOR AGES.
TUNK
THANKS, SQUID-FOR-BRAINS! BY THE WAY, WE'VE GOT CHAMELEON NOW.
YOU'RE DOWN TO THE SINISTER THREE. ONE MORE POINT FOR MY TEAM, CHUCKLES!
KRSHH
GRAHHH!
ENJOY YOUR BRIEF VICTORY, SPIDER-MAN...

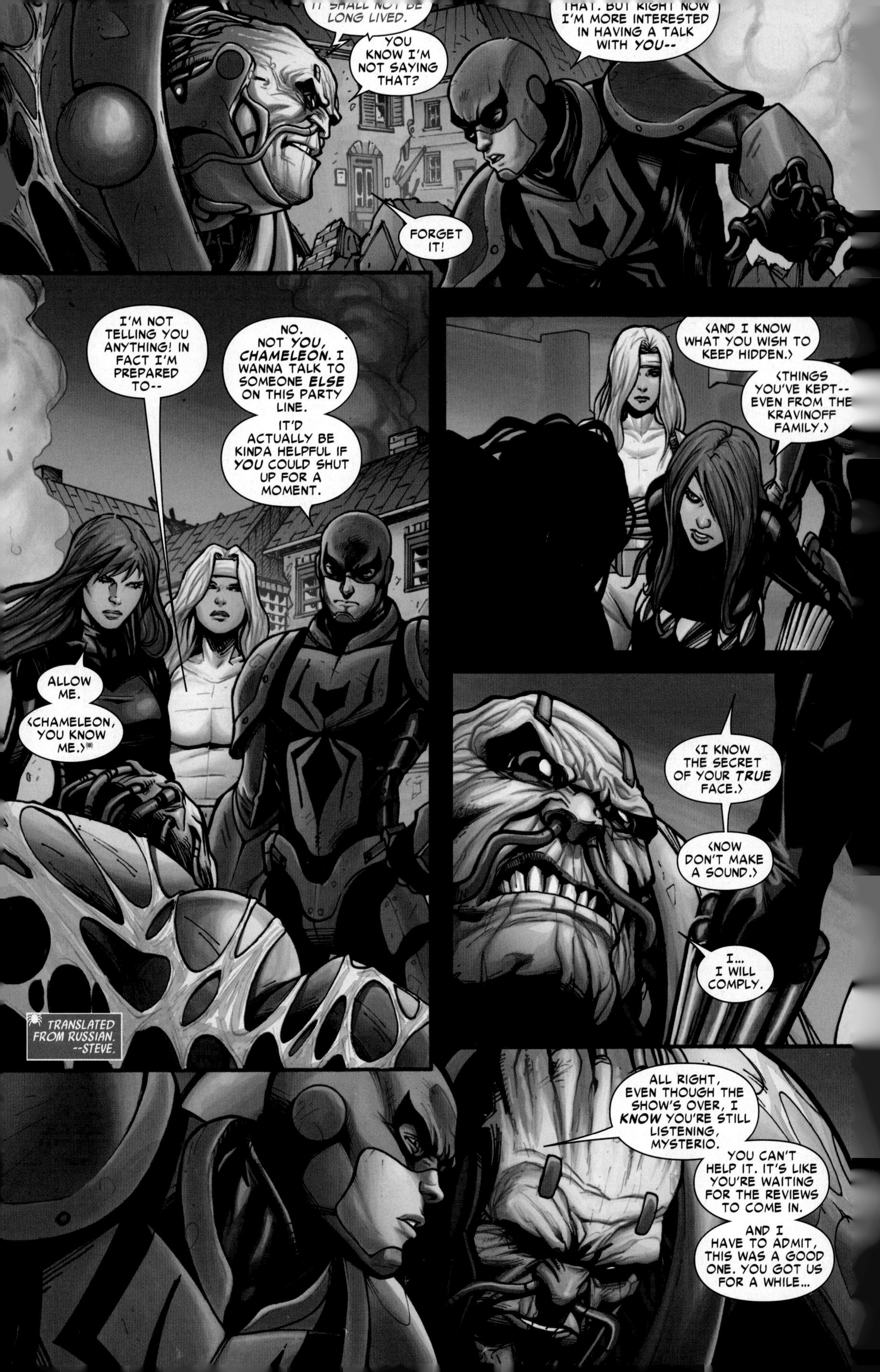
IT SHALL NOT BE LONG LIVED.
YOU KNOW I'M NOT SAYING THAT?
THAT. BUT RIGHT NOW I'M MORE INTERESTED IN HAVING A TALK WITH YOU--
FORGET IT!
I'M NOT TELLING YOU ANYTHING! IN FACT I'M PREPARED TO--
NO. NOT YOU, CHAMELEON. I WANNA TALK TO SOMEONE ELSE ON THIS PARTY LINE.
IT'D ACTUALLY BE KINDA HELPFUL IF YOU COULD SHUT UP FOR A MOMENT.
ALLOW ME.
‹CHAMELEON, YOU KNOW ME.›*
*TRANSLATED FROM RUSSIAN. --STEVE.
‹AND I KNOW WHAT YOU WISH TO KEEP HIDDEN.›
‹THINGS YOU'VE KEPT-- EVEN FROM THE KRAVINOFF FAMILY.›
‹I KNOW THE SECRET OF YOUR TRUE FACE.›
‹NOW DON'T MAKE A SOUND.›
I... I WILL COMPLY.
ALL RIGHT, EVEN THOUGH THE SHOW'S OVER, I KNOW YOU'RE STILL LISTENING, MYSTERIO.
YOU CAN'T HELP IT. IT'S LIKE YOU'RE WAITING FOR THE REVIEWS TO COME IN.
AND I HAVE TO ADMIT, THIS WAS A GOOD ONE. YOU GOT US FOR A WHILE...

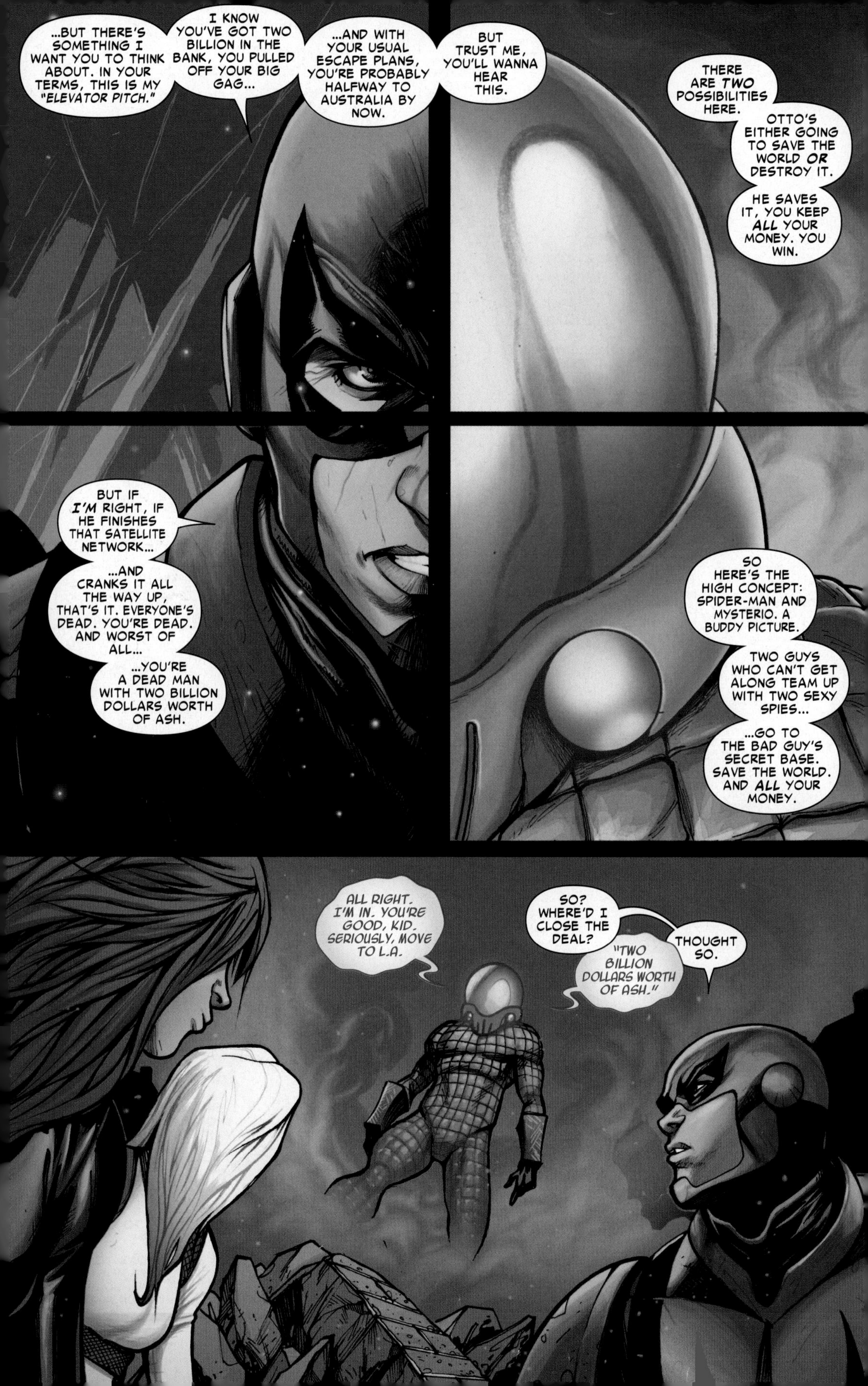

...BUT THERE'S SOMETHING I WANT YOU TO THINK ABOUT. IN YOUR TERMS, THIS IS MY "ELEVATOR PITCH."
I KNOW YOU'VE GOT TWO BILLION IN THE BANK, YOU PULLED OFF YOUR BIG GAG...
...AND WITH YOUR USUAL ESCAPE PLANS, YOU'RE PROBABLY HALFWAY TO AUSTRALIA BY NOW.
BUT TRUST ME, YOU'LL WANNA HEAR THIS.
THERE ARE TWO POSSIBILITIES HERE.
OTTO'S EITHER GOING TO SAVE THE WORLD OR DESTROY IT.
HE SAVES IT, YOU KEEP ALL YOUR MONEY. YOU WIN.
BUT IF I'M RIGHT, IF HE FINISHES THAT SATELLITE NETWORK...
...AND CRANKS IT ALL THE WAY UP, THAT'S IT. EVERYONE'S DEAD. YOU'RE DEAD. AND WORST OF ALL...
...YOU'RE A DEAD MAN WITH TWO BILLION DOLLARS WORTH OF ASH.
SO HERE'S THE HIGH CONCEPT: SPIDER-MAN AND MYSTERIO. A BUDDY PICTURE.
TWO GUYS WHO CAN'T GET ALONG TEAM UP WITH TWO SEXY SPIES...
...GO TO THE BAD GUY'S SECRET BASE. SAVE THE WORLD. AND ALL YOUR MONEY.
ALL RIGHT. I'M IN. YOU'RE GOOD, KID. SERIOUSLY, MOVE TO L.A.
SO? WHERE'D I CLOSE THE DEAL?
"TWO BILLION DOLLARS WORTH OF ASH."
THOUGHT SO.

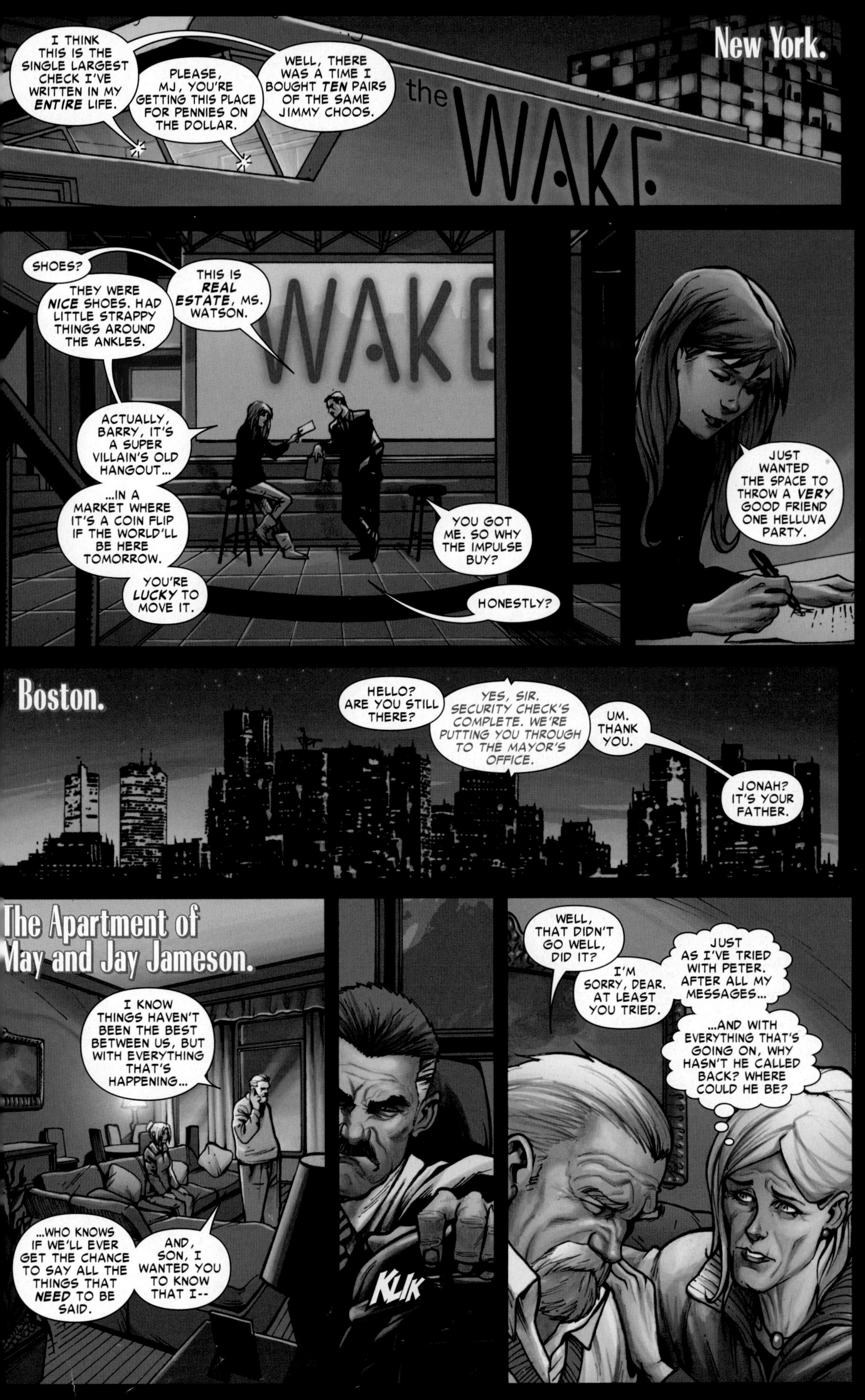
New York.
I THINK THIS IS THE SINGLE LARGEST CHECK I'VE WRITTEN IN MY ENTIRE LIFE.
PLEASE, MJ, YOU'RE GETTING THIS PLACE FOR PENNIES ON THE DOLLAR.
WELL, THERE WAS A TIME I BOUGHT TEN PAIRS OF THE SAME JIMMY CHOOS.
the WAKE
SHOES?
THEY WERE NICE SHOES. HAD LITTLE STRAPPY THINGS AROUND THE ANKLES.
THIS IS REAL ESTATE, MS. WATSON.
ACTUALLY, BARRY, IT'S A SUPER VILLAIN'S OLD HANGOUT...
...IN A MARKET WHERE IT'S A COIN FLIP IF THE WORLD'LL BE HERE TOMORROW.
YOU'RE LUCKY TO MOVE IT.
YOU GOT ME. SO WHY THE IMPULSE BUY?
HONESTLY?
JUST WANTED THE SPACE TO THROW A VERY GOOD FRIEND ONE HELLUVA PARTY.
Boston.
HELLO? ARE YOU STILL THERE?
YES, SIR. SECURITY CHECK'S COMPLETE. WE'RE PUTTING YOU THROUGH TO THE MAYOR'S OFFICE.
UM. THANK YOU.
JONAH? IT'S YOUR FATHER.
The Apartment of May and Jay Jameson.
I KNOW THINGS HAVEN'T BEEN THE BEST BETWEEN US, BUT WITH EVERYTHING THAT'S HAPPENING...
...WHO KNOWS IF WE'LL EVER GET THE CHANCE TO SAY ALL THE THINGS THAT NEED TO BE SAID.
AND, SON, I WANTED YOU TO KNOW THAT I--
KLIK
WELL, THAT DIDN'T GO WELL, DID IT?
I'M SORRY, DEAR. AT LEAST YOU TRIED.
JUST AS I'VE TRIED WITH PETER. AFTER ALL MY MESSAGES...
...AND WITH EVERYTHING THAT'S GOING ON, WHY HASN'T HE CALLED BACK? WHERE COULD HE BE?

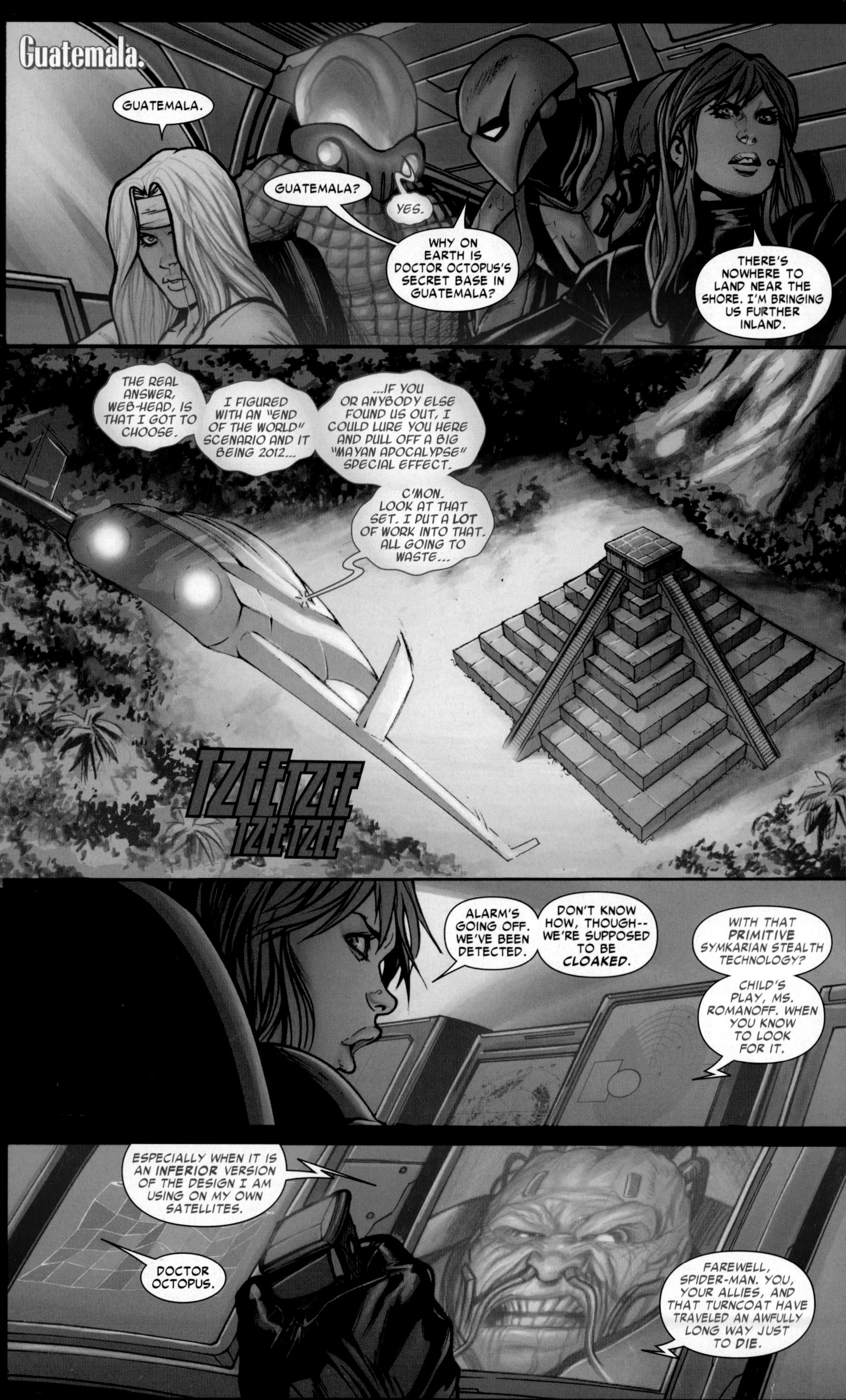
Guatemala.
GUATEMALA.
GUATEMALA?
YES.
WHY ON EARTH IS DOCTOR OCTOPUS'S SECRET BASE IN GUATEMALA?
THERE'S NOWHERE TO LAND NEAR THE SHORE. I'M BRINGING US FURTHER INLAND.
THE REAL ANSWER, WEB-HEAD, IS THAT I GOT TO CHOOSE.
I FIGURED WITH AN "END OF THE WORLD" SCENARIO AND IT BEING 2012...
...IF YOU OR ANYBODY ELSE FOUND US OUT, I COULD LURE YOU HERE AND PULL OFF A BIG "MAYAN APOCALYPSE" SPECIAL EFFECT.
C'MON. LOOK AT THAT SET. I PUT A LOT OF WORK INTO THAT. ALL GOING TO WASTE...
TZEETZEE TZEETZEE
ALARM'S GOING OFF. WE'VE BEEN DETECTED.
DON'T KNOW HOW, THOUGH-- WE'RE SUPPOSED TO BE CLOAKED.
WITH THAT PRIMITIVE SYMKARIAN STEALTH TECHNOLOGY?
CHILD'S PLAY, MS. ROMANOFF. WHEN YOU KNOW TO LOOK FOR IT.
ESPECIALLY WHEN IT IS AN INFERIOR VERSION OF THE DESIGN I AM USING ON MY OWN SATELLITES.
DOCTOR OCTOPUS.
FAREWELL, SPIDER-MAN. YOU, YOUR ALLIES, AND THAT TURNCOAT HAVE TRAVELED AN AWFULLY LONG WAY JUST TO DIE.

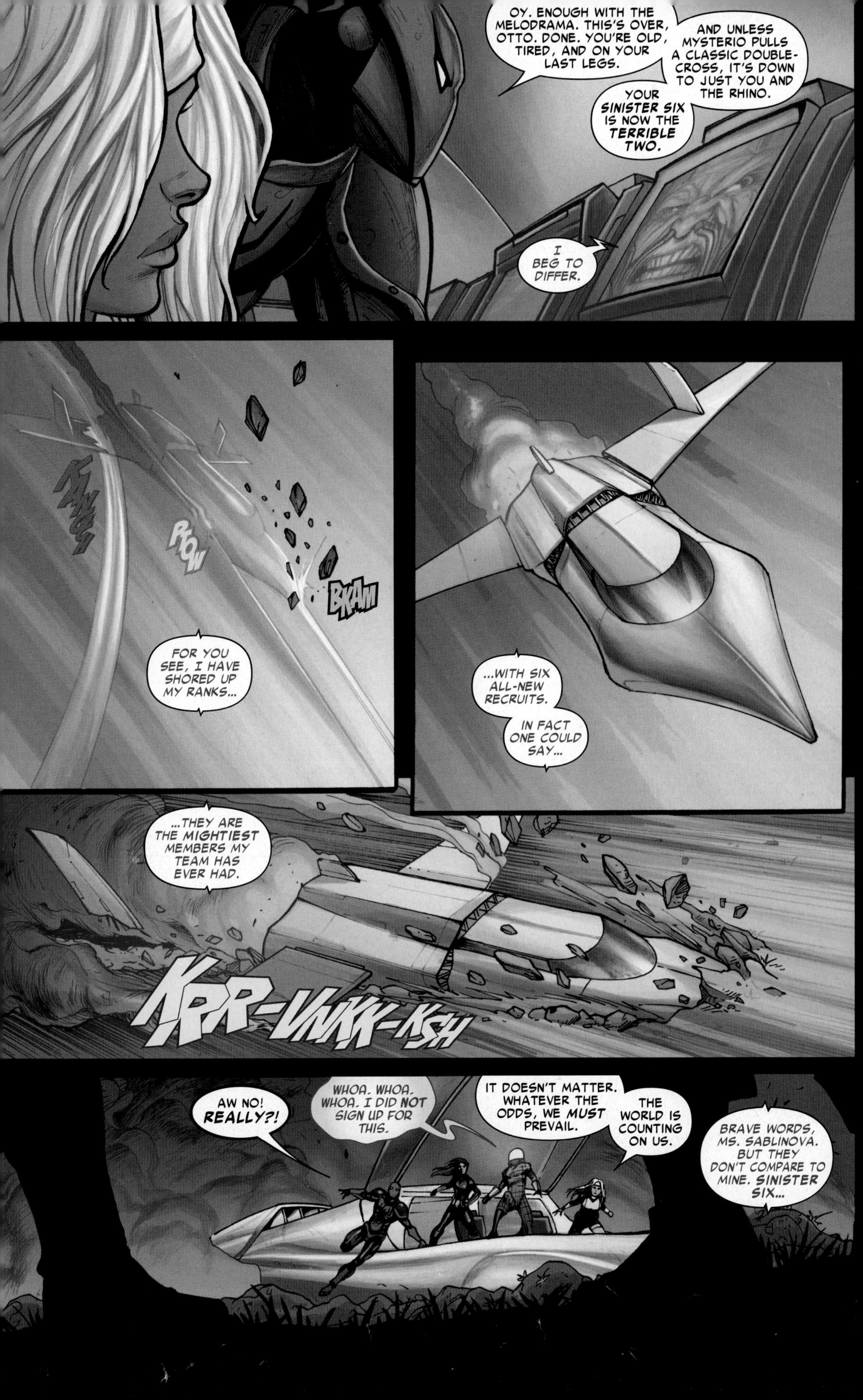
OY. ENOUGH WITH THE MELODRAMA. THIS'S OVER, OTTO. DONE. YOU'RE OLD, TIRED, AND ON YOUR LAST LEGS.
AND UNLESS MYSTERIO PULLS A CLASSIC DOUBLE-CROSS, IT'S DOWN TO JUST YOU AND THE RHINO.
YOUR SINISTER SIX IS NOW THE TERRIBLE TWO.
I BEG TO DIFFER.
KRAKOOM
PTOW
BKAM
FOR YOU SEE, I HAVE SHORED UP MY RANKS...
...WITH SIX ALL-NEW RECRUITS.
IN FACT ONE COULD SAY...
...THEY ARE THE MIGHTIEST MEMBERS MY TEAM HAS EVER HAD.
KRR-UNKK-KSH
AW NO! REALLY?!
WHOA. WHOA. WHOA. I DID NOT SIGN UP FOR THIS.
IT DOESN'T MATTER. WHATEVER THE ODDS, WE MUST PREVAIL.
THE WORLD IS COUNTING ON US.
BRAVE WORDS, MS. SABLINOVA. BUT THEY DON'T COMPARE TO MINE. SINISTER SIX...

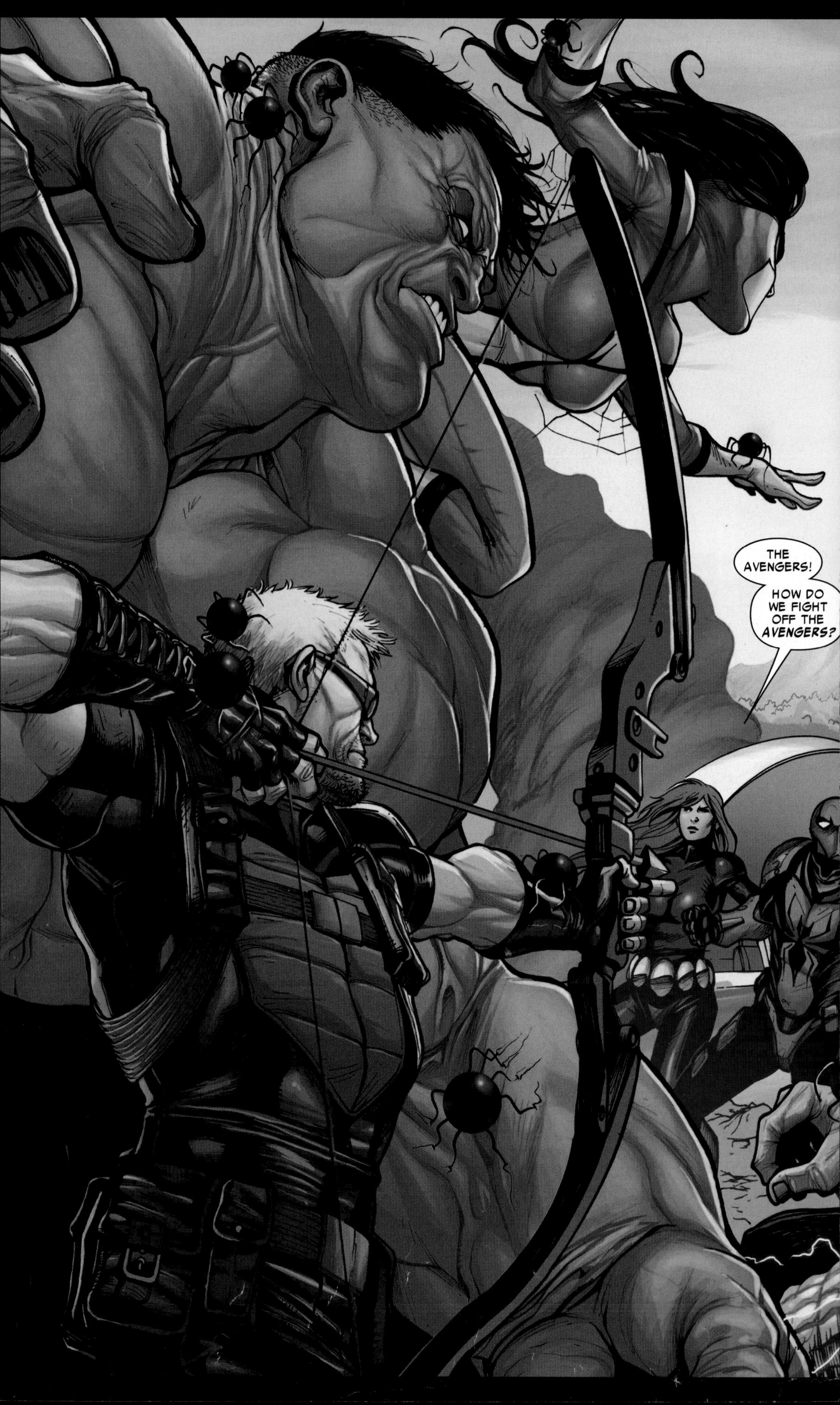
THE AVENGERS!
HOW DO WE FIGHT OFF THE AVENGERS?

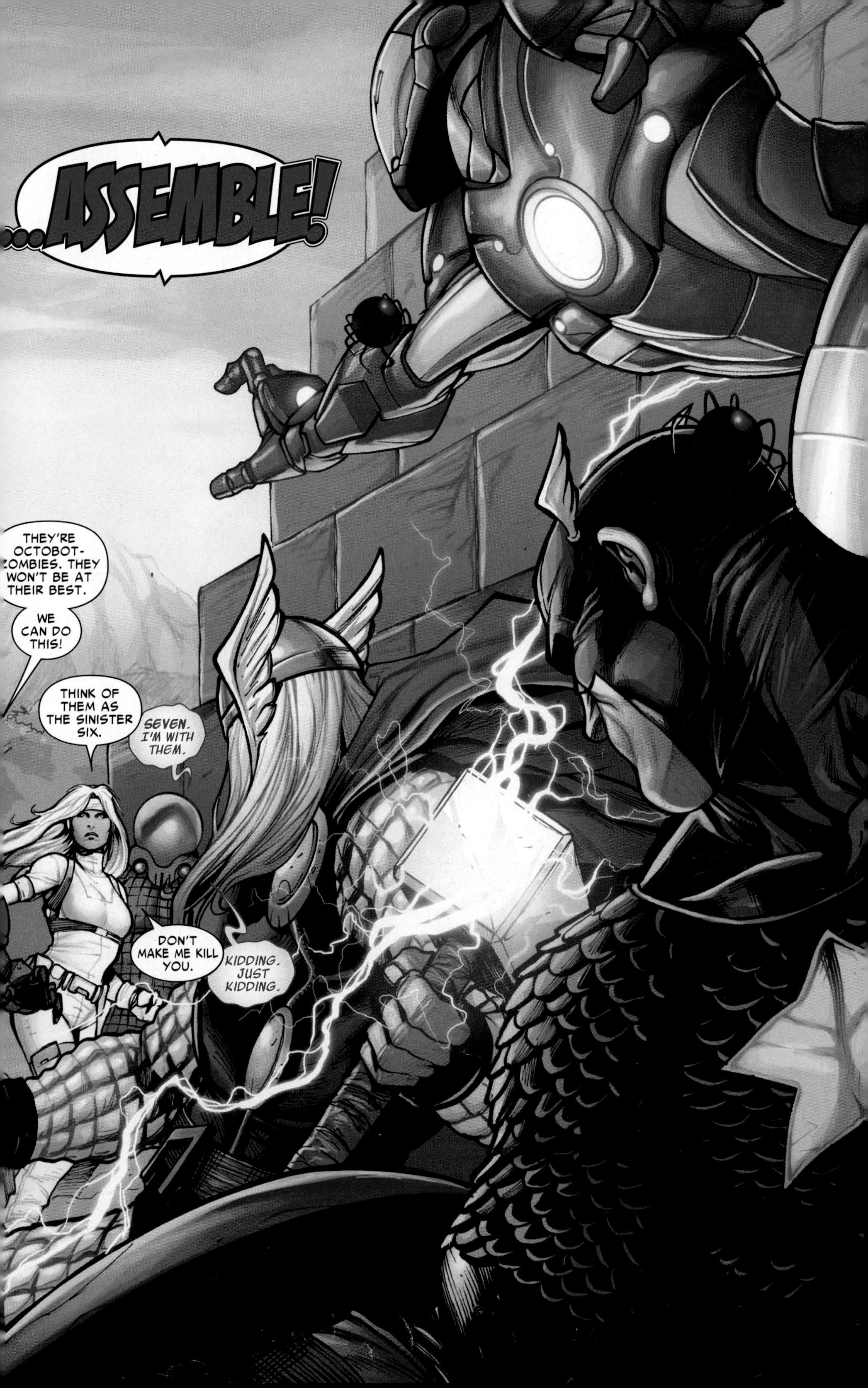

...ASSEMBLE!
THEY'RE OCTOBOT-ZOMBIES. THEY WON'T BE AT THEIR BEST.
WE CAN DO THIS!
THINK OF THEM AS THE SINISTER SIX.
SEVEN. I'M WITH THEM.
DON'T MAKE ME KILL YOU.
KIDDING. JUST KIDDING.

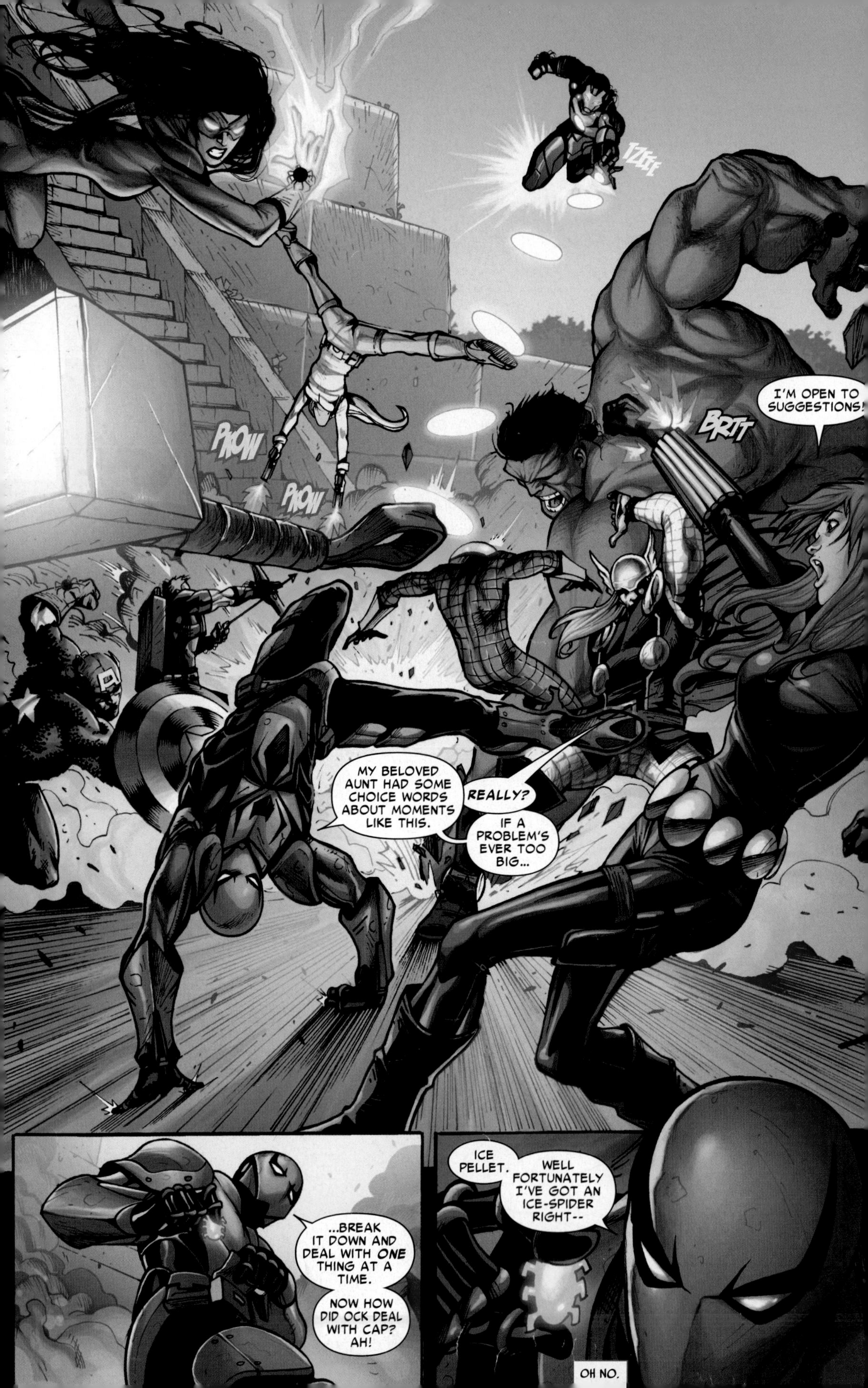
IZZEE
PROW
PROW
BRITT
I'M OPEN TO SUGGESTIONS!
MY BELOVED AUNT HAD SOME CHOICE WORDS ABOUT MOMENTS LIKE THIS.
REALLY?
IF A PROBLEM'S EVER TOO BIG...
...BREAK IT DOWN AND DEAL WITH ONE THING AT A TIME.
NOW HOW DID OCK DEAL WITH CAP? AH!
ICE PELLET.
WELL FORTUNATELY I'VE GOT AN ICE-SPIDER RIGHT--
OH NO.

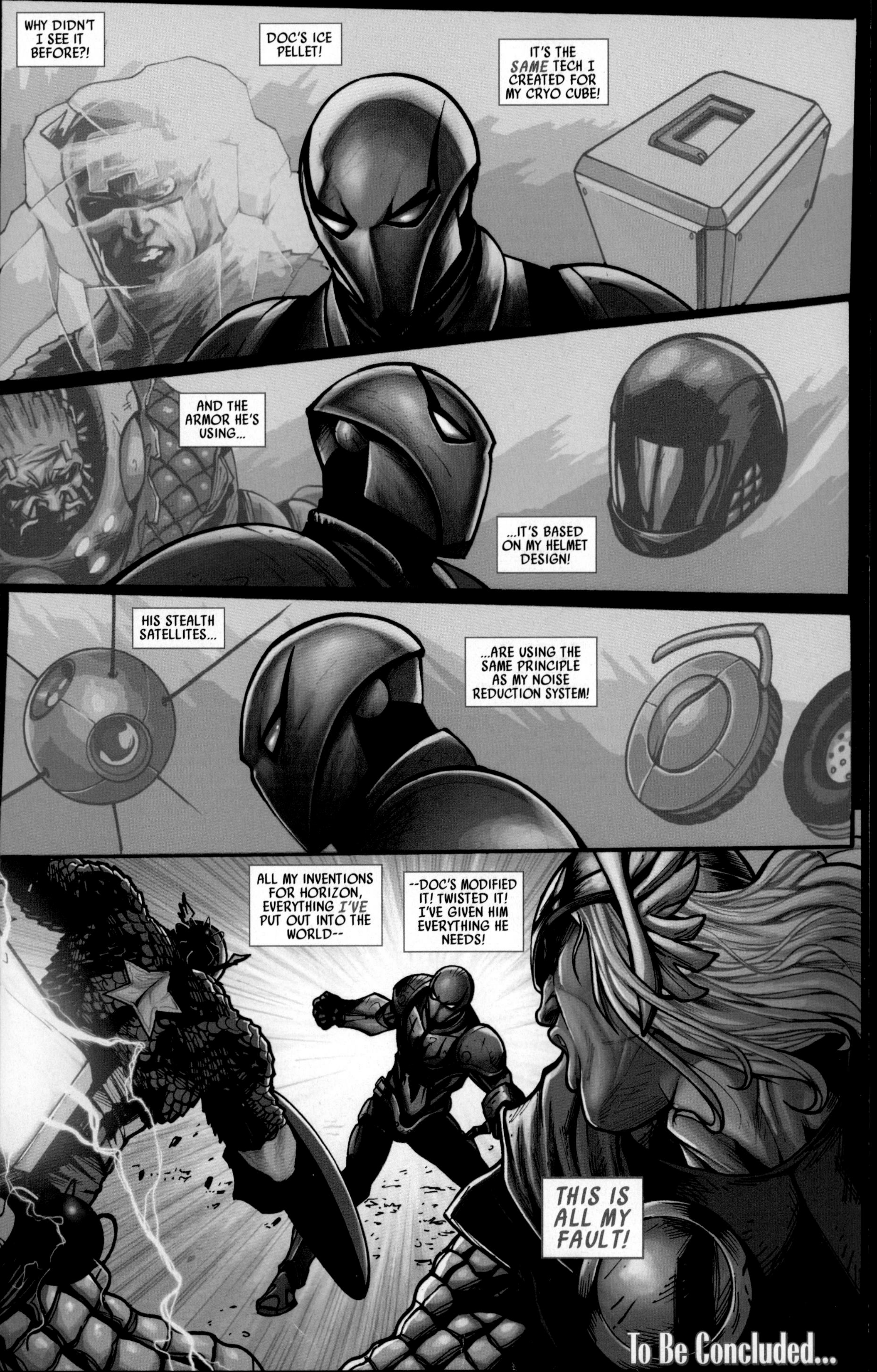
WHY DIDN'T I SEE IT BEFORE?!
DOC'S ICE PELLET!
IT'S THE SAME TECH I CREATED FOR MY CRYO CUBE!
AND THE ARMOR HE'S USING...
...IT'S BASED ON MY HELMET DESIGN!
HIS STEALTH SATELLITES...
...ARE USING THE SAME PRINCIPLE AS MY NOISE REDUCTION SYSTEM!
ALL MY INVENTIONS FOR HORIZON, EVERYTHING I'VE PUT OUT INTO THE WORLD--
--DOC'S MODIFIED IT! TWISTED IT! I'VE GIVEN HIM EVERYTHING HE NEEDS!
THIS IS ALL MY FAULT!
To Be Concluded...

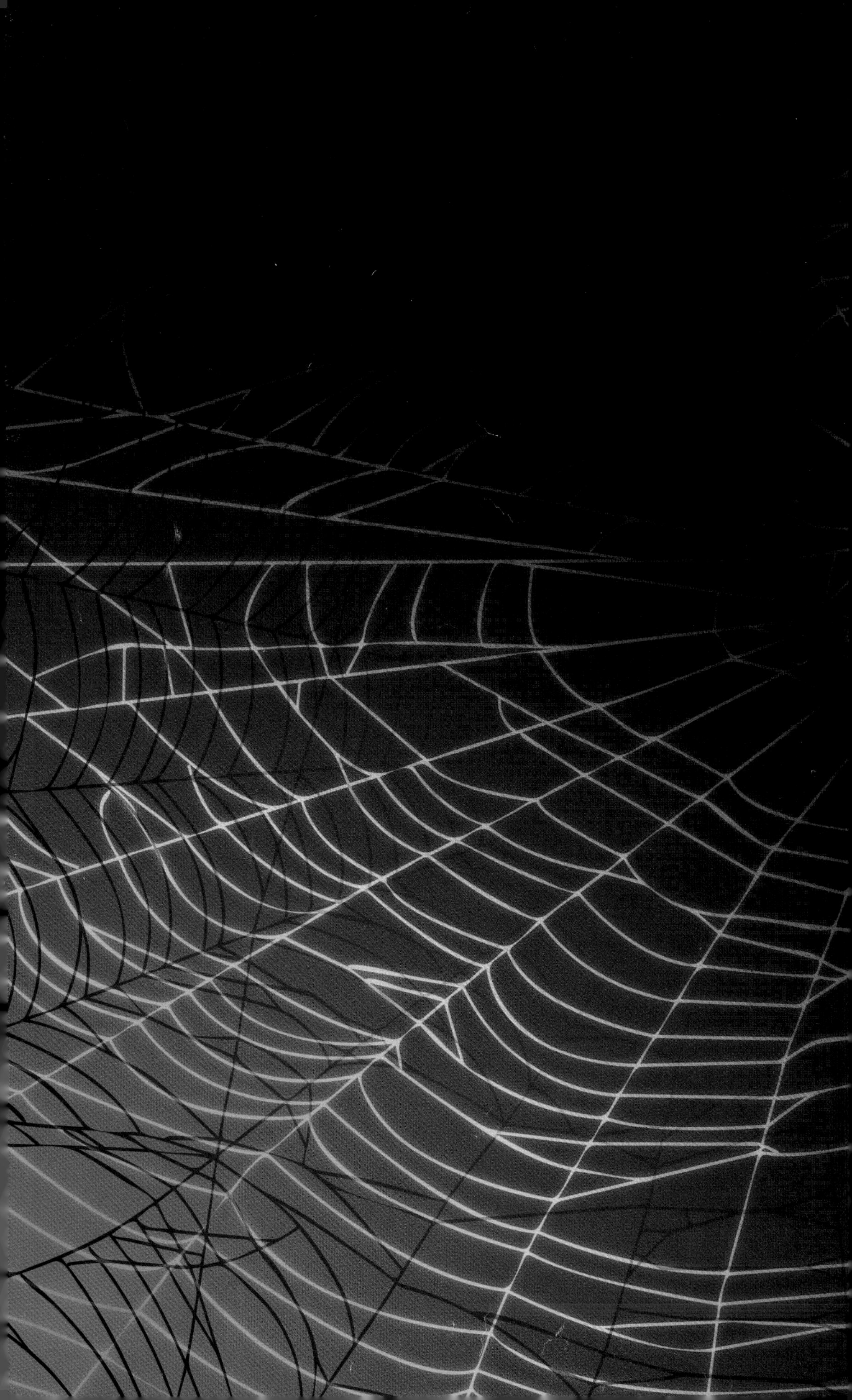

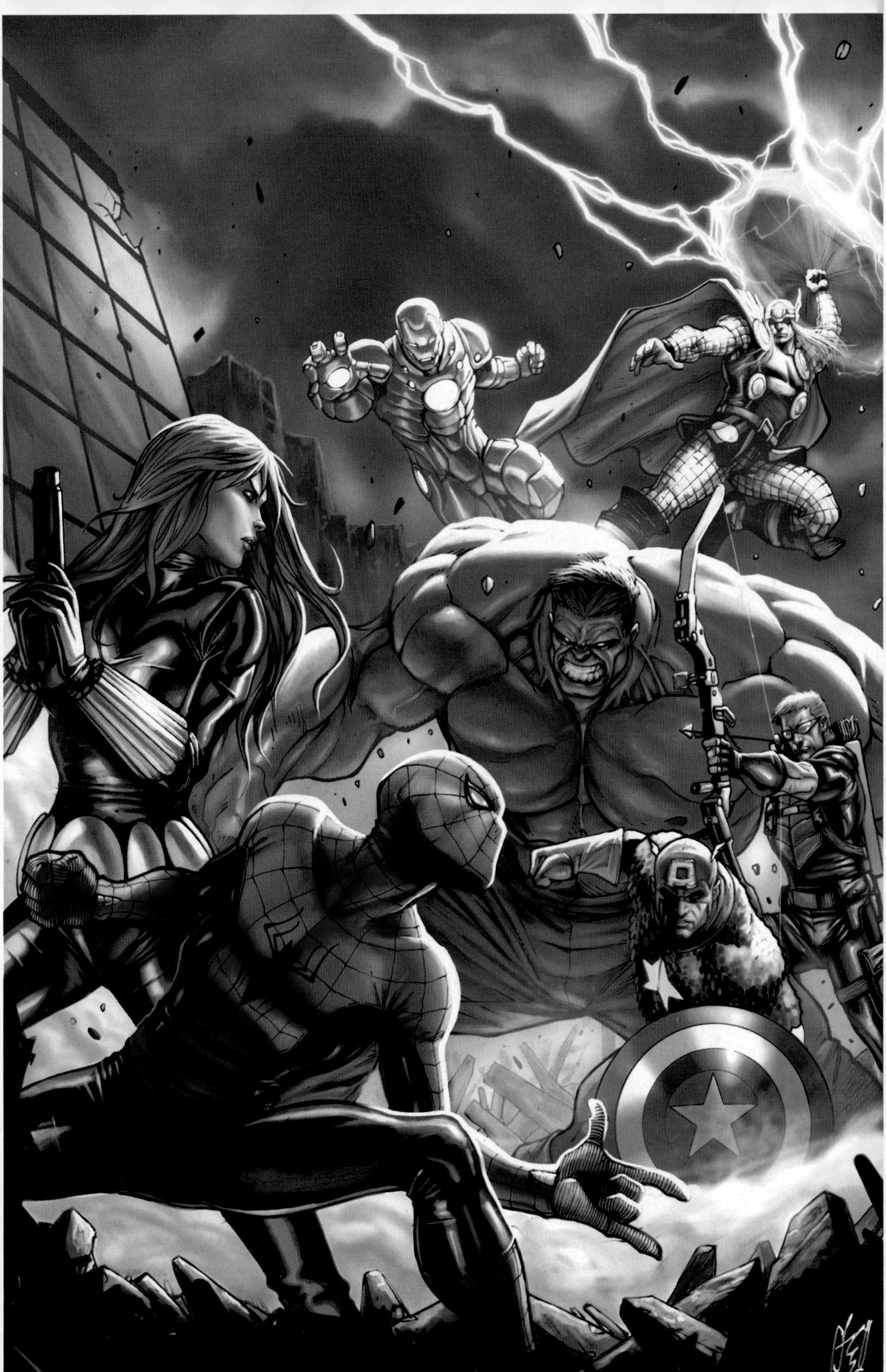

SPIDER-M
Y STEFANC

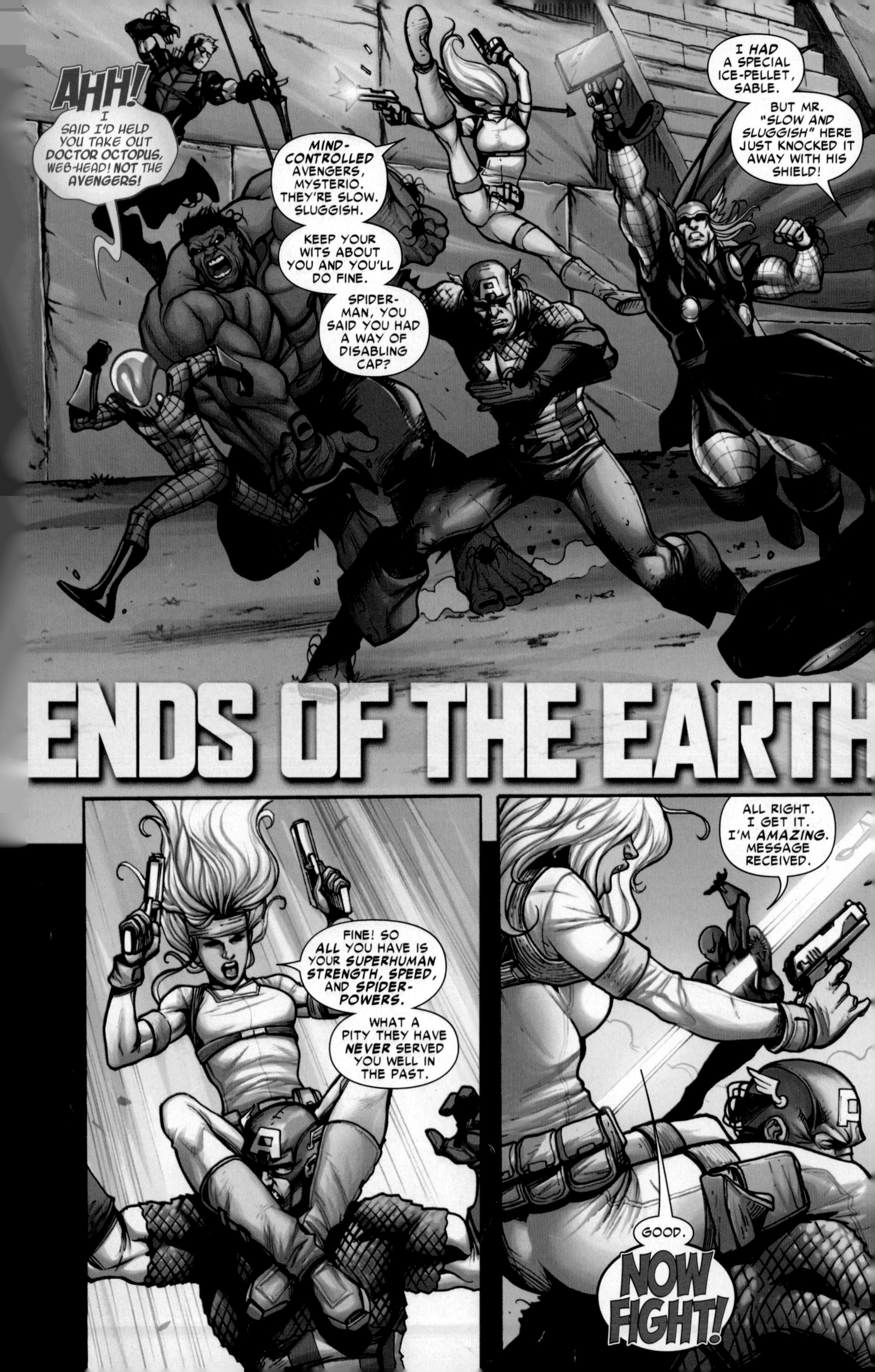
AHH!
I SAID I'D HELP YOU TAKE OUT DOCTOR OCTOPUS, WEB-HEAD! NOT THE AVENGERS!
MIND-CONTROLLED AVENGERS, MYSTERIO. THEY'RE SLOW. SLUGGISH.
KEEP YOUR WITS ABOUT YOU AND YOU'LL DO FINE.
SPIDER-MAN, YOU SAID YOU HAD A WAY OF DISABLING CAP?
I HAD A SPECIAL ICE-PELLET, SABLE.
BUT MR. "SLOW AND SLUGGISH" HERE JUST KNOCKED IT AWAY WITH HIS SHIELD!
ENDS OF THE EARTH
FINE! SO ALL YOU HAVE IS YOUR SUPERHUMAN STRENGTH, SPEED, AND SPIDER-POWERS.
WHAT A PITY THEY HAVE NEVER SERVED YOU WELL IN THE PAST.
ALL RIGHT. I GET IT. I'M AMAZING. MESSAGE RECEIVED.
GOOD.
NOW FIGHT!

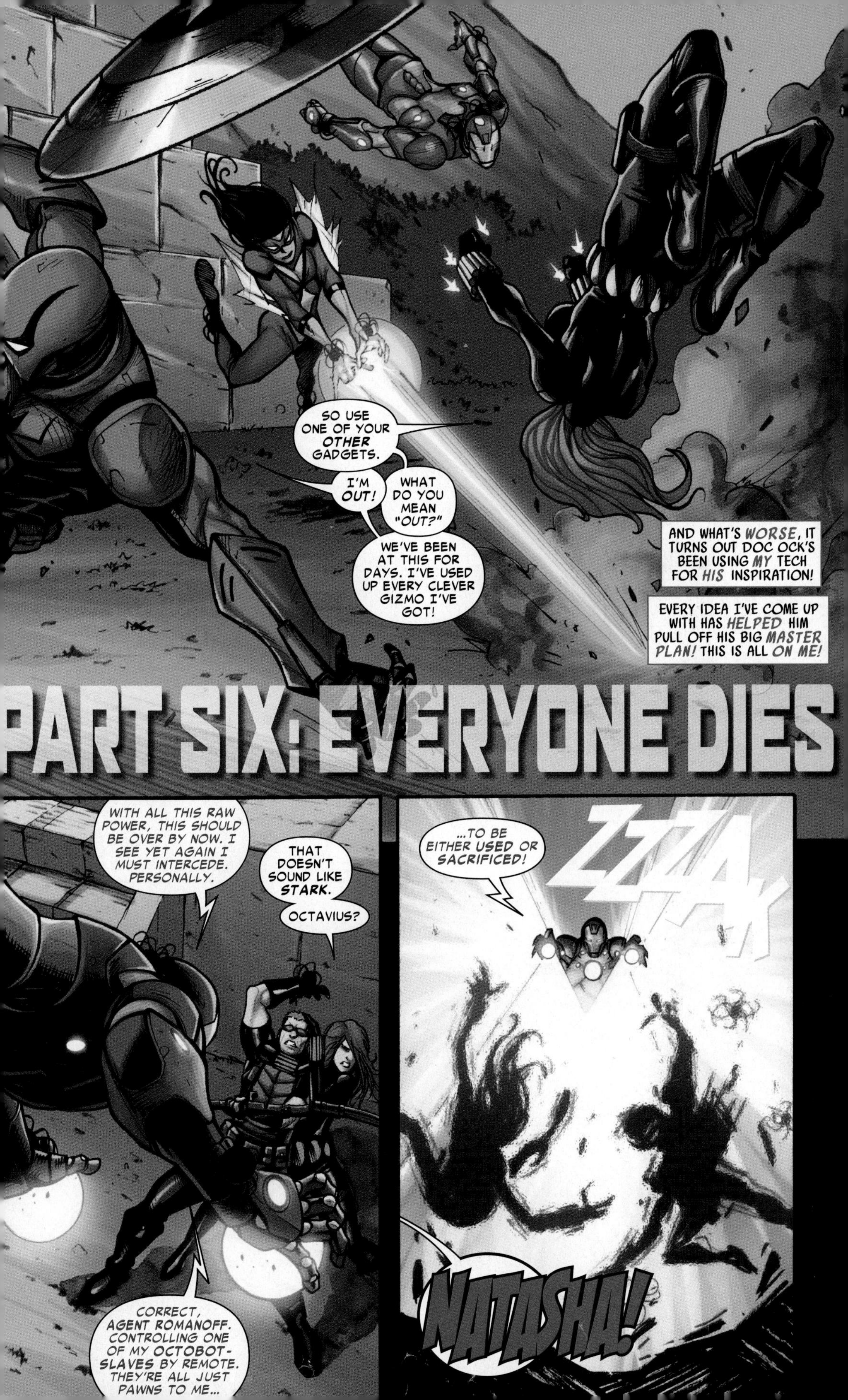
SO USE ONE OF YOUR OTHER GADGETS.
I'M OUT!
WHAT DO YOU MEAN "OUT?"
WE'VE BEEN AT THIS FOR DAYS. I'VE USED UP EVERY CLEVER GIZMO I'VE GOT!
AND WHAT'S WORSE, IT TURNS OUT DOC OCK'S BEEN USING MY TECH FOR HIS INSPIRATION!
EVERY IDEA I'VE COME UP WITH HAS HELPED HIM PULL OFF HIS BIG MASTER PLAN! THIS IS ALL ON ME!
PART SIX: EVERYONE DIES
WITH ALL THIS RAW POWER, THIS SHOULD BE OVER BY NOW. I SEE YET AGAIN I MUST INTERCEDE. PERSONALLY.
THAT DOESN'T SOUND LIKE STARK.
OCTAVIUS?
CORRECT, AGENT ROMANOFF. CONTROLLING ONE OF MY OCTOBOT-SLAVES BY REMOTE. THEY'RE ALL JUST PAWNS TO ME...
...TO BE EITHER USED OR SACRIFICED!
ZZZAK
NATASHA!

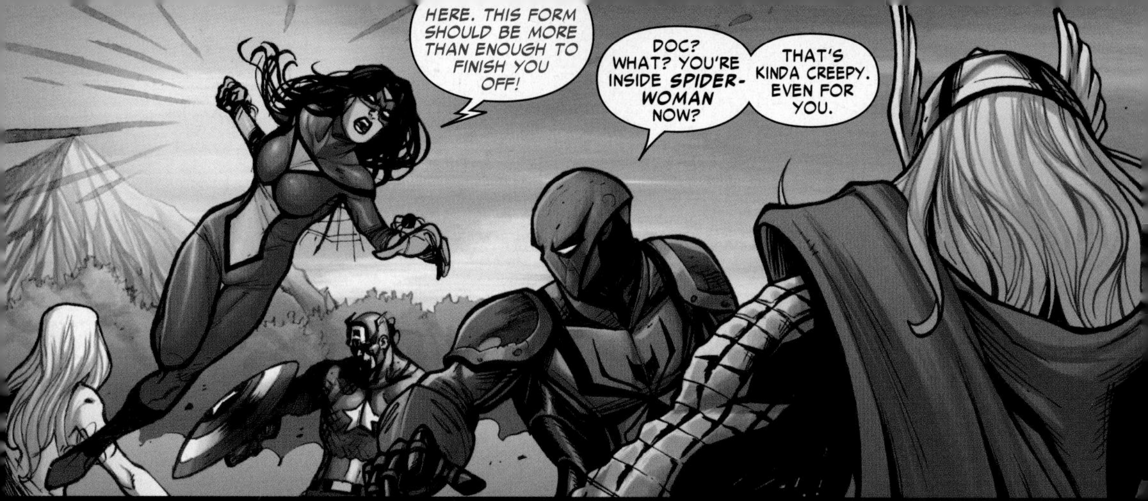
HERE. THIS FORM SHOULD BE MORE THAN ENOUGH TO FINISH YOU OFF!
DOC? WHAT? YOU'RE INSIDE SPIDER-WOMAN NOW?
THAT'S KINDA CREEPY. EVEN FOR YOU.

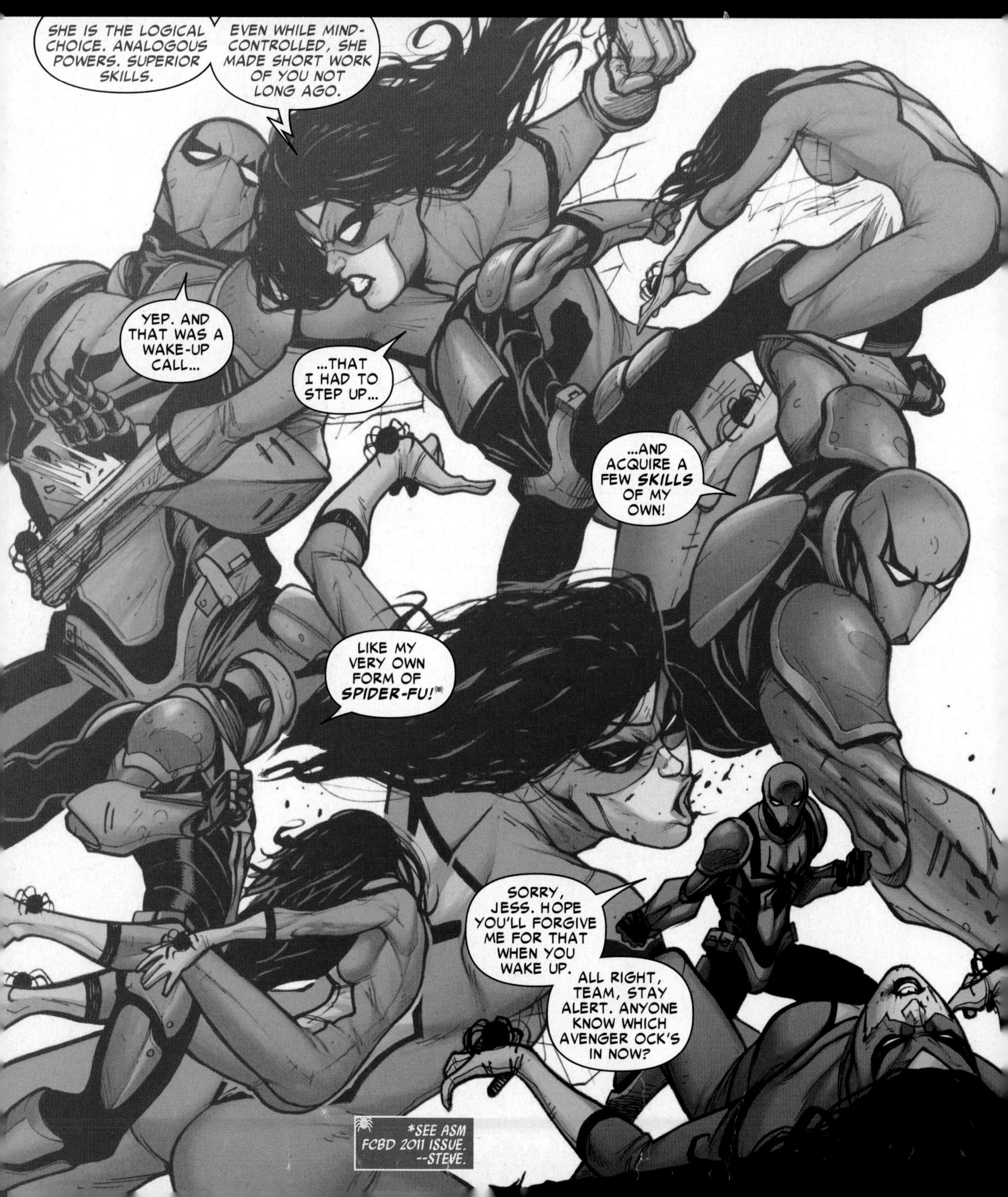
SHE IS THE LOGICAL CHOICE. ANALOGOUS POWERS. SUPERIOR SKILLS.
EVEN WHILE MIND-CONTROLLED, SHE MADE SHORT WORK OF YOU NOT LONG AGO.
YEP. AND THAT WAS A WAKE-UP CALL...
...THAT I HAD TO STEP UP...
...AND ACQUIRE A FEW SKILLS OF MY OWN!
LIKE MY VERY OWN FORM OF SPIDER-FU!*
SORRY, JESS. HOPE YOU'LL FORGIVE ME FOR THAT WHEN YOU WAKE UP.
ALL RIGHT, TEAM, STAY ALERT. ANYONE KNOW WHICH AVENGER OCK'S IN NOW?
*SEE ASM FCBD 2011 ISSUE. --STEVE.

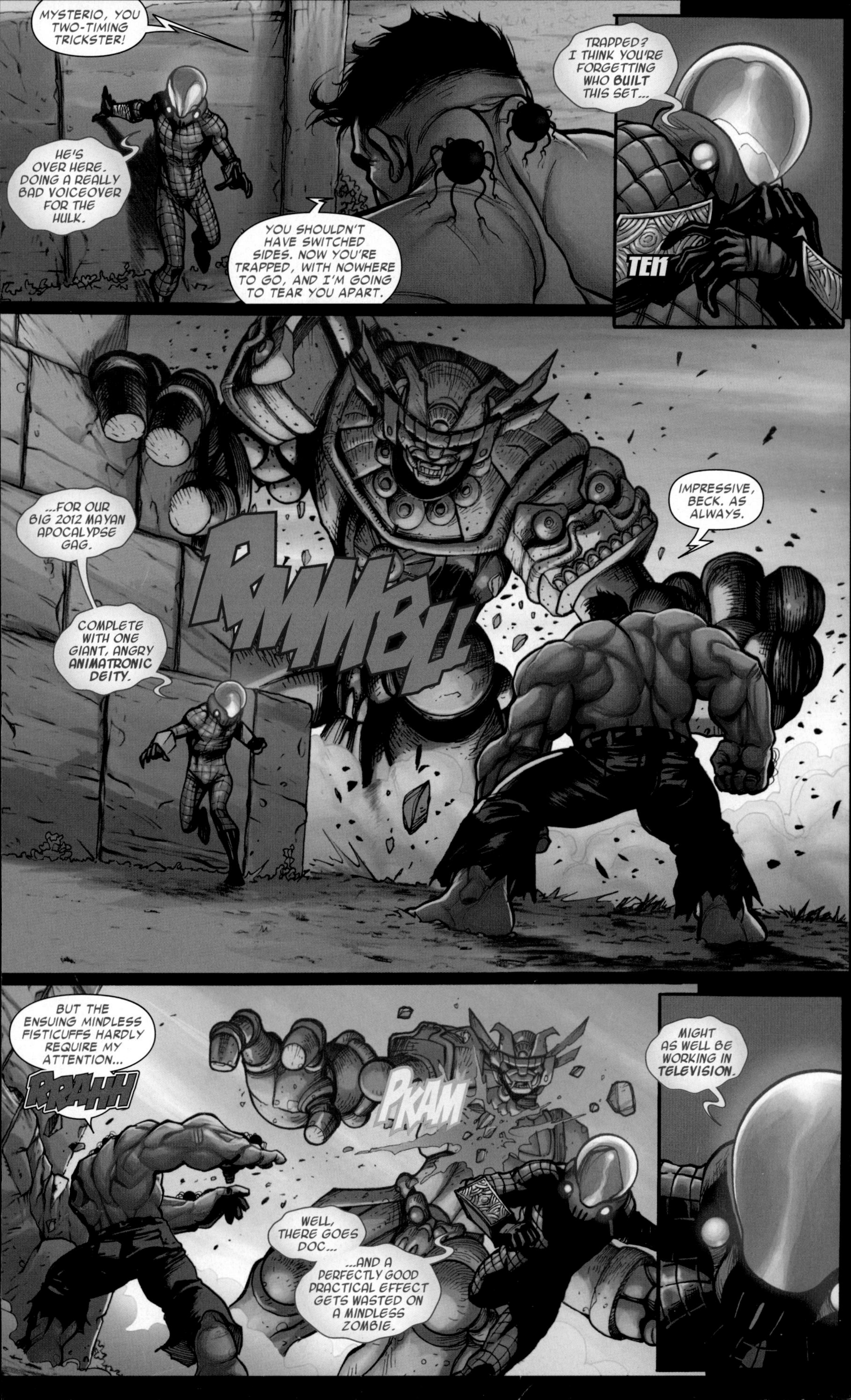
MYSTERIO, YOU TWO-TIMING TRICKSTER!
HE'S OVER HERE. DOING A REALLY BAD VOICEOVER FOR THE HULK.
YOU SHOULDN'T HAVE SWITCHED SIDES. NOW YOU'RE TRAPPED, WITH NOWHERE TO GO, AND I'M GOING TO TEAR YOU APART.
TRAPPED? I THINK YOU'RE FORGETTING WHO BUILT THIS SET...
TEK
...FOR OUR BIG 2012 MAYAN APOCALYPSE GAG.
COMPLETE WITH ONE GIANT, ANGRY ANIMATRONIC DEITY.
RMMBL
IMPRESSIVE, BECK. AS ALWAYS.
BUT THE ENSUING MINDLESS FISTICUFFS HARDLY REQUIRE MY ATTENTION...
RRAHH
PKAM
WELL, THERE GOES DOC...
...AND A PERFECTLY GOOD PRACTICAL EFFECT GETS WASTED ON A MINDLESS ZOMBIE.
MIGHT AS WELL BE WORKING IN TELEVISION.

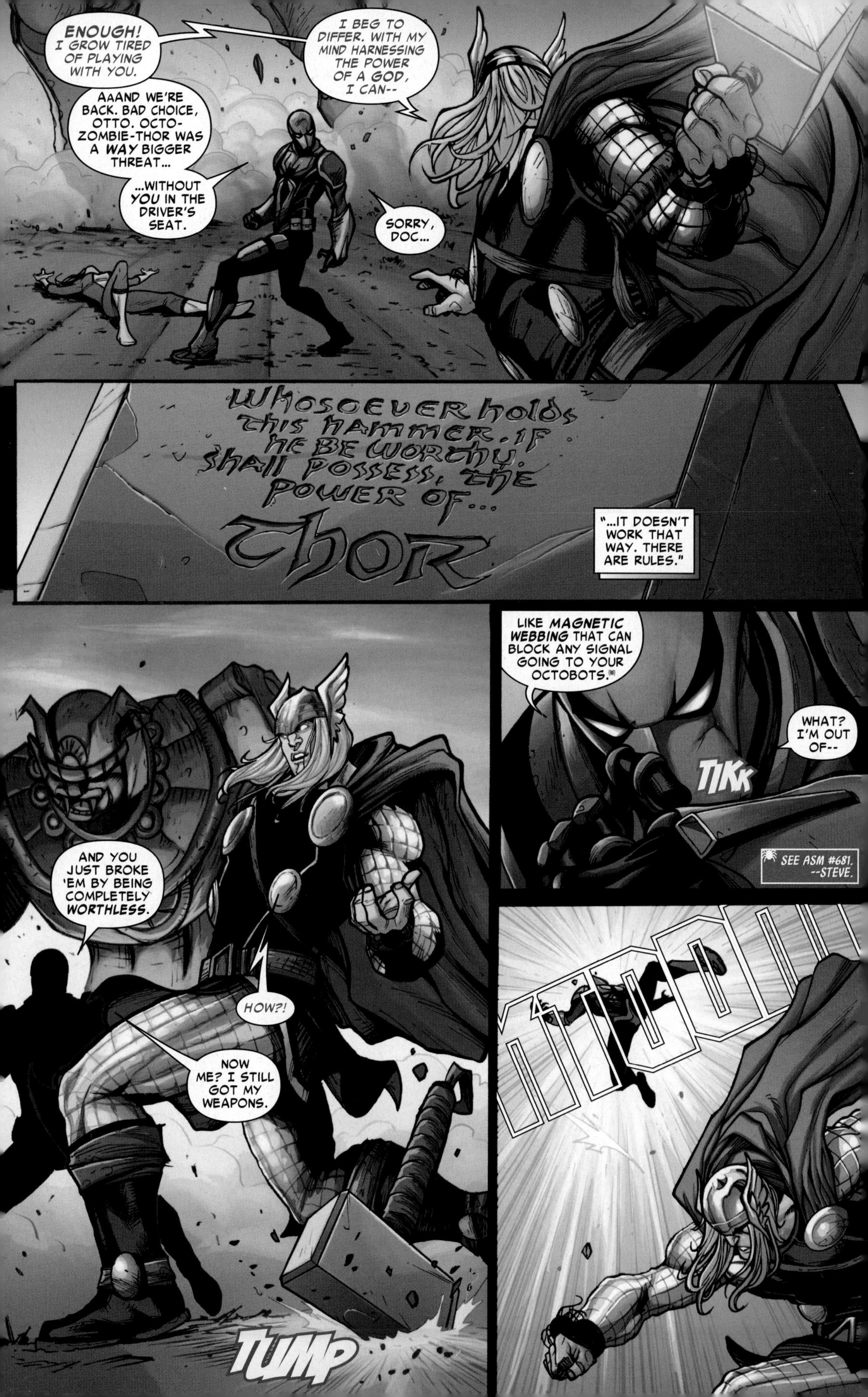
ENOUGH! I GROW TIRED OF PLAYING WITH YOU.
I BEG TO DIFFER. WITH MY MIND HARNESSING THE POWER OF A GOD, I CAN--
AAAND WE'RE BACK. BAD CHOICE, OTTO. OCTO-ZOMBIE-THOR WAS A WAY BIGGER THREAT...
...WITHOUT YOU IN THE DRIVER'S SEAT.
SORRY, DOC...
Whosoever holds this hammer, if he be worthy, shall possess, the power of... THOR
"...IT DOESN'T WORK THAT WAY. THERE ARE RULES."
AND YOU JUST BROKE 'EM BY BEING COMPLETELY WORTHLESS.
HOW?!
NOW ME? I STILL GOT MY WEAPONS.
TUMP
LIKE MAGNETIC WEBBING THAT CAN BLOCK ANY SIGNAL GOING TO YOUR OCTOBOTS.
WHAT? I'M OUT OF--
TIKK
SEE ASM #681. --STEVE.

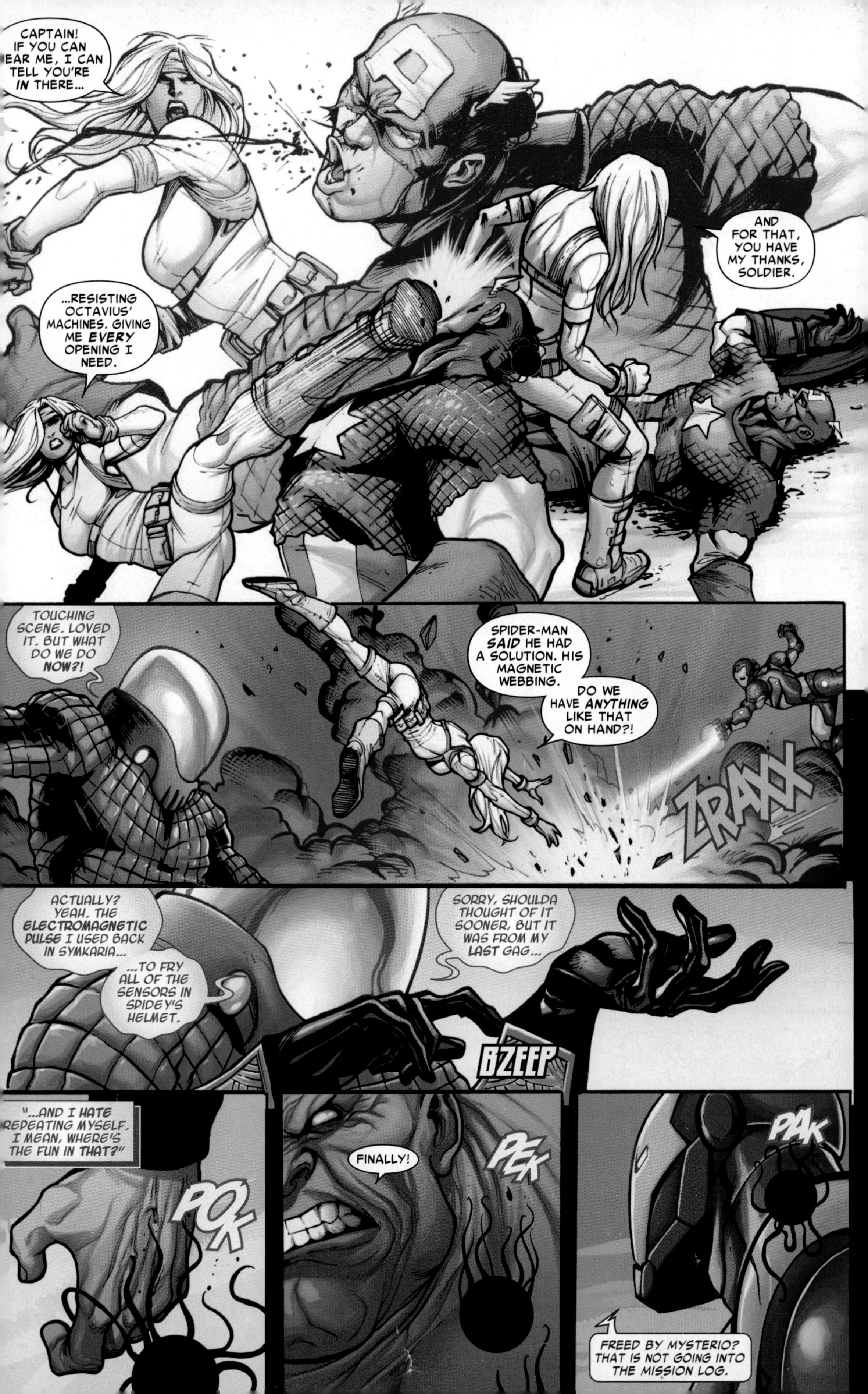
CAPTAIN! IF YOU CAN EAR ME, I CAN TELL YOU'RE IN THERE...
...RESISTING OCTAVIUS' MACHINES. GIVING ME EVERY OPENING I NEED.
AND FOR THAT, YOU HAVE MY THANKS, SOLDIER.
TOUCHING SCENE. LOVED IT. BUT WHAT DO WE DO NOW?!
SPIDER-MAN SAID HE HAD A SOLUTION. HIS MAGNETIC WEBBING.
DO WE HAVE ANYTHING LIKE THAT ON HAND?!
ZRAXX
ACTUALLY? YEAH. THE ELECTROMAGNETIC PULSE I USED BACK IN SYMKARIA...
...TO FRY ALL OF THE SENSORS IN SPIDEY'S HELMET.
SORRY, SHOULDA THOUGHT OF IT SOONER, BUT IT WAS FROM MY LAST GAG...
BZEEP
"...AND I HATE REPEATING MYSELF. I MEAN, WHERE'S THE FUN IN THAT?"
POK
FINALLY!
PEK
PAK
FREED BY MYSTERIO? THAT IS NOT GOING INTO THE MISSION LOG.

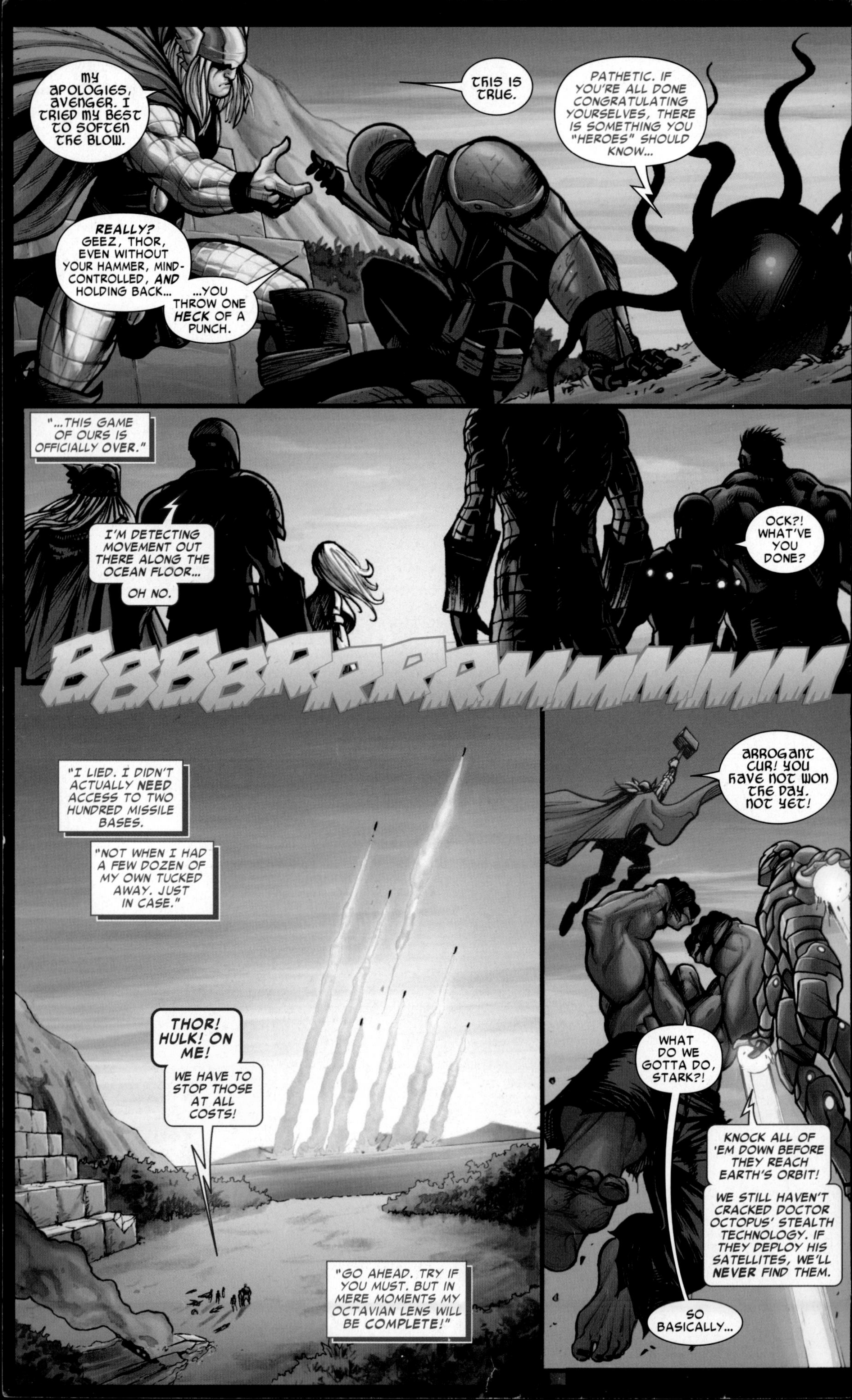
MY APOLOGIES, AVENGER. I TRIED MY BEST TO SOFTEN THE BLOW.
THIS IS TRUE.
REALLY? GEEZ, THOR, EVEN WITHOUT YOUR HAMMER, MIND-CONTROLLED, AND HOLDING BACK...
...YOU THROW ONE HECK OF A PUNCH.
PATHETIC. IF YOU'RE ALL DONE CONGRATULATING YOURSELVES, THERE IS SOMETHING YOU "HEROES" SHOULD KNOW...
"...THIS GAME OF OURS IS OFFICIALLY OVER."
I'M DETECTING MOVEMENT OUT THERE ALONG THE OCEAN FLOOR...
OH NO.
OCK?! WHAT'VE YOU DONE?
BBBBRRRRRMMMMMMM
"I LIED. I DIDN'T ACTUALLY NEED ACCESS TO TWO HUNDRED MISSILE BASES.
"NOT WHEN I HAD A FEW DOZEN OF MY OWN TUCKED AWAY. JUST IN CASE."
THOR! HULK! ON ME!
WE HAVE TO STOP THOSE AT ALL COSTS!
"GO AHEAD. TRY IF YOU MUST. BUT IN MERE MOMENTS MY OCTAVIAN LENS WILL BE COMPLETE!"
ARROGANT CUR! YOU HAVE NOT WON THE DAY. NOT YET!
WHAT DO WE GOTTA DO, STARK?!
KNOCK ALL OF 'EM DOWN BEFORE THEY REACH EARTH'S ORBIT!
WE STILL HAVEN'T CRACKED DOCTOR OCTOPUS' STEALTH TECHNOLOGY. IF THEY DEPLOY HIS SATELLITES, WE'LL NEVER FIND THEM.
SO BASICALLY...

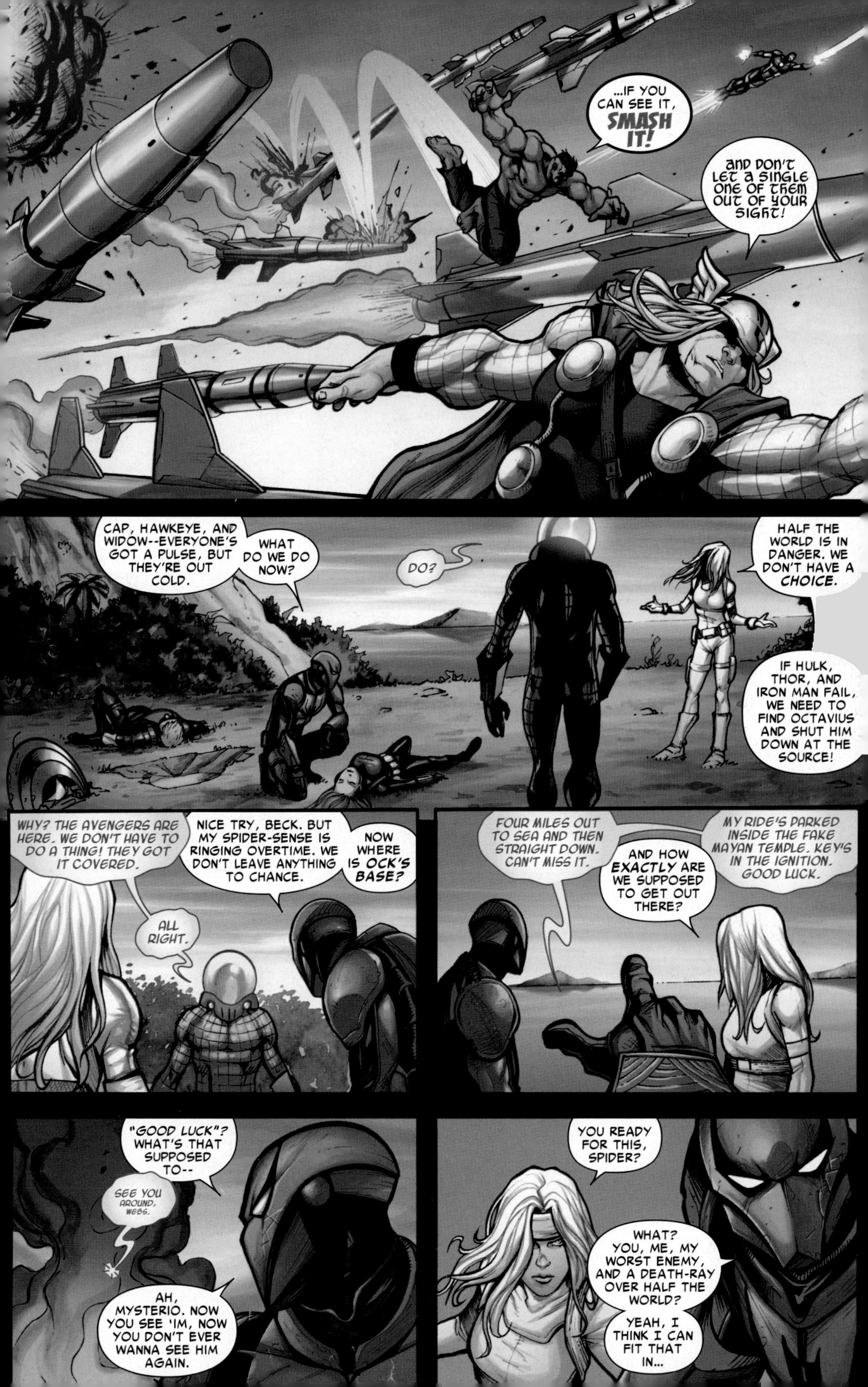

...IF YOU CAN SEE IT, SMASH IT!
AND DON'T LET A SINGLE ONE OF THEM OUT OF YOUR SIGHT!
CAP, HAWKEYE, AND WIDOW--EVERYONE'S GOT A PULSE, BUT THEY'RE OUT COLD.
WHAT DO WE DO NOW?
DO?
HALF THE WORLD IS IN DANGER. WE DON'T HAVE A CHOICE.
IF HULK, THOR, AND IRON MAN FAIL, WE NEED TO FIND OCTAVIUS AND SHUT HIM DOWN AT THE SOURCE!
WHY? THE AVENGERS ARE HERE. WE DON'T HAVE TO DO A THING! THEY GOT IT COVERED.
NICE TRY, BECK. BUT MY SPIDER-SENSE IS RINGING OVERTIME. WE DON'T LEAVE ANYTHING TO CHANCE.
NOW WHERE IS OCK'S BASE?
ALL RIGHT.
FOUR MILES OUT TO SEA AND THEN STRAIGHT DOWN. CAN'T MISS IT.
AND HOW EXACTLY ARE WE SUPPOSED TO GET OUT THERE?
MY RIDE'S PARKED INSIDE THE FAKE MAYAN TEMPLE. KEY'S IN THE IGNITION. GOOD LUCK.
"GOOD LUCK"? WHAT'S THAT SUPPOSED TO--
SEE YOU AROUND, WEBS.
AH, MYSTERIO. NOW YOU SEE 'IM, NOW YOU DON'T EVER WANNA SEE HIM AGAIN.
YOU READY FOR THIS, SPIDER?
WHAT? YOU, ME, MY WORST ENEMY, AND A DEATH-RAY OVER HALF THE WORLD?
YEAH, I THINK I CAN FIT THAT IN...

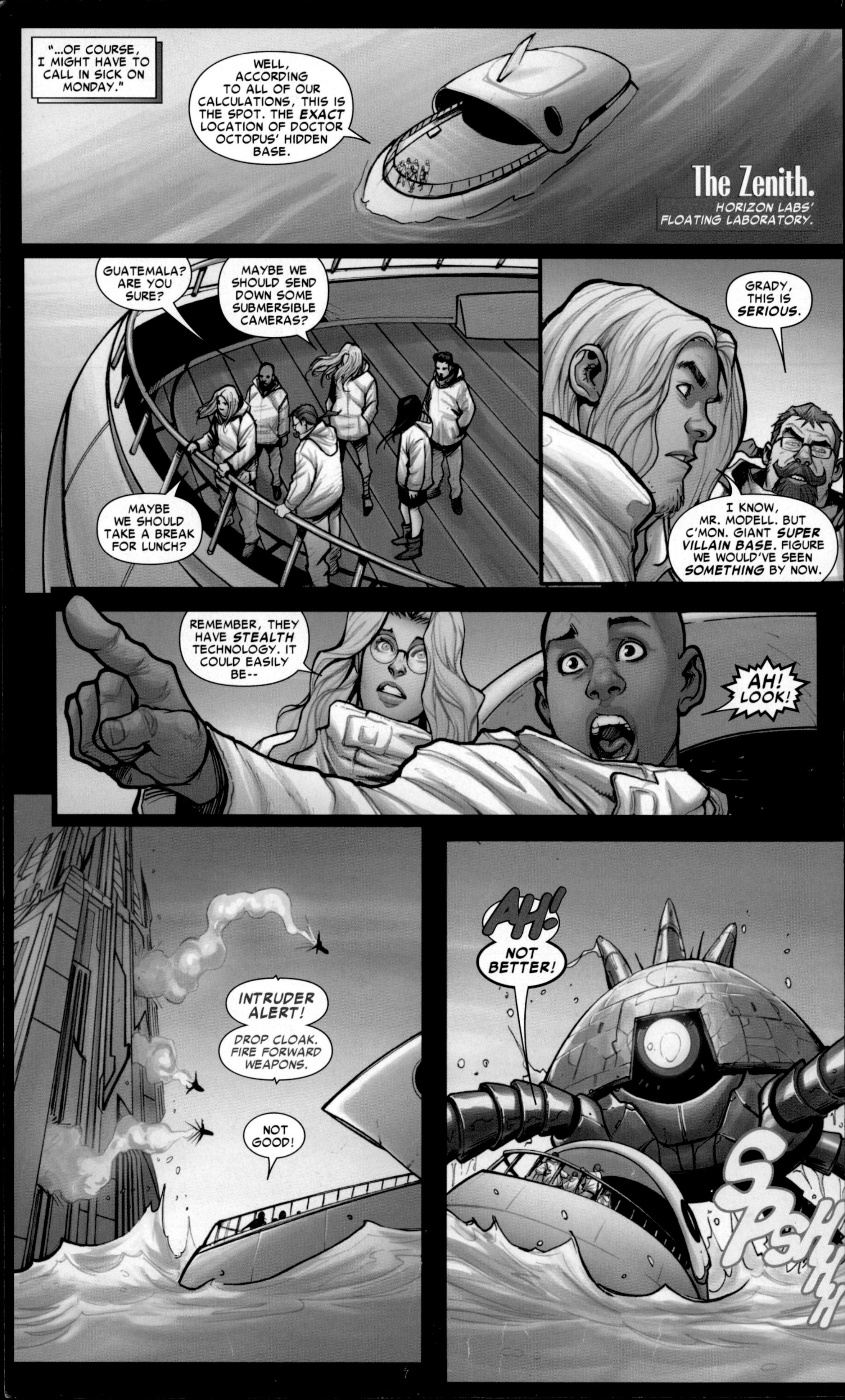

"...OF COURSE, I MIGHT HAVE TO CALL IN SICK ON MONDAY."
WELL, ACCORDING TO ALL OF OUR CALCULATIONS, THIS IS THE SPOT. THE EXACT LOCATION OF DOCTOR OCTOPUS' HIDDEN BASE.
The Zenith.
HORIZON LABS' FLOATING LABORATORY.
GUATEMALA? ARE YOU SURE?
MAYBE WE SHOULD SEND DOWN SOME SUBMERSIBLE CAMERAS?
MAYBE WE SHOULD TAKE A BREAK FOR LUNCH?
GRADY, THIS IS SERIOUS.
I KNOW, MR. MODELL. BUT C'MON. GIANT SUPER VILLAIN BASE. FIGURE WE WOULD'VE SEEN SOMETHING BY NOW.
REMEMBER, THEY HAVE STEALTH TECHNOLOGY. IT COULD EASILY BE--
AH! LOOK!
INTRUDER ALERT!
DROP CLOAK. FIRE FORWARD WEAPONS.
NOT GOOD!
AH!
NOT BETTER!
SPSHHH

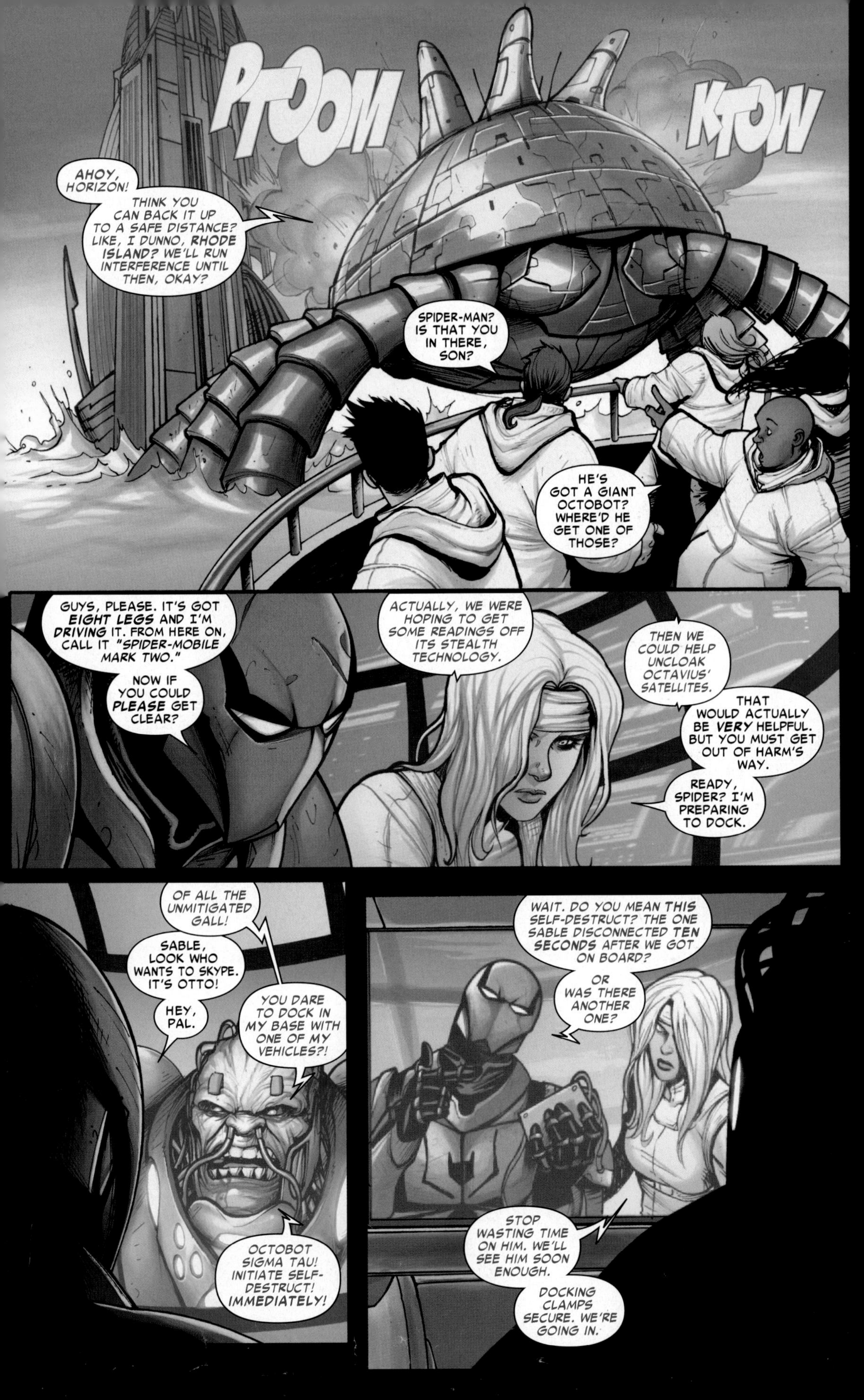
PTOOM
KTOW
AHOY, HORIZON!
THINK YOU CAN BACK IT UP TO A SAFE DISTANCE? LIKE, I DUNNO, RHODE ISLAND? WE'LL RUN INTERFERENCE UNTIL THEN, OKAY?
SPIDER-MAN? IS THAT YOU IN THERE, SON?
HE'S GOT A GIANT OCTOBOT? WHERE'D HE GET ONE OF THOSE?
GUYS, PLEASE. IT'S GOT EIGHT LEGS AND I'M DRIVING IT. FROM HERE ON, CALL IT "SPIDER-MOBILE MARK TWO."
NOW IF YOU COULD PLEASE GET CLEAR?
ACTUALLY, WE WERE HOPING TO GET SOME READINGS OFF ITS STEALTH TECHNOLOGY.
THEN WE COULD HELP UNCLOAK OCTAVIUS' SATELLITES.
THAT WOULD ACTUALLY BE VERY HELPFUL. BUT YOU MUST GET OUT OF HARM'S WAY.
READY, SPIDER? I'M PREPARING TO DOCK.
OF ALL THE UNMITIGATED GALL!
SABLE, LOOK WHO WANTS TO SKYPE. IT'S OTTO!
HEY, PAL.
YOU DARE TO DOCK IN MY BASE WITH ONE OF MY VEHICLES?!
OCTOBOT SIGMA TAU! INITIATE SELF-DESTRUCT! IMMEDIATELY!
WAIT. DO YOU MEAN THIS SELF-DESTRUCT? THE ONE SABLE DISCONNECTED TEN SECONDS AFTER WE GOT ON BOARD?
OR WAS THERE ANOTHER ONE?
STOP WASTING TIME ON HIM. WE'LL SEE HIM SOON ENOUGH.
DOCKING CLAMPS SECURE. WE'RE GOING IN.

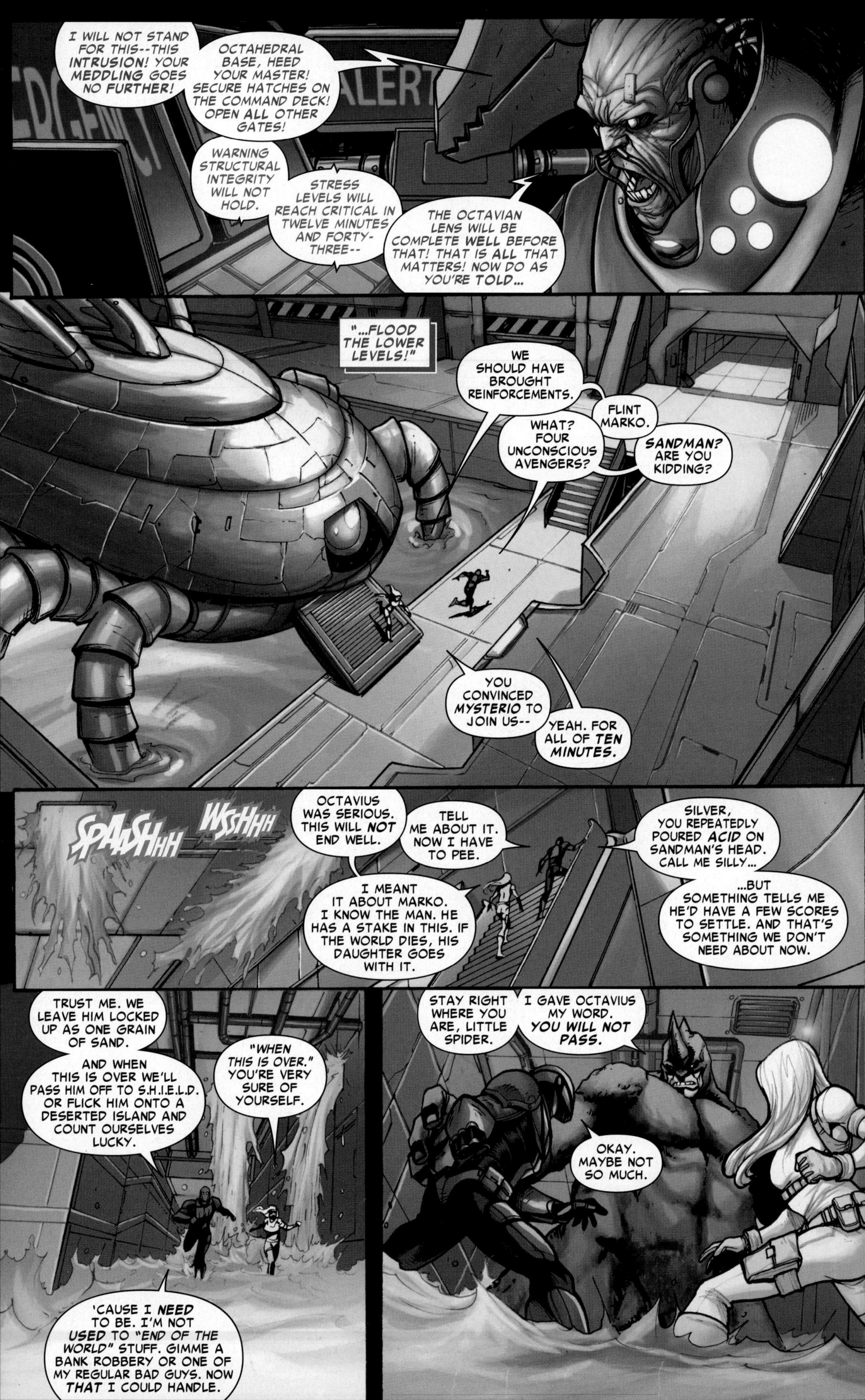
I WILL NOT STAND FOR THIS--THIS INTRUSION! YOUR MEDDLING GOES NO FURTHER!
OCTAHEDRAL BASE, HEED YOUR MASTER! SECURE HATCHES ON THE COMMAND DECK! OPEN ALL OTHER GATES!
WARNING STRUCTURAL INTEGRITY WILL NOT HOLD.
STRESS LEVELS WILL REACH CRITICAL IN TWELVE MINUTES AND FORTY-THREE--
THE OCTAVIAN LENS WILL BE COMPLETE WELL BEFORE THAT! THAT IS ALL THAT MATTERS! NOW DO AS YOU'RE TOLD...
"...FLOOD THE LOWER LEVELS!"
WE SHOULD HAVE BROUGHT REINFORCEMENTS.
WHAT? FOUR UNCONSCIOUS AVENGERS?
FLINT MARKO.
SANDMAN? ARE YOU KIDDING?
YOU CONVINCED MYSTERIO TO JOIN US--
YEAH. FOR ALL OF TEN MINUTES.
SPLAASHHH
WSSHHH
OCTAVIUS WAS SERIOUS. THIS WILL NOT END WELL.
TELL ME ABOUT IT. NOW I HAVE TO PEE.
I MEANT IT ABOUT MARKO. I KNOW THE MAN. HE HAS A STAKE IN THIS. IF THE WORLD DIES, HIS DAUGHTER GOES WITH IT.
SILVER, YOU REPEATEDLY POURED ACID ON SANDMAN'S HEAD. CALL ME SILLY...
...BUT SOMETHING TELLS ME HE'D HAVE A FEW SCORES TO SETTLE. AND THAT'S SOMETHING WE DON'T NEED ABOUT NOW.
TRUST ME. WE LEAVE HIM LOCKED UP AS ONE GRAIN OF SAND.
AND WHEN THIS IS OVER WE'LL PASS HIM OFF TO S.H.I.E.L.D. OR FLICK HIM ONTO A DESERTED ISLAND AND COUNT OURSELVES LUCKY.
"WHEN THIS IS OVER." YOU'RE VERY SURE OF YOURSELF.
'CAUSE I NEED TO BE. I'M NOT USED TO "END OF THE WORLD" STUFF. GIMME A BANK ROBBERY OR ONE OF MY REGULAR BAD GUYS. NOW THAT I COULD HANDLE.
STAY RIGHT WHERE YOU ARE, LITTLE SPIDER.
I GAVE OCTAVIUS MY WORD. YOU WILL NOT PASS.
OKAY. MAYBE NOT SO MUCH.

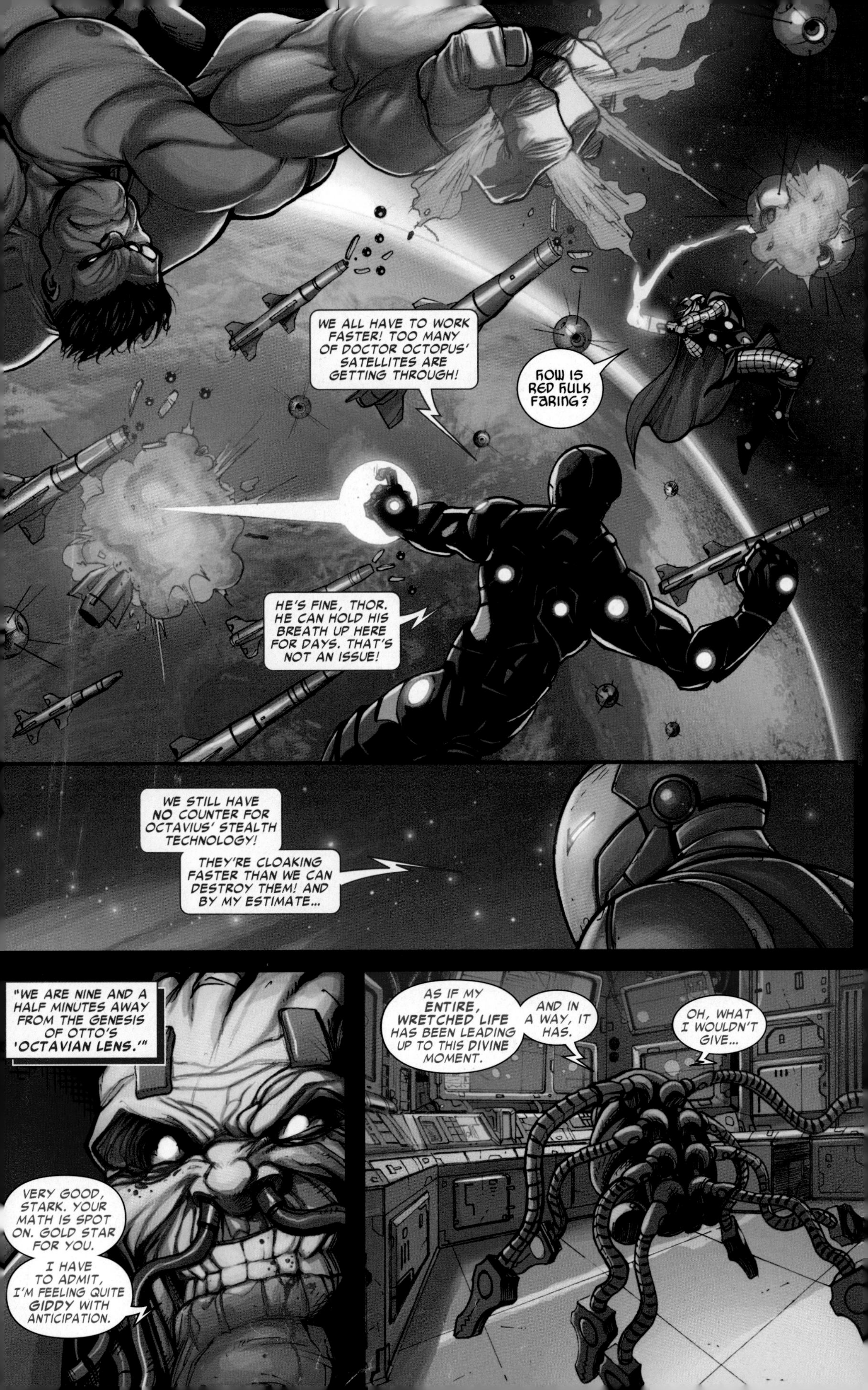
WE ALL HAVE TO WORK FASTER! TOO MANY OF DOCTOR OCTOPUS' SATELLITES ARE GETTING THROUGH!
HOW IS RED HULK FARING?
HE'S FINE, THOR. HE CAN HOLD HIS BREATH UP HERE FOR DAYS. THAT'S NOT AN ISSUE!
WE STILL HAVE NO COUNTER FOR OCTAVIUS' STEALTH TECHNOLOGY!
THEY'RE CLOAKING FASTER THAN WE CAN DESTROY THEM! AND BY MY ESTIMATE...
"WE ARE NINE AND A HALF MINUTES AWAY FROM THE GENESIS OF OTTO'S 'OCTAVIAN LENS.'"
VERY GOOD, STARK. YOUR MATH IS SPOT ON. GOLD STAR FOR YOU.
I HAVE TO ADMIT, I'M FEELING QUITE GIDDY WITH ANTICIPATION.
AS IF MY ENTIRE, WRETCHED LIFE HAS BEEN LEADING UP TO THIS DIVINE MOMENT.
AND IN A WAY, IT HAS.
OH, WHAT I WOULDN'T GIVE...

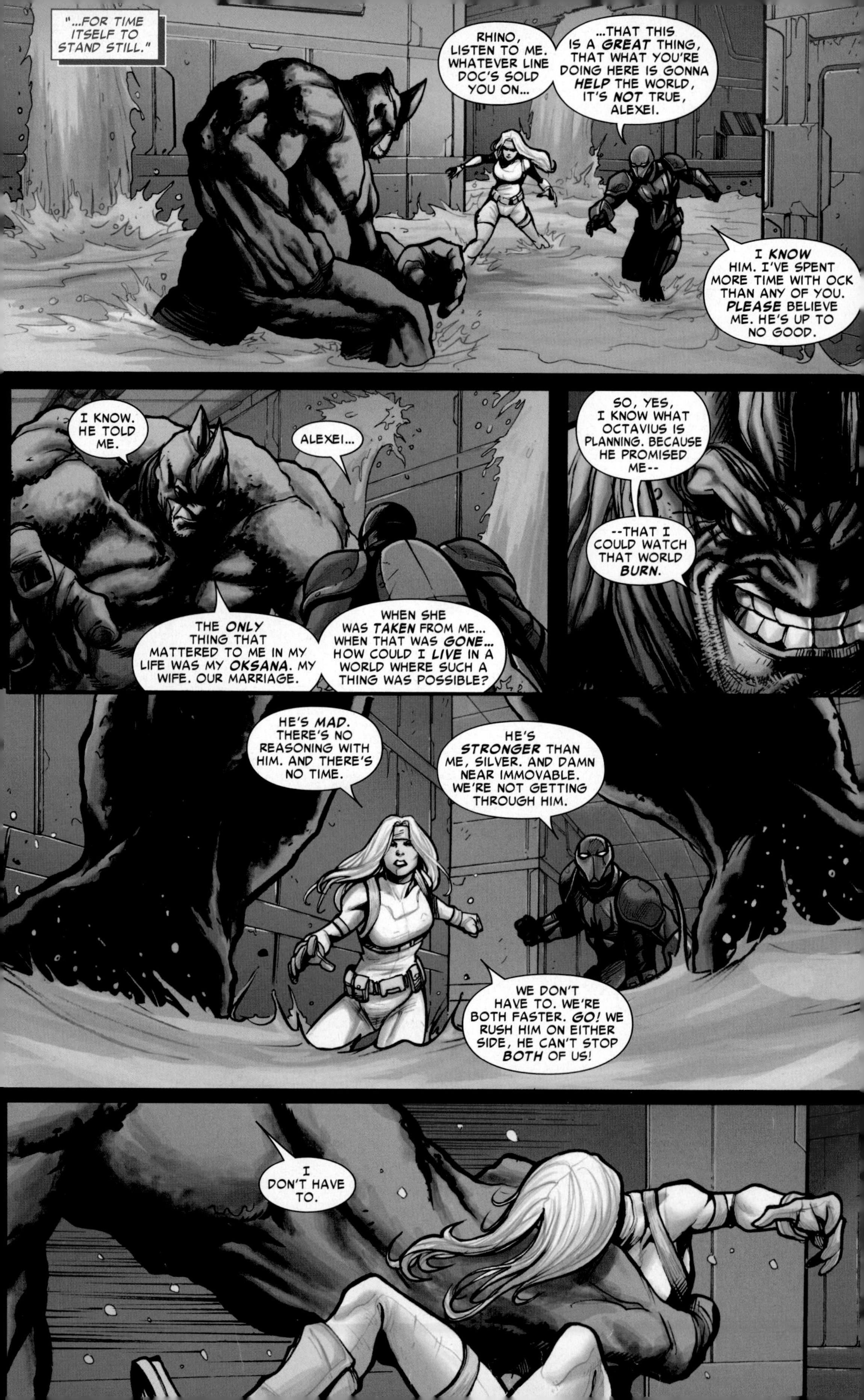
"...FOR TIME ITSELF TO STAND STILL."
RHINO, LISTEN TO ME. WHATEVER LINE DOC'S SOLD YOU ON...
...THAT THIS IS A GREAT THING, THAT WHAT YOU'RE DOING HERE IS GONNA HELP THE WORLD, IT'S NOT TRUE, ALEXEI.
I KNOW HIM. I'VE SPENT MORE TIME WITH OCK THAN ANY OF YOU. PLEASE BELIEVE ME. HE'S UP TO NO GOOD.
I KNOW. HE TOLD ME.
ALEXEI...
THE ONLY THING THAT MATTERED TO ME IN MY LIFE WAS MY OKSANA. MY WIFE. OUR MARRIAGE.
WHEN SHE WAS TAKEN FROM ME... WHEN THAT WAS GONE... HOW COULD I LIVE IN A WORLD WHERE SUCH A THING WAS POSSIBLE?
SO, YES, I KNOW WHAT OCTAVIUS IS PLANNING. BECAUSE HE PROMISED ME--
--THAT I COULD WATCH THAT WORLD BURN.
HE'S MAD. THERE'S NO REASONING WITH HIM. AND THERE'S NO TIME.
HE'S STRONGER THAN ME, SILVER. AND DAMN NEAR IMMOVABLE. WE'RE NOT GETTING THROUGH HIM.
WE DON'T HAVE TO. WE'RE BOTH FASTER. GO! WE RUSH HIM ON EITHER SIDE, HE CAN'T STOP BOTH OF US!
I DON'T HAVE TO.

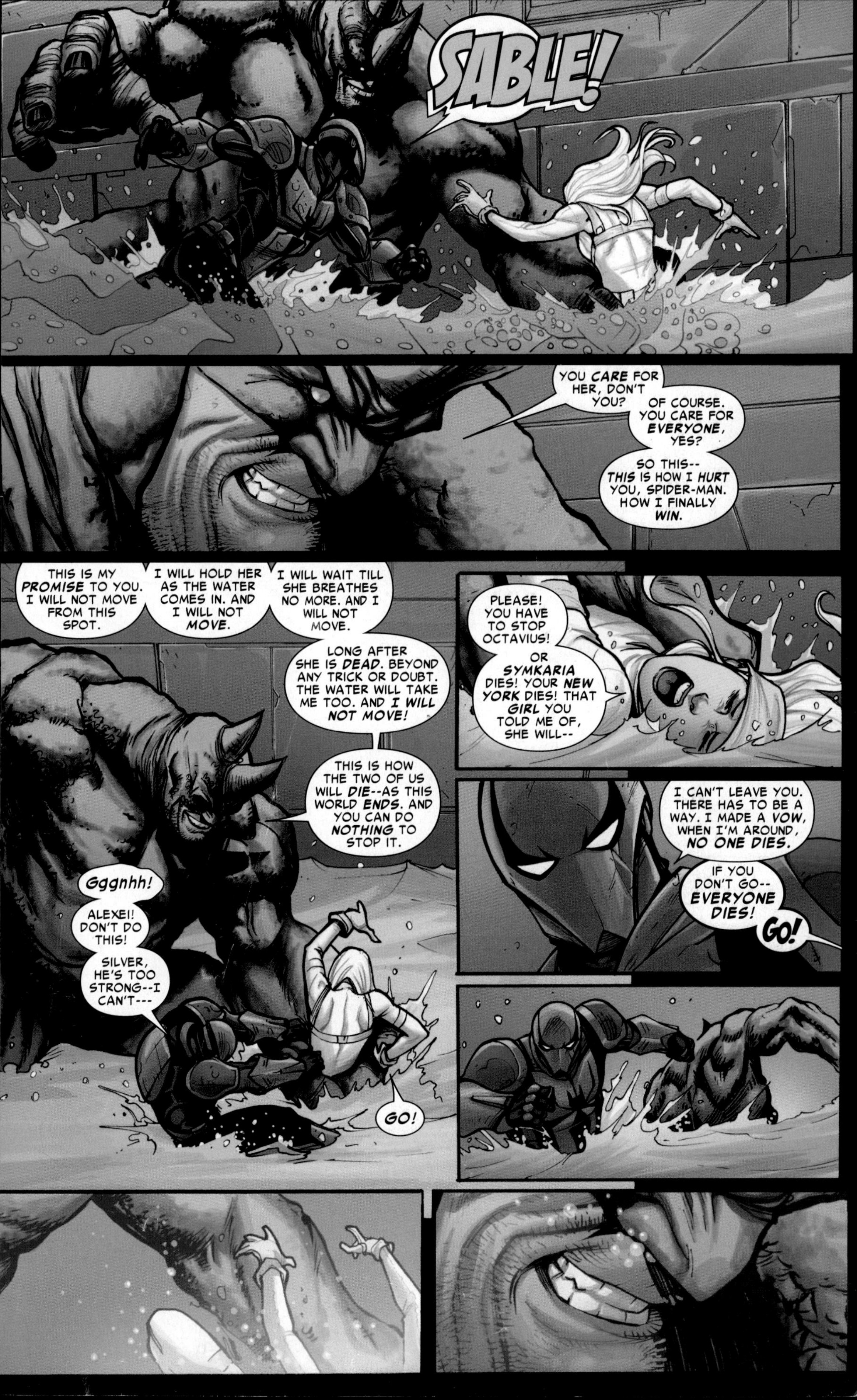
SABLE!
YOU CARE FOR HER, DON'T YOU?
OF COURSE. YOU CARE FOR EVERYONE, YES?
SO THIS-- THIS IS HOW I HURT YOU, SPIDER-MAN. HOW I FINALLY WIN.
THIS IS MY PROMISE TO YOU. I WILL NOT MOVE FROM THIS SPOT.
I WILL HOLD HER AS THE WATER COMES IN. AND I WILL NOT MOVE.
I WILL WAIT TILL SHE BREATHES NO MORE. AND I WILL NOT MOVE.
LONG AFTER SHE IS DEAD. BEYOND ANY TRICK OR DOUBT. THE WATER WILL TAKE ME TOO. AND I WILL NOT MOVE!
THIS IS HOW THE TWO OF US WILL DIE--AS THIS WORLD ENDS. AND YOU CAN DO NOTHING TO STOP IT.
Gggnhh!
ALEXEI! DON'T DO THIS!
SILVER, HE'S TOO STRONG--I CAN'T---
GO!
PLEASE! YOU HAVE TO STOP OCTAVIUS!
OR SYMKARIA DIES! YOUR NEW YORK DIES! THAT GIRL YOU TOLD ME OF, SHE WILL--
I CAN'T LEAVE YOU. THERE HAS TO BE A WAY. I MADE A VOW, WHEN I'M AROUND, NO ONE DIES.
IF YOU DON'T GO-- EVERYONE DIES!
GO!

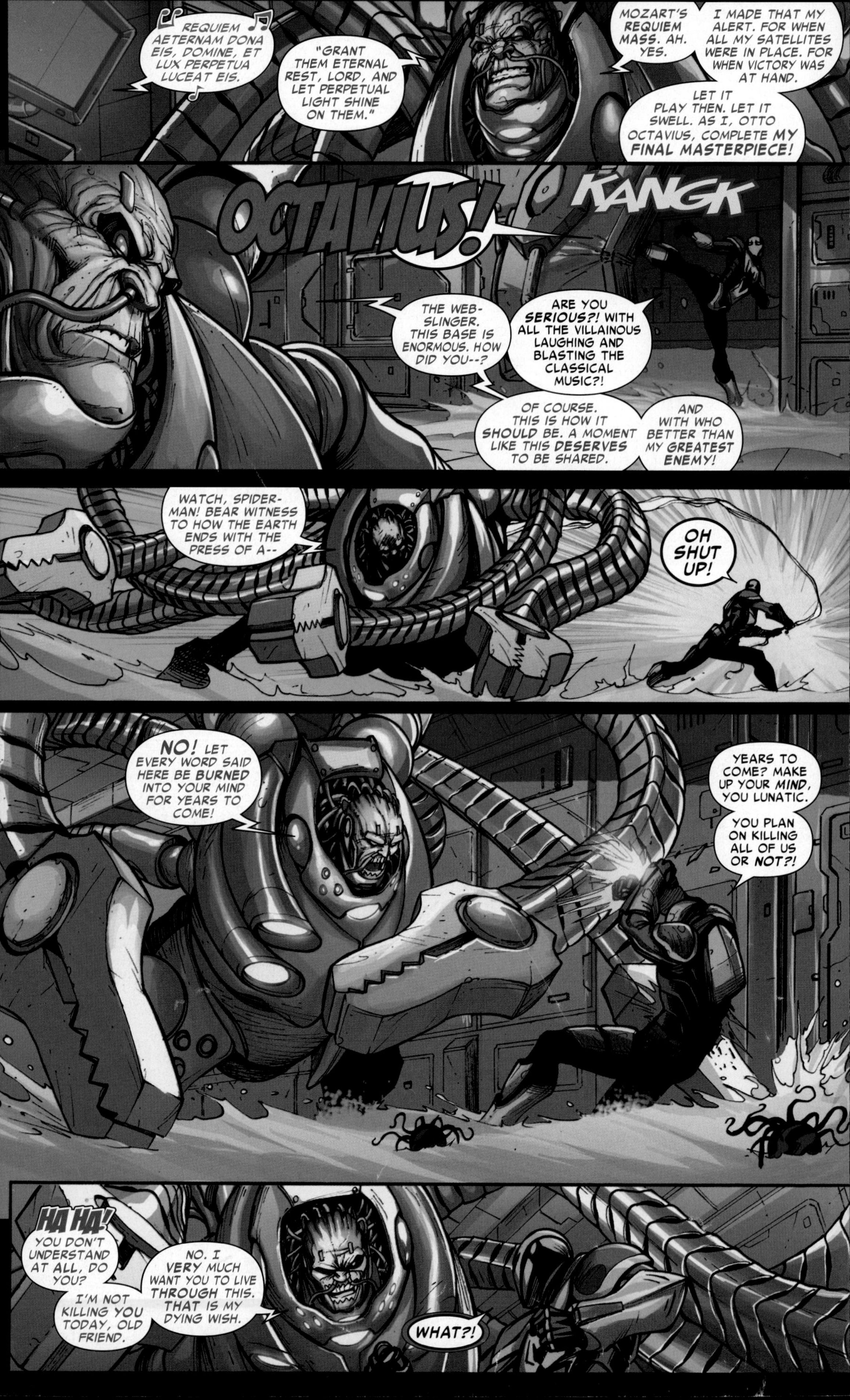
REQUIEM AETERNAM DONA EIS, DOMINE, ET LUX PERPETUA LUCEAT EIS.
"GRANT THEM ETERNAL REST, LORD, AND LET PERPETUAL LIGHT SHINE ON THEM."
MOZART'S REQUIEM MASS. AH. YES.
I MADE THAT MY ALERT. FOR WHEN ALL MY SATELLITES WERE IN PLACE. FOR WHEN VICTORY WAS AT HAND.
LET IT PLAY THEN. LET IT SWELL. AS I, OTTO OCTAVIUS, COMPLETE MY FINAL MASTERPIECE!
OCTAVIUS!
KANGK
THE WEB-SLINGER. THIS BASE IS ENORMOUS. HOW DID YOU--?
ARE YOU SERIOUS?! WITH ALL THE VILLAINOUS LAUGHING AND BLASTING THE CLASSICAL MUSIC?!
OF COURSE. THIS IS HOW IT SHOULD BE. A MOMENT LIKE THIS DESERVES TO BE SHARED.
AND WITH WHO BETTER THAN MY GREATEST ENEMY!
WATCH, SPIDER-MAN! BEAR WITNESS TO HOW THE EARTH ENDS WITH THE PRESS OF A--
OH SHUT UP!
NO! LET EVERY WORD SAID HERE BE BURNED INTO YOUR MIND FOR YEARS TO COME!
YEARS TO COME? MAKE UP YOUR MIND, YOU LUNATIC.
YOU PLAN ON KILLING ALL OF US OR NOT?!
HA HA!
YOU DON'T UNDERSTAND AT ALL, DO YOU?
I'M NOT KILLING YOU TODAY, OLD FRIEND.
NO. I VERY MUCH WANT YOU TO LIVE THROUGH THIS. THAT IS MY DYING WISH.
WHAT?!

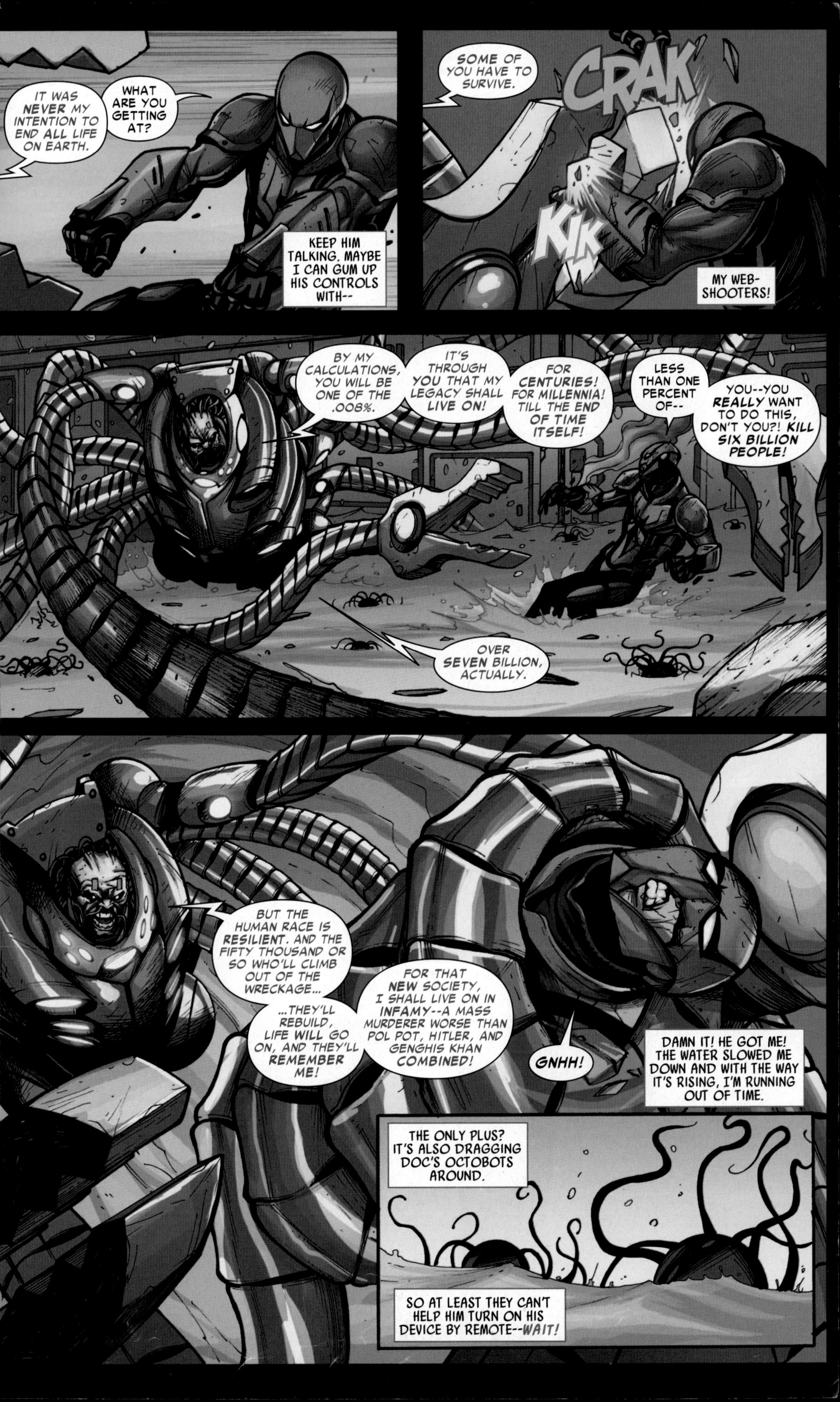
IT WAS NEVER MY INTENTION TO END ALL LIFE ON EARTH.
WHAT ARE YOU GETTING AT?
KEEP HIM TALKING. MAYBE I CAN GUM UP HIS CONTROLS WITH--
SOME OF YOU HAVE TO SURVIVE.
CRAK
KLIK
MY WEB-SHOOTERS!
BY MY CALCULATIONS, YOU WILL BE ONE OF THE .008%.
IT'S THROUGH YOU THAT MY LEGACY SHALL LIVE ON!
FOR CENTURIES! FOR MILLENNIA! TILL THE END OF TIME ITSELF!
LESS THAN ONE PERCENT OF--
YOU--YOU REALLY WANT TO DO THIS, DON'T YOU?! KILL SIX BILLION PEOPLE!
OVER SEVEN BILLION, ACTUALLY.
BUT THE HUMAN RACE IS RESILIENT. AND THE FIFTY THOUSAND OR SO WHO'LL CLIMB OUT OF THE WRECKAGE...
...THEY'LL REBUILD, LIFE WILL GO ON, AND THEY'LL REMEMBER ME!
FOR THAT NEW SOCIETY, I SHALL LIVE ON IN INFAMY--A MASS MURDERER WORSE THAN POL POT, HITLER, AND GENGHIS KHAN COMBINED!
GNHH!
DAMN IT! HE GOT ME! THE WATER SLOWED ME DOWN AND WITH THE WAY IT'S RISING, I'M RUNNING OUT OF TIME.
THE ONLY PLUS? IT'S ALSO DRAGGING DOC'S OCTOBOTS AROUND.
SO AT LEAST THEY CAN'T HELP HIM TURN ON HIS DEVICE BY REMOTE--WAIT!

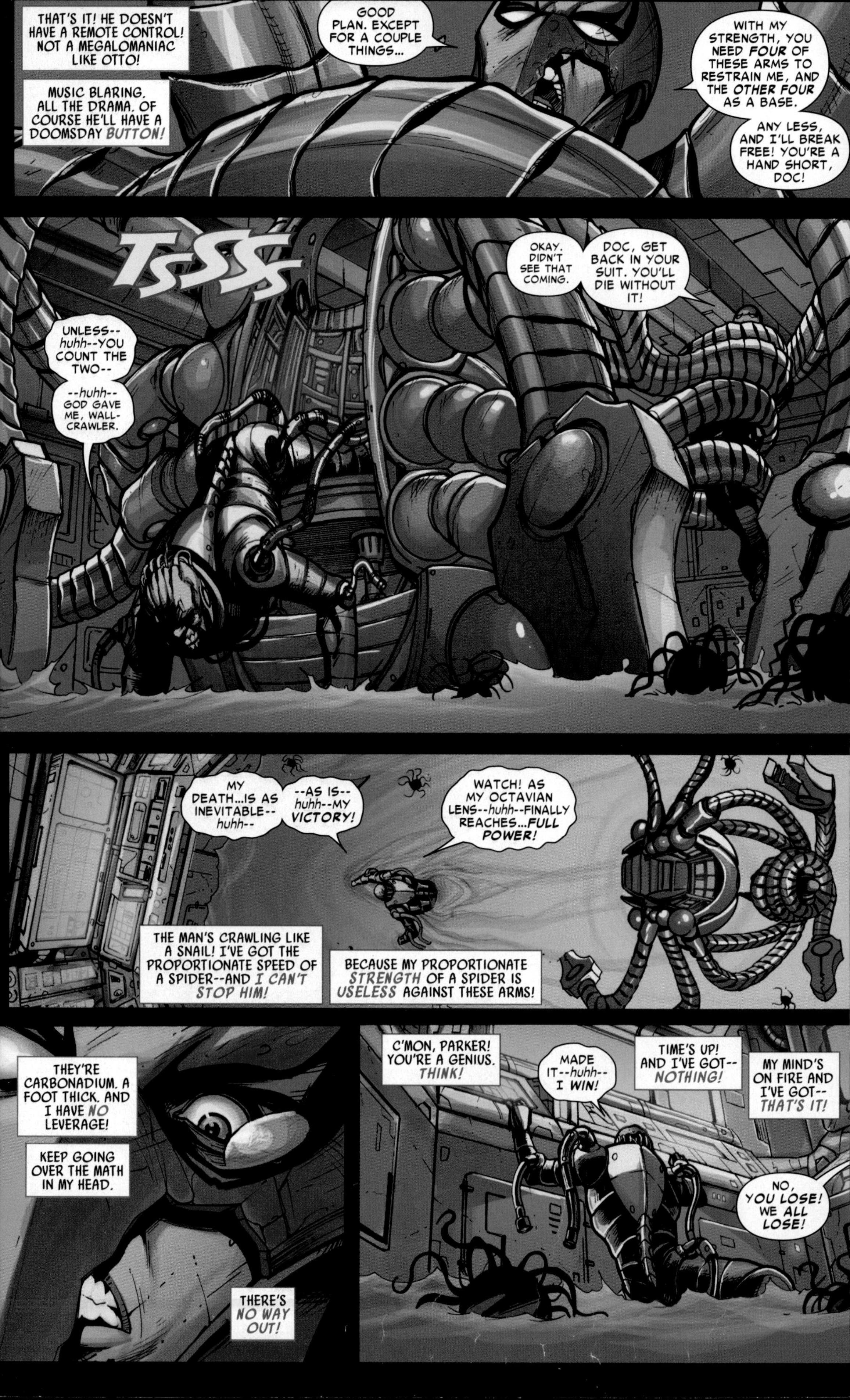
THAT'S IT! HE DOESN'T HAVE A REMOTE CONTROL! NOT A MEGALOMANIAC LIKE OTTO!
MUSIC BLARING. ALL THE DRAMA. OF COURSE HE'LL HAVE A DOOMSDAY BUTTON!
GOOD PLAN. EXCEPT FOR A COUPLE THINGS...
WITH MY STRENGTH, YOU NEED FOUR OF THESE ARMS TO RESTRAIN ME, AND THE OTHER FOUR AS A BASE.
ANY LESS, AND I'LL BREAK FREE! YOU'RE A HAND SHORT, DOC!
TSSSS
UNLESS--huhh--YOU COUNT THE TWO--
--huhh--GOD GAVE ME, WALL-CRAWLER.
OKAY. DIDN'T SEE THAT COMING.
DOC, GET BACK IN YOUR SUIT. YOU'LL DIE WITHOUT IT!
MY DEATH...IS AS INEVITABLE--huhh--
--AS IS--huhh--MY VICTORY!
WATCH! AS MY OCTAVIAN LENS--huhh--FINALLY REACHES...FULL POWER!
THE MAN'S CRAWLING LIKE A SNAIL! I'VE GOT THE PROPORTIONATE SPEED OF A SPIDER--AND I CAN'T STOP HIM!
BECAUSE MY PROPORTIONATE STRENGTH OF A SPIDER IS USELESS AGAINST THESE ARMS!
THEY'RE CARBONADIUM. A FOOT THICK. AND I HAVE NO LEVERAGE!
KEEP GOING OVER THE MATH IN MY HEAD.
THERE'S NO WAY OUT!
C'MON, PARKER! YOU'RE A GENIUS. THINK!
MADE IT--huhh--I WIN!
TIME'S UP! AND I'VE GOT--NOTHING!
MY MIND'S ON FIRE AND I'VE GOT--THAT'S IT!
NO, YOU LOSE! WE ALL LOSE!

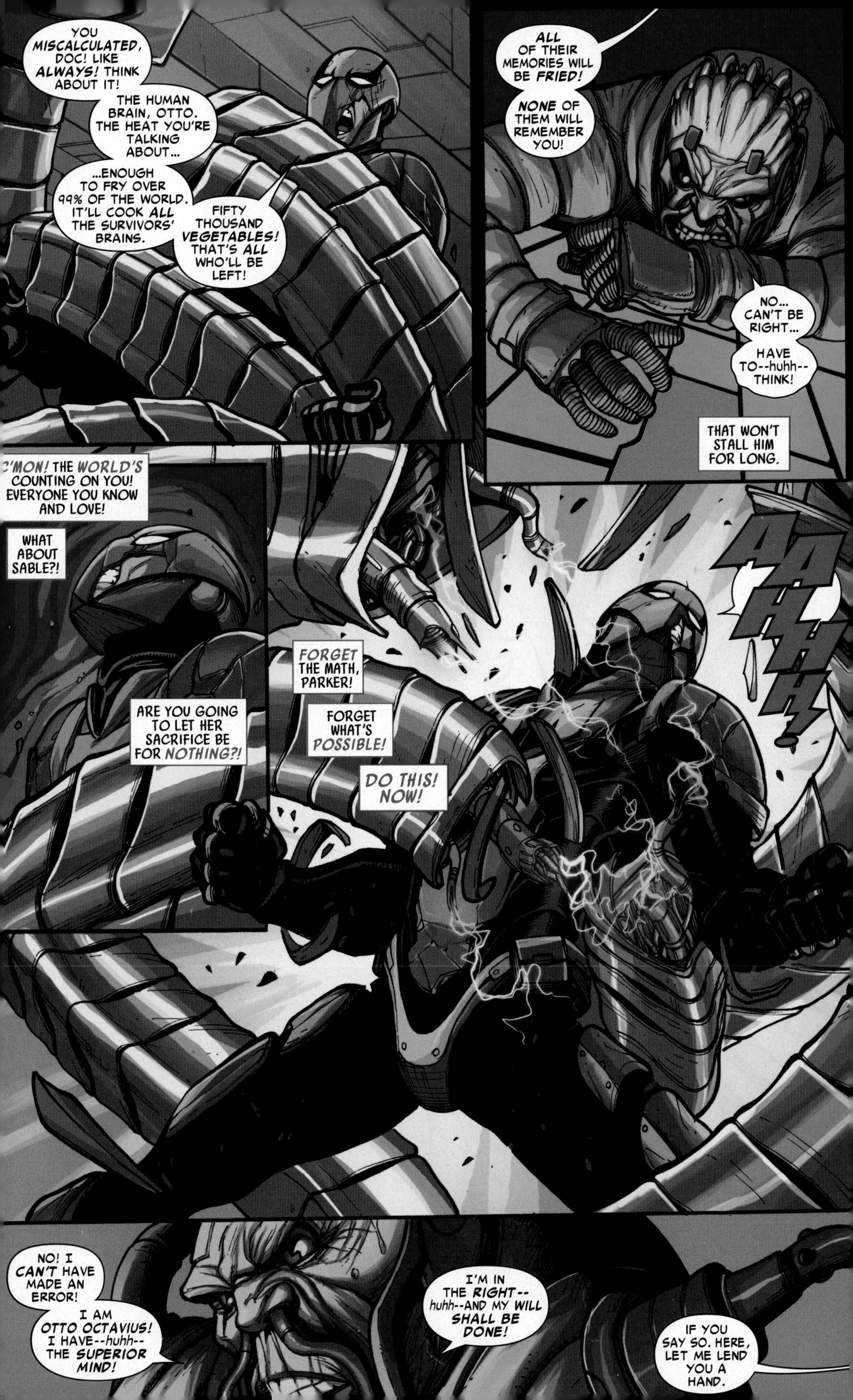

YOU MISCALCULATED, DOC! LIKE ALWAYS! THINK ABOUT IT!
THE HUMAN BRAIN, OTTO. THE HEAT YOU'RE TALKING ABOUT...
...ENOUGH TO FRY OVER 99% OF THE WORLD. IT'LL COOK ALL THE SURVIVORS' BRAINS.
FIFTY THOUSAND VEGETABLES! THAT'S ALL WHO'LL BE LEFT!
ALL OF THEIR MEMORIES WILL BE FRIED!
NONE OF THEM WILL REMEMBER YOU!
NO... CAN'T BE RIGHT...
HAVE TO--huhh--THINK!
THAT WON'T STALL HIM FOR LONG.
C'MON! THE WORLD'S COUNTING ON YOU! EVERYONE YOU KNOW AND LOVE!
WHAT ABOUT SABLE?!
ARE YOU GOING TO LET HER SACRIFICE BE FOR NOTHING?!
FORGET THE MATH, PARKER!
FORGET WHAT'S POSSIBLE!
DO THIS! NOW!
AAHHHH!
NO! I CAN'T HAVE MADE AN ERROR!
I AM OTTO OCTAVIUS! I HAVE--huhh--THE SUPERIOR MIND!
I'M IN THE RIGHT--huhh--AND MY WILL SHALL BE DONE!
IF YOU SAY SO. HERE, LET ME LEND YOU A HAND.

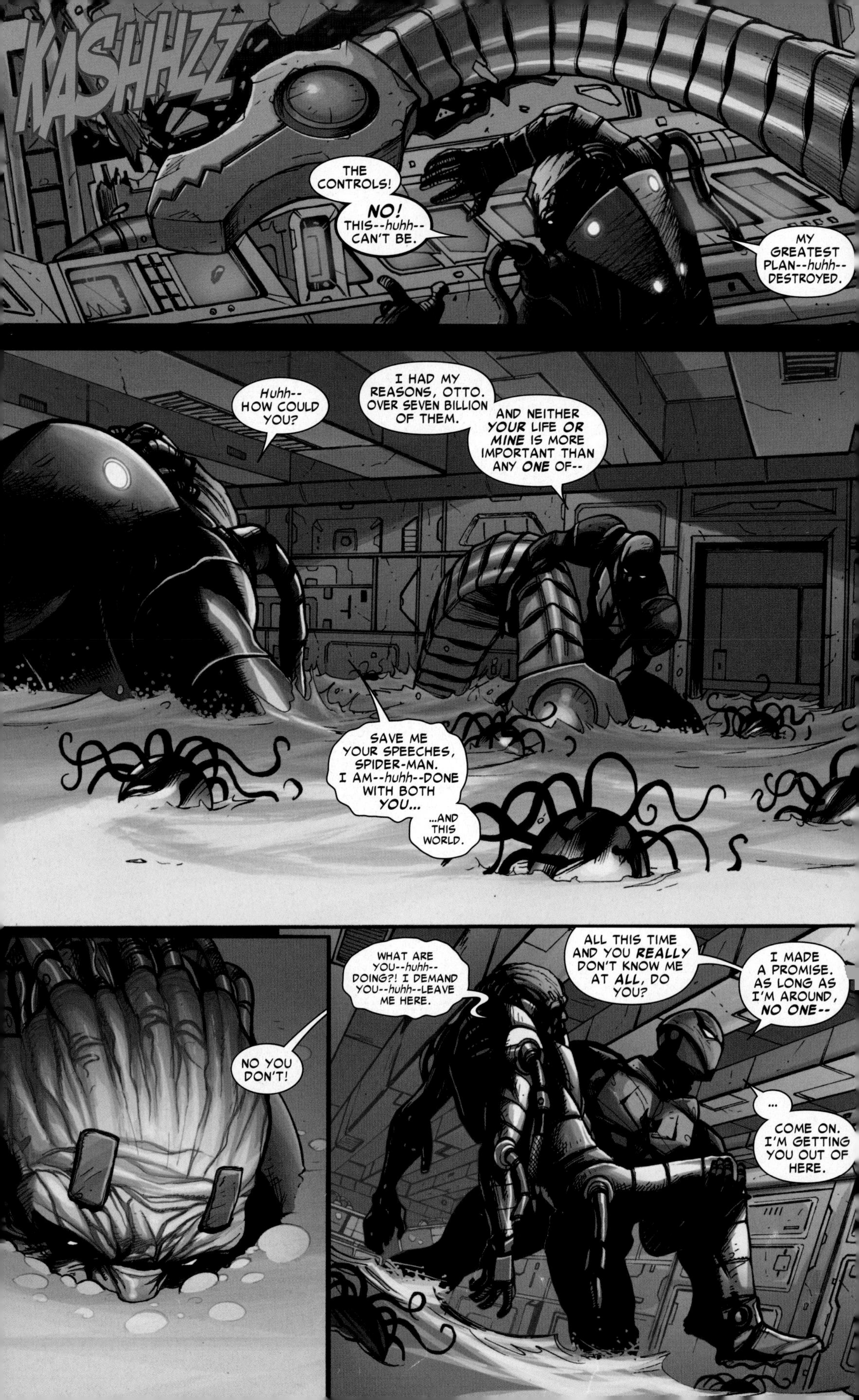
KASHHZZ
THE CONTROLS!
NO! THIS--huhh--CAN'T BE.
MY GREATEST PLAN--huhh--DESTROYED.
Huhh--HOW COULD YOU?
I HAD MY REASONS, OTTO. OVER SEVEN BILLION OF THEM.
AND NEITHER YOUR LIFE OR MINE IS MORE IMPORTANT THAN ANY ONE OF--
SAVE ME YOUR SPEECHES, SPIDER-MAN. I AM--huhh--DONE WITH BOTH YOU...
...AND THIS WORLD.
NO YOU DON'T!
WHAT ARE YOU--huhh--DOING?! I DEMAND YOU--huhh--LEAVE ME HERE.
ALL THIS TIME AND YOU REALLY DON'T KNOW ME AT ALL, DO YOU?
I MADE A PROMISE. AS LONG AS I'M AROUND, NO ONE--
...
COME ON. I'M GETTING YOU OUT OF HERE.

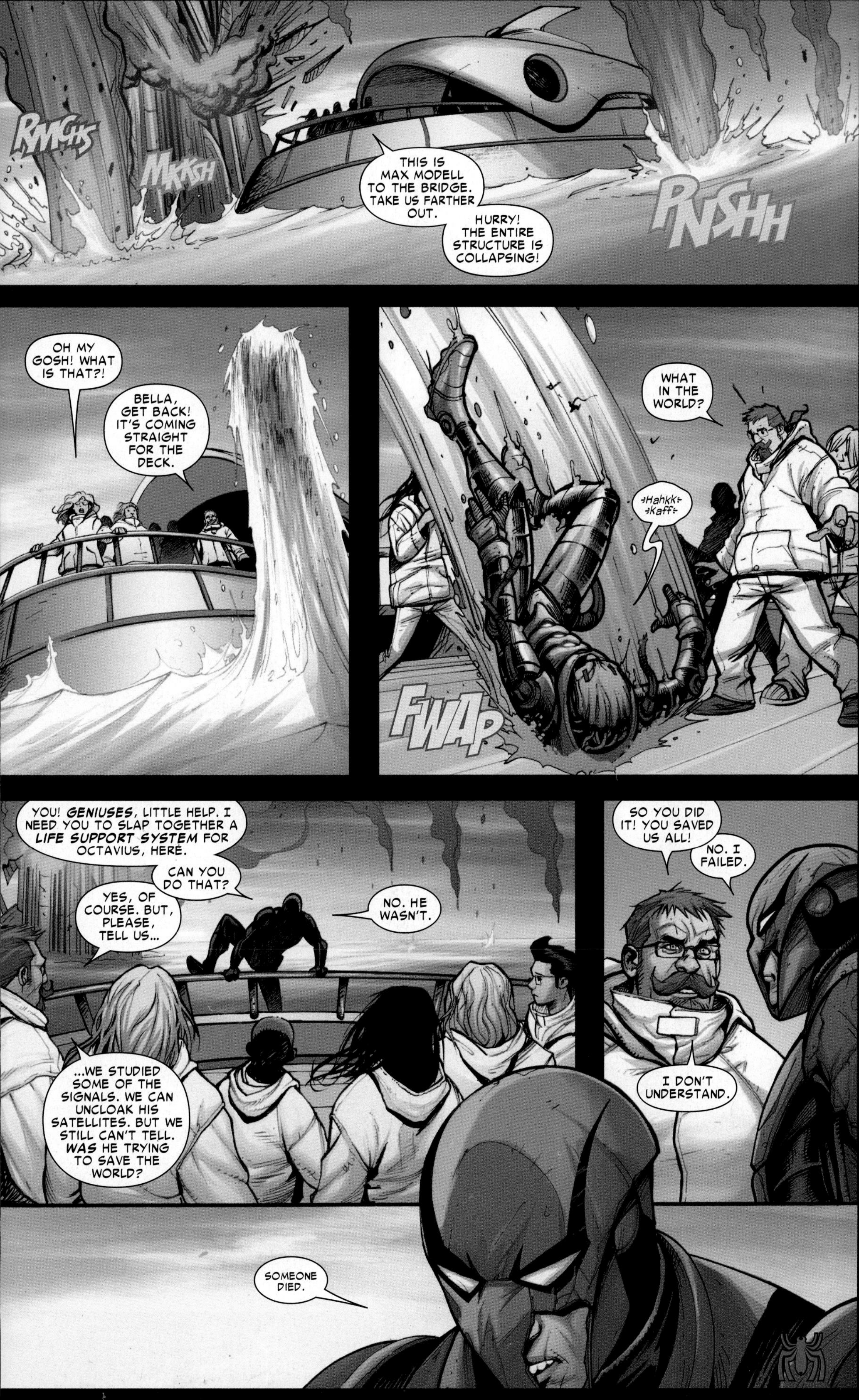
RMCHS
MKKSH
THIS IS MAX MODELL TO THE BRIDGE. TAKE US FARTHER OUT.
HURRY! THE ENTIRE STRUCTURE IS COLLAPSING!
PNSHH
OH MY GOSH! WHAT IS THAT?!
BELLA, GET BACK! IT'S COMING STRAIGHT FOR THE DECK.
WHAT IN THE WORLD?
Hahkk Kaff
FWAP
YOU! GENIUSES, LITTLE HELP. I NEED YOU TO SLAP TOGETHER A LIFE SUPPORT SYSTEM FOR OCTAVIUS, HERE.
CAN YOU DO THAT?
YES, OF COURSE. BUT, PLEASE, TELL US...
...WE STUDIED SOME OF THE SIGNALS. WE CAN UNCLOAK HIS SATELLITES. BUT WE STILL CAN'T TELL. WAS HE TRYING TO SAVE THE WORLD?
NO. HE WASN'T.
SO YOU DID IT! YOU SAVED US ALL!
NO. I FAILED.
I DON'T UNDERSTAND.
SOMEONE DIED.

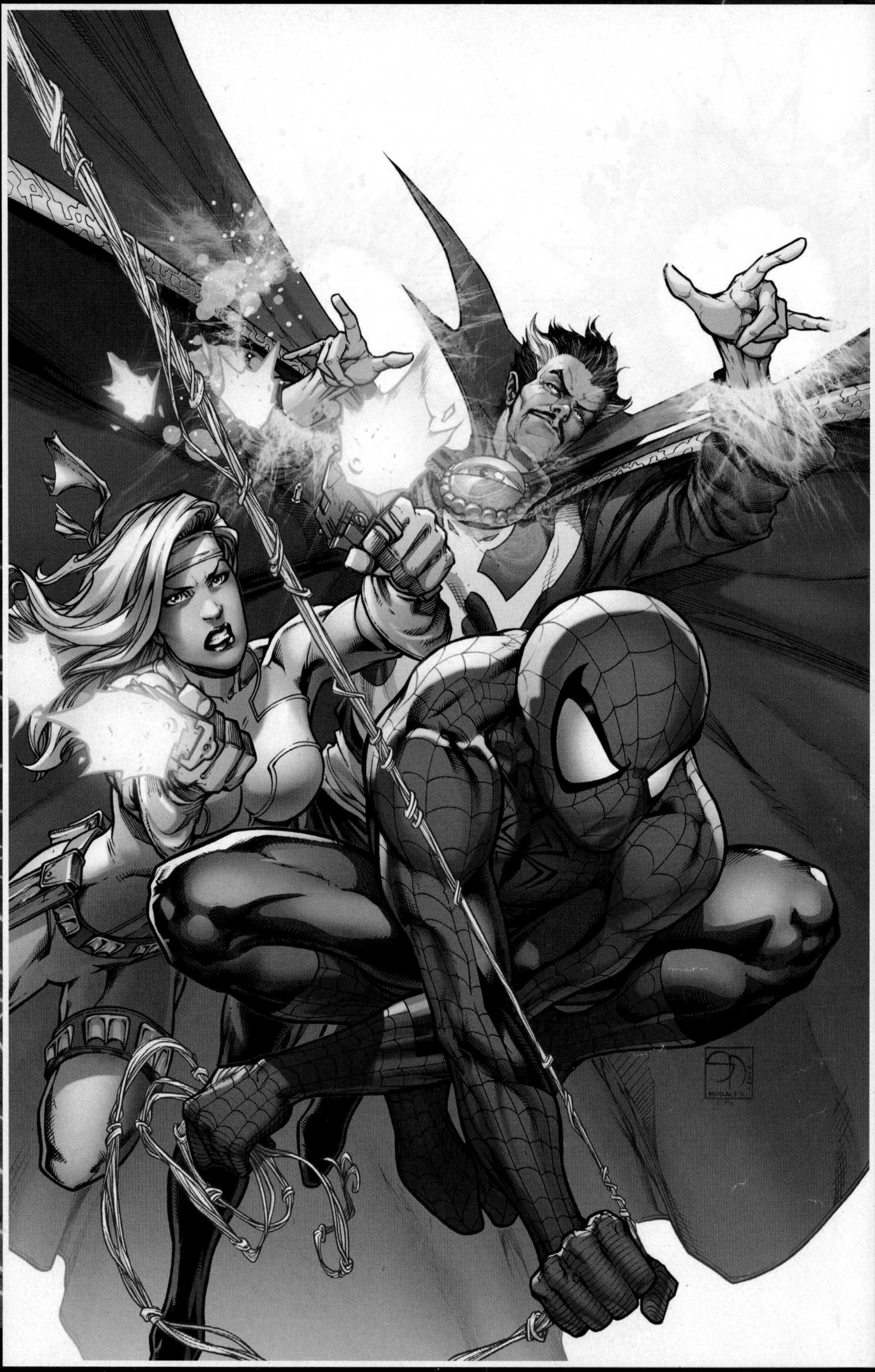

AVENGING SPIDER-MAN #8
COVER BY SHANE DAVIS, MARK MORALES & JUSTIN PONSOR

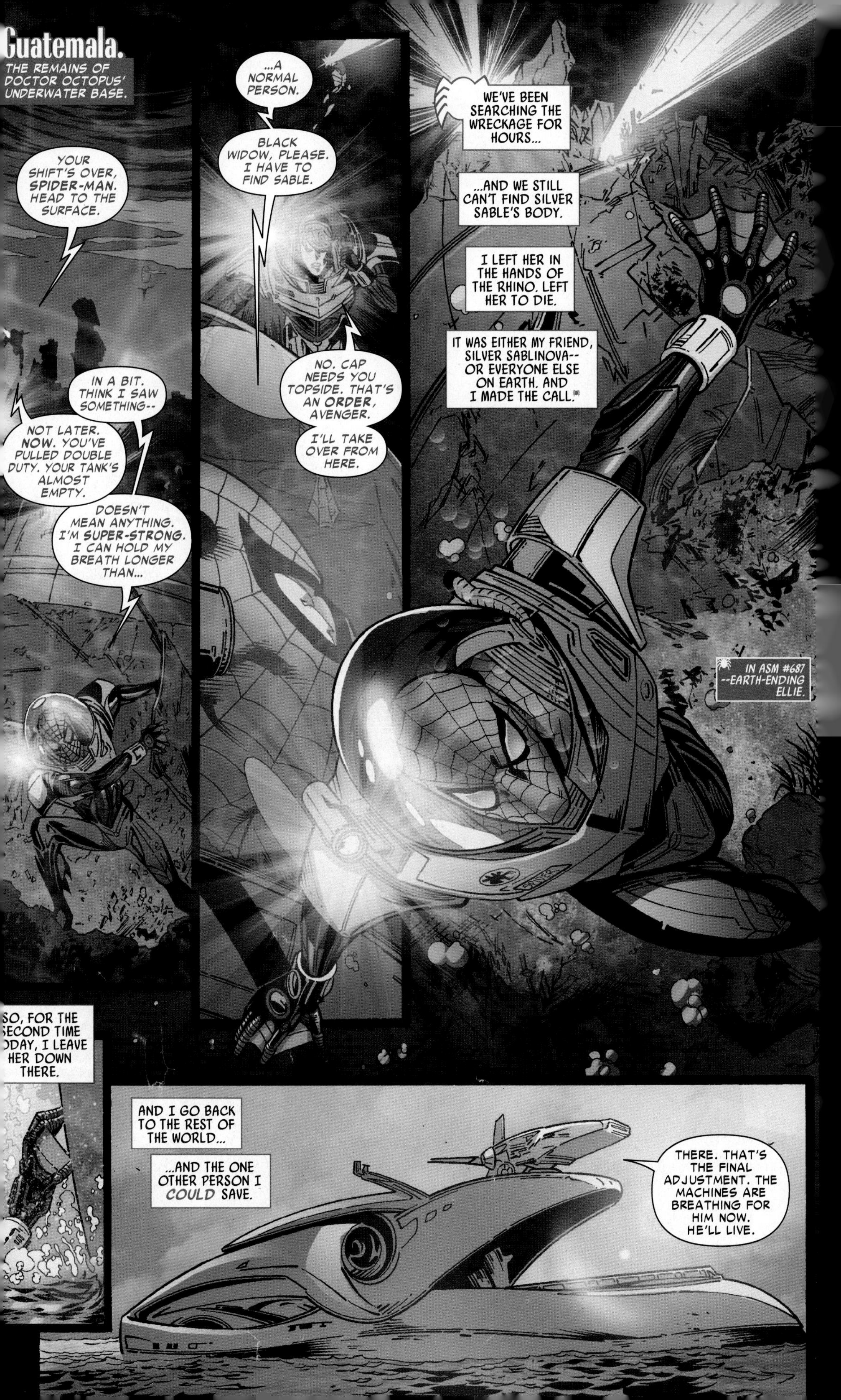

Guatemala.
THE REMAINS OF DOCTOR OCTOPUS' UNDERWATER BASE.
YOUR SHIFT'S OVER, SPIDER-MAN. HEAD TO THE SURFACE.
IN A BIT. THINK I SAW SOMETHING--
NOT LATER. NOW. YOU'VE PULLED DOUBLE DUTY. YOUR TANK'S ALMOST EMPTY.
DOESN'T MEAN ANYTHING. I'M SUPER-STRONG. I CAN HOLD MY BREATH LONGER THAN...
...A NORMAL PERSON.
BLACK WIDOW, PLEASE. I HAVE TO FIND SABLE.
NO. CAP NEEDS YOU TOPSIDE. THAT'S AN ORDER, AVENGER.
I'LL TAKE OVER FROM HERE.
WE'VE BEEN SEARCHING THE WRECKAGE FOR HOURS...
...AND WE STILL CAN'T FIND SILVER SABLE'S BODY.
I LEFT HER IN THE HANDS OF THE RHINO. LEFT HER TO DIE.
IT WAS EITHER MY FRIEND, SILVER SABLINOVA-- OR EVERYONE ELSE ON EARTH. AND I MADE THE CALL.
IN ASM #687 --EARTH-ENDING ELLIE.
SO, FOR THE SECOND TIME TODAY, I LEAVE HER DOWN THERE.
AND I GO BACK TO THE REST OF THE WORLD...
...AND THE ONE OTHER PERSON I COULD SAVE.
THERE. THAT'S THE FINAL ADJUSTMENT. THE MACHINES ARE BREATHING FOR HIM NOW. HE'LL LIVE.

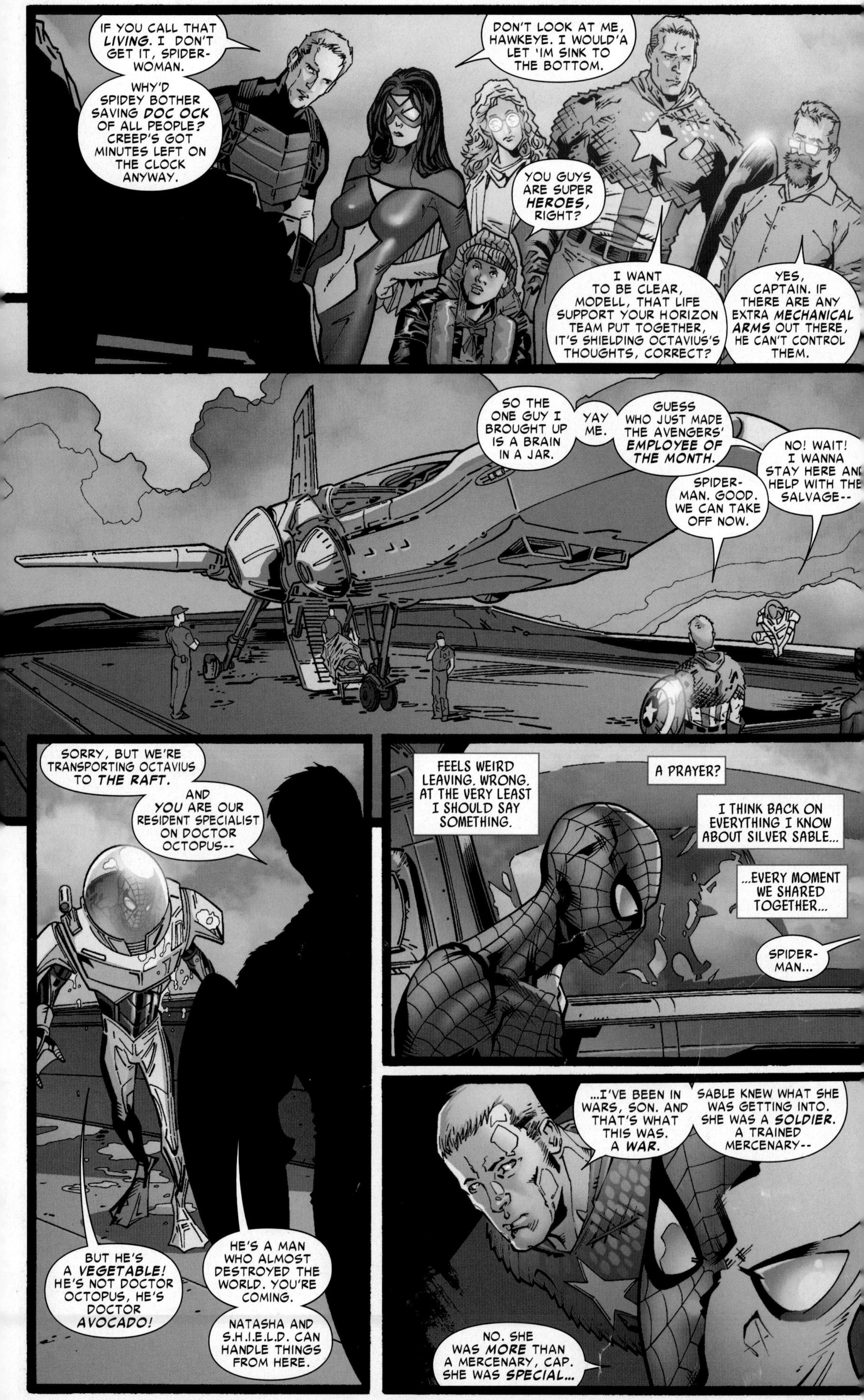
IF YOU CALL THAT LIVING. I DON'T GET IT, SPIDER-WOMAN.
WHY'D SPIDEY BOTHER SAVING DOC OCK OF ALL PEOPLE? CREEP'S GOT MINUTES LEFT ON THE CLOCK ANYWAY.
DON'T LOOK AT ME, HAWKEYE. I WOULD'A LET 'IM SINK TO THE BOTTOM.
YOU GUYS ARE SUPER HEROES, RIGHT?
I WANT TO BE CLEAR, MODELL, THAT LIFE SUPPORT YOUR HORIZON TEAM PUT TOGETHER, IT'S SHIELDING OCTAVIUS'S THOUGHTS, CORRECT?
YES, CAPTAIN. IF THERE ARE ANY EXTRA MECHANICAL ARMS OUT THERE, HE CAN'T CONTROL THEM.
SO THE ONE GUY I BROUGHT UP IS A BRAIN IN A JAR.
YAY ME.
GUESS WHO JUST MADE THE AVENGERS' EMPLOYEE OF THE MONTH.
SPIDER-MAN. GOOD. WE CAN TAKE OFF NOW.
NO! WAIT! I WANNA STAY HERE AND HELP WITH THE SALVAGE--
SORRY, BUT WE'RE TRANSPORTING OCTAVIUS TO THE RAFT.
AND YOU ARE OUR RESIDENT SPECIALIST ON DOCTOR OCTOPUS--
BUT HE'S A VEGETABLE! HE'S NOT DOCTOR OCTOPUS, HE'S DOCTOR AVOCADO!
HE'S A MAN WHO ALMOST DESTROYED THE WORLD. YOU'RE COMING.
NATASHA AND S.H.I.E.L.D. CAN HANDLE THINGS FROM HERE.
FEELS WEIRD LEAVING. WRONG. AT THE VERY LEAST I SHOULD SAY SOMETHING.
A PRAYER?
I THINK BACK ON EVERYTHING I KNOW ABOUT SILVER SABLE...
...EVERY MOMENT WE SHARED TOGETHER...
SPIDER-MAN...
...I'VE BEEN IN WARS, SON. AND THAT'S WHAT THIS WAS. A WAR.
SABLE KNEW WHAT SHE WAS GETTING INTO. SHE WAS A SOLDIER. A TRAINED MERCENARY--
NO. SHE WAS MORE THAN A MERCENARY, CAP. SHE WAS SPECIAL...

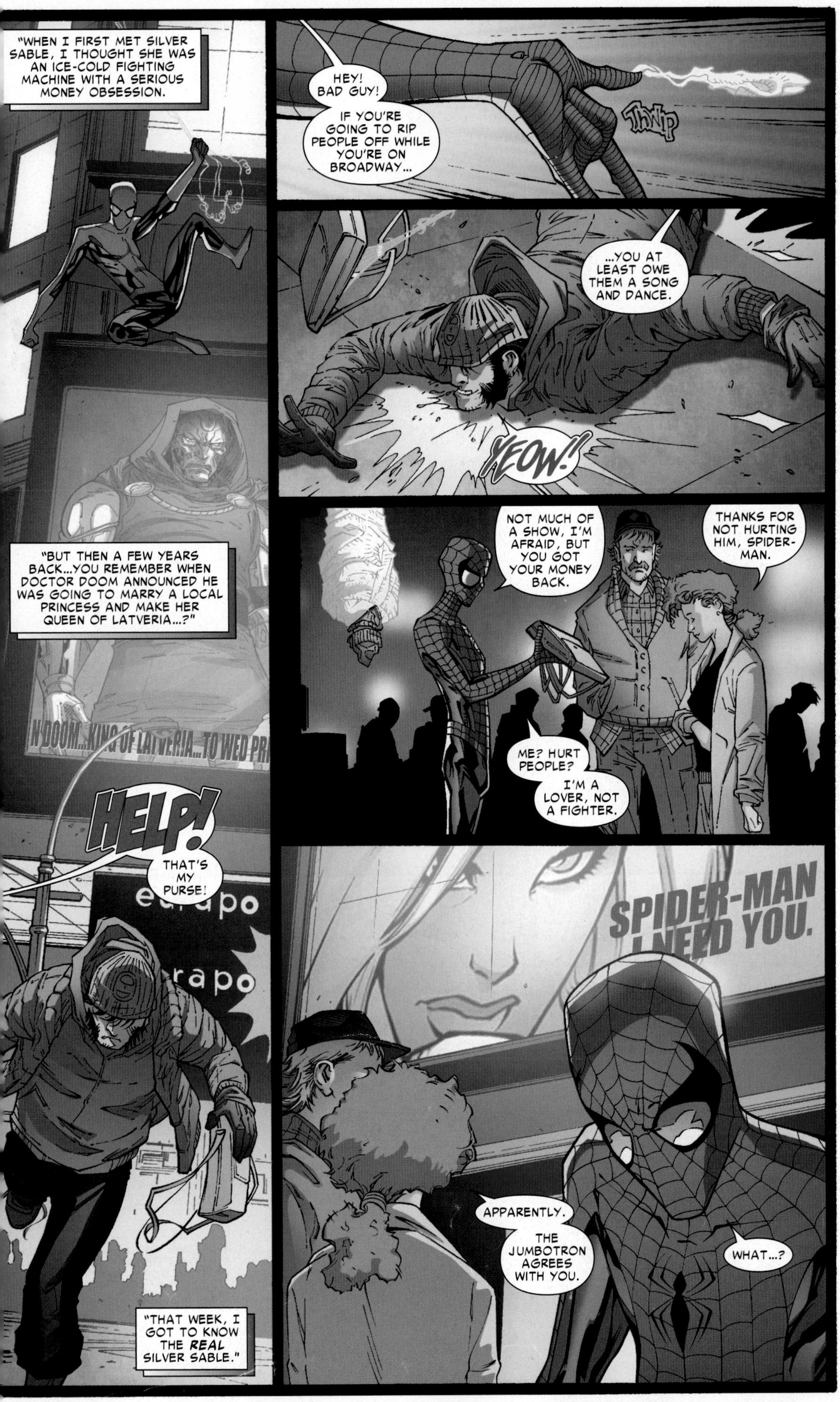
"WHEN I FIRST MET SILVER SABLE, I THOUGHT SHE WAS AN ICE-COLD FIGHTING MACHINE WITH A SERIOUS MONEY OBSESSION.
"BUT THEN A FEW YEARS BACK...YOU REMEMBER WHEN DOCTOR DOOM ANNOUNCED HE WAS GOING TO MARRY A LOCAL PRINCESS AND MAKE HER QUEEN OF LATVERIA...?"
N DOOM...KING OF LATVERIA...TO WED PR
HELP!
THAT'S MY PURSE!
"THAT WEEK, I GOT TO KNOW THE REAL SILVER SABLE."
HEY! BAD GUY!
IF YOU'RE GOING TO RIP PEOPLE OFF WHILE YOU'RE ON BROADWAY...
THWIP
...YOU AT LEAST OWE THEM A SONG AND DANCE.
YEOW!
NOT MUCH OF A SHOW, I'M AFRAID, BUT YOU GOT YOUR MONEY BACK.
THANKS FOR NOT HURTING HIM, SPIDER-MAN.
ME? HURT PEOPLE?
I'M A LOVER, NOT A FIGHTER.
SPIDER-MAN I NEED YOU.
APPARENTLY.
THE JUMBOTRON AGREES WITH YOU.
WHAT...?

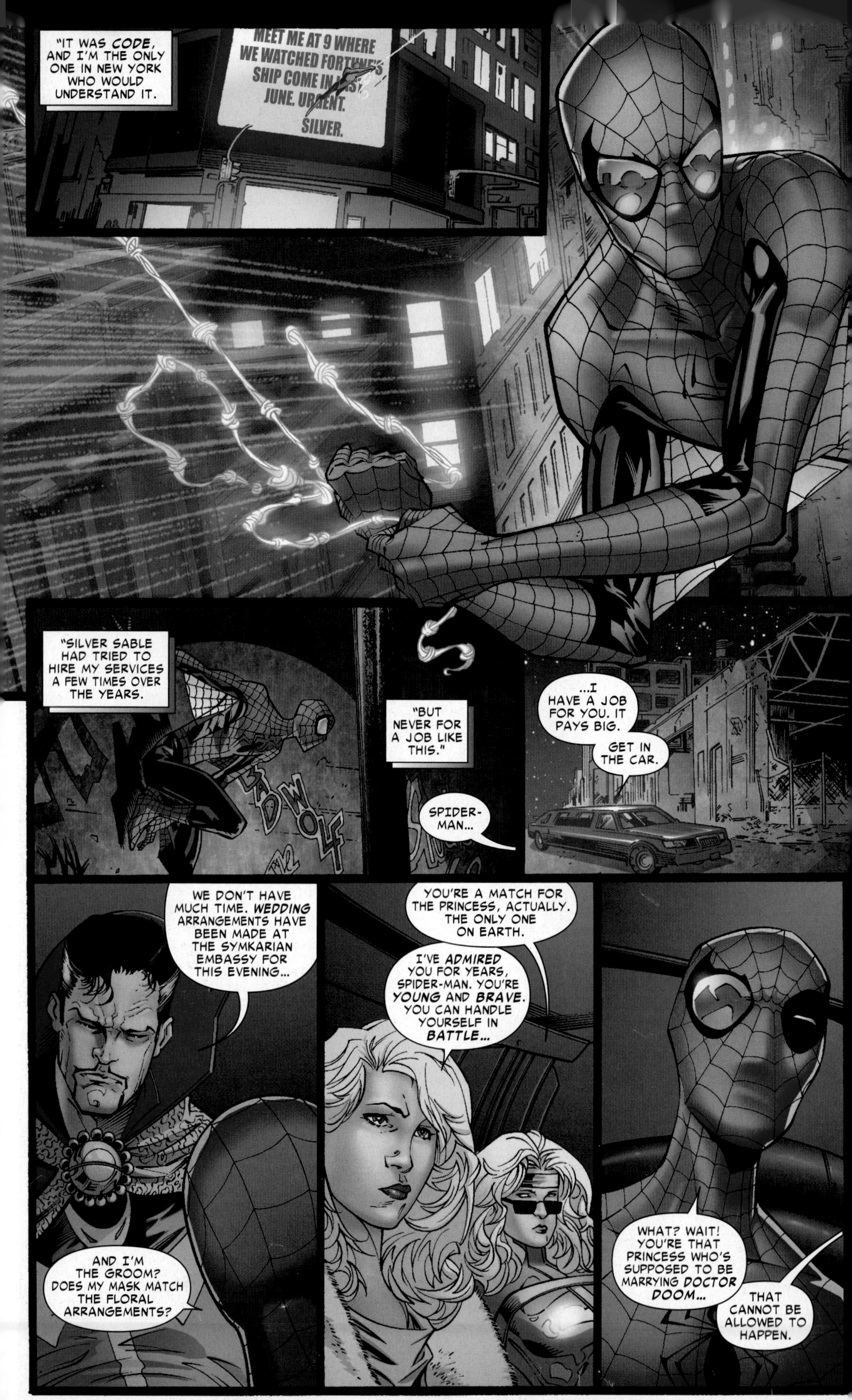
"IT WAS CODE, AND I'M THE ONLY ONE IN NEW YORK WHO WOULD UNDERSTAND IT.
MEET ME AT 9 WHERE WE WATCHED FORTUNE'S SHIP COME IN LAST JUNE. URGENT. SILVER.
"SILVER SABLE HAD TRIED TO HIRE MY SERVICES A FEW TIMES OVER THE YEARS.
"BUT NEVER FOR A JOB LIKE THIS."
SPIDER-MAN...
...I HAVE A JOB FOR YOU. IT PAYS BIG.
GET IN THE CAR.
WE DON'T HAVE MUCH TIME. WEDDING ARRANGEMENTS HAVE BEEN MADE AT THE SYMKARIAN EMBASSY FOR THIS EVENING...
AND I'M THE GROOM? DOES MY MASK MATCH THE FLORAL ARRANGEMENTS?
YOU'RE A MATCH FOR THE PRINCESS, ACTUALLY. THE ONLY ONE ON EARTH.
I'VE ADMIRED YOU FOR YEARS, SPIDER-MAN. YOU'RE YOUNG AND BRAVE. YOU CAN HANDLE YOURSELF IN BATTLE...
WHAT? WAIT! YOU'RE THAT PRINCESS WHO'S SUPPOSED TO BE MARRYING DOCTOR DOOM...
THAT CANNOT BE ALLOWED TO HAPPEN.

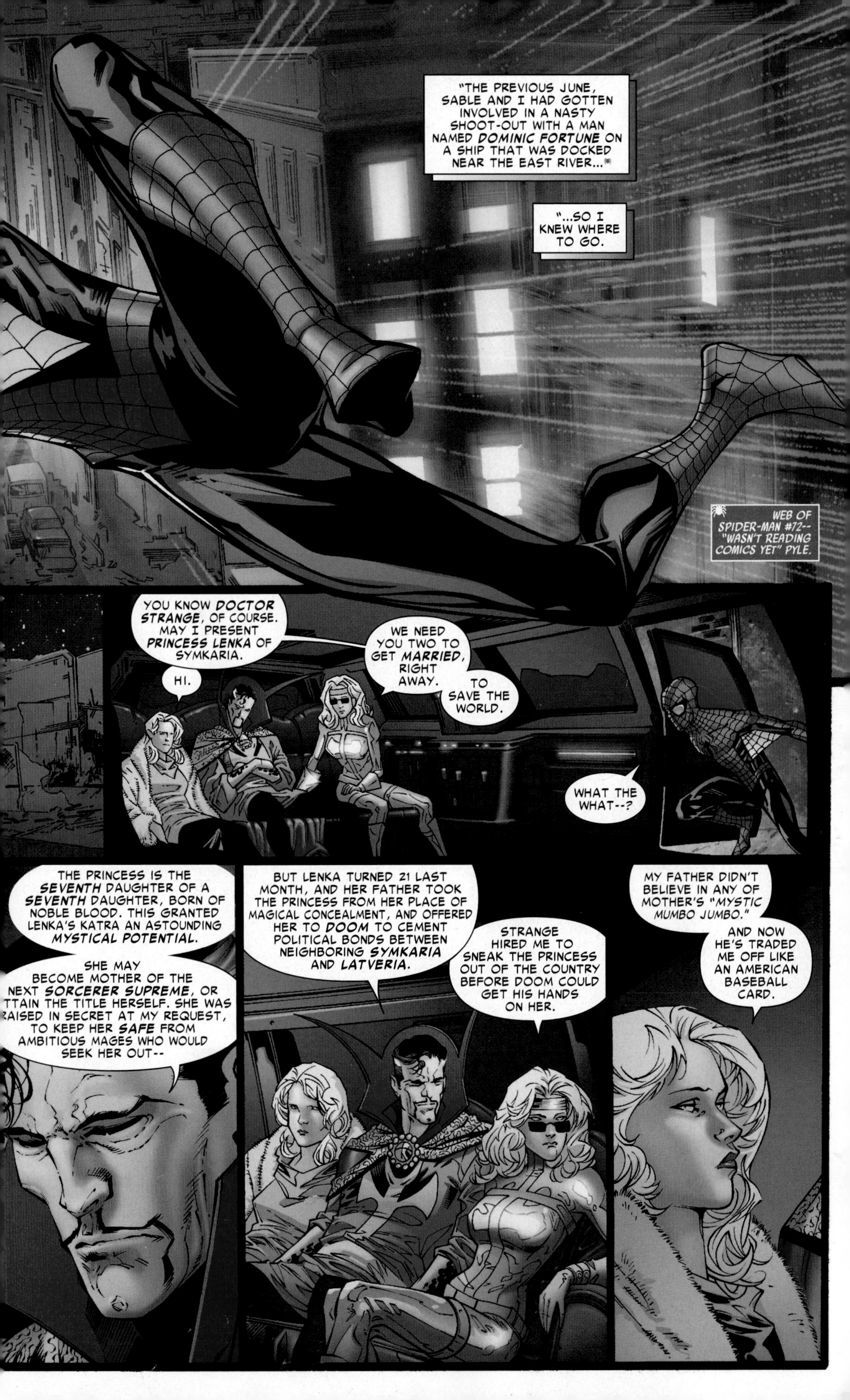
"THE PREVIOUS JUNE, SABLE AND I HAD GOTTEN INVOLVED IN A NASTY SHOOT-OUT WITH A MAN NAMED DOMINIC FORTUNE ON A SHIP THAT WAS DOCKED NEAR THE EAST RIVER...*
"...SO I KNEW WHERE TO GO.
*WEB OF SPIDER-MAN #72-- "WASN'T READING COMICS YET" PYLE.
YOU KNOW DOCTOR STRANGE, OF COURSE. MAY I PRESENT PRINCESS LENKA OF SYMKARIA.
HI.
WE NEED YOU TWO TO GET MARRIED, RIGHT AWAY.
TO SAVE THE WORLD.
WHAT THE WHAT--?
THE PRINCESS IS THE SEVENTH DAUGHTER OF A SEVENTH DAUGHTER, BORN OF NOBLE BLOOD. THIS GRANTED LENKA'S KATRA AN ASTOUNDING MYSTICAL POTENTIAL.
SHE MAY BECOME MOTHER OF THE NEXT SORCERER SUPREME, OR TTAIN THE TITLE HERSELF. SHE WAS RAISED IN SECRET AT MY REQUEST, TO KEEP HER SAFE FROM AMBITIOUS MAGES WHO WOULD SEEK HER OUT--
BUT LENKA TURNED 21 LAST MONTH, AND HER FATHER TOOK THE PRINCESS FROM HER PLACE OF MAGICAL CONCEALMENT, AND OFFERED HER TO DOOM TO CEMENT POLITICAL BONDS BETWEEN NEIGHBORING SYMKARIA AND LATVERIA.
STRANGE HIRED ME TO SNEAK THE PRINCESS OUT OF THE COUNTRY BEFORE DOOM COULD GET HIS HANDS ON HER.
MY FATHER DIDN'T BELIEVE IN ANY OF MOTHER'S "MYSTIC MUMBO JUMBO."
AND NOW HE'S TRADED ME OFF LIKE AN AMERICAN BASEBALL CARD.

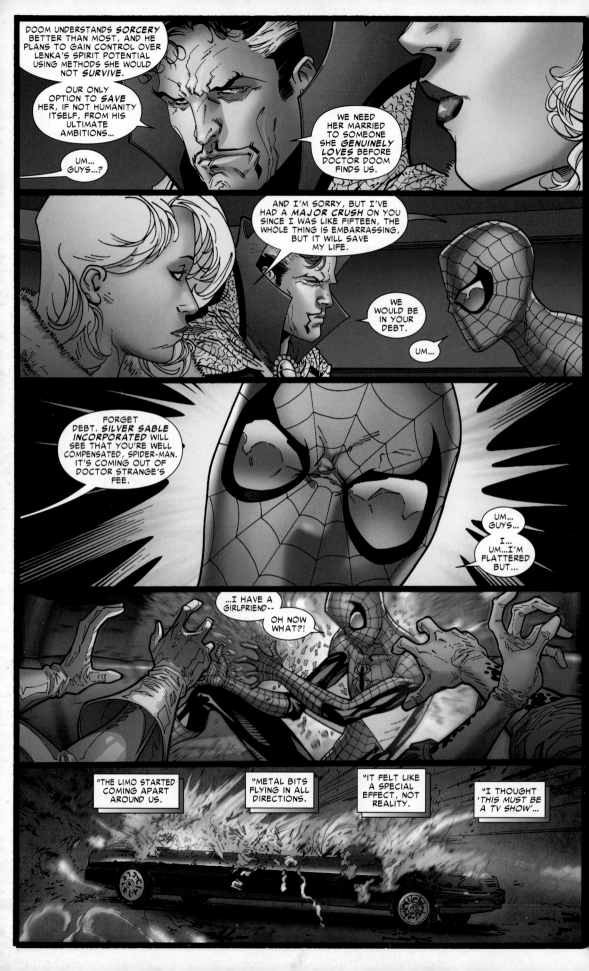

DOOM UNDERSTANDS **SORCERY** BETTER THAN MOST, AND HE PLANS TO GAIN CONTROL OVER LENKA'S SPIRIT POTENTIAL USING METHODS SHE WOULD NOT **SURVIVE**.

OUR ONLY OPTION TO **SAVE** HER, IF NOT HUMANITY ITSELF, FROM HIS ULTIMATE AMBITIONS...

UM... GUYS...?

WE NEED HER MARRIED TO SOMEONE SHE **GENUINELY LOVES** BEFORE DOCTOR DOOM FINDS US.

AND I'M SORRY, BUT I'VE HAD A **MAJOR CRUSH** ON YOU SINCE I WAS LIKE FIFTEEN, THE WHOLE THING IS EMBARRASSING, BUT IT WILL SAVE MY LIFE.

WE WOULD BE IN YOUR DEBT.

UM...

FORGET DEBT. **SILVER SABLE INCORPORATED** WILL SEE THAT YOU'RE WELL COMPENSATED, SPIDER-MAN. IT'S COMING OUT OF DOCTOR STRANGE'S FEE.

UM... GUYS... I... UM...I'M FLATTERED BUT...

...I HAVE A GIRLFRIEND--

OH NOW WHAT?!

"THE LIMO STARTED COMING APART AROUND US.

"METAL BITS FLYING IN ALL DIRECTIONS.

"IT FELT LIKE A SPECIAL EFFECT, NOT REALITY.

"I THOUGHT 'THIS MUST BE A TV SHOW'...

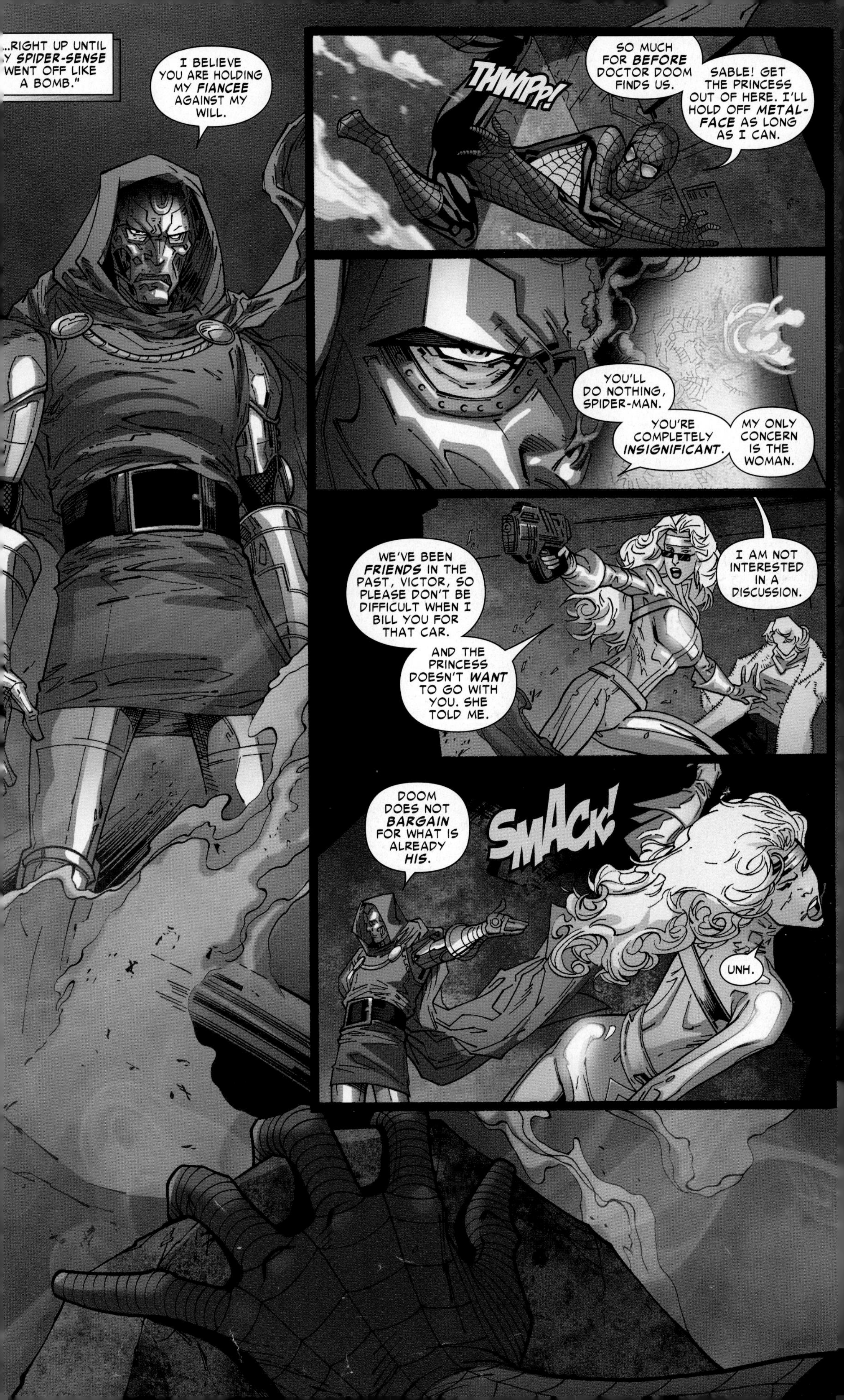

...RIGHT UP UNTIL Y SPIDER-SENSE WENT OFF LIKE A BOMB."
I BELIEVE YOU ARE HOLDING MY FIANCEE AGAINST MY WILL.
THWIPP!
SO MUCH FOR BEFORE DOCTOR DOOM FINDS US.
SABLE! GET THE PRINCESS OUT OF HERE. I'LL HOLD OFF METAL-FACE AS LONG AS I CAN.
YOU'LL DO NOTHING, SPIDER-MAN.
YOU'RE COMPLETELY INSIGNIFICANT.
MY ONLY CONCERN IS THE WOMAN.
I AM NOT INTERESTED IN A DISCUSSION.
WE'VE BEEN FRIENDS IN THE PAST, VICTOR, SO PLEASE DON'T BE DIFFICULT WHEN I BILL YOU FOR THAT CAR.
AND THE PRINCESS DOESN'T WANT TO GO WITH YOU. SHE TOLD ME.
DOOM DOES NOT BARGAIN FOR WHAT IS ALREADY HIS.
SMACK!
UNH.

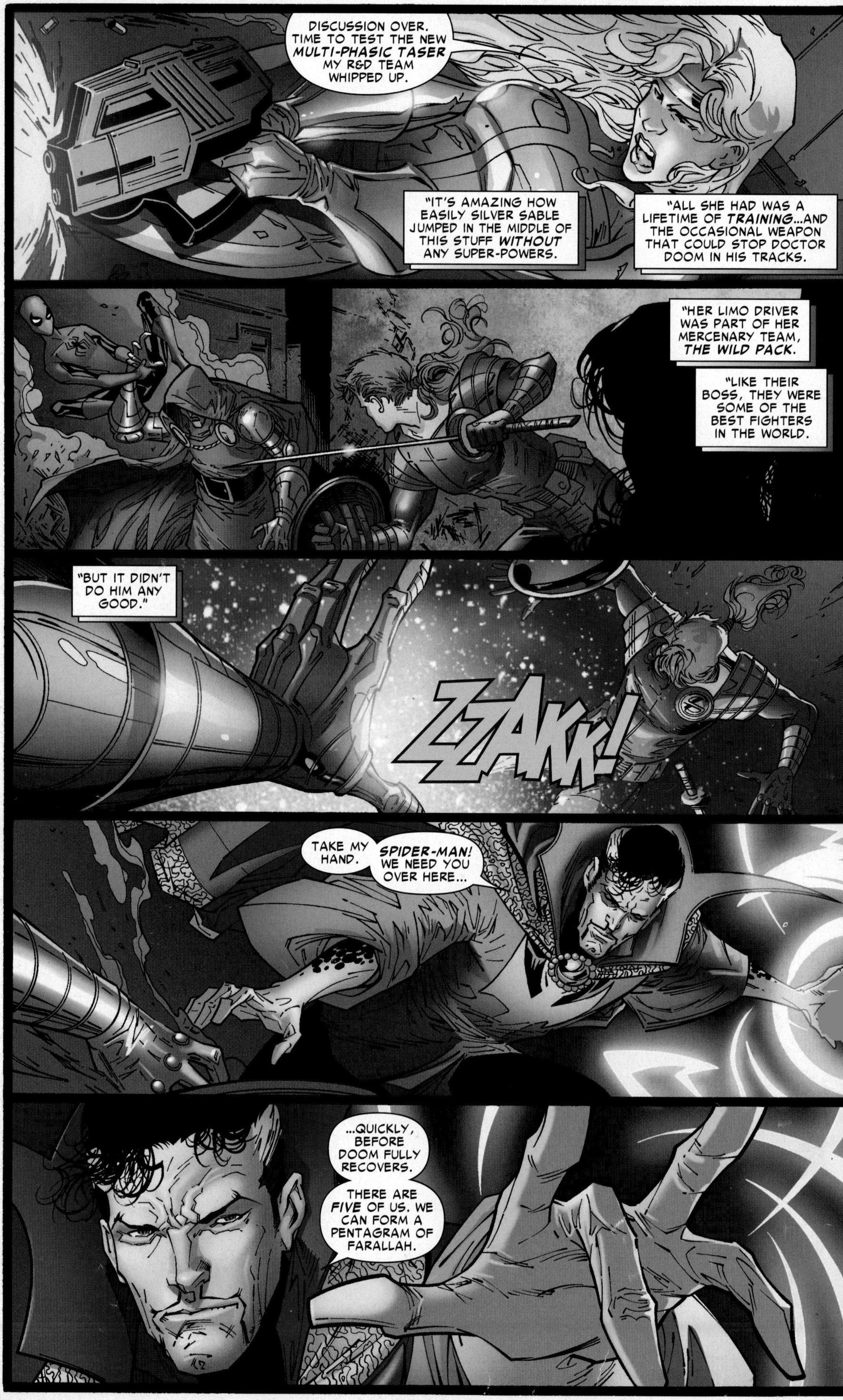
DISCUSSION OVER. TIME TO TEST THE NEW MULTI-PHASIC TASER MY R&D TEAM WHIPPED UP.
"IT'S AMAZING HOW EASILY SILVER SABLE JUMPED IN THE MIDDLE OF THIS STUFF WITHOUT ANY SUPER-POWERS.
"ALL SHE HAD WAS A LIFETIME OF TRAINING...AND THE OCCASIONAL WEAPON THAT COULD STOP DOCTOR DOOM IN HIS TRACKS.
"HER LIMO DRIVER WAS PART OF HER MERCENARY TEAM, THE WILD PACK.
"LIKE THEIR BOSS, THEY WERE SOME OF THE BEST FIGHTERS IN THE WORLD.
"BUT IT DIDN'T DO HIM ANY GOOD."
ZZAKK!
TAKE MY HAND.
SPIDER-MAN! WE NEED YOU OVER HERE...
...QUICKLY, BEFORE DOOM FULLY RECOVERS.
THERE ARE FIVE OF US. WE CAN FORM A PENTAGRAM OF FARALLAH.

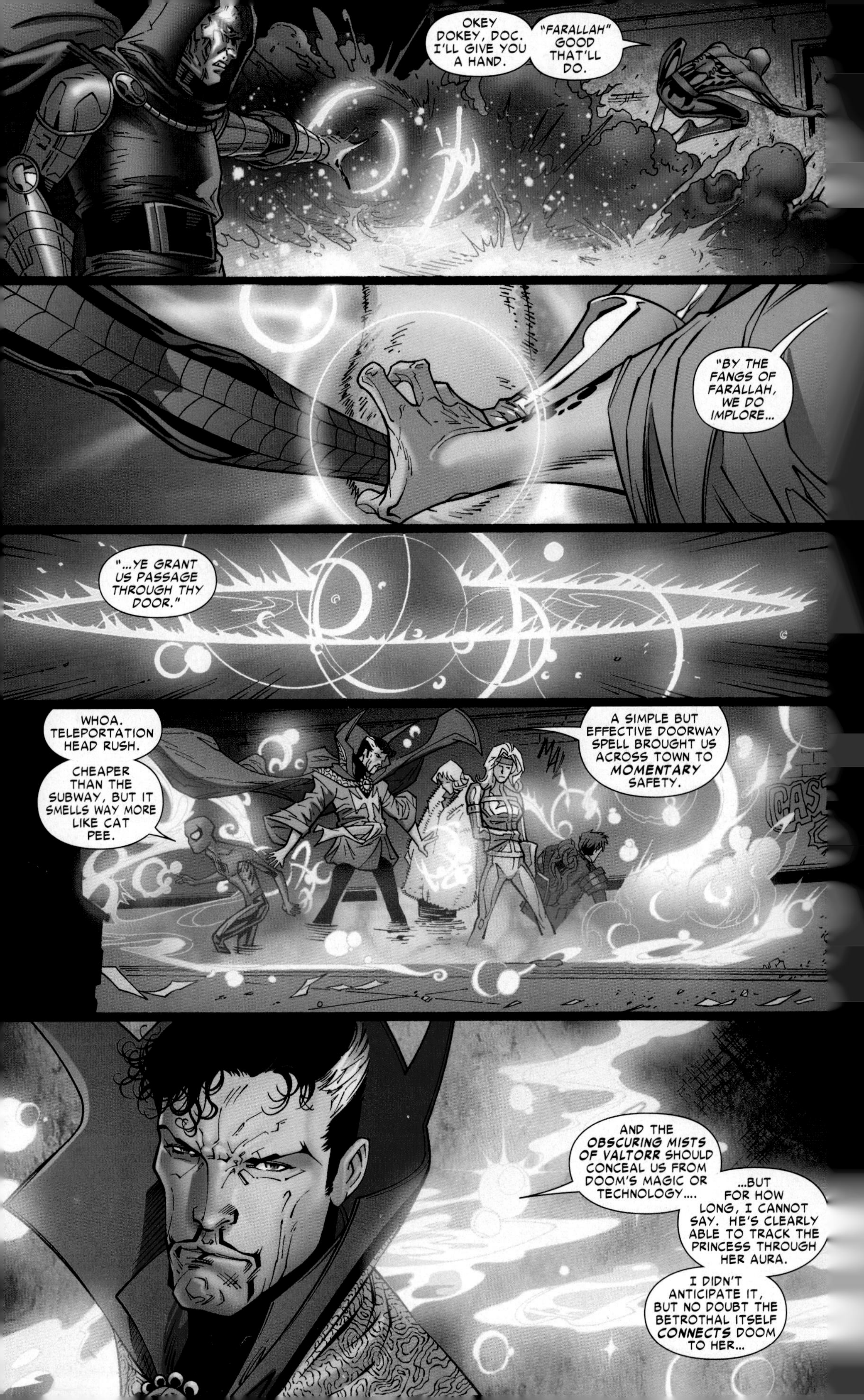
OKEY DOKEY, DOC. I'LL GIVE YOU A HAND.
"FARALLAH" GOOD THAT'LL DO.
"BY THE FANGS OF FARALLAH, WE DO IMPLORE...
"...YE GRANT US PASSAGE THROUGH THY DOOR."
WHOA. TELEPORTATION HEAD RUSH.
CHEAPER THAN THE SUBWAY, BUT IT SMELLS WAY MORE LIKE CAT PEE.
A SIMPLE BUT EFFECTIVE DOORWAY SPELL BROUGHT US ACROSS TOWN TO MOMENTARY SAFETY.
AND THE OBSCURING MISTS OF VALTORR SHOULD CONCEAL US FROM DOOM'S MAGIC OR TECHNOLOGY....
...BUT FOR HOW LONG, I CANNOT SAY. HE'S CLEARLY ABLE TO TRACK THE PRINCESS THROUGH HER AURA.
I DIDN'T ANTICIPATE IT, BUT NO DOUBT THE BETROTHAL ITSELF CONNECTS DOOM TO HER...

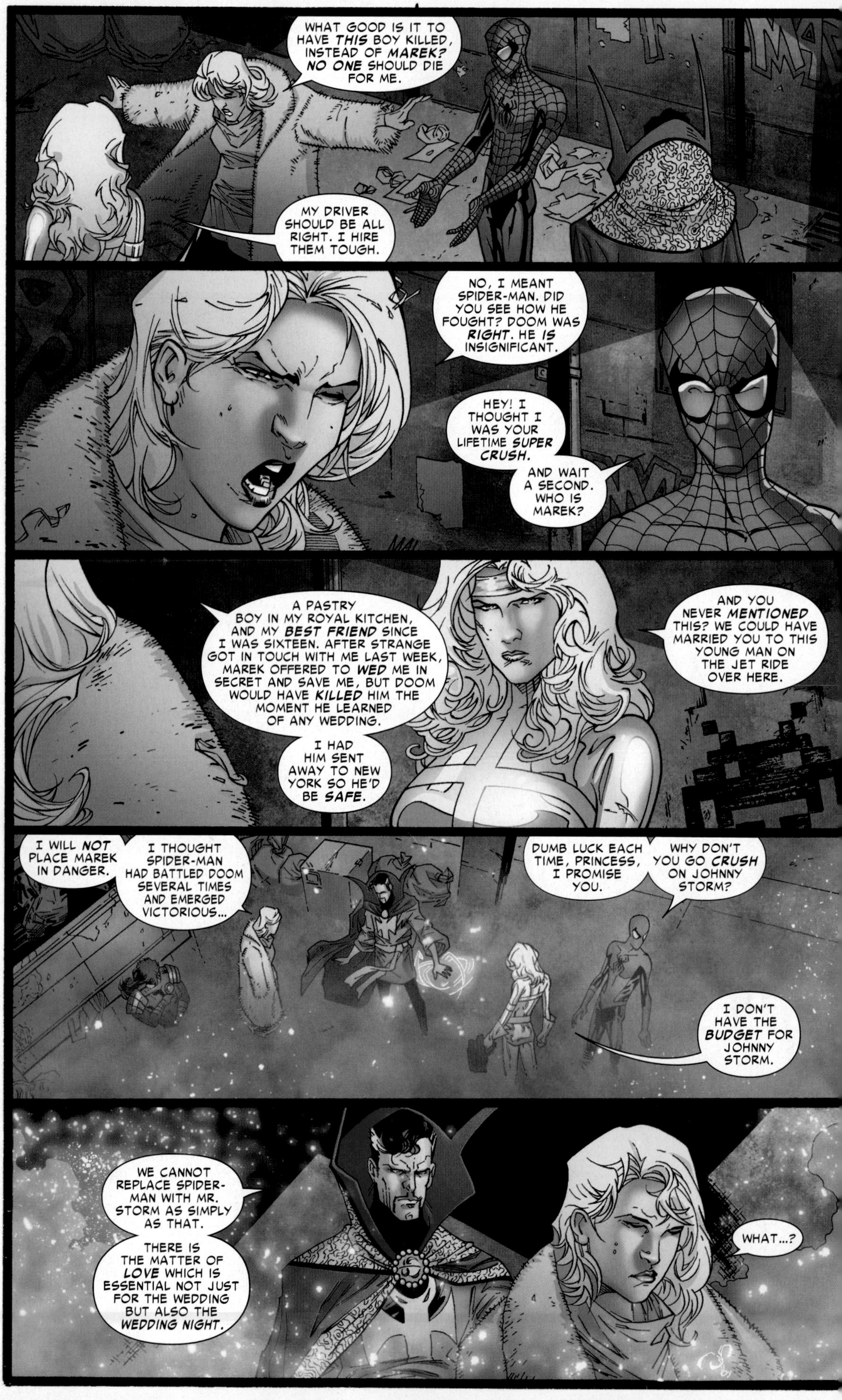
WHAT GOOD IS IT TO HAVE THIS BOY KILLED, INSTEAD OF MAREK? NO ONE SHOULD DIE FOR ME.
MY DRIVER SHOULD BE ALL RIGHT. I HIRE THEM TOUGH.
NO, I MEANT SPIDER-MAN. DID YOU SEE HOW HE FOUGHT? DOOM WAS RIGHT. HE IS INSIGNIFICANT.
HEY! I THOUGHT I WAS YOUR LIFETIME SUPER CRUSH.
AND WAIT A SECOND. WHO IS MAREK?
A PASTRY BOY IN MY ROYAL KITCHEN, AND MY BEST FRIEND SINCE I WAS SIXTEEN. AFTER STRANGE GOT IN TOUCH WITH ME LAST WEEK, MAREK OFFERED TO WED ME IN SECRET AND SAVE ME, BUT DOOM WOULD HAVE KILLED HIM THE MOMENT HE LEARNED OF ANY WEDDING.
I HAD HIM SENT AWAY TO NEW YORK SO HE'D BE SAFE.
AND YOU NEVER MENTIONED THIS? WE COULD HAVE MARRIED YOU TO THIS YOUNG MAN ON THE JET RIDE OVER HERE.
I WILL NOT PLACE MAREK IN DANGER.
I THOUGHT SPIDER-MAN HAD BATTLED DOOM SEVERAL TIMES AND EMERGED VICTORIOUS...
DUMB LUCK EACH TIME, PRINCESS, I PROMISE YOU.
WHY DON'T YOU GO CRUSH ON JOHNNY STORM?
I DON'T HAVE THE BUDGET FOR JOHNNY STORM.
WE CANNOT REPLACE SPIDER-MAN WITH MR. STORM AS SIMPLY AS THAT.
THERE IS THE MATTER OF LOVE WHICH IS ESSENTIAL NOT JUST FOR THE WEDDING BUT ALSO THE WEDDING NIGHT.
WHAT...?

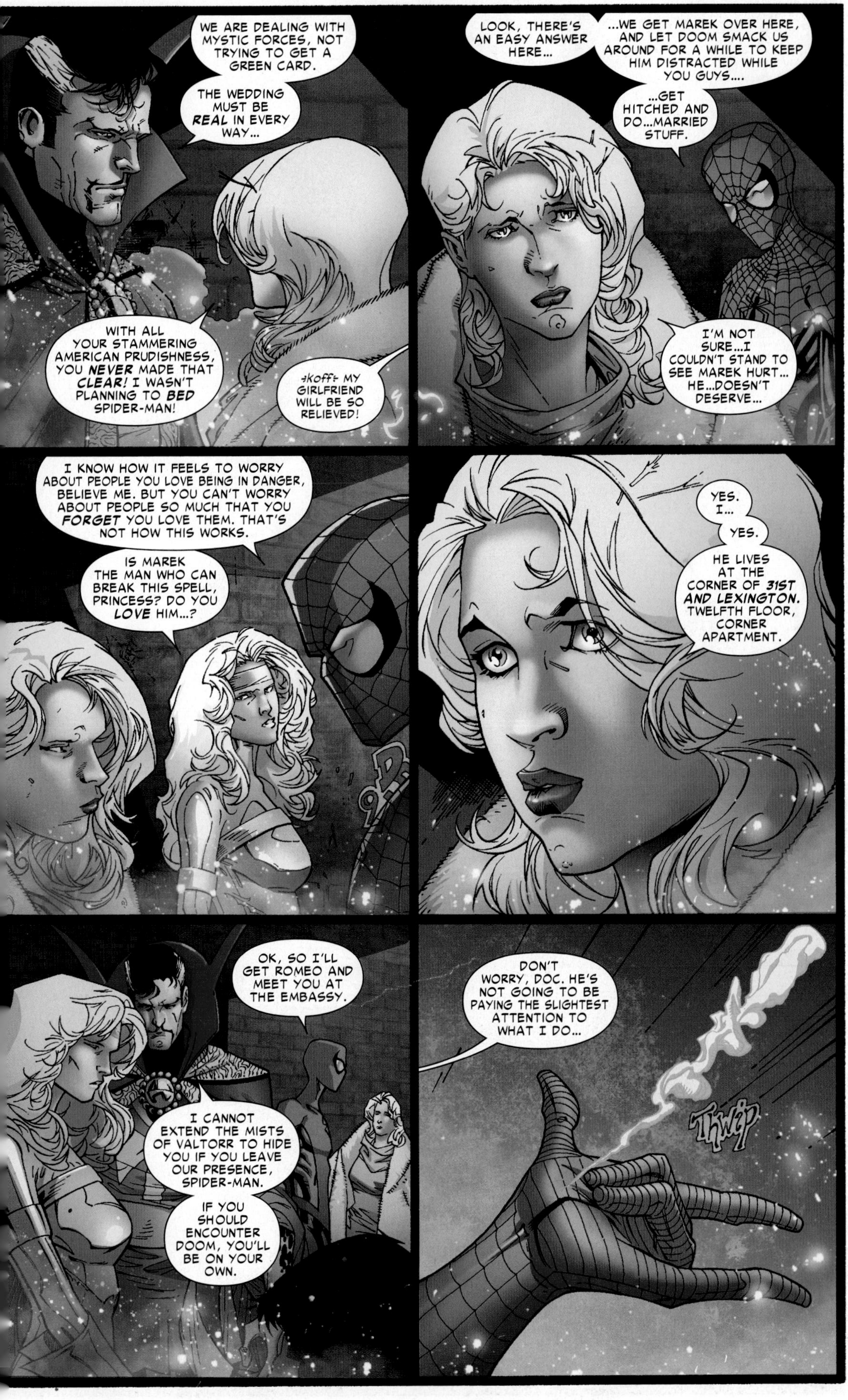
WE ARE DEALING WITH MYSTIC FORCES, NOT TRYING TO GET A GREEN CARD.
THE WEDDING MUST BE REAL IN EVERY WAY...
WITH ALL YOUR STAMMERING AMERICAN PRUDISHNESS, YOU NEVER MADE THAT CLEAR! I WASN'T PLANNING TO BED SPIDER-MAN!
KOFF MY GIRLFRIEND WILL BE SO RELIEVED!
LOOK, THERE'S AN EASY ANSWER HERE...
...WE GET MAREK OVER HERE, AND LET DOOM SMACK US AROUND FOR A WHILE TO KEEP HIM DISTRACTED WHILE YOU GUYS....
...GET HITCHED AND DO...MARRIED STUFF.
I'M NOT SURE...I COULDN'T STAND TO SEE MAREK HURT... HE...DOESN'T DESERVE...
I KNOW HOW IT FEELS TO WORRY ABOUT PEOPLE YOU LOVE BEING IN DANGER, BELIEVE ME. BUT YOU CAN'T WORRY ABOUT PEOPLE SO MUCH THAT YOU FORGET YOU LOVE THEM. THAT'S NOT HOW THIS WORKS.
IS MAREK THE MAN WHO CAN BREAK THIS SPELL, PRINCESS? DO YOU LOVE HIM...?
YES. I...
YES.
HE LIVES AT THE CORNER OF 31ST AND LEXINGTON. TWELFTH FLOOR, CORNER APARTMENT.
OK, SO I'LL GET ROMEO AND MEET YOU AT THE EMBASSY.
I CANNOT EXTEND THE MISTS OF VALTORR TO HIDE YOU IF YOU LEAVE OUR PRESENCE, SPIDER-MAN.
IF YOU SHOULD ENCOUNTER DOOM, YOU'LL BE ON YOUR OWN.
DON'T WORRY, DOC. HE'S NOT GOING TO BE PAYING THE SLIGHTEST ATTENTION TO WHAT I DO...
THWIP

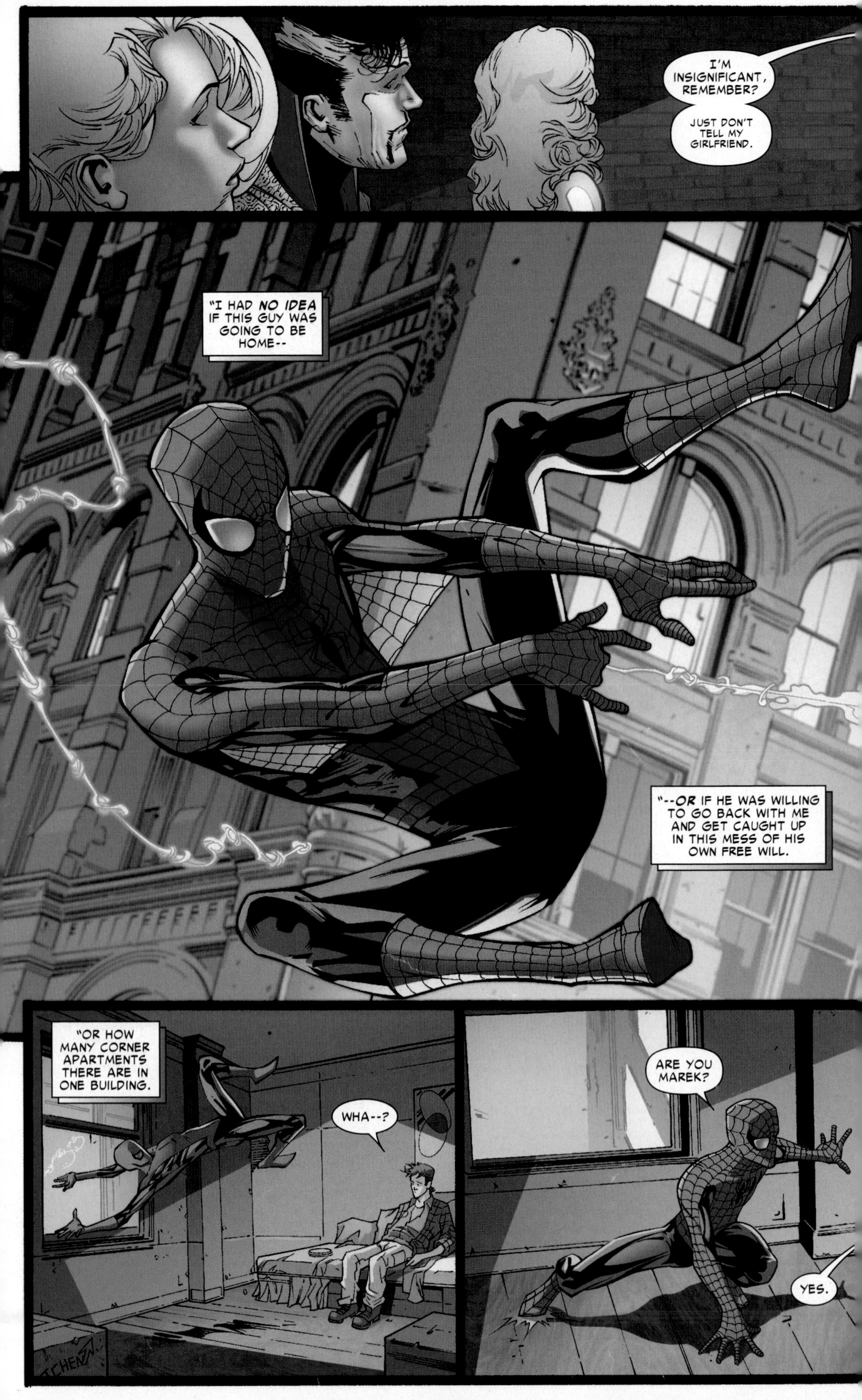
I'M INSIGNIFICANT, REMEMBER?
JUST DON'T TELL MY GIRLFRIEND.
"I HAD NO IDEA IF THIS GUY WAS GOING TO BE HOME--
"--OR IF HE WAS WILLING TO GO BACK WITH ME AND GET CAUGHT UP IN THIS MESS OF HIS OWN FREE WILL.
"OR HOW MANY CORNER APARTMENTS THERE ARE IN ONE BUILDING.
WHA--?
ARE YOU MAREK?
YES.

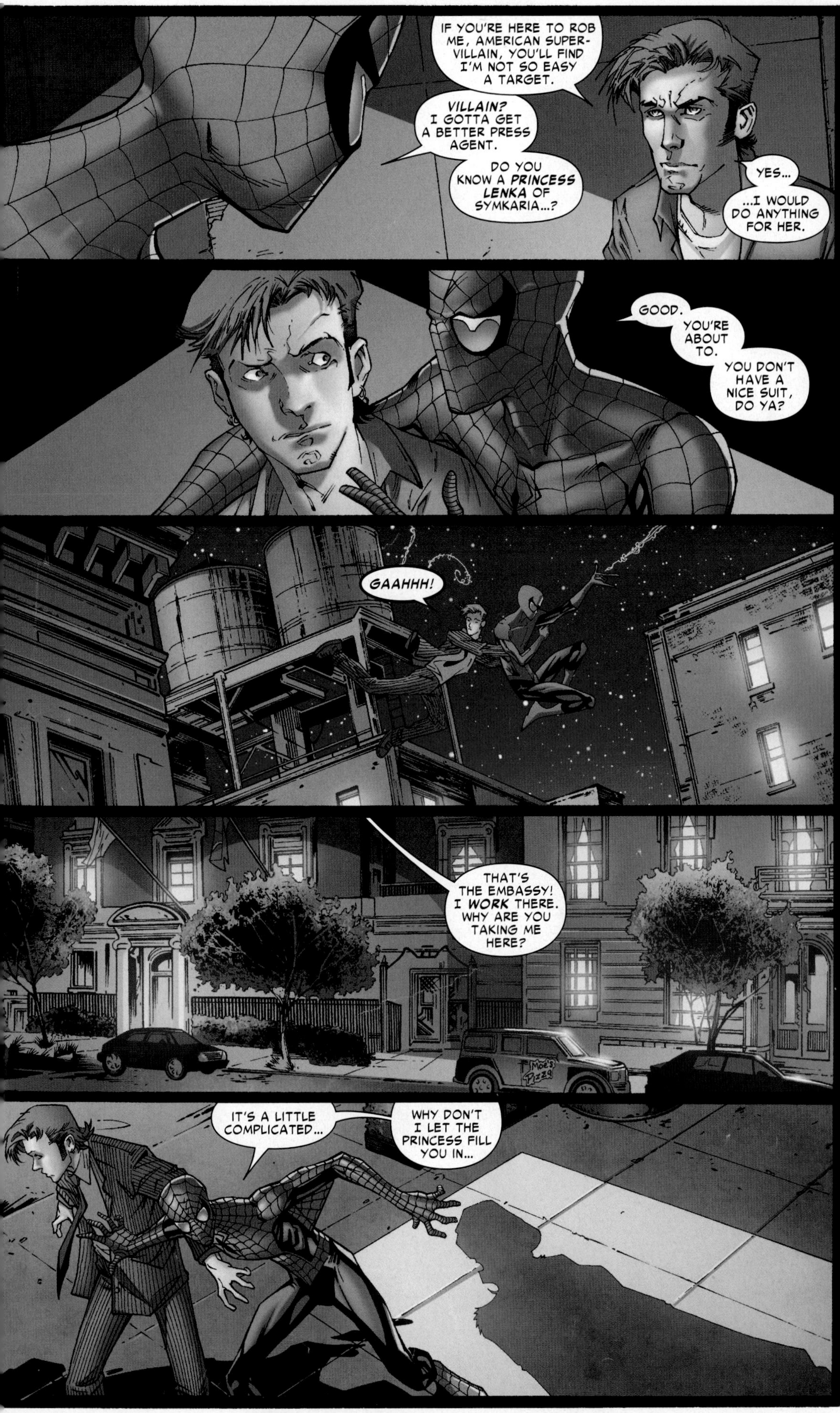

IF YOU'RE HERE TO ROB ME, AMERICAN SUPER-VILLAIN, YOU'LL FIND I'M NOT SO EASY A TARGET.
VILLAIN? I GOTTA GET A BETTER PRESS AGENT.
DO YOU KNOW A PRINCESS LENKA OF SYMKARIA...?
YES...
...I WOULD DO ANYTHING FOR HER.
GOOD.
YOU'RE ABOUT TO.
YOU DON'T HAVE A NICE SUIT, DO YA?
GAAHHH!
THAT'S THE EMBASSY! I WORK THERE. WHY ARE YOU TAKING ME HERE?
IT'S A LITTLE COMPLICATED...
WHY DON'T I LET THE PRINCESS FILL YOU IN...

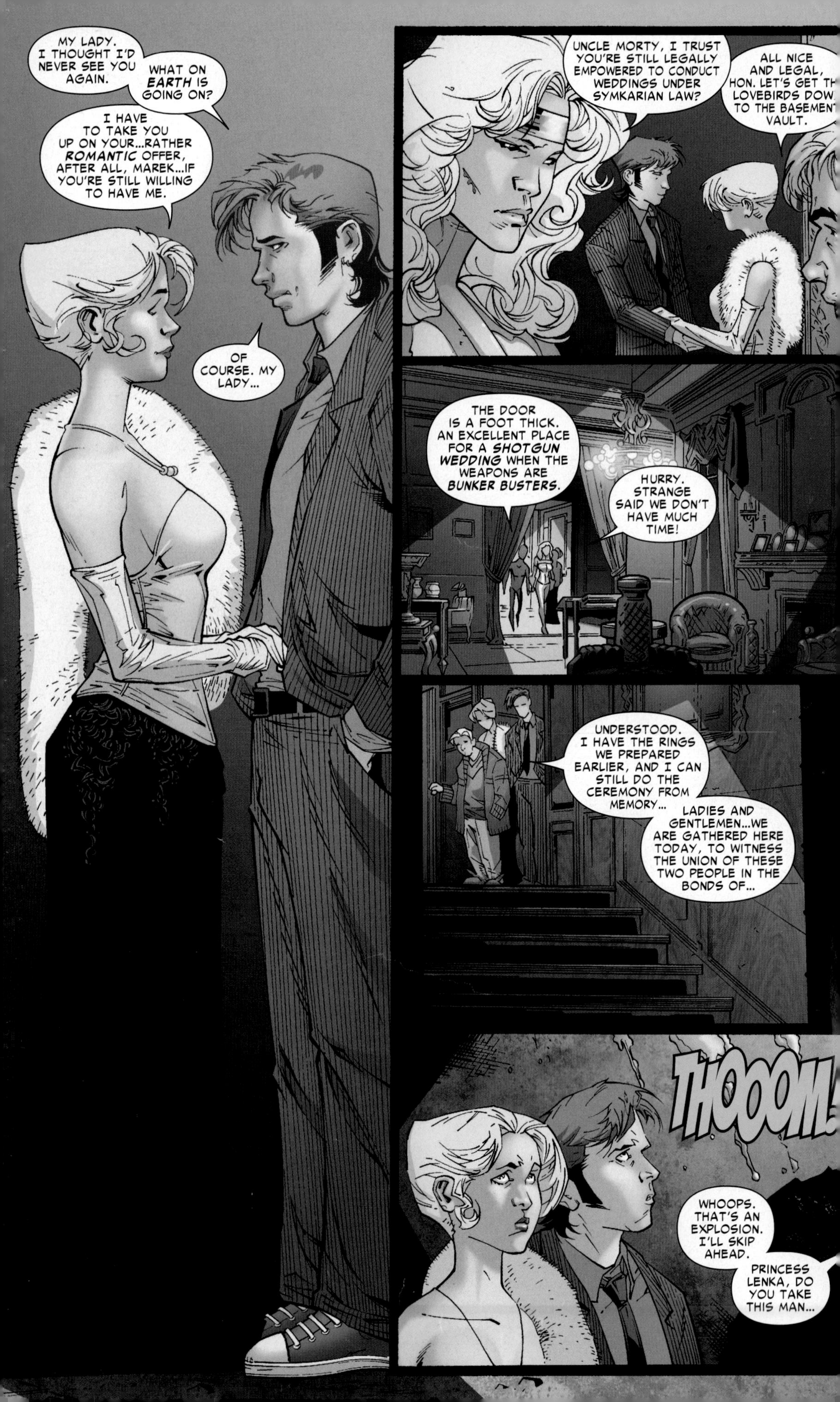
MY LADY. I THOUGHT I'D NEVER SEE YOU AGAIN.
WHAT ON EARTH IS GOING ON?
I HAVE TO TAKE YOU UP ON YOUR...RATHER ROMANTIC OFFER, AFTER ALL, MAREK...IF YOU'RE STILL WILLING TO HAVE ME.
OF COURSE. MY LADY...
UNCLE MORTY, I TRUST YOU'RE STILL LEGALLY EMPOWERED TO CONDUCT WEDDINGS UNDER SYMKARIAN LAW?
ALL NICE AND LEGAL, HON. LET'S GET TH LOVEBIRDS DOW TO THE BASEMENT VAULT.
THE DOOR IS A FOOT THICK. AN EXCELLENT PLACE FOR A SHOTGUN WEDDING WHEN THE WEAPONS ARE BUNKER BUSTERS.
HURRY. STRANGE SAID WE DON'T HAVE MUCH TIME!
UNDERSTOOD. I HAVE THE RINGS WE PREPARED EARLIER, AND I CAN STILL DO THE CEREMONY FROM MEMORY...
LADIES AND GENTLEMEN...WE ARE GATHERED HERE TODAY, TO WITNESS THE UNION OF THESE TWO PEOPLE IN THE BONDS OF...
THOOOM!
WHOOPS. THAT'S AN EXPLOSION. I'LL SKIP AHEAD.
PRINCESS LENKA, DO YOU TAKE THIS MAN...

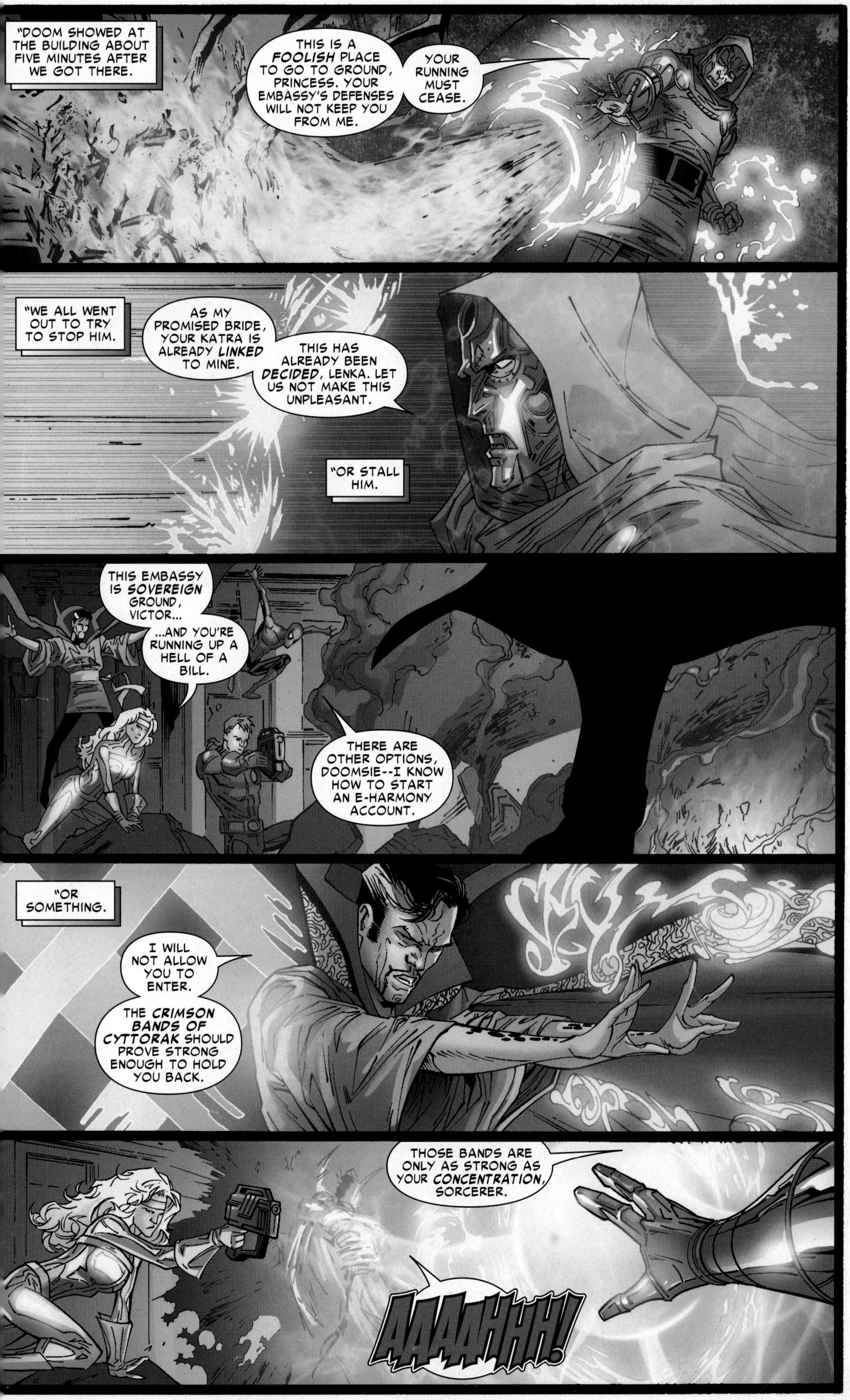
"DOOM SHOWED AT THE BUILDING ABOUT FIVE MINUTES AFTER WE GOT THERE.
THIS IS A FOOLISH PLACE TO GO TO GROUND, PRINCESS. YOUR EMBASSY'S DEFENSES WILL NOT KEEP YOU FROM ME.
YOUR RUNNING MUST CEASE.
"WE ALL WENT OUT TO TRY TO STOP HIM.
AS MY PROMISED BRIDE, YOUR KATRA IS ALREADY LINKED TO MINE.
THIS HAS ALREADY BEEN DECIDED, LENKA. LET US NOT MAKE THIS UNPLEASANT.
"OR STALL HIM.
THIS EMBASSY IS SOVEREIGN GROUND, VICTOR...
...AND YOU'RE RUNNING UP A HELL OF A BILL.
THERE ARE OTHER OPTIONS, DOOMSIE--I KNOW HOW TO START AN E-HARMONY ACCOUNT.
"OR SOMETHING.
I WILL NOT ALLOW YOU TO ENTER.
THE CRIMSON BANDS OF CYTTORAK SHOULD PROVE STRONG ENOUGH TO HOLD YOU BACK.
THOSE BANDS ARE ONLY AS STRONG AS YOUR CONCENTRATION, SORCERER.
AAAAHHHH!

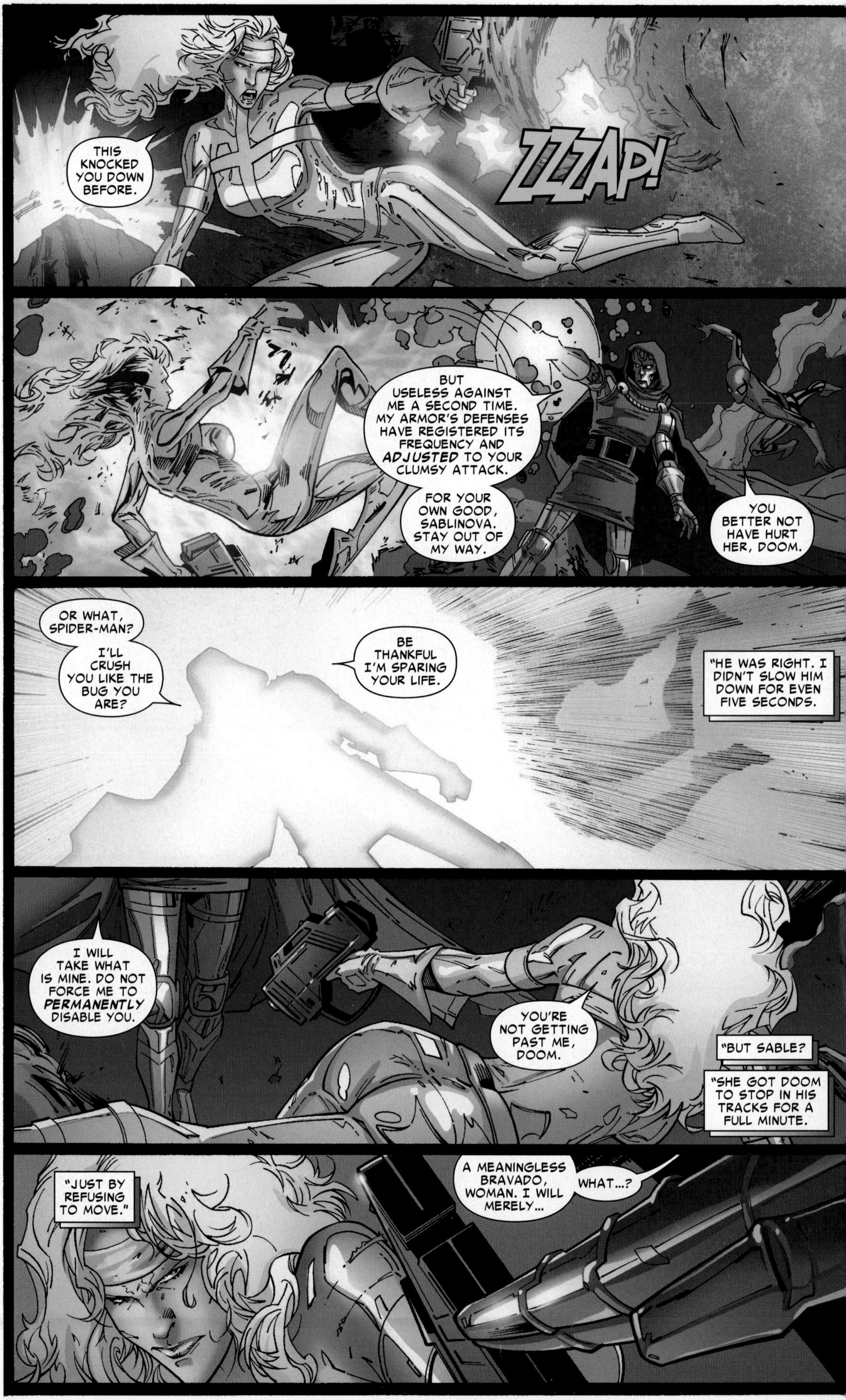
THIS KNOCKED YOU DOWN BEFORE.
ZZZAP!
BUT USELESS AGAINST ME A SECOND TIME. MY ARMOR'S DEFENSES HAVE REGISTERED ITS FREQUENCY AND ADJUSTED TO YOUR CLUMSY ATTACK.
FOR YOUR OWN GOOD, SABLINOVA. STAY OUT OF MY WAY.
YOU BETTER NOT HAVE HURT HER, DOOM.
OR WHAT, SPIDER-MAN?
I'LL CRUSH YOU LIKE THE BUG YOU ARE?
BE THANKFUL I'M SPARING YOUR LIFE.
"HE WAS RIGHT. I DIDN'T SLOW HIM DOWN FOR EVEN FIVE SECONDS.
I WILL TAKE WHAT IS MINE. DO NOT FORCE ME TO PERMANENTLY DISABLE YOU.
YOU'RE NOT GETTING PAST ME, DOOM.
"BUT SABLE?
"SHE GOT DOOM TO STOP IN HIS TRACKS FOR A FULL MINUTE.
"JUST BY REFUSING TO MOVE."
A MEANINGLESS BRAVADO, WOMAN. I WILL MERELY...
WHAT...?

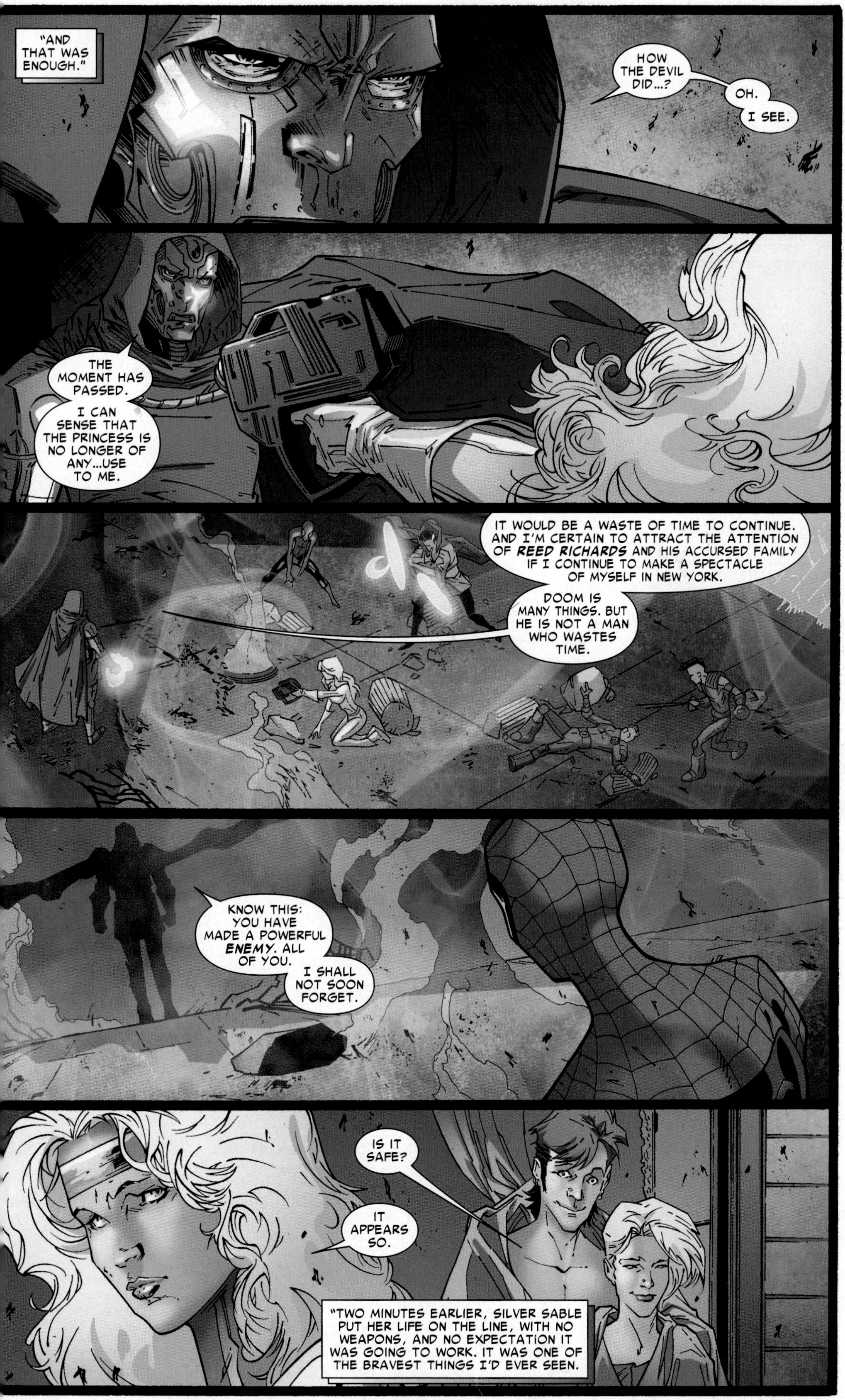
"AND THAT WAS ENOUGH."
HOW THE DEVIL DID...?
OH.
I SEE.
THE MOMENT HAS PASSED.
I CAN SENSE THAT THE PRINCESS IS NO LONGER OF ANY...USE TO ME.
IT WOULD BE A WASTE OF TIME TO CONTINUE. AND I'M CERTAIN TO ATTRACT THE ATTENTION OF REED RICHARDS AND HIS ACCURSED FAMILY IF I CONTINUE TO MAKE A SPECTACLE OF MYSELF IN NEW YORK.
DOOM IS MANY THINGS. BUT HE IS NOT A MAN WHO WASTES TIME.
KNOW THIS: YOU HAVE MADE A POWERFUL ENEMY. ALL OF YOU.
I SHALL NOT SOON FORGET.
IS IT SAFE?
IT APPEARS SO.
"TWO MINUTES EARLIER, SILVER SABLE PUT HER LIFE ON THE LINE, WITH NO WEAPONS, AND NO EXPECTATION IT WAS GOING TO WORK. IT WAS ONE OF THE BRAVEST THINGS I'D EVER SEEN.

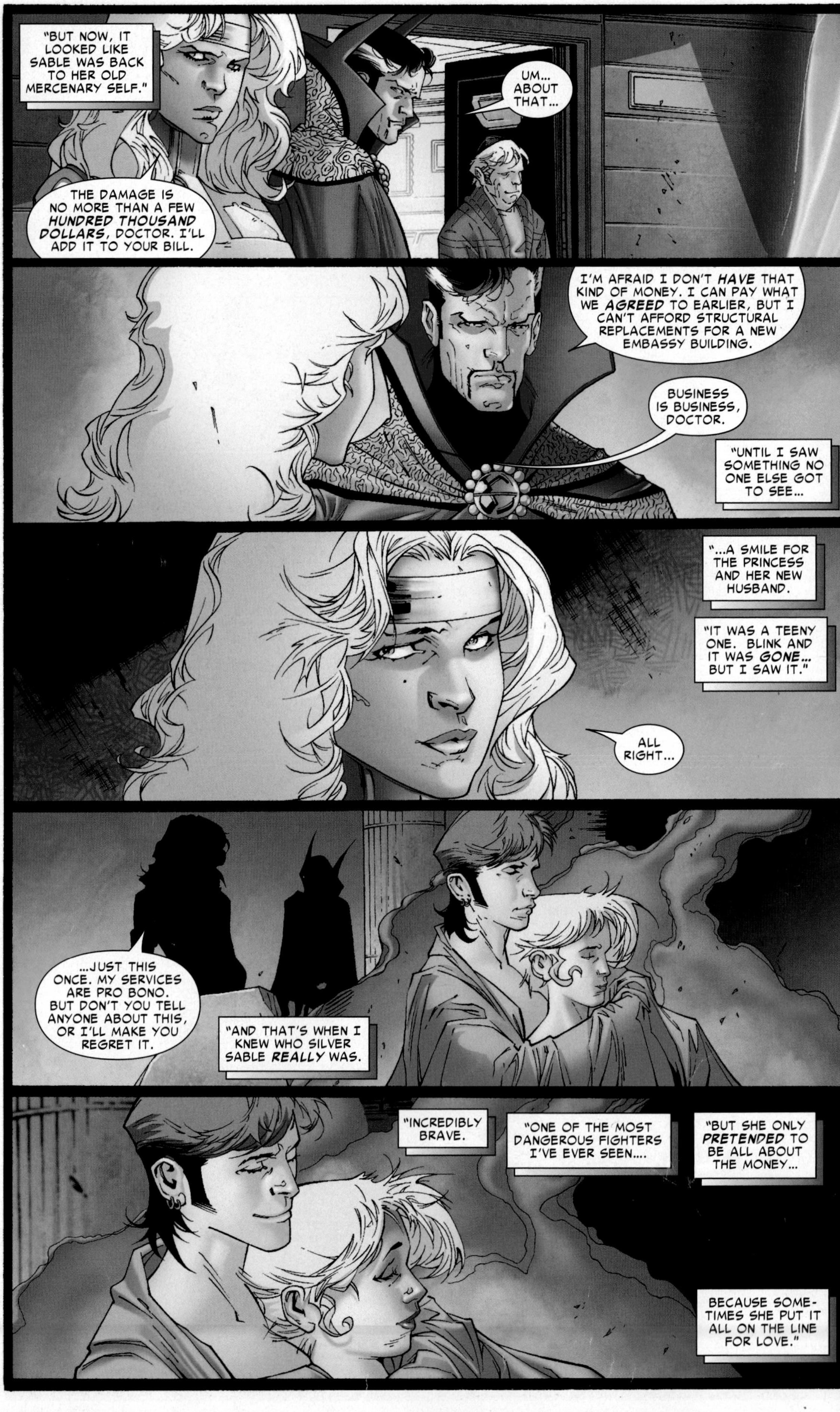
"BUT NOW, IT LOOKED LIKE SABLE WAS BACK TO HER OLD MERCENARY SELF."
UM... ABOUT THAT...
THE DAMAGE IS NO MORE THAN A FEW HUNDRED THOUSAND DOLLARS, DOCTOR. I'LL ADD IT TO YOUR BILL.
I'M AFRAID I DON'T HAVE THAT KIND OF MONEY. I CAN PAY WHAT WE AGREED TO EARLIER, BUT I CAN'T AFFORD STRUCTURAL REPLACEMENTS FOR A NEW EMBASSY BUILDING.
BUSINESS IS BUSINESS, DOCTOR.
"UNTIL I SAW SOMETHING NO ONE ELSE GOT TO SEE...
"...A SMILE FOR THE PRINCESS AND HER NEW HUSBAND.
"IT WAS A TEENY ONE. BLINK AND IT WAS GONE... BUT I SAW IT."
ALL RIGHT...
...JUST THIS ONCE. MY SERVICES ARE PRO BONO. BUT DON'T YOU TELL ANYONE ABOUT THIS, OR I'LL MAKE YOU REGRET IT.
"AND THAT'S WHEN I KNEW WHO SILVER SABLE REALLY WAS.
"INCREDIBLY BRAVE.
"ONE OF THE MOST DANGEROUS FIGHTERS I'VE EVER SEEN....
"BUT SHE ONLY PRETENDED TO BE ALL ABOUT THE MONEY...
BECAUSE SOMETIMES SHE PUT IT ALL ON THE LINE FOR LOVE."

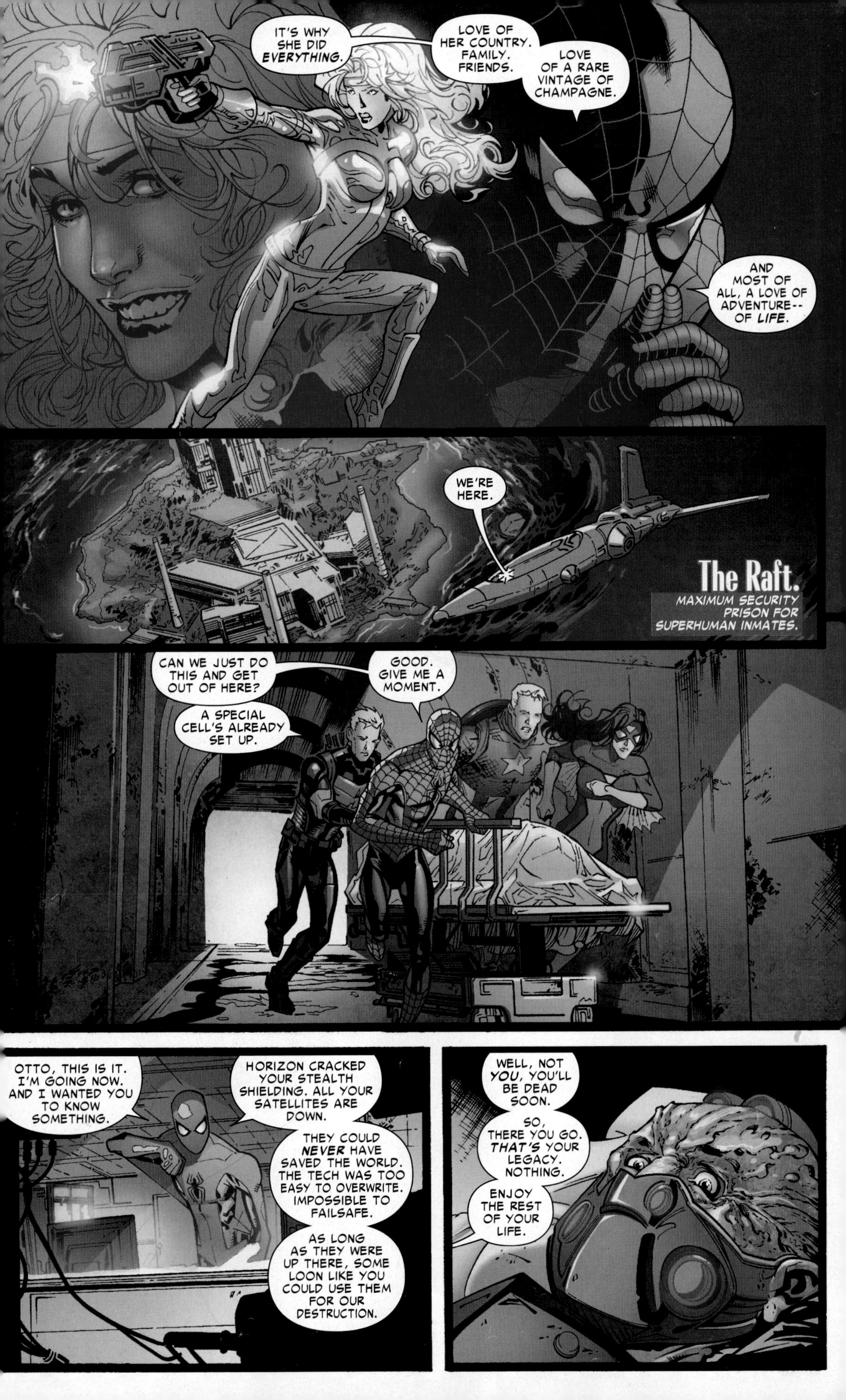

IT'S WHY SHE DID EVERYTHING.
LOVE OF HER COUNTRY. FAMILY. FRIENDS.
LOVE OF A RARE VINTAGE OF CHAMPAGNE.
AND MOST OF ALL, A LOVE OF ADVENTURE-- OF LIFE.
WE'RE HERE.
The Raft.
MAXIMUM SECURITY PRISON FOR SUPERHUMAN INMATES.
CAN WE JUST DO THIS AND GET OUT OF HERE?
A SPECIAL CELL'S ALREADY SET UP.
GOOD. GIVE ME A MOMENT.
OTTO, THIS IS IT. I'M GOING NOW. AND I WANTED YOU TO KNOW SOMETHING.
HORIZON CRACKED YOUR STEALTH SHIELDING. ALL YOUR SATELLITES ARE DOWN.
THEY COULD NEVER HAVE SAVED THE WORLD. THE TECH WAS TOO EASY TO OVERWRITE. IMPOSSIBLE TO FAILSAFE.
AS LONG AS THEY WERE UP THERE, SOME LOON LIKE YOU COULD USE THEM FOR OUR DESTRUCTION.
WELL, NOT YOU, YOU'LL BE DEAD SOON.
SO, THERE YOU GO. THAT'S YOUR LEGACY. NOTHING.
ENJOY THE REST OF YOUR LIFE.

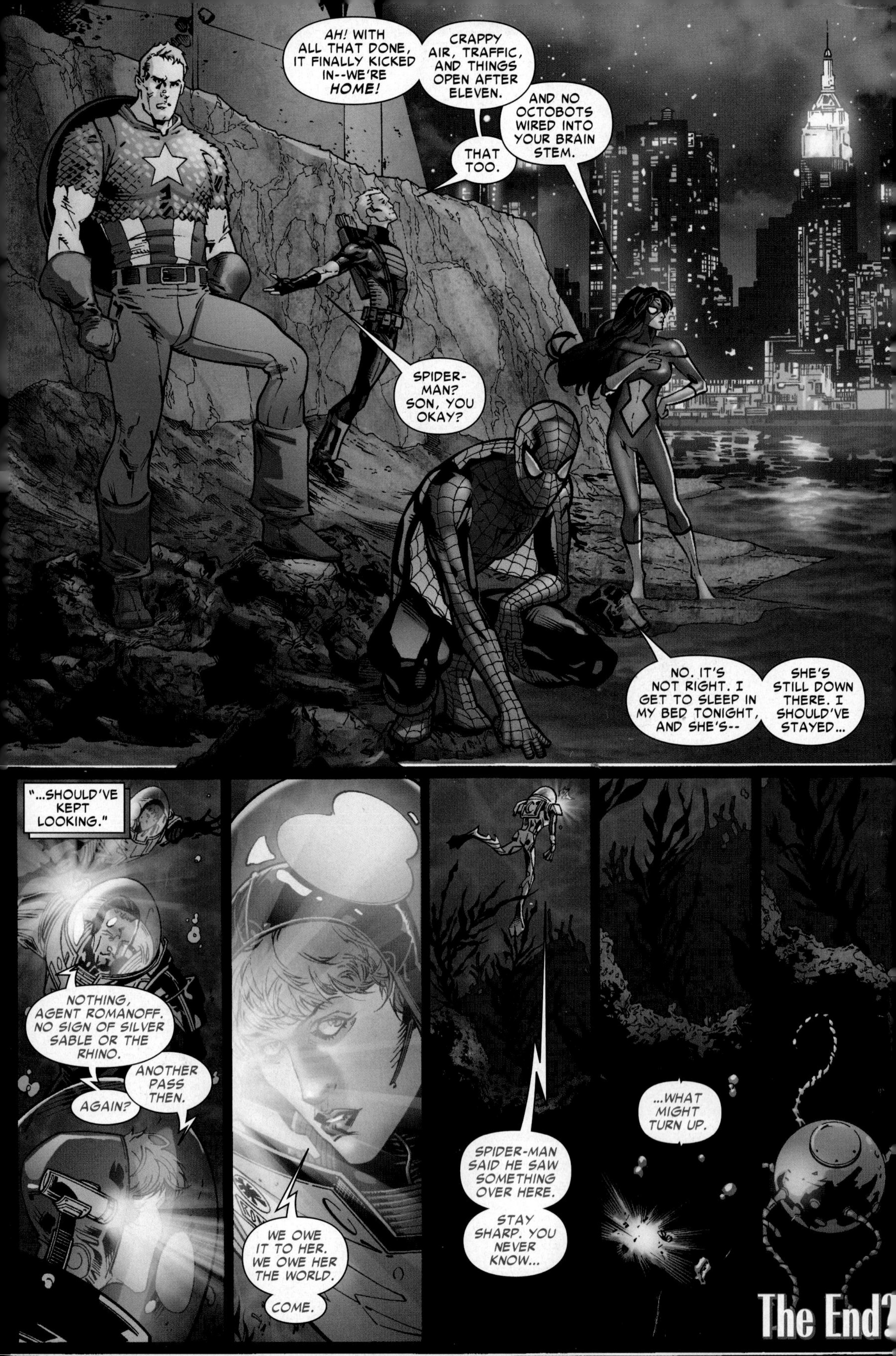
AH! WITH ALL THAT DONE, IT FINALLY KICKED IN--WE'RE HOME!
CRAPPY AIR, TRAFFIC, AND THINGS OPEN AFTER ELEVEN.
THAT TOO.
AND NO OCTOBOTS WIRED INTO YOUR BRAIN STEM.
SPIDER-MAN? SON, YOU OKAY?
NO. IT'S NOT RIGHT. I GET TO SLEEP IN MY BED TONIGHT, AND SHE'S--
SHE'S STILL DOWN THERE. I SHOULD'VE STAYED...
"...SHOULD'VE KEPT LOOKING."
NOTHING, AGENT ROMANOFF. NO SIGN OF SILVER SABLE OR THE RHINO.
AGAIN?
ANOTHER PASS THEN.
WE OWE IT TO HER. WE OWE HER THE WORLD.
COME.
SPIDER-MAN SAID HE SAW SOMETHING OVER HERE.
STAY SHARP. YOU NEVER KNOW...
...WHAT MIGHT TURN UP.
The End?

Next: Captain Marvel!

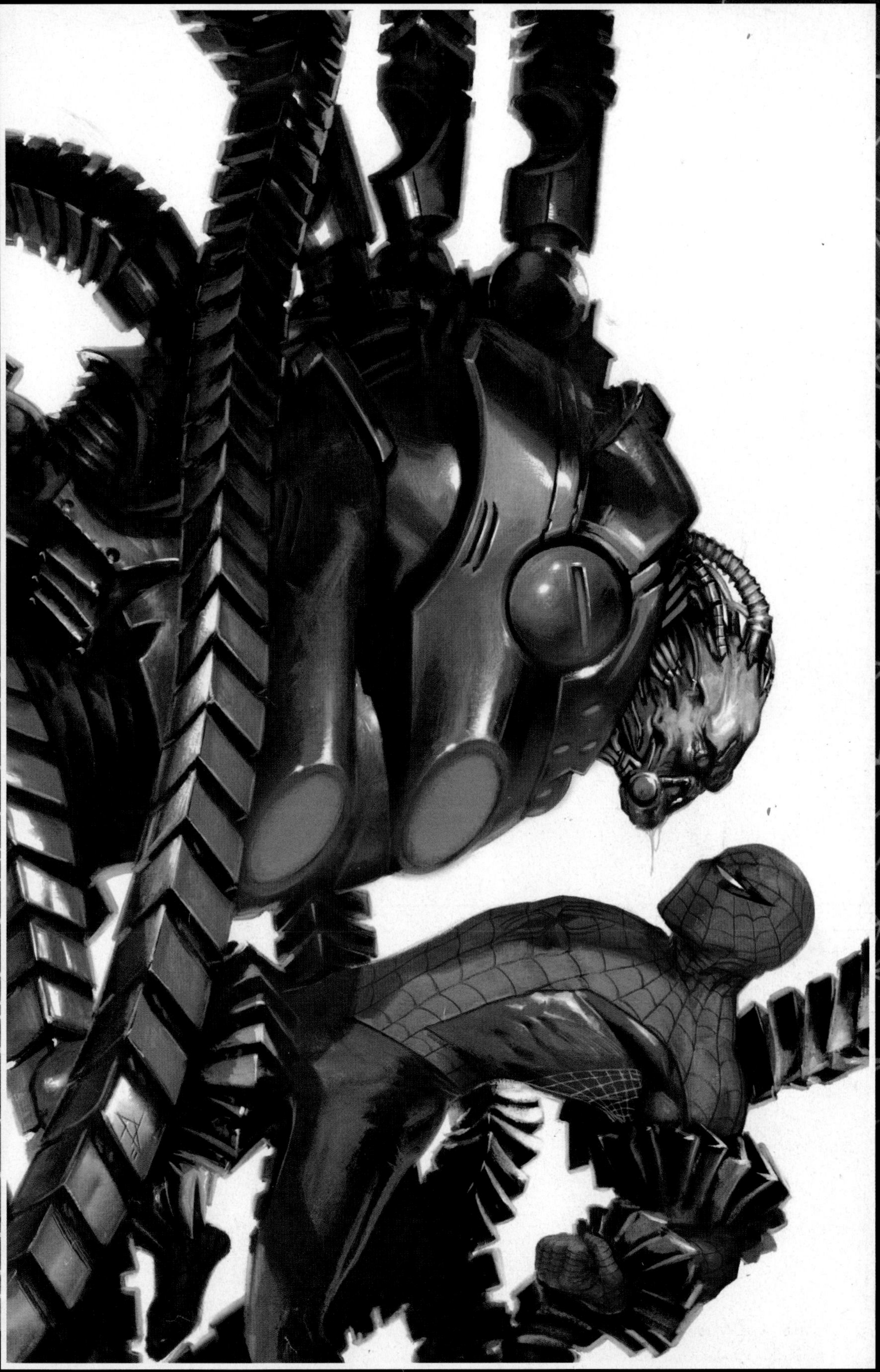

AMAZING SPIDER-MAN #682 VARIANT
COVER BY GABRIELE DELL'OTTO

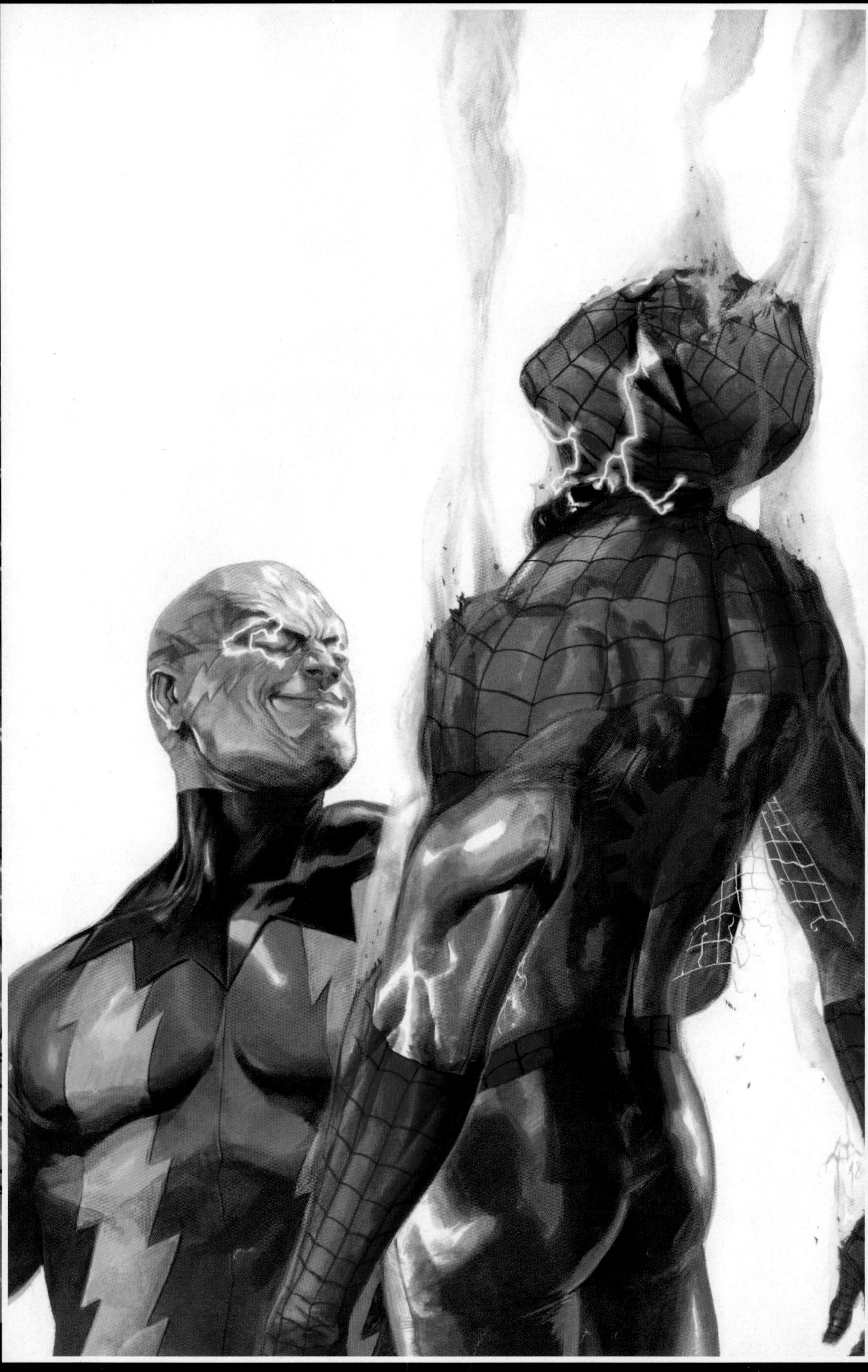

AMAZING SPIDER-MAN #683 VARIANT
COVER BY GABRIELE DELL'OTTO

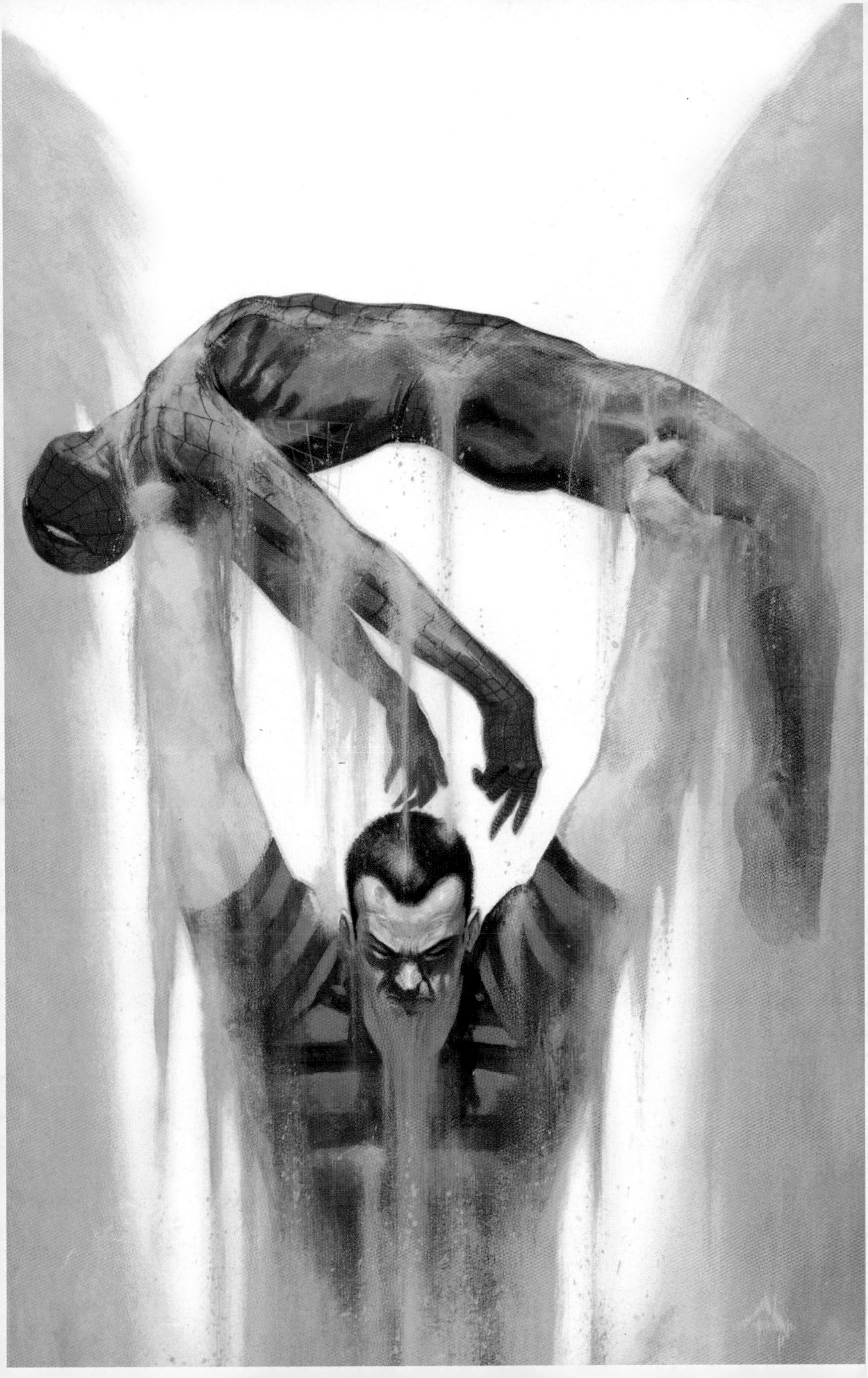

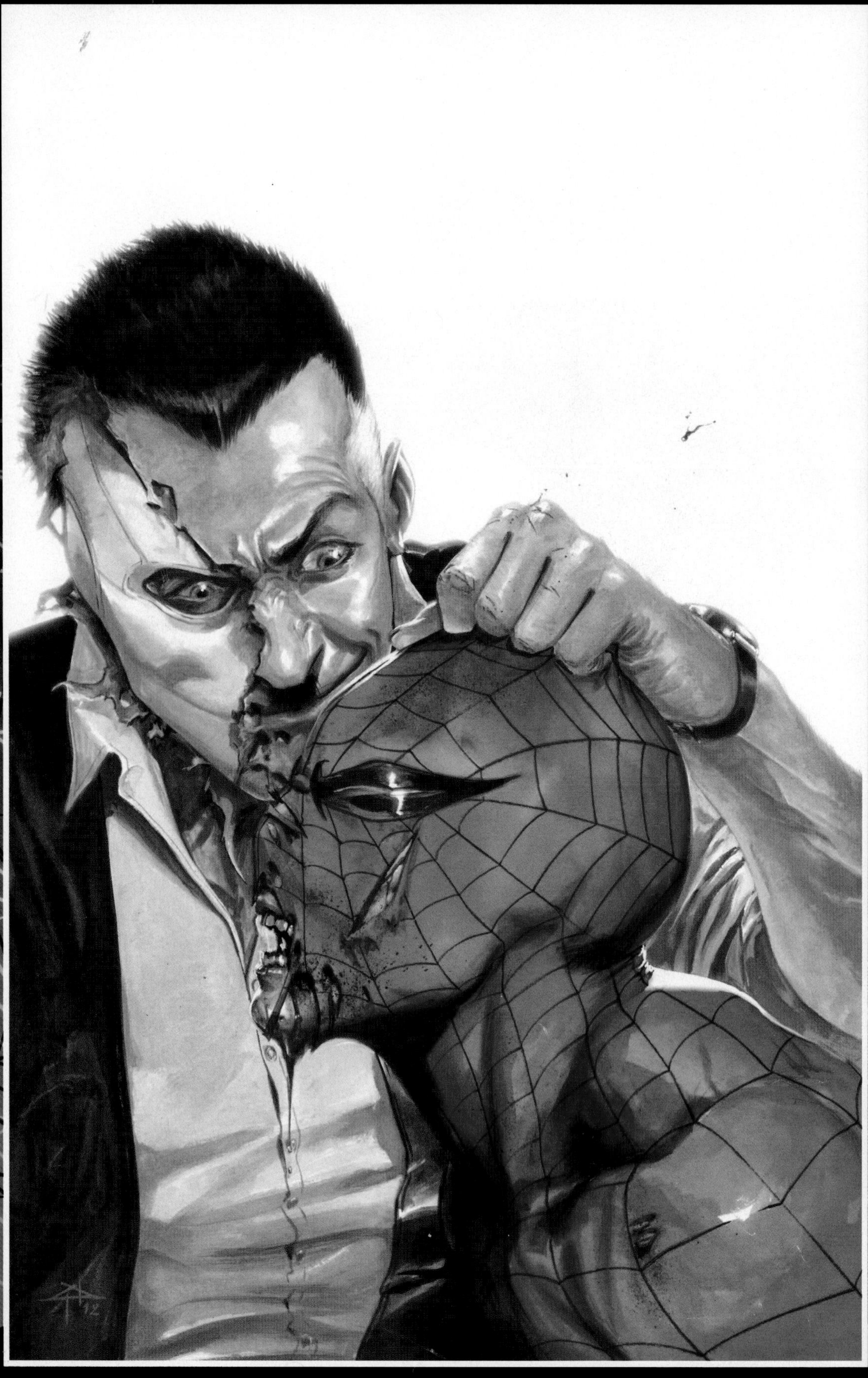

AMAZING SPIDER-MAN #685 VARIANT
COVER BY GABRIELE DELL'OTTO

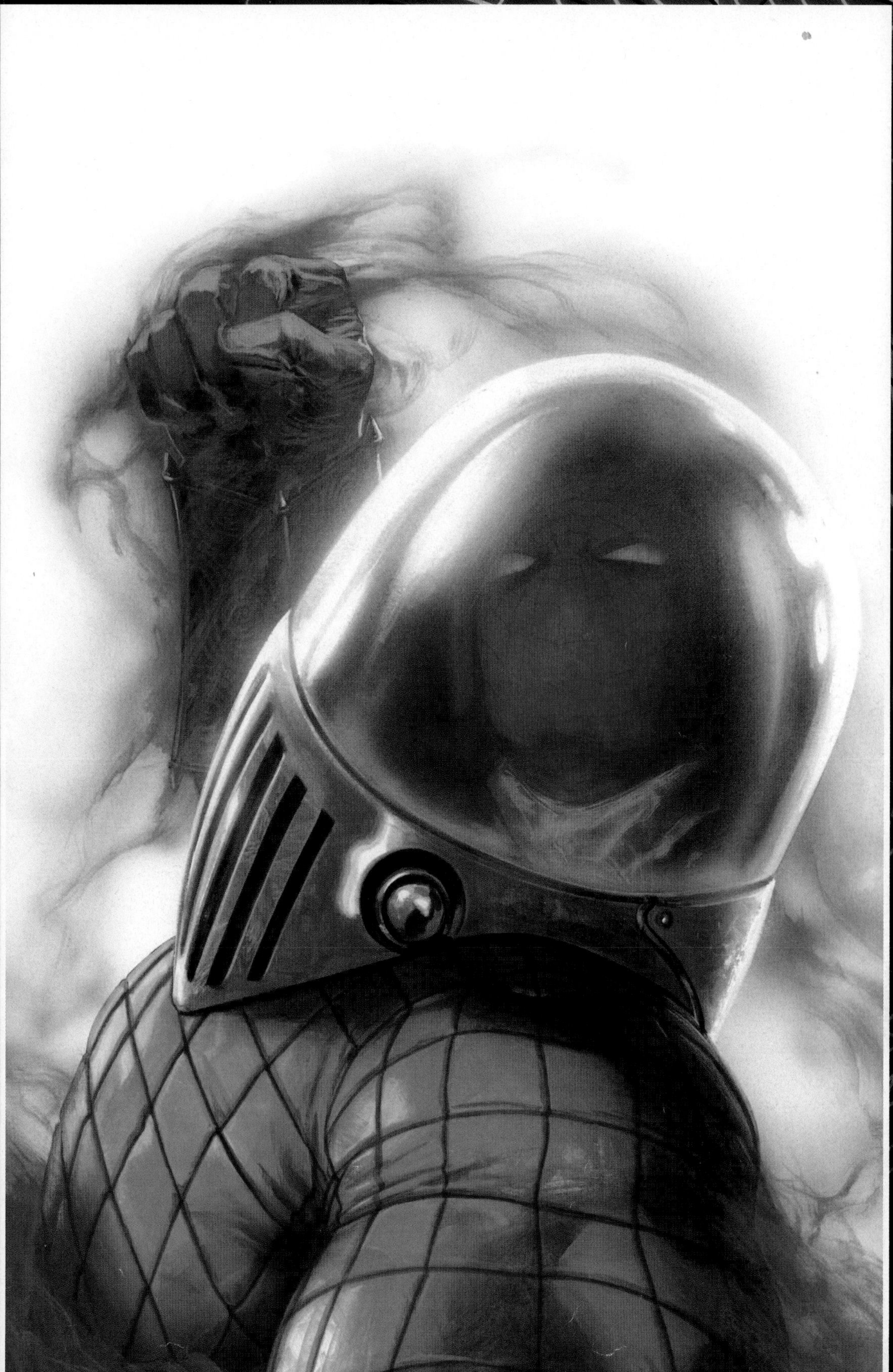

AMAZING SPIDER-MAN #686 VARIANT
COVER BY GABRIELE DELL'OTTO

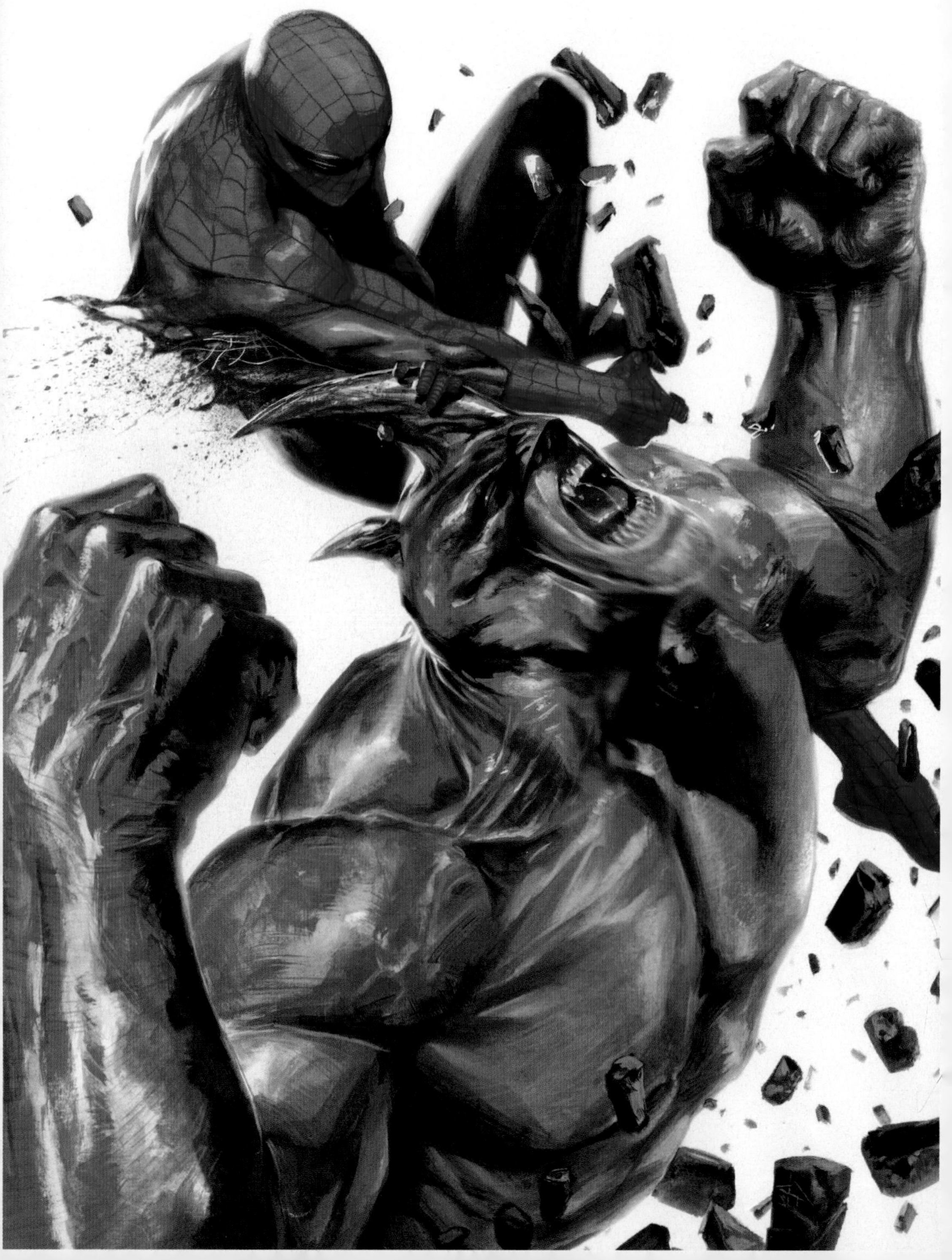

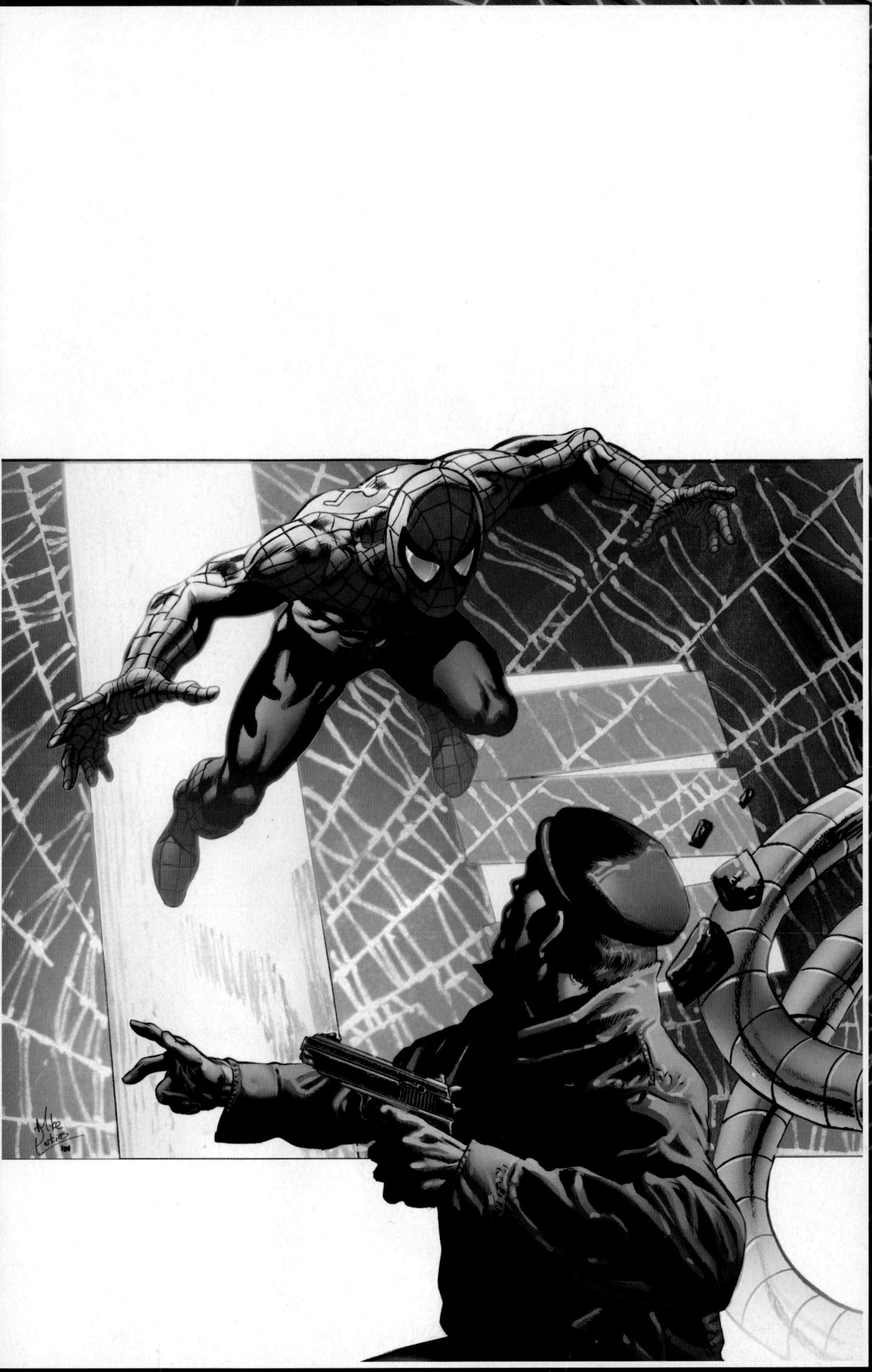

AMAZING SPIDER-MAN #687 SPIDER-MAN IN MOTION VARIANT
COVER BY MIKE PERKINS & FRANK D'ARMATA

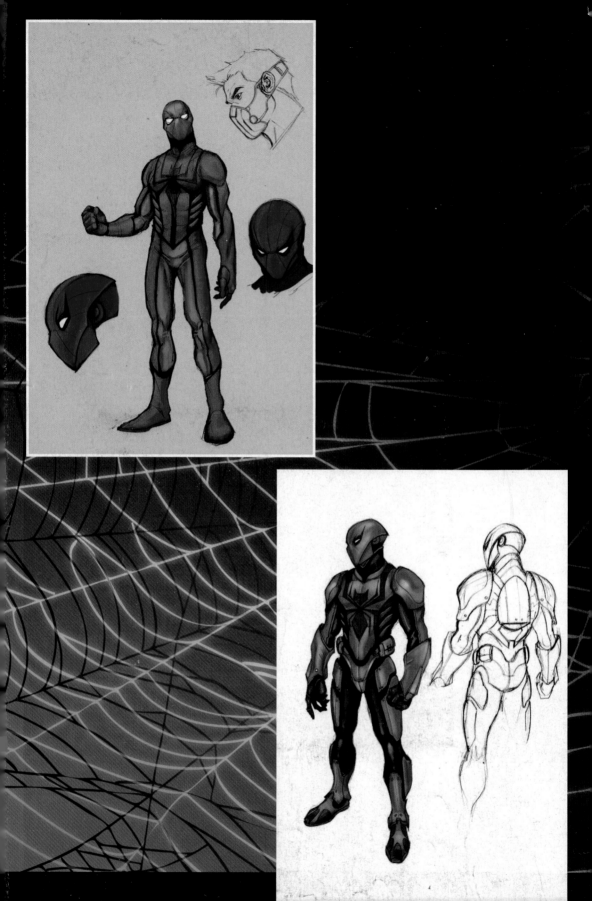

ARMOR DESIGNS
BY STEFANO CASELLI